CHRISTIAN ENGLAND

Born in 1929, David L. Edwards was educated at the King's School, Canterbury, and after reading history at Oxford was elected a Fellow of All Souls College. He later taught in the Divinity Faculty at Cambridge, where he was Dean of King's College. He is the author of more than a dozen books but has, however, been chiefly occupied with his work as a clergyman of the Church of England. For eight years he was Editor and Managing Director of the SCM Press, and later served for another eight years as Sub-Dean of Westminster Abbey, Rector of St Margaret's, the Speaker's Chaplain in the House of Commons, and chairman of Christian Aid, until becoming Dean of Norwich in 1978. Early in 1983 he returned to London again to become Provost of Southwark Cathedral.

DAVID L. EDWARDS

CHRISTIAN ENGLAND

(Volume Three)

FROM THE EIGHTEENTH CENTURY TO THE FIRST WORLD WAR

Collins
FOUNT PAPERBACKS

First published in Great Britain in 1984
by William Collins Sons & Co Ltd, London
Published by Fount Paperbacks, London in 1985

© David L. Edwards 1984

Made and printed in Great Britain by
William Collins Sons & Co Ltd, Glasgow

To Sybil

Contents

Preface

With this book I bring to an end my attempt to write the first ecumenical history of English Christianity, trying to serve the general reader as well as the student and to do justice to Catholics and Evangelicals, Anglicans and Nonconformists, conservatives and radicals, poets and preachers, intellectuals and the people. Earlier volumes were *Christian England: Its Story to the Reformation* (1981) and *Christian England: From the Reformation to the Eighteenth Century* (1983).

This book tells the story of how the Evangelical revival brought a new power to personal religion for many of the English including Methodists and other Nonconformists. It was followed by a Catholic revival both in the Church of England and in the enlarged Roman Catholic community, together with a new determination to respond to the needs of the larger population in the world's first industrial nation. Such revivals made Victorian England as religious as it was, with a faith which sustained poets from Wordsworth to Hopkins and much philanthropy – and which spread (like the connected British empire and commerce) into all the continents. Even this mere sketch of the Victorian age brings together many outstanding men and women. For all its faults it was an age full of courage and creativity, one of the peaks of Christian civilization; only people not fit to be compared with the Victorians will sneer at them.

More Victorian detail may be found in many other books, and I should have liked to give as much detail as was sometimes possible in the earlier volumes of *Christian England*, but readers will appreciate the necessary limits of space. A fully comprehensive volume would have been too daunting. Greater scholars have with more authority expounded the themes which I combine in this sketch, but they have tended to do so from a denominational standpoint. (I made a contribution myself in my book of 1971, *Leaders of the Church of England 1828–1944*, but my treatment of those characters here has been entirely reworked.) As I surveyed the other literature available, I reached the conclusion that I could make myself useful more easily by telling the story as a whole rather than by going into detail.

Finally I outline the often very bitter controversies between the English Christians in the early years of the twentieth century and the decline of conventional Christianity which the sudden outbreak of the First World War partly revealed and partly caused. That great war began the period to which we belong. It is a period in which English religion has not died but has declined in its importance for society. Over almost all the period which I have covered in three volumes the rich story of English religion was right at the centre of the people's history, with worldwide results.

I need not repeat the thanks which I offered in the Preface to the second volume of *Christian England*, for my thanks remain the same, most of this book having been written when I was Dean of Norwich. Nor need I repeat my apologies for failures. But I am above all thankful that I have completed, however unsatisfactorily, a fascinating project. I have found to be profoundly true something which Edward Gibbon, a sceptic, wrote: 'For the man who can raise himself above the prejudices of party and sect, the history of religion is the most interesting part of the history of the human spirit.'

Southwark Cathedral   D.L.E.

Part One

REVIVAL

CHAPTER ONE

CHALLENGES TO ORTHODOXY

THE NEW QUESTIONING

The England over which George III began to reign in 1760 was a great power for the first time in its history, thanks partly to its union with Scotland and its occupation of Ireland. Its manufacturing industry was the most advanced in the world. Its navy ruled the waves. Its army had conquered the heartland of Canada; the whole east coast of America down to Florida lay under its rule; and its merchants were extracting great wealth out of an India which was at the mercy of the East India Company's small forces. Its population was growing fast (more children were surviving and more adults were eating fresh meat during the winter) but was not yet dependent on imported food. Its roads were being improved and the network of canals – the greatest engineering feat in its history so far – was being constructed. Its aristocracy lived in splendour, and many landowners, financiers, manufacturers and merchants were probably more comfortable. The menace of the London mob was a reminder of the underworld of poverty to be found in the towns. It was also true that a bad harvest resulted in people starving, and that the low prices caused by a glut of corn were almost as disastrous for the countryside. But the poverty was worse in every other country in the world.

The new king, aged twenty-two and full of ideals, himself added to the official draft of his first speech to Parliament: 'I glory in the name of Britain.' His reign was to see many changes. Both he and his people in Britain and Ireland were to suffer much, while the Americans departed to fulfil their own manifest destiny. But before his death in 1820, the kingdom of George III had stood against the empire of Napoleon and had made the decisive naval, military and financial contributions to that empire's disappearance; and the colonies acquired during the course of that great war had been added to a second British empire.[1]

Much of English life remained stable and pleasant. The Church of England certainly looked well established in many rural parishes. To this day handsome Georgian rectories bear witness to the prosperity of many of the clergy, and there are books which show what some of them were doing. *The Natural History and Antiquities of Selborne*, published by its rector, Gilbert White, in 1789, the year of the French Revolution, was a beautifully written record of close observation of the Hampshire countryside. A diary for the years 1758–1803 preserved much of the life of James Woodforde – a conscientious man by the standards of his day, taking a service once a week, helping the poor with charity and elementary medicine, inviting neighbours to share the bounty of his table. No new idea ever disturbed the tranquillity of his days in Norfolk.[2] He was not unique.[3]

But it was also a time of new questions. The independence achieved by the Americans was matched by a radicalism in England. Some radicals continued to voice discontent although driven underground when all the conservative forces rallied to defend the old social order in responses to the major shocks of the French Revolution, the war against France and the post-war slump. New questions asked under the young George III and never forgotten probed the necessity of kings, the moral authority of a Parliament which did not represent the people, the whole alliance of Church and State. Some affluent Whigs now belonged to a society called 'the Friends of the People'. More alarmingly, radical agitators urged the people to be their own friends.

Essentially what happened in politics was that the stability

[1] Good introductions include Ian Christie, *Wars and Revolutions 1760–1815* (London, 1982), and Marilyn Butler, *Romantics, Rebels and Reactionaries* (Oxford, 1981), on the literature.

[2] James Woodforde's *Diary of a Country Parson*, edited by John Beresford, was first published in 5 vols. (Oxford, 1924–31). A one-volume selection appeared in 1935.

[3] A. Tindal Hart drew together many studies in *The Country Priest in English History* (London, 1959), *Clergy and Society 1600–1800* (London, 1968), and *The Curate's Lot* (London, 1970).

accepted after England's 'glorious revolution' of 1688–89 ceased to seem perfect even to those who had prospered. The social order could not satisfy all the new ambitions stirring the enlarged population. Change was becoming more revolutionary in the modern sense. In the arts, too, there was change. 'Sense' had been prized – often a trivial sense, or, when serious in intent, a satirical sense. Reason, decorum and elegance had been admired as the cultural equivalents of the political stability which had been such a relief after the turmoils of the seventeenth century. Now the sunny afternoon was over and the climate of opinion was stormy. A new restlessness and a new individualism emerged. Within the eighteenth century, 'sensibility' (what a later generation would call sensitiveness – but it could also mean an unhealthy selfishness) was usually kept well under control. What mattered most was still 'sense'; for self-discipline must be the stable framework of a rational, prosperous life. But gradually the new stirring became the nineteenth century's faith in intuition, emotion, energy and heroism. The day of the heroic ego, or at least of the sensitive self, had arrived. It became a cultural revolution, to be called Romanticism.

Even the clergy, whose lives often seemed so sheltered, could be vulnerable. In rural Norfolk Parson Woodforde, for all the stability of his public existence, was deeply troubled by anxieties in his heart, making him an unhappy recluse in his last years; and two short books by soul-searching country clergymen were minor landmarks in the wider movement of emotions. Edward Young's *Night Thoughts* was a poem about death reckoned by the Methodist hymn-writer Charles Wesley the most useful book ever published apart from the Bible. Laurence Sterne's *Sentimental Journey* (into France) recorded 'a quiet journey of the heart in pursuit of *Nature*, and those affections which rise out of her' – at a time when he, too, had night thoughts, for he knew that he was dying. And not all who questioned the old comfortable certainties remained within the Christian fold, as those literary clergymen did. Not everyone who observed the poverty in village or slum felt inclined to describe it in gentle poetry using heroic couplets, as another parson, George Crabbe, did. Some put their deep-probing questions with a fierce contempt for all that the clergy represented.

William Hogarth, who died in 1764, engraved an immensely popular series of prints which were hilarious or ferocious (or both at the same time). In his vision of town life the pleasures of the rich were empty, the consolations of the poor were coarse, politics was a brawl, and selfishness reigned everywhere. One level of society saw the harlot's progress to misery; another, the rake's progress. The English prided themselves on their manly freedom but used it to be cruel to each other and to animals. Public executions were popular recreations and the Englishman's favourite sport was cock-fighting (to the death, with heavy gambling). Hogarth felt no need to offer a cure for these social diseases; he was a satirist. But in so far as he had a cure, this seems to have been inspired by his patriotic trust in roast beef, hard work and freedom. Some of his paintings – of his servants, for example – show a real love of the people. With all their vices the English were the world's best; and with more roast beef, more industry and more freedom, they would be better. Hogarth (who painted an amazingly frank portrait of Bishop Benjamin Hoadly as a self-complacent criminal in his splendid robes) certainly did not rely on religion for reformation or consolation. His print of a parish church in 1728, 'The Sleeping Congregation', was contemptuous – but it was genial in comparison with the coarsely savage prints which attacked popular religion in the early 1760s: 'Enthusiasm Delineated' and 'Credulity, Superstition and Fanaticism'.[4]

In 1761 Peter Annet, a schoolmaster, brought out the *Free Inquirer*, the first journal openly to ridicule Christianity; and in the 1790s there was a ready public for Tom Paine's two books *The Rights of Man* and *The Age of Reason*, although every effort was made by the authorities to suppress them. The first was so favourable to the French Revolution that Paine had to flee to France. The first part of *The Age of Reason*, written in Paris, was a vigorous summary of Deism, the belief in an impersonal and

---

[1] See Derek Jarrett, *England in the Age of Hogarth* (London, 1974), and Ronald Paulson (ed. Anne Wilde), *Hogarth: His Life, Art and Times* (New Haven, Conn., 1974).

now inactive Creator which was probably all that was left of the personal religion of the majority of Englishmen at the time – so far from the truth was it that Deism had been 'defeated' by the theology of Bishop Joseph Butler. Tom Paine compared the Church's God with 'a passionate man who killed his son when he could not revenge himself in any other way'. In Paris he founded a society of Theophilanthropists, lovers of God and man; it had its own temple. But the second part of *The Age of Reason*, written in prison while Paine was awaiting execution at the hands of the extreme revolutionaries, savagely attacked the errors in the Bible and Christianity. In the end he openly advocated that 'the churches be sold, and the money arising therefrom be invested as a fund for the education of children of poor parents of every profession'.

'The only idea man can affix to the name of God', wrote Paine, 'is the first cause, the cause of all things. . . . The true Deist has but one Deity; and his religion consists in contemplating the power, wisdom and benignity of the Deity in his works, and in endeavouring to imitate him in everything moral, scientific and mechanical. . . . The Almighty Lecturer, by displaying the principles of science in the structure of the universe, has invited man to study and to imitation. . . . Religion, therefore, being the belief of a God and the practice of moral truth, cannot have any connection with mystery. The belief of God, so far from having anything of mystery in it, is of all beliefs the most easy, because it arises to us, as it is observed, out of necessity.' Or at least this kind of belief arose easily for Tom Paine, the son of devout Quakers.[5]

Others found even Deism difficult. The earthquake which devastated Lisbon on All Saints Day 1755 inspired Voltaire's *Candide* and much other scepticism. David Hume, for one, found no 'principles of science' or of morality taught by the 'Almighty Lecturer'. In his essay on miracles, published seven years before the earthquake, he had scarcely troubled to conceal his agnosticism beneath his irony. He concluded that 'the Christian Religion not only was at first attended with

---

[5] See Audrey Williamson, *Thomas Paine* (London, 1973), and James Boulton, *The Language of Politics in the Age of Paine and Burke* (London, 1963).

miracles, but even at this day cannot be believed by any reasonable person without one. Mere reason is insufficient to convince us of its veracity: and whoever is moved by Faith to assent to it, is conscious of a continued miracle in his own person, which subverts all the principles of his understanding, and gives him a determination to believe what is most contrary to custom and experience.'

Hume was one of the Scots who reaped the advantages of the union with England. He found friends and patrons there, and when he was given charge of the lawyers' library in Edinburgh he used it to write the first systematic history of England, which in the end made him 'not only independent but opulent'. In his early twenties he had, like many intelligent young men, been the victim of introspective despair, and he had proceeded to question all external and conventional realities and moralities; but his mature and placidly comfortable policy was 'inattention' to the ultimate questions. It has been well described. 'He rightly judged that, if he pretended to instruct the world by a reason he had declared bankrupt, no one would notice the inconsistency. . . . What he would have approved of is the "carelessness and inattention" of generations of Anglo-Saxons who have pursued their business, or their studies, without regard to anything more than a vague utilitarianism. . . . That was his religion – a religion of sympathy, but not too much of it, and a great perseverance in caution.'[6]

Towards the end of the 1750s Edward Gibbon read Hume's philosophy and it confirmed his own rejection of dogmatic religion. He also began to see himself as an historian with Hume as his closest model. In his *History of the Decline and Fall of the Roman Empire* he never attacked the memory of that empire's victim and conqueror, Jesus of Nazareth. Instead, he patronized Jesus, whose 'progress from infancy to youth and manhood was marked by a regular increase in stature and wisdom; and after a painful agony of mind and body, he expired on the cross. He lived and died for the service of mankind. . . .' Gibbon could even bring himself to pay a few stately compli-

---

[6] C. H. Sisson, *David Hume* (Edinburgh, 1976), pp. 95–6. Antony Flew studied *Hume's Philosophy of Belief* (London, 1961).

ments to the Christian religion – particularly when the new religion of reason and revolution in France had dismayed him by its excesses. When himself middle-aged, he assured a pious aunt that 'I consider religion as the best guide to youth and the best support of old age'. But he had no real respect for Christianity; he had suffered too much from it while young. What Richard Porson wrote about him was accurate. 'He often makes, when he cannot readily find, an occasion to insult our religion; which he hates so cordially that he might seem to revenge some personal injury.'

The injury was this. During his second year at Magdalen College, Oxford, Gibbon came across a recently published *Free Enquiry* by Conyers Middleton into the miracles said to have occurred in the Christian Church in its first five centuries. The sceptical onslaught had the unintended effect of persuading this unhappy, lonely and bored student that if he was prepared to accept the ancient Church's miracles – as he then was – he might as well accept its dogmas. His conversion to Roman Catholicism meant that he could not return to Oxford. Instead he was packed off to Lausanne, to stay with a Protestant pastor – with good success. He acquired in Switzerland the command of French and the industrious love of history that were to be the foundations of his literary triumphs. He also acquired a hatred of the Catholicism which had been about to exclude him for ever from the cultured world.[7]

TWO TROUBLED CHRISTIANS

A conservative response to such challenges was possible, but it could look like a desperate clinging. Two examples were Samuel Johnson, the king of literary London, and King George III.

How near Samuel Johnson was to madness is not known. The most intimate documents which he left unburned were his

---

[7] The best biography is D. M. Low, *Edward Gibbon 1737–1794* (London, 1937). See also S. T. McCloy, *Gibbon's Antagonism to Christianity and the Discussions that it has Provoked* (London, 1933); J. W. Swain, *Edward Gibbon the Historian* (London, 1966); Sir Gavin de Beer, *Gibbon and his World* (London, 1968).

prayers, but the self-accusations in them revealed little that was exceptional. Probably the only person in whom he confided freely was Mrs Thrale. She left behind evidence that he thought he was close to insanity; but she had neither the medical nor the literary equipment to go into details. The men with whom he drank and talked, evening after evening, saw that he needed their company because he was unhappy; but most of them left only slight records behind. James Boswell never lacked either effrontery or the industry to record its achievements, but he could not extract from the cantankerous old sage the full story of his early years and of their psychological consequences.

Boswell did, however, find the solution to a puzzle which must otherwise perplex all who read his great *Life of Samuel Johnson*: why did people tolerate the Doctor's rudeness? It has never been enough to offer an explanation in terms of the wit and wisdom, since men so rude are usually left to be witty and wise by themselves. But Boswell propounded the solution: 'his loud explosions are guns of distress'. The unspoken fact in the famous conversations was that his shadowy companions, whose comments on questions seemed to be of value only in so far as they provoked the Doctor's genius, were more fortunate than he was – and they knew it.

Most of them knew also that Johnson's true nature was expressed in his constant kindness to those who were, as he was, miserable. Mrs Thrale reckoned that while she knew him he never spent more than £80 a year on himself or less than £200 a year on others. His home was a refuge for the destitute, and on his way to and from dinner he would empty his pockets for beggars or put pennies into the hands of children asleep on doorsteps. This tyrant of the dinner table would go out to buy oysters for his sick cat, Hodge. In his will he made his Negro servant his residuary legatee. Gruffly compassionate, disliking to be called 'Doctor' and seldom calling his friends 'Sir' (those were touches which Boswell added to make him sound more magisterial), Johnson was not joking when he told Sir Joshua Reynolds that the great business of his life was to escape from himself. He could not find sufficient relief in writing: he wrote surprisingly little which was deeply his own, although he produced prolific journalism, most of which he did not trouble to read through before it went to the printer. His distress drove him to his fellow men in taverns. But fate, kinder than he thought it was, sent him Boswell to preserve some glimpses of his wounded personality and, with these, some echoes of the English language's best talk.

Born in 1709, the son of an incompetent bookseller in Lichfield, Johnson was marked for life by tuberculosis leading to scrofula (the 'king's evil'). A visit to London to be touched by Queen Anne failed to cure him. Surgery done clumsily on him while a baby scarred his face; one ear was deaf and one eye almost blind. And there were psychological scars. His involuntary tics and other compulsive movements became grotesque. He usually looked unkempt and habitually lived in disorder. Poverty wounded him also. It drove him from Oxford, where he was laughed at because his toes showed through his shoes.

Having conquered a prolonged breakdown brought about by that setback, he walked to London in 1737 and for nine years earned his living as a hack journalist. Then he undertook to compile the first comprehensive *Dictionary of the English Language*, and after great toils its publication secured his fame. He went on to edit Shakespeare and to make another major contribution as a critic by his *Lives of the Poets*. But the wounds of battle did not heal easily. His poem on *London*, a rather conventional performance modelled on Juvenal's satire on the corruption of Rome, might have been followed by creative greatness. There were only magnificent fragments – a poem on *The Vanity of Human Wishes*, also imitating Juvenal; *Rasselas*, a story written in order to pay for his mother's funeral; some two hundred essays written for the *Rambler* and amounting to an exposition of morality as he understood it. For at least four years he felt close to insanity, and his great *Preface to Shakespeare* was written in the midst of that hell. Hating to be alone, he fell into habits which, while not the 'sloth' he often called them, were not conducive to the creation of great books. He would dine in a tavern at four in the afternoon, drink tea and read on his return home, get off to sleep at about four in the morning, and rise for work at noon.

His pessimistic philosophy fed an austere religion. *Rasselas*, published in the same year as Voltaire's *Candide*, attacked shallow optimism as the savagely witty Frenchman did – but it reached the conclusion that man's only perfect happiness lay in heaven. It was not an easy conclusion to reach or retain; he once said that 'he never had a moment when death was not terrible to him'. He lived in constant horror of the possibility of his own eternal damnation. His main argument for the immortality of the soul was that without it human life would make no sense at all: 'the only thinking being of this globe is doomed to think merely to be wretched, and to pass his time from youth to age in fearing or suffering calamities.'

He respected clergymen, and wrote about forty solid, if dull, sermons for some less eloquent friends to preach (just as he wrote lectures on law to rescue a friend who had been made a professor at Oxford). He was invited to accept ordination and a parish, but could not face the 'assiduous and familiar instruction of the vulgar and the ignorant'. He had learning and piety enough for a bishop, except that he reckoned that no one could be made a bishop for learning and piety. In return for his respect he wanted clergymen to be orthodox, hard-working and decorous. 'I do not envy the clergyman's life as an easy life,' he once declared, 'nor do I envy the clergyman who makes it an easy life.' Once in a tavern he complained loudly about some of the company; 'the merriment of parsons is mightily offensive.' He refused to allow religion to be mocked, or vice to be paraded, in his company. He was always chaste and, although a greedy eater, for much of his life abstained from alcohol. This was all the more remarkable because he preferred laymen who would be merry.

He was by nature a sceptic; Mrs Thrale remarked on his 'fixed incredulity of everything he heard'. When a companion confessed to 'shocking, impious thoughts', he replied: 'If I was to divide my life into three parts, two of them would have been filled with such thoughts.' Rightly he thought that for most Christians doubt must always accompany faith; 'nothing is granted in this world beyond rational hope.' But he was never open about his doubts or precise about their theological solutions; he never wrote on religion at any length, and when he spoke about it in company he tended to bluster. It was his custom to receive Holy Communion at Easter only, having fasted on Good Friday; but even then he was usually late in church, unable to sit still in a pew, fearful of hearing nonsense from the pulpit (or music which he detested almost as much). He often accused himself of having neglected to 'take pleasure in public worship' or to make a proper study of the Bible. He had the habit of writing down beautifully expressed prayers – a habit fairly common in his age, but one which did not suggest intimacy with a heavenly Father.

It was only when he knew he was dying that he talked freely to his friends about personal religion. 'Let me exhort you', he said to a young Italian, 'always to think of my situation, which must one day be yours; always remember that life is short and eternity never ends.' When assured that David Hume had died happily, he refused to believe it. Hume 'had a vanity in being thought easy', he assured Boswell. His own deathbed creed was addressed to the question which he had faced all his life:

> Must helpless Man, in Ignorance sedate,
> Roll darkling down the Torrent of his Fate?[8]

In the autumn of 1788 George III suffered a severe illness which included delirium and nearly included death. He recovered but was similarly afflicted in 1801 and 1804. In 1811 his mind finally gave way and he lived in a world of his own until his death in 1820. Large sums were spent on the best medical skill of the time, but diagnosis proved impossible, let alone cure. Almost certainly this mental disease had a physical origin, since no evidence suggests that the King's behaviour was unbalanced during the first fifty years of his life. On the contrary, he was the most popular monarch since Elizabeth I, mixing freely and well with many people of all classes. He loved

---

[8] Among the many books on Johnson, the most useful for our present purpose are Robert Voitle, *Samuel Johnson the Moralist* (Cambridge, Mass., 1961); Maurice Quinlan, *Samuel Johnson: A Layman's Religion* (Madison, Wisc., 1963); Charles Chapin, *The Religious Thought of Samuel Johnson* (Ann Arbor, Minn., 1968); James Gray, *Johnson's Sermons* (Oxford, 1972); Charles Pierce, *The Religious Life of Samuel Johnson* (London, 1983). W. Jackson Bate, *Samuel Johnson* (London, 1978), is the best short life. James Clifford did not live to complete his standard modern life, but achieved *Young Samuel Johnson* and *Dictionary Johnson* (London, 1955–80).

both hunting and music, and collected a large library. He was a faithful husband, the concerned father of a large family, a sober and self-disciplined man driven by a sense of his duty. He broke away entirely from the licentious habits of the first two Georges and would not live in Kensington Palace or Hampton Court, which he thought they had disgraced. Although he bought a house on the site of the later Buckingham Palace, he preferred to live quietly as a country gentleman at Windsor or Kew.

George III's character is relevant to our story because his respectability was based on his religion. He received the Holy Communion twelve times a year; it was symbolic that he took off his crown before communicating at his coronation. Thus inspired, he consistently opposed his age's vicious fashions. Soon after his accession the standard proclamation appeared 'for the encouragement of piety and virtue'. More surprisingly he reissued it in a strengthened version in 1784. He rebuked an aristocrat who occupied the Archbishopric of Canterbury from 1768 to 1783 (Frederick Cornwallis) for planning a ball in Lambeth Palace; he made no secret of his detestation of the morals of able politicians such as Charles James Fox; and his long quarrel with his own son and heir was inflamed by anger at the prince's sexual promiscuity, gambling losses and general irresponsibility (encouraged by Fox). He liked to believe that his relapse into mental illness in 1801 was caused by William Pitt's proposal to allow Roman Catholics the vote – as the King maintained, in defiance of his own coronation oath to preserve the Protestant religion – and Pitt had to promise never to mention the subject again. While insane the King was put under the brutal care of a clergyman, Francis Willis, who without being a qualified physician kept a private asylum and promised (as the qualified doctors did not) to effect a cure if given a free hand. At their first meeting the King rebuked Willis for changing from clerical to medical interests. According to the diarist Greville, he told him: 'You have quitted a profession I have always loved, and you have embraced one I most heartily detest.'

Samuel Johnson's pension which rescued him from poverty came from the secret service fund with the King's ready consent, and the two men approved of each other when they met. Johnson declared that it did a man good to be talked to by his sovereign. They had much in common. Their loyalty to the Church of England was defiantly old-fashioned. The Established Church seemed a precious part of the world of order and sanity; and they clung to its prayers because in their dark distresses they knew how it felt to be in hell.[9]

WILLIAM PALEY AND THE FAILURE OF COMPLACENT BELIEF

A more complacent defence of the Church could be offered, but in a time of questions and troubles its very complacency made it ultimately implausible.

William Paley happened to be born (in 1743) outside Yorkshire but his father was for forty-four years the schoolmaster in his native parish of Giggleswick. He spoke all through his life with a Yorkshire accent and never ceased to be blunt in his self-confident arguments. He spent seventeen years in Cambridge, first as a brilliant student, then as an effective college tutor, before holding a variety of ecclesiastical posts until his death in 1805. Three books of his were adopted as virtually the text books of the academic and ecclesiastical Establishment. The most important was *A View of the Evidences of Christianity* (1794); all Cambridge undergraduates were examined on their knowledge of this book from 1822 until 1920, unless they preferred the elementary logic or chemistry allowed as an alternative during the twentieth century. Paley also expounded the preliminaries to Christianity in his *Natural Theology* and its consequences in his *Principles of Moral and Political Philosophy*.

It may seem puzzling that such an influential champion of the Church of England's established role in society was not made a bishop; but the explanation is, like everything else about Paley, reasonable. He was happy to accumulate a large income from several humbler but less onerous positions which he held simultaneously. For their part, the bishop-makers

---

[9] The best biography is John Brooke, *George III* (London, 1974).

could not help noticing with alarm that he was no smooth courtier. He had retained his outspoken independence, especially in his talk, although the tendency of his writings was consistently conservative. Various private flippancies were repeated and did him no good. In a book he wrote that 'the divine right of kings is, like the divine right of constables . . . a right ratified, we humbly presume, by the divine approbation, so long as obedience to their authority appears to be necessary, or conducive to the common welfare.' The same book also referred to 'those futile arts and decorations which compose the business and recommendations of a court.' Obedience to rulers was usually expedient, Paley taught, even if the ruler were 'a child, a woman, a driveller or a lunatic'; and respect for property was usually also expedient, even if the property system resembled a flock all collecting grain to feed one superior pigeon. George III was said to have met William Pitt's recommendation of this philosopher for a bishopric with: 'What? Pigeon Paley? Not orthodox, not orthodox.'

Paley defended Christianity and the Church on the ground that they increased human happiness. Jesus was a man whose status as the Son of God was attested by the fact that although he 'had visited no polished cities' he was a surprisingly civilized teacher of religion and morality; 'there was no heat in his piety, or in the language in which he expressed it.' The religion taught by Jesus was, of course, the religion taught by William Paley. It had been temporarily commended by miracles but they had long ago ceased. It was successful and had led to the establishment of National Churches. Although the wealth of some clergymen put them in contrast with the Galilean fishermen, 'rich and splendid situations in the Church have been justly regarded as prizes held out to invite persons of good hopes and ingenuous attainments to enter into its service.'

The religious message which Jesus delivered with such elegance concerned the benevolence of God. Paley took it for granted that the order in the universe demonstrated its creation. Like a man finding a watch on the ground when crossing a heath, the student of nature could know that what lay before him had been designed by a maker. Paley dwelt on the

admirable design of the human body and on the many pleasures of human life, but also celebrated the happiness of God's
other creatures. 'It is a happy world after all. The air, the earth,
the water, teem with delighted existence. In a spring noon, or a
summer evening, on whichever side I turn, myriads of happy
beings crowd on my view. . . . If we look to what the waters
produce, shoals of the fry of fish frequent the margins of rivers,
of lakes, and of the sea itself. These are so happy that they do
not know what to do with themselves. Their attitudes, their
vivacity, their leaps out of the water, their frolics in it (which I
have noticed a thousand times with equal attention and
amusement), all conduce to show their excess of spirits. . . .'

The moral message of Jesus was the encouragement among
men of a benevolence similar to God's, with the promise of a
suitable reward. Paley defined virtue as 'the doing good to
mankind, in obedience to the will of God, and for the sake of
everlasting happiness.' An important part of happiness in
human life was to be busy, and Archdeacon Paley, observing
that many of his fellow clergymen were idle and therefore
bored, suggested suitable hobbies for them; for example, they
should fill in the time by gardening but add to their pleasure by
acquiring some knowledge of botany. He praised an interest in
politics; not only did this afford a harmless and intelligent topic
of conversation, but in politics men could do God's will 'as
collected from expediency'. The one test of political or private
morality for Paley was the increase of happiness. Sir Leslie
Stephen wrote that Paley had taught that 'Christ came into the
world to tell us that we should go to hell if our actions did not
tend to promote the greatest happiness of the greatest number.'
His modern biographer who has a liking for Paley comments
about this summary: 'it is not wholly unfair'.[10]

[10] M. L. Clarke, *Paley: Evidence for the Man* (London, 1974), p. 72.

JOSEPH PRIESTLEY AND
THE FAILURE OF RATIONAL DISSENT

It was possible to argue that Paley's mistake was to defend too much of the old orthodoxy and the old Establishment in Church and State; that Christianity could be shown to be a suitable religion for rationally happy men if only it could be rationalized more radically.

Another Yorkshireman, Joseph Priestley, was born to humble and pious parents in 1733. At the age of nineteen he entered the only higher education open to him since his parents had rejected the Church of England, and this was an 'academy' for the sons of such Dissenters. There he was taught by a minister who, although orthodox, encouraged young men both to debate theology freely and to develop many non-theological interests; and so Priestley entered the movement which came to be called 'Rational Dissent'.

After two ill-paid pastorates as a Dissenting minister he became a tutor in another Dissenting academy, and by publishing textbooks built up a national reputation. Later in his life he returned to preaching, in London and Birmingham. His religious views moved further and further away from the stern orthodoxy of Calvinism, with its doctrine that some were predestined to heaven and others (the majority) to hell – but his well-to-do congregations were far from dismayed. He came before them on Sundays to preach sermons which seemed eminently sensible, and he took trouble in explaining the Bible to their children. During the week he was at work in his library and his laboratory, and they took a pride in his wide-ranging intellectual distinction. This distinction was so marked that the Earl of Shelburne persuaded Priestley to spend seven years as his librarian and companion.

The scientific work was not all of the same quality. Priestley had received no proper training; in his early years he was so poor that the purchase of basic books and instruments was a major difficulty, and he always had many non-scientific interests to distract him. But he wrote on electricity, and made important contributions. He excelled as a chemist. He was the first to explain oxygen, chlorine, ammonia, hydrogen chloride and sulphur dioxide. His researches into the properties of iron, carbon and steam became of use to manufacturers and he was scientific adviser to Josiah Wedgwood, the brilliant developer and salesman of superior pottery – while his invention of soda water, originally intended to help sailors on long voyages, has given many millions a lighter kind of pleasure. He was acknowledged as the intellectual king of the expanding town of Birmingham, where James Watt had recently built a steam engine.

His deepest interests were, however, in religious and political thought. He fully shared Paley's conviction that the marvels of nature all pointed to the existence of the Creator. But 'have nothing to do with a parliamentary religion', he urged, 'or a parliamentary God.' Reading and reflection persuaded him that, just as some of the airs which he investigated had become noxious by the decay of vegetable matter, so orthodox Christianity had been corrupted; and he was determined to say that it smelt.

While a student he read David Hartley's *Observations on Man* (1749). That book acquired an astonishing prestige in the second half of the eighteenth century – astonishing because the nineteenth and twentieth centuries have agreed that its observations could be forgotten. Hartley seemed to Priestley to reveal the truth about the word 'soul', which was that it was a confusing way of talking. The reality was that the mind received impressions through the senses and associated several impressions to form ideas; but when the brain died, the mind died. It remained dead until resurrected at the end of time. And what was true about other men was true about Jesus.

After becoming a minister, Priestley read books about the divinity of Christ. They made him, by the end of the 1760s, a full-blooded Unitarian. Jesus, 'as much a creature of God as a loaf of bread', was now dead, but he had taught the truth about God's benevolence and man's duties and therefore had been the Messiah. Worshipping him had been nothing better than idolatry. There had been no need to make Atonement for the sins of the whole world, since God himself was responsible for the existence of evil, as of everything else, in a world where men necessarily behaved as instructed by their senses. In *The Doctrine of Philosophical Necessity*, Priestley wrote: 'A Necessarian cannot accuse himself of having done wrong in the ultimate sense of the word. He has, therefore, in the strict sense, nothing to do with repentance or confession or pardon, which are all adapted to a different, imperfect, fallacious view of things.' It was not that Priestley advocated vice, whatever his opponents might say. But he wished to set the improvement of human behaviour in its proper context, for he believed that 'the whole series of events from the beginning of the world to the consummation of all things makes one connected chain of events, originally established by the Deity.' The universe was as progressive as was Priestley himself.

He also experimented in political theory. He assured his well-to-do audiences that he was no violent radical, and certainly he had no wish to extend the powers of the State. His *Essay on the First Principles of Government* urged the State 'never to interfere, without the greatest caution, in things that do not immediately affect the lives, liberty or property of members of the community.' But he sought the admission of consistent Dissenters (such as those audiences) to the universities, to local government and to Parliament; and he sought electoral reform. He derided a corrupt system which meant that Birmingham's inhabitants (more than thirty thousand) had no representative in the Commons.

In the early 1780s it was possible to expect gradual progress for such rational radicalism. The Earl of Shelburne became prime minister in 1782 and negotiated the recognition of the Americans whose war for independence had been welcomed by Priestley and many other Dissenters. Many other political reforms were being talked about. Under such patronage the cause of Rational Dissent, corresponding with the educated opinion of the day, would surely prevail. Priestley was present when his friend Theophilus Lindsey, who had abandoned the Anglican priesthood, opened a Unitarian chapel in Essex Street, London, and was delighted when the chapel was filled with a distinguished congregation. In 1772 the House of Commons was petitioned by an ultra-liberal group of London clergy for more doctrinal freedom. Although this petition was rejected, the requirement (very rarely enforced) that Dissenting ministers should assent to the doctrinal articles was soon abolished. Within Dissent, the appeal of Unitarianism was so strong that members of the General Baptist denomination who objected to it split off to form a 'New Connexion' during the 1770s. The old word 'Presbyterian' was becoming more and more infrequent in every-day speech. Roman Catholicism seemed powerless to cause any trouble; in 1780 Priestley urged that it should be tolerated since 'it is cowardly to kick an old and dying lion'. The controversies of the previous century seemed to be so safely buried that in 1789 a motion for the total repeal of the legislation penalizing Dissent in the Test and Corporation Acts was defeated in the Commons by a mere twenty votes (122–102). Sermons and pamphlets poured out, mocking the idea that a modern government should be expected to enforce medieval doctrines.[11]

The popularity for a time of proposals for a radical and rational simplification of Christianity can be seen in the career of Richard Watson. In 1782 he was made Bishop of Llandaff by Lord Shelburne. The son of the schoolmaster at Hawkshurst (Wordsworth's school), he had won the highest honours in mathematics at Cambridge. Remaining in the university to teach, he had been appointed professor of chemistry. Although he made no secret of the fact that he had 'never read a syllable on the subject', Cambridge must not leave science to the Dissenters. Then he had been elected professor of divinity. He was no great heretic; he lived to write an *Apology for Christianity*, replying to Edward Gibbon, and an *Apology for the Bible*, replying to Tom Paine ('apology' meant 'defence'). Paine had announced that 'my belief in the perfection of the Deity will not permit me to believe that a book so manifestly obscure, disorderly and contradictory can be his work. I can write a better book myself.' But Watson was an admirer of the Bible, partly because it saved him from further theological work. 'I reduced the study of divinity into as narrow a compass as I could, for I determined to study nothing but my Bible, being

---

[11] This campaign was studied by R. B. Barlow in *Citizenship and Conscience* (Philadelphia, Pa., 1962).

unconcerned about the opinions of councils, fathers, churches, bishops and other men as little inspired as myself.'

However, any hopes that this uninspired bishop would be promoted to a leading position in the Established Church, and that Dissenters would be put on terms of political equality with its members, were wrecked. In 1789 Watson retired to a mansion on the banks of Windermere and there spent the rest of his life (he died in 1816). He visited his Welsh diocese, sometimes as often as once a year, and he kept in touch by letter with his deputy in Cambridge, where he remained a professor; and he also kept a benevolent, if remote, eye on the parishes which provided him with additional incomes. But he explained to inquirers that he felt an obligation to concentrate on the improvement of his estate for the benefit of his family since he could hope for no further advancement in the Church. Meanwhile radicalism went down to defeat. In the House of Commons, when the motion for the repeal of the Test and Corporation Acts came back in 1790, it was thrown out by 294 votes to 105. The Earl of Shelburne, already excluded from office since 1783, was driven into the political wilderness. The Tories entered what was to be almost exactly half a century of power.

Much of this swing to conservatism in Church and State was a reaction against the French Revolution. In 1789, only two months after the narrow defeat of the motion in favour of the Dissenters in Westminster, the Bastille was stormed in Paris. The overthrow of oppression which this symbolized was welcomed by Dissenters such as Richard Price, the minister of the congregation in London to which Priestley had preached. In a much-discussed sermon Price compared events in France with the English Revolution of 1688 and announced that all kings owed their crowns to the people. But a reaction far more typical among those of the English who enjoyed privileges came from Bishop Watson: he announced that the news from France had caused him to 'fly with terror and abhorrence from the altar of liberty'.

Price's radical challenge inspired Edmund Burke to write a classic of counter-revolutionary rhetoric. In *Reflections on the Revolution in France*, he declared that 'the glory of Europe is extinguished for ever' if the old alliance of the orthodox Church with the monarchical State was to be destroyed by mob violence and if the old religious emphasis on duty was to be replaced by an atheist philosophy extolling the rights of man.

Back in 1773 Burke, then fresh from a visit to the sceptical aristocrats of Paris, had poured out all his Irish eloquence in a warning to the House of Commons not to tolerate atheism. In the fifteen years since that warning his eloquence had grown richer, but so rich as to be a bore, the 'dinner-bell' of the Commons; and the causes which he had defended had not amounted to a simple righteousness. While he was advocating the freedom of the Americans, he was drawing pay from them. While he was urging the punishment of the 'plunderers' of India such as Warren Hastings, he was defending his brother who was a swindler. He had shown courage, and had taken pride, in being a 'friend of liberty'. He had sought a recognition of the religious rights of the Irish Catholics, for example. In 1773, while defending the Church of England against change, he had assured the Commons that he also wished to defend the rights of individuals to dissent from it; he would 'have toleration a part of establishment'. But he had always taken it for granted that such rights as he advocated would not destroy the fabric of society – or, to put it more bluntly, the class system – of the England where the Church was to remain established.

This vital qualification to his advocacy of freedom now came to the fore in his reaction to the French Revolution. The 'morality' of a community was more important than any individual's rights: 'men are qualified for civil liberty in exact proportion to their disposition to put moral chains upon their own appetites.' The class system was what the realities of human nature demanded; in comparison, talk about the natural rights of the individual was mere 'theory'. A society was made up of imperfect men, but 'he censures God who quarrels with the imperfections of men' and in order that imperfect, unruly men might be disciplined God had willed the State: 'he who gave our nature to be perfected by our virtue willed also the necessary means of its perfection.' The State was a sacred partnership, but that did not mean that it was a mere agreement between individuals for their private and temporary purposes. It was 'a partnership in all science, a partnership in all art, a partnership in every virtue and in all perfection . . . a partnership . . . between those who are living, those who are dead and those who are to be born.' And it was impious to change the terms of such a partnership to suit 'floating fancies or fashions' or the 'swinish multitude'. As Burke was to write in a sequel to these anti-revolutionary *Reflections*, 'the awful Author of our being is the Author of our place in the order of existence'.[12]

This passionate philosophy appealed to the religious, as well as to the other, convictions of those inclined to conservatism. George III said that every gentleman should read it, and the doomed Louis XVI translated it into French. It was a book which made or reflected a whole new mood. Among those many Englishmen who could not read the old Tory cry 'Church and King!' was heard more loudly than it had been for a century. William Pitt, who had at first seemed rather close to reformers such as Shelburne, found his destiny as a war minister, implacably resisting the aggressive French until he lived to see England secured by Nelson's victory at Trafalgar. In the England of Pitt and Nelson, bracing itself for the greatest war it had ever endured, Burke's creed of nation and class, of God and duty, was an inspiration. Rational Dissenters and any others who could be suspected of a Frenchified republicanism ('Jacobinism') were the inevitable targets of hostility at every level of a nation absorbed in what seemed to be a crusade.

But alarm about the French Revolution was not the only cause of the defeat of all that Joseph Priestley advocated. He was also unpopular because of his religious radicalism, which he expressed with an insensitive arrogance. He made almost no contact with the average clergyman or churchgoer, let alone with the poor, and his theology made almost no contact with the Christian tradition. It was criticized by Richard Price and other Dissenters as well as by a number of very angry Anglicans. These conservatives exaggerated the extent to which the

---

[12] Recent studies include Charles Parkin, *The Moral Basis of Burke's Political Thought* (Cambridge, 1956); Alfred Cobban, *Edmund Burke and the Revolt against the Eighteenth Century* (revised, London, 1960); B. T. Wilkins, *The Problem of Burke's Political Philosophy* (Oxford, 1967); Michael Freeman, *Edmund Burke and the Critique of Political Radicalism* (Oxford, 1981).

developed doctrine of the Trinity could be found in the New
Testament and the early Church, but their replies could not be
answered solely at the academic level. There, Priestley could
score debating points. But the real strength of their replies was
emotional. For many centuries Christians had prayed to the
Father through the Son, and they had worshipped the Son as
the divine Saviour. All the saints had encouraged them to do
so. That had been the heartbeat of the Christian tradition.
Priestley's comparison of God the Son with a loaf of bread
seemed mightily offensive.

It is not surprising that this insensitive radical's Unitarian
creed, contemptuous of Christian orthodoxy, was thought to
be a new religion, hostile to all the institutions of England –
without being friendly to England's poor. A modern biographer of Lord Shelburne has summed up Priestley's influence
on that radical politician. 'According to the scale of values
which he imparted to Shelburne, virtue was to be found in the
middling station in life, liberty of conscience, private secular
education, self-help, thrift and respect for property as the trust
of the righteous and the test of political responsibility; vice was
to be found in idleness, luxury, established religion, pauper-
ism, and the life of the English poor generally'.[13] Such values
could never inspire a popular religious movement in England;
and when proclaimed in pamphlets and addresses sympathetic
with revolution in France, they could seem aggressively unpat-
riotic and anti-social as well as anti-Christian. Edward Gibbon, for example, coldly rejected Priestley's attempt to form an
alliance and in his memoirs called him a 'trumpet of sedition'.
And Priestley's unpopularity now exploded into mob violence.

In Birmingham on the warm evening of 14 July 1791 a
dinner inaugurating a 'Constitutional Society' was surrounded
by a riotous crowd, inflamed by the appearance of the slogan
'This useless barn to be let or sold' chalked on Anglican church
doors – and by the publication of a pamphlet recalling the fall
of the Bastille on 14 July, and remarking on the venal, hypocritical, extravagant and oppressive British system of Church and
State. These provocative acts were disowned by Priestley and

---

[13] John Norris, *Shelburne and Reform* (London, 1963), p. 84.

his friends, but the impression had been created that on that 14 July revolution was being planned in Birmingham. The diners escaped that evening but the mob moved off from the tavern to burn down the elegant chapel where Priestley preached and another meeting house occupied by Rational Dissenters. After that it proceeded to wreck the preacher's house, library and laboratory, together with almost twenty other homes belonging to leading Dissenters. All over Birmingham was scrawled the Tory slogan, 'Church and King for ever!' Those responsible for law and order – including the King – were acutely embarrassed by the riot, sent in troops to quell it, and hanged two of its ringleaders. But the principal victim must have known that King George, honestly declaring himself 'pleased that Priestley is the sufferer', voiced public opinion.

The preacher-scientist tried to resume his work in England, but could not. It was a time when Burke could assure the Commons that many thousands of daggers had been ordered for a revolution to begin in Birmingham. A bookseller received four years' imprisonment for selling Paine's *Rights of Man*. Priestley's position in England was not helped when he was made an honorary citizen of the First Republic in France, which a few days after guillotining Louis XVI declared war on England. In 1794 he decided to emigrate to tolerant Pennsylvania, where his sons settled as farmers. He spent the last ten years of his life in America. He was honoured by three Presidents; he took tea with George Washington, John Adams was polite, and Thomas Jefferson declared that he had read *The Corruptions of Christianity* with agreement 'over and over again'. In exile Joseph Priestley preached, he experimented, and he was correcting the proofs of a pamphlet an hour before his death. But he knew that in his own country his attempt to make religion 'rational' and radical was, for the time being, smashed along with his Birmingham home and laboratory.[14]

---

[14] F. W. Gibbs, *Joseph Priestley* (London, 1965), is mainly scientific and may be supplemented by Sir Anthony Lincoln, *Some Political and Social Ideas of English Dissent 1763–1800* (London, 1938).

CHAPTER TWO

THE EVANGELICAL REVIVAL

THE GREAT AWAKENING IN AMERICA

Had English Christianity remained entirely in hands such as Paley's or Priestley's, presumably it would have declined as Paine, Hume or Gibbon expected. It would have lacked emotional strength. When frightened people such as Burke turned to the Christian religion in reaction against the French Revolution, they would have found little remaining in it but the belief in benevolence and progress, a belief not very likely to flourish as the revolution plunged Europe into chaos and a long war, and as other political and emotional tempests raged. But in fact Christianity gained power among the English as it rose to the challenge. The nineteenth century was to be far more Christian than the eighteenth – both in England and in those large areas of North America which were still united with England culturally. Democracy was to grow; but the Christian Church in its many branches was to make strenuous efforts to grow with the people, to talk as the people talked and to form congregations where the people lived, fanning into flame the still glowing religious emotions or memories. Scientific knowledge was to expand, a science-based industrial revolution was to make life new and urban, and the popular mind was to become largely secular. The Christian religion, however, was to be redefined for those who remained faithful to it. It was to be made exciting. It was to be able to transform individuals and to inspire new groups of tightly knit friends. Among thoughtful believers, it was to be the surrender of self-sufficiency in exchange for an emotional assurance beyond the reach of the cold hand of science. It was to be the entry into a world beautified by the Creator, a world more glorious than any industrial city. A reborn faith was to be given authority in those mysterious depths of the heart which were to be explored in literature by the Romantic movement and its successors. A revitalized congregation was to be far more conscious that it believed in the revealed God and wished to worship him, while the surrounding society became increasingly godless. In the cities created by industry there were to be faithful congregations, even if not many members of the new working class belonged to them for profoundly religious reasons. This recovery was to enable Christian soldiers to march against secularization; to fight and sometimes to conquer.

There was a widespread reaction against the French Revolution's bloody chaos in the 1790s, and with that came a reaction against the revolutionaries' religion of reason. In many areas of Europe the reaction produced a positive intensity in belonging to the Catholic Church (even Napoleon had to come to terms with the Papacy in order to be an emperor) and in Germany the rebirth of nationalism in the struggle against the French was accompanied by a revival of Lutheranism. The psychological forces which rallied against the French Revolution had, however, begun to grow long before the 1800s or 1790s. Emotionally the strongest form of Lutheranism was 'Pietism', a movement which had been started as long ago as the 1660s. Pietism was always marked by a warmly personal devotion to Jesus as Saviour, by private Bible study, and by enthusiasm in hymn-singing and other forms of worship. The old faith had been given a new life. In the English-speaking world, when the reaction against the excesses of the French Revolution needed to be expressed in a powerful, conservative religion, the Evangelical movement already existed and reaped the benefit. It was a renewal of conservative religion in many ways parallel with the Pietism of the German Lutherans, but its first large successes were achieved when Calvinism burst into flame in colonial America.

In Pennsylvania and other American 'middle colonies' in the 1730s, Presbyterian preachers breathed life into a Calvinism which had become a dull orthodoxy, while in New England others revived the religion (without the politics) of the Puritans. But the greatest name was that of Jonathan Edwards. The son and grandson of Puritan preachers of the old school, his own power was fresh when at Northampton in western Massachusetts he proclaimed the revived faith in God's sovereignty. A widely distributed public lecture of 1731 was entitled 'God Glorified in the Work of Redemption by the Greatness of Man's Dependence upon him in the Whole of It'. By the summer of 1735, Edwards later recalled, 'the town seemed to be full of the presence of God'.

Although his style was not that of a popular preacher, he was willing to disturb the emotions in his offer of salvation. Indeed, his *Treatise concerning Religious Affections* argued with skill that true religion consisted of emotions, stirred by the Spirit of God. In a particularly famous sermon he spoke of what befell 'Sinners in the Hands of an Angry God' and since he believed that people who did not repent of their sins before death would be condemned to the endless tortures of hell ('the God that holds you over the pit of hell, much as one holds a spider, or some loathsome insect over the fire, abhors you . . .'), he could scarcely be expected to remain unemotional when preaching. But with this frank appeal to the heart went careful reasoning.

In a series of books published in the 1750s he expounded a Calvinist view of man by attempting to answer the claims of the rationalist enlightenment with its own weapons. Pondering the freedom of the will, or the nature of sin, or the character of 'benevolence' in the virtuous man, he deepened the discussion. He presented man as a whole person who had to choose between darkness and light; as a figure in a tragedy, in that he habitually chose darkness; but also as potentially a son of God, filled by God's grace with God's light. In many ways this ardent Calvinist was a civilized member of the eighteenth century, standing in the tradition of many of the English Puritans of the previous century but fully aware of more recent thought; his death in 1758 (soon after becoming president of the recently founded college at Princeton) was caused by his willingness to be inoculated against smallpox. And because his theology had this thoughtful quality, it had an enduring influence. It has been pointed out that 'in western Christendom, the Pietist movement did not generally produce a theological school. . . . Re-awakened piety in New England, however, thanks to the genius of Jonathan Edwards, was followed by and incorporated in a theological school; it thereby stands unique; it thereby survived.'[1]

For Jonathan Edwards life was far from serene. He had to leave his church at Northampton in 1750; most people in his congregation had become intolerably irritated by his habits – by his aloofness (he read or wrote for thirteen hours a day), by his refusal to admit new church members until they had first given an account of their faith which satisfied him, by his frequent absences as the spiritual leader of a revival which seemed questionable, and even by the salary he sought in order to maintain a handsome wife and family. He simply did not fit into a little community devoted to food, drink and gossip. So he moved to the frontier settlement of Stourbridge in the glorious Berkshire mountains. There he wrote his great books but also acted as a missionary to the Indians. More controversial still were some of those who assisted and followed Edwards. Lacking altogether his spiritual refinement and intellectual interests, these men became the founders of the notorious traditions of a debased revivalism or fundamentalism, exploiting the guilt and fear of simple people, welcoming hysteria and making a commercial profit. Such were some of the problems surrounding the Great Awakening which was called the 'new light'.[2]

The Calvinist awakening did not really touch the well-educated gentlemen who were the founding fathers of American independence – Washington and Jefferson the Virginian plantation owners, Franklin and Adams among the intellectuals. To them, as to many of the clergy, the new enthusiasm was irrational and its popularity was dangerous to the whole order of a respectable society. Nor should the popularity of Calvinism, or of any other kind of religion, be exaggerated. Harvard, Yale and other colleges adhered to the more peaceful 'old light' during and after the revivals. It is reckoned that by 1790 only about a tenth of the thirteen colonies' four million or

---

[1] E. S. Gausted, *The Great Awakening in New England* (New York, 1957), p. 138.

[2] See Perry Miller, *Jonathan Edwards* (New York, 1949), and *Jonathan Edwards: A Profile*, ed. David Levin (New York, 1969). The more human side was presented by Elisabeth Dodds, *Marriage to a Difficult Man: 'The Uncommon Union' of Jonathan and Sarah Edwards* (Philadelphia, Pa., 1975).

more inhabitants (three-quarters of whom were white) definitely belonged to a Christian congregation. But the orthodoxy of the new preaching did show that the coldly 'rational' religion was not going to have an unopposed victory; it did arouse the interest, however superficial, of hundreds of thousands; and it did convert thousands of individuals. In the southern colonies Baptist congregations began to multiply, providing a permanently popular alternative to an Anglicanism still aristocratic in its ethos. This warm-hearted version of Christianity provided a religion to which slaves could become converted, and it troubled the consciences of slave-owners sufficiently to prompt a few of them to encourage such conversions. More easily it appealed to the poor whites who had found themselves in virtual slavery as 'indentured servants', labouring to pay for their passages. In the middle colonies and in New England the revival led to the insistence of many congregations on taking responsibility for their own spiritual life, without control by the local group of ministers; since these independent congregations had now usually come to believe that baptism should be restricted to believing adults, they helped to make the Baptist denomination the largest in America.

This religious revival dramatically challenged the sheer materialism which, after the decay of Puritanism, had become the philosophy of free settlers rapidly getting richer. Americans had come to respect what was practical, what worked, what was self-evident; but now it seemed possible to demonstrate that Christian experience was in that category. A love of the Bible, an enthusiasm for personal improvement, a belief that the true Christian must be 'born again' – all these convictions began to be associated with the American character. They were to be transported into the wilderness as the Frontier moved west. Preachers also changed. They now depended far less on their status in society or on their theological scholarship, and far more on their down-to-earth appeal to the people.[3]

National unity was awakened. Because preachers travelled

---

[3] W. T. Youngs studied *God's Messengers: Religious Leadership in Colonial New England* (Baltimore, Md., 1976).

from church to church and from colony to colony, speaking in glowing terms about revivals in the places from which they had come, holding up a vision of Christian America, the lines of communication up and down the Atlantic coast were strengthened, challenging the inherent tendency of British imperialism to link each colony direct with 'home'. The awakening pushed the colonies towards a future in which the culture was to be still basically Christian, but proud of the new freedom enjoyed by many denominations; still indebted to the religious heritage of Europe, but newly confident in its own vigour. Although Calvinism was to become only one star on the theological flag, the whole American idea owed much to this contribution. 'The Awakenings were not the sole source of the American sense of destiny,' a leading historian has written, 'but they made it convincing to masses of men and women, and they often intensified the feeling in the soul of a people.'[4]

The results were seen in the 1770s. The cutting of the political links with England might have been traumatic for all American religion – had the religion been as feeble, as dependent on initiatives from the old country, as it had been before the Calvinist awakening. As it was, the problems of independence seem to have been severe only for the 'Loyalists' who adhered to the Crown and the Church of England. Their churches and rectories now became obvious targets for some mob violence, and in the northern American colonies the situation was so tense that many thousands moved northwards. But American Anglicans had for long enjoyed a practical independence and were now determined to be faithful to the 'Episcopal' church order without remaining loyal to the English king or to the English bishops who had so long hindered Anglican expansion by their refusal to supply an American bishop. Most of the signatures on the Declaration of Independence (including Washington's) were of men who had been members of the Church of England in its days of privilege. A clergyman acceptable to these rebels, although he had denounced the rebellion, was sent over with strict instructions to

---

    [4] Robert T. Handy, *A History of the Churches in the United States and Canada* (New York, 1976), p. 115.

return as a bishop. His name was Samuel Seabury. Having been denied consecration in London (on the ground that he would not swear allegiance to George III), he achieved it in 1784 at the hands of Scottish bishops in Aberdeen. Three years later two others were made bishops in London to shepherd the American Episcopal Church, an Act of Parliament having recognized that the step was inevitable – a century and a half too late.[5]

The other American denominations had fewer formal ties with England, and in these there was far less confusion of conscience about the rebellion. As the Declaration of Independence proclaimed, the truths on which it was based were 'self-evident' (in the original draft, 'sacred and undeniable'). The justification of England's own revolution of 1688–89 was well known, particularly in the philosophy of John Locke. In Locke was the key argument that a contract between the ruler and the ruled could be broken. However, it is clear that Calvinist theology also inspired men to rebel against a 'tyrant', in America in the 1770s as in England in the 1640s. The only clergyman to sign the Declaration of Independence was John Witherspoon, a Calvinist who had succeeded Edwards in the presidency of the Princeton college; but his signature did represent a revived tradition that a people was divinely destined to freedom. Indeed, when the fires of the Calvinist revival began to die down in the 1740s, some of the vision of the coming reign of Christ on earth was still retained and translated into American patriotic idealism. It has been observed that 'amid the shifting intellectual currents of eighteenth-century New England, one theme above all others maintained its hold on the clergy. It was the solid conviction that their own community had been chosen as a special people of God.'[6]

[5] See Carl Bridenbaugh, *Mitre and Sceptre: Transatlantic Faiths, Ideas, Personalities and Politics 1689–1775* (New York, 1962), and for an English acknowledgement of guilt H. G. G. Herklots, *The Church of England and the American Episcopal Church* (London, 1966).

[6] Nathan O. Hatch, *The Sacred Cause of Liberty* (New Haven, Conn., 1977), p. 59. Other recent studies include Alan Heimest, *Religion and the American Mind: From the Great Awakening to the Revolution* (Cambridge, Mass., 1966); Bernard Bailyn, *The Intellectual Origins of the American Revolution* (Cambridge, Mass., 1967); Robert Middlekauff, *The Glorious Cause: The American Revolution 1763–1789* (New York, 1982).

After independence some efforts were made to preserve the legally established Churches with the plea that the alternative was atheism. In Virginia Patrick Henry defended the Anglican establishment against James Madison, but Thomas Jefferson's Bill for Establishing Religious Freedom was finally passed in 1786. The same period saw the end of the privileges of the Church of England in the other colonies, as the first written state constitutions in history were adopted. In Massachusetts, Connecticut and New Hampshire, however, the Congregationalist heirs of the Puritans delayed the change, merely offering other Protestant denominations a share in the taxes. The matter was settled by the First Amendment to the Constitution, which came into effect in 1791: 'Congress shall make no law respecting an establishment of religion, or prohibiting the free exercise thereof.' That was a bold new step; in Europe the Church had enjoyed privileges from the State ever since Constantine had established his own authority as the first Christian (or semi-Christian) emperor by the battle near the Milvian Bridge over the Tiber in 312. But in the infant United States the churches generally expressed confidence that they could flourish since they had a vital Gospel to preach.[7]

Surveying the deeply emotional appeal to individuals made by preachers such as Jonathan Edwards, H. Richard Niebuhr offered this assessment. 'The Awakening arose in the new world of emancipated individuals who had become their own political masters to an uncommon degree. It dealt with men and families who through the acquisition of free or cheap land had been made economically independent. It confronted men who were being intellectually emancipated from the dogmas of the past by the filtering down into common life of ideas developed by scientists and philosophers. It spoke to people who had been freed to no small extent from the bonds of customary morality. . . . It was no wholly new beginning, for the Christianity expressed in it was a more venerable thing

---

[7] The standard survey is A. P. Stokes and L. Pfeffer, *Church and State in the United States* (revised, New York, 1964).

than the American nation. Yet for Americans it was a new beginning; it was our national conversion.'[8]

With the achievement of American independence in politics and religion, a history of English Christianity must end its coverage of the United States. But an Englishman yet to be mentioned had been the greatest preacher of the Calvinist awakening in colonial America; and George Whitefield's work did much to suggest what would be the future of the Christian religion on both shores of the Atlantic.

GEORGE WHITEFIELD
AND THE SECOND BIRTH

George Whitefield crossed the Atlantic thirteen times. The feat was then very rare outside the ranks of professional sailors. Almost as rare were his American journeys between north and south. He made the greatest appeal to the public while still in his twenties, and the accounts of the hysterical adulation surrounding the 'boy preacher' in the 1740s have their closest parallels in the history of popular musicians. He was good-looking, although his eyes had a squint and he was satirized in a London play 'Dr Squintum', a nickname which stuck. And he was loud. People were fascinated by the extraordinary power of his voice without any artificial amplification; Benjamin Franklin, who became his friend but did not take seriously what he had to say, once calculated during a sermon that such a voice could reach thirty thousand people if the wind was favourable. Those who listened to the words found a delightful new style. 'He has', said that old cynic Lord Boling-broke, 'the most commanding eloquence I ever heard.'

Whitefield preached extempore in an age when the reading of sermons had become standard. He was a powerful story-teller; he once had Lord Chesterfield crying out in excitement during one of his many anecdotes. He was colloquial and controversial; in a pamphlet he wrote that Archbishop Tillot-

---

[8] H. Richard Niebuhr, *The Kingdom of God in America* (New York, 1935), pp. 99, 126.

son (still the idol of sensible Church of England men) knew as little about the all-important doctrine of justification by faith 'as Mahomet'. He expected emphatic approval or disapproval; a complaint was made to the Bishop of Gloucester who had just made him a deacon that his very first sermon 'drove fifteen mad'. Many, of course, disapproved of him; the gentle Isaac Watts rebuked his closest friend, Philip Doddridge, for 'sinking the character of a minister, and especially of a tutor among the Dissenters, so low as to collaborate with Whitefield.' But Whitefield was well received when he visited the dying Watts. David Garrick the actor said that such an orator could make people weep or cheer by the way he pronounced the word 'Mesopotamia'. But any entertainment provided by the sermon almost always ended up with a message which made the preacher weep as he delivered it. It was the message of the 'new birth', of a union with the Christ who had preached from the cross. That was what entitled Whitefield to be called 'the greatest evangelist of the British race'.[9]

Although a Calvinist, he seems never to have made any close study of John Calvin's works. His doctrine flowed out of his own experience. As a lad he had served beer in the inn kept by his widowed mother in Gloucester. At Oxford he had been a poor 'servitor' who waited on his fellow students, and away from the beery applause of the inn he had become socially insecure, lonely and morbidly introspective. His attempts to lead a rigidly pious and priggish life, his incessant self-examination and his very severe fasting had brought him to a collapse, like Martin Luther as a young monk in the 1510s. The turning point for George Whitefield had come when he had read a meditation by a seventeenth-century bishop, Joseph Hall, about Christ's words from the cross, 'I thirst'. He saw then that the helplessness of the sinner must be greater than the helplessness of the Saviour. All that could be essential was the prayer of naked faith, the total reliance on the merits of the Saviour who by the sacrifice of his death had satisfied the

---

    [9] Albert D. Belden, *George Whitefield the Awakener* (revised, London, 1953), p. 3. For contrasting styles in the pulpit, see *The English Sermon, 1750–1850*, ed. Robert Nye (London, 1976).

justice of the angry God. And he saw this for himself without any living man's help, believing that his life had been changed solely by God's fully sovereign mercy, by the predestinating decree which saved some while damning others. The 'new birth' had redeemed this self-condemning, poor, isolated student when all his natural resources had broken down. The experience became the dominant, almost the only, theme of his preaching; and he began preaching less than a year after his crisis, which occurred soon after Easter 1735.

The pattern of his work was formed with an astonishing rapidity. He refused to be tied to any one parish, or to do general pastoral work. By talk and by letter he told individuals about the new birth and urgently invited them to share it; and if he was not allowed to preach in church he was ready to preach out of doors. This was not a completely novel action. George Fox, other Quakers and other radicals had preached out of doors in the previous century. A Welsh layman, Howell Harris, had begun such preaching soon after his conversion in 1735, and by 1739 there were nearly thirty little societies of converts, the origins of Welsh Calvinistic Methodism. But the Conventicle and Toleration Acts were still the law, forbidding preaching outside churches and licensed Dissenters' meeting houses; and at first a respectable clergyman such as John Wesley thought 'field-preaching' a 'mad action'. Within little more than three years of his own 'new birth' Whitefield had crossed the Atlantic and had caught the vision of all the American colonies 'ablaze for God'. He published a journal of this voyage – the first of much journalism about his mission. Returning home in order to be ordained priest, he had become an itinerant evangelist and as such had felt responsible for the souls of the notorious miners of Kingswood, near Bristol. On a Saturday afternoon in 1739, he advanced towards a little knot of them and called out: 'Blessed are the poor in spirit!' Before the end of his open-air sermon the miners' tears were making white rivers down their faces.

Inevitably such preaching was despised and rejected by many. David Hume (who held that Calvinism 'divinized cruelty, wrath, fury, vengeance and all the blackest vices') wrote to Gibbon: 'Among many marks of decline, the prevalence of superstition in England prognosticates the fall of philosophy and the decay of taste.' The Duchess of Buckingham thought it 'monstrous to be told that you have a heart as sinful as the common wretches that crawl on the earth.' Samuel Johnson objected on other grounds: 'I believe he did good. But when familiarity and noise claim the praise due to knowledge, art and elegance, we must beat down such pretensions.' Many popular satirists depicted him as 'a grotesque figure, a buffoon – contemptible and ridiculous . . . lewdly squinting at this congregation as he picks their pockets'.[10] But large audiences trembled when reminded of the angry God or wept when told of the Saviour's self-sacrifice.

Part of the impact of the message was due to the preacher's own willingness to sacrifice everything to it. He defied the authorities of his Church by being willing to preach in other men's parishes uninvited – or in non-Anglican chapels. He faced many journeys, perils and blows. And in part his success was due to his ruthlessness. The southernmost English colony of Georgia, with its little capital Savannah, had been founded by General James Oglethorpe in 1732. The chief aim had been to provide a refuge for Englishmen imprisoned for debt (a subsidiary aim being the defence of the older English colonies against the Spaniards in Florida). Oglethorpe had insisted that no slaves – not even 'indentured' English servants – should be used. The Georgians were to do their own work in clearing the land for agriculture. Whitefield was soon appointed rector of Savannah and might have been expected to have become the idealistic colony's chief pastor. Instead he was seldom in his own church, and his main contribution to the colony was to insist that slaves were needed to develop the land around his favourite project, an orphanage which was to train missionaries. But Whitefield could also be ruthless with his fellow whites. When he proposed marriage by post to an English lady, his letter to her was preoccupied by her future duties in the orphanage. To her parents he wrote: 'I am free from the foolish passion which the world calls *Love*. I write only because I believe it is the will of God that I should alter my state; but your

---

[10] Albert M. Lyles, *Methodism Mocked* (London, 1960), p. 138.

denial will finally convince me that your daughter is not the person appointed for me.' It did.

At first he regarded the still more famous evangelist John Wesley as his spiritual father. When he had won fame as a preacher, he thought of Wesley as his successor first in Bristol and then in all England; he would concentrate on America. By 1740, however, the split between the two men had led to pamphlets issued on the two sides of the Atlantic and when they met again in the following year there was no deep reconciliation. On the surface the split was due to Whitefield's Calvinism. Wesley thought it monstrous to teach that God could predestine the majority of the human race to hell, and said so. He also thought it very dangerous to believe that one was among God's favourites, the 'elect', however one behaved; he had in mind his own brother-in-law Westley Hall, a fervent preacher who fled to the West Indies with one of his many mistresses. Whitefield, in his turn, warned Wesley about the dangers in his optimistic teaching that converted Christians could and should be 'perfect'; this preacher knew that he was not perfect himself and never expected others to be. However, it may be doubted whether a theological disagreement was the fundamental cause of the split. There was a clash of personalities.

Whitefield was not a rival organizer to Wesley; he knew that his talents did not lie in that field. He was delighted when a masterful woman appeared on the scene with strong Calvinist convictions and great wealth – Selina, Countess of Huntingdon. He accepted her money for two buildings, a 'tabernacle' for his preaching at Moorfields in London and a larger 'chapel' in Tottenham Court Road, and wrote to his patron: 'A *Leader* is wanting. This honour has been put upon your Ladyship by the Great Head of the Church.'[11] He never set himself up as a leader to whom a network of societies should be attached. He often said: 'Let the name of Whitefield perish!' He once catalogued his own faults: 'I have been too rash and hasty in giving characters, both of places and persons. . . . Being fond of Scripture language, I have often used a style too apostolical.

---

[11] See J. B. Figgis, *The Countess of Huntingdon and her Connexion* (London, 1982).

. . . I have been too bitter in my zeal. . . . I have published too soon and too explicitly what had been better kept in longer or told after my death. . . .' (The last confession rightly lamented the indiscretion of publishing his journals up to 1741 as a naïve autobiography – a gift to the wits.) But of one thing Whitefield was sure. He had been called by God to preach the new birth. Trying to conquer asthma in the bedroom of the Presbyterian minister's house in a little town in Massachusetts, he told a young assistant: 'A good pulpit sweat today may give me relief; I shall be better after preaching.' The young man expressed the friendly wish that he would conserve his energies and not preach so often. This evangelist who longed to be in the pulpit again had, after all, preached about a thousand times a year for some thirty years. He had probably spoken to more people than anyone else in the world's history. But he was obstinate when his young companion warned him against over-exertion. 'I had rather wear out than rust out', replied George Whitefield.[12]

THE CONVERSION OF THE WESLEYS

In his native England the only plainly visible results of all George Whitefield's preaching were the congregations of a few chapels registered as Dissenting meeting houses. The contrast is great with Methodism, led by John Wesley. When he died in 1791 the *Gentleman's Magazine* paid John Wesley a generous tribute, while implying that he had little to offer a gentleman. 'By the humane endeavours of him and his brother Charles a sense of decency in morals and religion was introduced into the lowest classes of mankind. . . . He was one of the few characters who outlived enmity and prejudice, and received in his later years every mark of esteem from every denomination. . . . His personal influence was greater than any private gentleman in the country. . . . Instead of being an ornament to literature he was a blessing to his fellows; instead of the genius of his age, he was the servant of God.'

---

[12] See Arnold Dallimore, *George Whitefield* (2 vols., London, 1970–80), and John Pollock, *George Whitefield and the Great Awakening* (London, 1973).

John Wesley's dominance over Methodism made it Arminian, not Calvinist; its journal, founded in 1778, was for many years called the *Arminian Magazine*. At first sight it is bewildering that the Arminian theology condemned by James I as a Dutch heresy, but adopted by Charles I and the Cavaliers, should now become the creed of a popular religious movement. But it is clear that for almost all the early Methodists what mattered about Arminianism was that it inspired much evangelism, and released many converts from nightmares, by its insistence that Christ had died in order to save *all*, not merely the predestined elect, from hell. The 'all' which had attracted the prosperous early disciples of the Dutch professor named Arminius, and which had then attracted the court of Charles I as a slogan to defend civilization against religious fanatics, was now a trumpet-blast to summon English sinners from all kinds of feckless living. Certainly the early Methodists, who responded to that 'all' with changed lives, were not absorbed in theological speculations. On the contrary, Methodism was a vibrant and often vulgar form of popular religion, thanks to two brothers. One was an organizer of religion, more effective than any other Englishman had been in that role since William the Conqueror's archbishop, Lanfranc; the other was a poet who wrote seven thousand hymns which the people could sing. When we study the origins of Methodism, we study an appeal to the people – in principle, to 'all' – made by John and Charles Wesley.

We also study the effects of the training which they had received in Epworth Rectory in Lincolnshire. John Wesley often repeated that he was a High Churchman and the son of a High Churchman. Charles Wesley wrote hymns which taught a more Catholic understanding of the Eucharist than could be heard from any Anglican bishop or professor in that age. Their father, Samuel Wesley, Rector of Epworth for thirty-eight years from 1697, was a convert to this high Anglicanism from Dissent. He was also rigid, dictatorial and hot-tempered, resolved to do his pastoral duty as he saw it although many of his parishioners responded with insults or physical violence. The remote and water-logged area where his parish lay had been drained in the reign of Charles I, and the parishioners had then lost many of their ancestors' rights. That seems to be one reason why the cause of Church and King was locally unpopular. But the rector's arrogance did not help. After his own ordination, John Wesley always insisted on managing the affairs of anyone who was at all willing to allow him to interfere. He gave people spiritual, moral, financial, political and medical instruction. Although he was supremely unqualified for this role, he even distributed marriage guidance. He could not help preaching, even when talking or writing to women who were hoping to hear from him some profession of love. When his mother died, he wrote to his brother: 'My heart does not, and I am absolutely sure God does not, condemn me for any want of duty towards her in any kind, except only that I have not reproved her so plainly and fully as I should have done.' And he was never willing to collaborate with anyone who might be an equal.

Yet in the final analysis, his power was spiritual – and his spiritual greatness was forged in the heat of his relationships with these parents. His father loved going to London as a member of the militantly Tory House of Clergy in the Convocation; and his patron was Queen Anne's favourite, Archbishop Sharp. When the Convocation was suspended and Queen Anne dead, he still clung to an orthodoxy imbibed in Oxford in the 1680s. When in 1724 John Wesley had graduated and was preparing for ordination, Samuel sent him a long list of standard theology to absorb; and he added: 'If you have any scruples about any point of Revelation or the scheme of the Church of England (which I think exactly agreeable to it) I can answer 'em.' Less amusing is the way in which Samuel Wesley treated the most beautiful and the cleverest of his daughters, Hetty, who became pregnant as a result of a night with a lawyer whom she wrongly believed was going to marry her the next morning. Her father never forgave her, drove her into a wretched and totally unsuitable marriage, and was unmoved when her first child and three others died. John tried to reconcile his father to his sister, but we can see how he formed his own early image of God as the unmerciful Judge.

Samuel Wesley married Susanna Annesley (and had to leave the parish which he held before moving to Epworth because he objected to the squire's mistress talking to his respectable wife). Susanna was the twenty-fifth child of a clergyman who possessed a private fortune and an independent mind, ending up as one of the leading Dissenting preachers. Defoe said that 'nothing in him was little or mean'. Although from the age of thirteen Susanna dissented from Dissent, her father's standards were passed on to her own nineteen children – or to those of them who survived infancy. She was as inflexible as her father or her husband. As a Jacobite she refused to say 'Amen' when Samuel Wesley prayed for William III, and did not yield even when Samuel left home for a prolonged period of sulks and threatened to enlist as a chaplain in the navy. John Wesley was born in 1703, nine months after their reconciliation.

Samuel mismanaged his affairs (he was once imprisoned for debt) and consoled himself by writing books which very few people wanted to read. He was a clumsy poet and his great work was a Latin treatise on the Book of Job. (This work, which he was sure would make his fame and fortune, was presented to the Queen after his death. She observed that it was 'bound prettily'.) His rectory was twice burned down, perhaps by hostile parishioners, and John Wesley was nearly left to perish in the flames in 1709 – which was why he thought of himself as a 'brand plucked out of the burning'. The much more practical Susanna rebuilt home and family after these disasters, although their furniture and clothing were never grand, and food and heat were often problems. She conducted family life with the routine to be expected in a very strict boarding school, and undertook the religious instruction of each of her children in private. As an adult John Wesley still recalled his Thursday evenings alone with her, and wrote to her for guidance. She also instructed the parishioners on a Sunday evening in her kitchen, while her husband was away and she disapproved of the curate. She was widely read. Her own missionary work in this fenland parish was inspired by reading about what Danish missionaries were doing in India, and her religion of the heart was fed by the *Pensées* of Blaise Pascal. It was characteristic of her that, while her husband urged John to study standard Anglican theology before ordination, she begged him to concentrate on 'practical divinity'. By that she meant partly the writings of her father's fellow Puritans, but also a larger literature. Both she and her son grew to be deeply interested in Pascal's fellow Catholics in seventeenth-century France. In the 1730s John Wesley, still encouraged by Susanna, was fast becoming an authority on the literature of mysticism.[13]

Between them, therefore, Samuel and Susanna Wesley conveyed a complex heritage. Such a childhood produced three priests of the Church of England who in many ways resembled their parents – John, Charles and their elder brother Samuel (a schoolmaster who disapproved of Methodism as a novelty). It is impressive that these parents, although so often in debt, managed to send their sons to public schools and to the university for the best education then available in England, and it should never be forgotten that one great advantage possessed by the Wesleys was that they were the intellectual equals or superiors of their critics. But a terrible price was paid. The parents were not able to be of much help in the general emotional development of their children. Of all of them, only Charles made a happy marriage. And even the religion on which all the family's efforts were concentrated was bound to lead to an explosion.

In the eighteenth century comfortable and rational Anglicans often regretted that, with such parents, John and Charles Wesley were bound to be enthusiasts or fanatics. In the years 1745–48, an eminent churchman (who called himself 'John Smith' but almost certainly was Thomas Secker, later Archbishop of Canterbury) wrote a series of six thoughtful public letters to John Wesley about the dangers in the movement he had started. Typical was the warning: 'The son of a Wesley and an Annesley is in no danger of *lukewarmness*, but ought to take great care on the side of *impetuosity* and *zeal*.'

---

[13] John A. Newton has presented *Susanna Wesley and the Puritan Tradition in Methodism* (London, 1968). Maximin Piette, S. J., *John Wesley and the Evolution of Protestantism* (English translation, London 1937), stressed the interest in Catholic spirituality which she also encouraged, while Elsie Harrison's highly readable *Son to Susanna* (London, 1937) claimed that she had altogether too much influence emotionally.

Actually, however, before the religion of Epworth Rectory could explode into nationwide Methodism, it had to implode inwards, into a very distressing psychological crisis produced by the understanding of religion as a life of strict obedience to a stern law.

Both John and Charles Wesley seem to have been fairly normal at school and as university freshmen. While at Oxford, however, they studied devotional books; John recalled Jeremy Taylor in 1725, Thomas à Kempis next year, and William Law 'a year or two after'. These books summoned them back to the strict standards which had been impressed on them as little boys. So they tried their utmost to be obedient to the law of holiness – but as they tried, their very successes seemed failures to their over-active consciences. They had to suffer much before love could liberate them from absorption in the question whether they were sufficiently obedient. Guilt accumulated – and the price to be paid for the removal of guilt seemed to be the total renunciation of the ordinary pleasures of life. Against this price they rebelled, being intelligent, energetic, strongly sexed and often attractive young men. They were plunged more miserably into themselves. A desperate longing for love and joy, rather than the stern logic of a law which all must in measure disobey, was the meaning of Charles Wesley's famous hymn:

> Love divine, all loves excelling,
> Joy of heaven, to earth come down. . . .

And the contrasting vision of Christ as Judge of the World has never been expressed better than in his Advent hymn, 'Lo, he comes with clouds descending'.

The brothers' self-absorbed religion seems to have made them incapable of ordinary friendships. In Oxford, for example, the 'Holy Club' was founded by Charles and directed by John from 1729. It did indeed cultivate personal holiness and did dispense charity with religious instruction to prisoners and other poor people. But the extravagance in fasting contributed to, or caused, George Whitefield's breakdown and the actual death of another member, William Morgan. No member of the club was of any real help to Whitefield in his spiritual torments, while the average undergraduate regarded the whole lot of them as exhibitionist prigs.

Soon after their father's death in 1735 both John and Charles accepted invitations to serve in the new colony of Georgia – the former as a missionary to the Red Indians, the latter (who was far more reluctant) as General Oglethorpe's secretary. John's motive was 'to save my soul' and 'to learn the true sense of the Gospel of Christ by preaching it to the heathen'. Finding that his main duties lay among the white settlers, he was so naïve as to believe that they would be willing to live like members of the Holy Club, while in his few contacts with the Indians he was surprised to find that they were not the innocent children of nature he had expected. Both the brothers were extraordinarily clumsy in their relationships with women. The feckless Charles sorely tried his employer, and despite a reconciliation, asked to be sent home. John had to make his escape having outraged the little colony by refusing to give Holy Communion to the girl who a few months previously had seemed about to become his wife, on the ground that her church attendance had lately been too infrequent. The whole of their missionary journey was a disaster.

After this humiliation in Georgia (where Whitefield became popular), it was evident to the brothers that they needed something. Worldly contemporaries thought that they needed common sense. They were, however, nothing if not religious, God-conscious, and they were sure that their need was to feel the forgiving love of God before they could preach that love effectively. They also knew that this assurance had to come from God alone; they could not earn it. They were ripe for the message that human morality or philosophy must be forgotten in the presence of the all-holy God; that forgiveness from this God must be accepted in penitence and joy, and could never be earned by keeping a law; that true holiness was not the cause of true faith in God, but the fruit of that faith; that everything depended on God being love, not wrath. The Wesleys already knew all this teaching as a theory. It was the Reformation doctrine of justification by faith alone, still proclaimed by the official documents of the Church of England although not much taught in this period. (John Wesley understood the great

Bishop Joseph Butler as saying of faith that it 'is a good work; it is a virtuous temper of mind'.) But the point was that the Wesleys had not felt the power of this doctrine for themselves.

In a state of physical and spiritual collapse, Charles Wesley went to lodge in a devout working-class home in London. He heard his hostess's sister say outside his door: 'In the name of Jesus of Nazareth, arise and believe, that thou mayest be healed of thy infirmities.' He then opened his Bible at random (a dangerous practice to which the brothers were always addicted) and fortunately found the words: 'He hath put a new song in my mouth, even a thanksgiving unto our God. Many shall see it, and fear, and shall put their trust in the Lord.' Before he slept Charles wrote in his journal: 'I now found myself at peace with God . . . I saw that by faith I stood. . . .' The day was Whitsunday 1738.

Within three days, on 24 May, John Wesley who was also in London, and also near to a complete breakdown, had a closely similar experience. That afternoon he attended Evensong in St Paul's Cathedral, where the anthem matched his mood: 'Out of the deep have I called unto thee, O Lord. . . .' That evening he went reluctantly to a meeting in Aldersgate Street of one of London's religious societies, and heard a visiting German preacher. The sermon was an exposition of a key document dating from the Reformation of the sixteenth century, Martin Luther's Preface to St Paul's letter to the Romans. And that night John Wesley was taken by friends in triumph to Charles's sickroom, exclaiming: 'I believe!' In the famous words of his journal: 'About a quarter before nine o'clock while he was describing the change which God works in the heart through faith in Christ, I felt my heart strangely warmed. I felt I did trust in Christ, Christ alone for salvation; and an assurance was given me that He had taken away *my* sins, even *mine*, and saved me from the law of sin and death.'

The experience which John and Charles Wesley underwent in 1738 was not totally transforming. Both brothers continued to know paralysing moods of depression and self-condemnation. 'I do not love God,' John wrote to Charles in 1766, 'I never did. I am only an honest heathen. . . . If I have any fear, it is not of falling into hell, but of falling into nothing.'

But in that same letter may be found words more typical of the thoroughly converted, thoroughly dictatorial, preacher whom England had come to know: 'O insist everywhere on full redemption, receivable by *faith alone*; consequently to be looked for *now*. . . . We must have a thorough *reform of the preachers*.' In 1738 John Wesley preached on 'Salvation by Faith' in the university church at Oxford eighteen days after the warming of his heart; and he preached at length and with power. And some four years later, Charles put the brothers' experience into a hymn which is a classic:

> Come O thou Traveller unknown,
> Whom still I hold, but cannot see,
> My company before is gone,
> And I am left alone with thee. . . .
>
> 'Tis Love, 'tis Love! Thou dieds't for me,
> I hear thy whisper in my heart!
> The morning breaks, the shadows flee;
> Pure Universal Love thou art. . . .[14]

JOHN WESLEY AND THE METHODISTS

John Wesley is said to have travelled about a quarter of a million miles on horseback or, when old, in a simple coach; it is the distance of the moon from the earth. He is also thought to have preached about forty thousand times. A bibliography published in 1896 listed 233 books or tracts by him, more than a hundred others edited by him, and English, French, Latin, Greek and Hebrew grammars which he compiled. The subjects which he handled included tea, electricity and the history

---

[14] The best introductory biographies are V. H. H. Green, *John Wesley* (London, 1964), and Stanley Ayling, *John Wesley* (London, 1979), both rather hostile. They need to be supplemented by Martin Schmidt's 'theological biography', *John Wesley* in 3 vols. (London, 1962–73), and by the background provided in *A History of the Methodist Church in Great Britain*, edited by Rupert Davies and Gordon Rupp (vol. 1, London, 1965). More details are in V. H. H. Green, *The Young Mr Wesley* (London, 1961); J. E. Rattenbury, *The Conversion of the Wesleys* (London, 1937); and J. S. Simon, *John Wesley* (5 vols., London, 1921–34). Frederic C. Gill studied *Charles Wesley the First Methodist* (London, 1964).

of Rome. He spent about three-quarters of the year on the road and was not deterred by the prohibitions of his fellow clergy, by the suspicions of the magistrates, by rioting mobs, by illness, by rain or by snow. He arose each morning at four, conducted a service at five on most days of his life, spent about ten hours a day riding (and usually reading or even writing at the same time), preached and dispensed pastoral guidance most evenings and was fast asleep soon after ten. He earned about £30,000 as an author but lived on under £30 a year, giving the rest away. In his old age the bitter unpopularity he had undergone was little more than material for his frequent reminiscences, and crowds flocked to see his snowy hair and his baby-like complexion. He had become a major celebrity, although many still scoffed at the irrationality of his message and at the low company he preferred. In 1791, the year of his death, there were 72,476 full members of 'societies' in the British Isles owing allegiance to him, with a much larger number of associates. Almost two centuries later there were in the world about eighteen million full Methodists, two-thirds of them in the United States.

When we come to assess John Wesley we are overwhelmed by the evidence. His *Journal* was published three or four years after the events being narrated, and a supplementary diary recorded his activities hour by hour. He wrote many letters in addition to all the material he put into print, and collected and polished up forty-four sermons which would provide an epitome of his theology. And the heart of Methodism beats still more audibly in *A Collection of Hymns for the Use of the People Called Methodists* which he edited in 1780; 480 of the 525 hymns were by his brother Charles. But the evidence still leaves a mystery. He never wrote a systematic treatise on theology or the Church, and it may be doubted if he was ever certain about his long-term aims.

What was the 'scriptural holiness' he wanted to 'spread throughout the land'? His experience in Aldersgate Street in 1738 was not often referred to in his lifetime, and the explanation may be that it suggested that a convert must simply be quiet and still. He was far too much of an activist to be still or quiet for very long, and when he had moved away from the

Moravians he said many harsh things about 'mysticism'. His understanding of faith was not Lutheran, although illumination had come to him through Luther. In his journal for 1741 he called Luther 'muddy and confused . . . deeply tinctured with mysticism'. He included none of Luther's works in the fifty-volume *Christian Library* which he edited between 1749 and 1755. And while the warming of his heart in 1738 brought assurance to him personally (in most moods), he came to reject the claim that a Christian could not be 'justified' if he or she had not been similarly assured. A conversion of his own type was, he came to see, only the 'common privilege'. It was not essential to salvation; the only essential was holiness, with love as its fruit. He welcomed dramatic evidences of conversion and when he preached a university sermon at Oxford in 1744, on the text 'And they were all filled with the Holy Ghost', he was so close to the New Testament that he was never asked to preach there again. But particularly after 1744 his main interest lay not in the eager beginnings of a Christian life but in growth in 'holiness' and 'knowledge'. It is one of the many paradoxes of his life that he who had braved so much hostility in order to preach salvation by faith alone lived to write (in his *Thoughts on Salvation by Faith*, 1779) that 'no man is finally saved without works'.

He was not entirely clear about the holiness he expected. He often spoke about 'the life of God in the soul of man', echoing the title of a book by a seventeenth-century Scotsman, Henry Scougal, that had meant much to him as a young man. He constantly taught converts to pray for 'Christian perfection' and seemed to his enemies to be reviving the folly of believing that converts did not need the conventional moral restraints. But he also taught that a strict and persevering self-discipline was absolutely necessary, and that without it a convert who had once been assured about his Saviour could still fall from 'grace' into hell. This teaching offended Calvinists, laying him open to further accusations that he still taught 'works-righteousness'. He defined sin in a limited way as the voluntary transgression of a known law, and it followed that his idea of 'perfection' was only freedom from sin so defined, a freedom which might prove temporary. On this basis he accepted claims made by some Methodists that they had achieved 'entire sanctification' and loved to record 'triumphant' death-beds. If he could, he would ask the dying: 'Do you see Jesus?' But he never claimed to be 'perfect' himself and what he meant about these Methodists was, it seems clear, the Catholic idea of the saint. Referring to the seventeenth-century Catholic saint, he once asked in a sermon: 'Who has spoken of sanctification in a stronger or more scriptural fashion than Francis of Sales?' But eighteenth-century England was not a place where it was easy to talk about the Catholic saints. Nor was Wesley willing to adopt the entire Catholic understanding of sanctity, since he did not believe that souls could be made holy in purgatory after death. Demanding of himself and others a real righteousness before death, rejoicing in the lives and holy deaths of the Methodists, he clung to this unsatisfactory term 'perfection'.[15]

About one thing he was absolutely clear. Holiness must be 'perfect love' – a transformed life with, and for, others. Therefore it must be 'social holiness', expressed by active membership of the visible Church and issuing in honest and loving behaviour in the world. In practical terms Methodism meant joining a Methodist 'society' – and for many years that meant, at least in John Wesley's eyes, fasting on Wednesday and Friday and attending two services every Sunday, before and after the two services to be attended in the parish church. It also meant being willing to be questioned and instructed about intimately personal matters of belief and behaviour. In effect the term 'Methodist', used in Oxford in the early 1730s to refer to men thought to be ridiculously methodical in their observance of the customs enjoined in the Book of Common Prayer, had come by the middle of the 1740s to mean people methodically Wesleyan. Preaching from a balcony in Philadelphia, Whitefield once cried out: 'Father Abraham, whom have you in heaven? Any Episcopalians? . . . Presbyterians? . . . Independents or Seceders? . . . Have you any Methodists?' And the answer from heaven came, according to Whitefield: 'We don't

---

[15] Methodist discussion includes R. N. Flew, *The Idea of Perfection in Christian Theology*, (London, 1934); W. E. Sangster, *The Path to Perfection* (London, 1941); C. W. Williams, *Wesley's Theology Today* (London, 1962).

know those names here.' It seems unlikely that John Wesley would have heard that answer.

It was his unique ability as an organizer and pastor that distinguished John Wesley from all his contemporaries – not only from Whitefield or the Welsh revivalists, but also from men such as Benjamin Ingham, who had been with him in the Holy Club and in Georgia and who returned to become an independent evangelist in the north of England. John Wesley's pastoral oversight was accepted by so many individuals after 1738 because it was accompanied by joy and love, as it had not been before 1738; and it endured after his death because while taking endless trouble over individuals he also created a system which would uphold them when he had gone. The central paradox of his life is that 'while he may have lacked a creative mind, he was a genius at adaptation' and therefore 'his religious conservatism harboured ecclesiastical radicalism'.[16]

His genius at adaptation may be seen in his dealings with the Moravians. The preacher whose exposition of Luther had warmed his heart in 1738, Peter Böhler, was a Moravian. Descended from some of the disciples of the fifteenth-century reformer of religion in Bohemia, John Huss, this group had retained its Protestant faith and had been revitalized by the Pietist movement.[17] In 1722 it had settled on one of the estates of Count Nikolaus von Zinzendorf, at Herrnhut in Saxony. Five years later it had undergone a corporate religious experience out of which had come a clear call to a worldwide mission – something without precedent in Christian history apart from the Jesuits. Zinzendorf had become a bishop and the dictatorial, but richly creative, leader in this mission. The Wesleys had already come across the movement; there had been Moravians on the ship bound for Georgia. The agitated brothers had been impressed by their calm courage during the voyage and by their wisdom during the missionary work. Soon after his Aldersgate Street experience John Wesley went to Germany to examine their organization more closely. He learned much: the

---

[16] V. H. H. Green, *John Wesley*, p. 155.
[17] See A. J. Lewis, *Zinzendorf the Ecumenical Pioneer* (London, 1962), and C. W. Towlson, *Moravian and Methodist* (London, 1957).

importance of hymn-singing, the practice of the almost monthly 'love-feast' (where the fare was cake and water and the main nourishment came through testimonies of spiritual progress), the 'watch-night' service (on the Friday night nearest the full moon), the division of the larger congregations into 'bands' of four or five people (of the same sex and marital status) for the purpose of spiritual edification. All these Moravian customs were copied, to the enrichment of Methodism. But John Wesley was no mere imitator. A believer in fasting and restraint, he rejected Moravian practices which he thought worldly, unhealthy or over-ambitious: the indulgence in the delights of wealth (particularly on the part of Zinzendorf himself), the lushly sentimental details about the suffering of Christ, the physical contact involved in the 'kiss' of peace or in footwashing, the ambition to build a worldwide movement within a generation. Indeed, he gradually came to regard the Moravians as 'German wolves'.

To the Moravian elements which he favoured, Wesley added his own practices, developed from old Puritan ideas. Many Puritans had stressed the spiritual fellowship to be enjoyed by a group of like-minded ministers, often called a *classis* from the learned Latin. Now Wesley developed 'classes' or groups of about a dozen lay men or women who would meet weekly in order to question and encourage each other about spiritual and material matters. The idea sprang out of the offer of one Captain Foy to collect a penny a week from poor Methodists towards the liquidation of the debt on the 'New Room' at Bristol in 1741, but by the time he had ridden back to London after the meeting where that offer had been made Wesley had seen that the idea could solve problems deeper than finance. Many Puritans had also believed in the covenant between members of a congregation. Now Wesley developed a 'covenant' service, when each Methodist bound himself or herself anew to the Lord Jesus. Later it was used on the first Sunday in the new year.[18]

As Methodism grew, Wesley relied on methods which Whitefield, the Welsh revivalists and the Moravians had

---

[18] Robert C. Monk studied *John Wesley: His Puritan Heritage* (London, 1966).

already introduced in a smaller way. In 1789 he defined the four essentials of the Methodist system, on which he would insist despite the disapproval of bishops and parish priests:

1. to preach in the open air
2. to pray extempore
3. to form societies
4. to accept the assistance of lay preachers.

Although he was nervous about following Whitefield's example in 'field-preaching' in Bristol in 1739, he soon saw that his exclusion from almost all the pulpits of the Church of England was not an unmitigated disaster. Preaching in the open air helped to recreate a New Testament atmosphere, and like the apostles of old John Wesley was not surprised if lives were changed dramatically, miraculous healings took place, and devils were expelled from shouting or writhing hearers. Nor was he dismayed if mobs assaulted him, as they had assaulted St Paul; it was his own way of doing battle against Satan. He believed that God controlled in detail not only the responses of his hearers but also the journey and the weather. He believed that good angels watched over the proceedings and their consequences. Although he loved to use the services of the Book of Common Prayer indoors (and was a frequent communicant), he also found that a blessing attended extempore prayer for the people in the open air. Indeed, the impression left by his *Journal* is that he was well aware that by being preached out of doors his sermons (which in themselves were not nearly so emotional as Whitefield's) attracted a publicity, and secured a response, which would not have come to him on anything like the same scale had he restricted himself to occasions when the parish priest invited him to preach during or after a Prayer Book service.

But John Wesley was not primarily a preacher. He was an organizer. In 1743 he determined not to preach where he could not organize – 'not to strike one stroke in any place where I cannot follow the blow'.

He formed societies – not everywhere, but wherever his preaching aroused a sufficient response or wherever someone else's preaching had led to the formation of a group willing to be taken over by him. His main bases were London and Bristol. He was also successful in other areas undergoing the beginnings of industrialization – in Newcastle and Sunderland where collieries had been developed, in Hull, Leeds and the West Riding of Yorkshire, in Cornwall among the tin-miners, in the still disorganized industrial towns in the middle of England such as Manchester, in the growing port of Liverpool. The rural south-east and south midlands were almost untouched by Methodism – while in East Anglia, although there was a popular welcome for a religion which would not be controlled by the rich squires and merchants, there was far more independence than John Wesley experienced elsewhere.

His speciality was to form societies of industrial workers and their families. Most of these had quite recently been uprooted from the countryside; the 'cake of custom' had been broken and they were ready for a new message. But industrialization had not yet created that anonymous mass, the proletariat. Nor had it bred atheism. These were men and women who could be recalled by a sermon to a sense of their own spiritual importance, to a sense of themselves as sinners accountable to God.

Of course the Wesleys often met with hostility or indifference, but it is striking how often these Oxford clergymen full of religious emotions, men for whom assurance of forgiveness by God was the chief need, found hearers who understood among these industrial workers. And the Wesleys did not withdraw their converts from these communities. Unlike the Quakers, the Methodists were not to be made conspicuous and ridiculous by unusual dress or other habits. But (again unlike the Quakers) they were given plenty of firm instructions about how to behave; decisions were not left to their agreement after silence. For example, they were instructed always to dress plainly; to 'gain all you can; save all you can; give all you can'. John Wesley insisted on honesty, writing *A Word to a Smuggler* and *A Word to a Freeholder* (against bribery in elections). He insisted on temperance (he forbade spirits although he enjoyed wine – and he was equally severe and self-denying about the expense of tea). He also insisted on the chastity of the single life or on faithfulness to vows (men and women always worshipped separately when under his control). He was equally emphatic about cleanliness and hygiene generally. And he gave these working men and women a new vision of what life could be. He lavished on them all the spiritual riches accumulated by his reading and experience. He taught them to believe that God had been so gracious to them that they could be perfect in love.

He encouraged them to read the Bible day by day – and much else, ordering his preachers to carry books and pamphlets around with them. For his people's benefit he supplied concise guides to the Bible, history, literature, philosophy, politics, economics, medicine and science, with a Dictionary. He encouraged them to educate their children. As early as 1739 he founded his own school for the children of the poor at Kingswood near Bristol, and opened another near it as a boarding school for the sons of his preachers: and in the 1780s he began being enthusiastic about Sunday schools for the children of the poor. He encouraged them to explore each other's hearts in their classes, so that they became psychologists and moralists; and to care for each other when physically ill, so that their 'stewards' collected and distributed considerable funds for the sick. He encouraged them to hope for heaven and meanwhile to work for heaven on earth, transfiguring their daily labours in the spirit of Charles Wesley's hymn 'Forth in thy name, O Lord, I go'. Those who were not willing to live and to labour in this spirit were told to go forth more rudely. There was a membership card renewable every quarter, and one of John Wesley's main tasks was expelling backsliders.

Joseph Priestley, although he deplored John Wesley's superstitions, wrote in his *Address to the Methodists* (1791): 'To you is the civilization, the industry and sobriety of great numbers of the labouring part of the community owing.' Had Priestley been interested in monasteries or sanctification, he could have added that somehow Wesley had created out of these working people a fellowship under semi-monastic discipline, a school for saints. Methodists had made the surrender which still echoes in the hymn by one of their preachers, Edward Perronet: 'All hail the power of Jesus' name'. George Lavington, Bishop of Exeter, included much which was abusive and much which was untrue in an attack on John Wesley's influence published in three volumes (1749–51), but the title of this onslaught implied a just estimate of John Wesley's spiritual influence as a leader fit to be compared with the great founders of the religious orders of the Catholic Church. The bishop's title was *The Enthusiasm of Methodists and Papists Compared.*

John Wesley's assistants were almost all laymen. The Church of England also used laymen, but only as churchwardens who were not expected to be spiritual men. Through sheer necessity Methodism had to use laymen to preach – and had to use men of lesser social status than the average churchwarden. Some were itinerant preachers, very modestly paid, the first being Thomas Maxfield in 1741; and for years John Wesley struggled to avoid allowing these preachers to receive any money at all since the gospels taught that food and clothing ought to be enough. Others conducted their neighbours' worship, or led a class of a dozen, without any material reward. This use of laymen aroused further ridicule; Laurence Sterne commented that Methodist preachers were 'much fitter to make a pulpit than to get into one'. But it released many talents hitherto buried. And in a Methodist congregation there were no gradations according to the worshippers' status in the world. In the eighteenth century both the parish churches and the Dissenters' meeting houses were often filled with pews, allocated according to rank (and the ability to pay rent for them). Seating parishioners in this style was a question which preoccupied churchwardens. But Methodist chapels had benches.

We should not, however, think that John Wesley was in any way a democrat. He accepted the class system outside the chapels, and within them he created a new one, arranged according to people's status in his eyes. His preachers, appointed and not infrequently dismissed by him, were divided into two classes; the more select and trusted 'Assistants' were superior to the 'Helpers'. He discouraged worldly ambition. One of his rules read: 'Do not affect the gentleman. You have no more to do with this character than with that of a dancing master.' He published his own sermons to guide theirs. He issued many other instructions to reshape their lives in the image he desired – and they accepted this supervision, far closer than any bishop's. They were his 'sons in the Gospel'.

In particular they accepted his exhortations because he lived like that himself. It was no prelate in the House of Lords who ordered them in 1745: 'You have nothing to do but to save souls. Therefore spend and be spent in this work. And go always, not only to those who want you, but to those who want you most.'

Among the souls to whom these preachers were to pay special attention were the class leaders, whose subordination was made clear: 'they are employed by the Assistant as long and as far as he pleases.' From 1744 (when ten of them gathered) onwards, Wesley summoned an annual national conference of his preachers. No one was entitled to attend without his invitation, and when in 1784 he decided that the legal powers of the conference should be limited to a hundred preachers (less than half the total), he simply selected those he wanted. The conference never included any representatives of the congregations. Under its control, local meetings of preachers, stewards and class leaders (the 'Circuit Meetings') took place every quarter from 1748 onwards. These meetings regulated the affairs of the 'societies'. Wesley completely rejected any notion that the laity of a particular congregation should have any such power.

It is indeed hard to see how the separation of this thoroughly Wesleyan organization from the Church of England could have been avoided. What postponed the formal recognition of the split until after John Wesley's death was the fact that, together with an obstinate refusal to be deterred or in any other way influenced by any bishop or parish priest, Methodism's dictator also frequently expressed an obstinate refusal to separate from the Church of which he was a priest. His mature attitude was defined (in so far as it could be defined) in his sermon preached in Newcastle in 1749 on 'The Catholic Spirit'. Catholicism he wanted; it spoke to him of the universal love of God, manifest in many times and places. But he advocated its generous spirit, not its traditional safeguards. His text was: 'Is thine heart right, as my heart is with thy heart? If it be, give me thine hand' (2 Kings 10:15). He had travelled far from Epworth and from Oxford, although he was very reluctant to admit it.

Clearly John Wesley, when he set out on his missionary

journeys, had no intention of founding a denomination. He took a pride in the blessing (however guarded) of the Archbishop of Canterbury, John Potter. In his interview with Bishop Gibson of London, one of the bishop's worries was about his practice of re-baptizing Dissenters, for at this stage John Wesley still believed that there was 'no salvation outside the Church'. In his historic interview with Bishop Joseph Butler on 16 August 1739 he seems to have tried to reassure the philosopher-bishop. The 'pretending to extraordinary gifts and revelations of the Holy Ghost' to which Butler objected – 'a horrid thing, a very horrid thing' – was not defended by Wesley, according to his own note of the meeting (we have no record of it from Butler). He replied that he claimed only 'what every Christian may receive and ought to expect and pray for'. Some of what the bishop objected to was blamed on Whitefield, some on hysterical women whom Wesley said he could control. When Butler said that he had been informed that Holy Communion was celebrated in Methodist meetings, Wesley simply said that the information was wrong. When he objected to Wesley preaching in the diocese of Bristol without a licence, the preacher claimed (incorrectly) that he was entitled to do this as a Fellow of Lincoln College, Oxford.

But one step was taken when in 1740 Wesley led his own followers out of the Fetter Lane Society (founded in 1738 and including Moravians too much inclined to 'mysticism'). This London group formed the nucleus of the congregation which now met in a previously disused building in Moorfields, the 'Foundery'. For many years almost all Methodist societies met in their members' cottages or barns, always avoiding the 'church hours' so as to show that they had no wish to be rivals with the parish churches. But gradually John Wesley had to acknowledge that many of the parish clergy insulted Methodists when they appeared in church – and that Methodists were willing to pay for their own simple buildings. He yielded, too, by permitting Holy Communion at Methodist meetings (first in 1743). However, he caused a legal problem by being unwilling before 1787 to see the buildings registered as Dissenting 'meeting houses' (except as a temporary measure in response to the riots of the 1740s). If the Methodists were not Dissenters, they were not entitled to the liberties specified in the Toleration Act of 1689. Even when he had yielded that point, Wesley still tried to retain the modest terms 'preaching house' and 'chapel'. There were about 470 such buildings when he died. In 1778 he led his London congregation out of the Foundery into the far more handsome New Chapel in City Road, complete with a burial ground.

Charles Wesley, although he preached there Sunday by Sunday before his death in 1788, refused to be buried in that ground. A parish churchyard must be his last resting place. For long he had struggled (in vain) to persuade his brother to restrict membership of Methodist societies to members of the Church of England. Many others warned John Wesley of the sin of schism, and he issued many assurances that he was not contemplating it. From time to time admirers would suggest that he ought to be made a bishop in the Church of England – either of a diocese or of the Methodists as a kind of religious order. But it was in practice inconceivable that he would accept the restrictions of a diocesan bishopric. It was equally inconceivable that the authorities would formally bless a situation where he exercised a detailed personal control over societies in many hundreds of parishes – even in the parishes of Evangelicals whose preaching he approved. His claim to take the world as his parish inevitably seemed alarming arrogance to the bishops (and to the politicians who appointed them). The Methodists could be compared with the medieval Franciscans who had also gone to the poor, but their disregard of ecclesiastical authority went far beyond anything permitted to any religious order under any Catholic system.

The crisis came through the need to make provision for the leadership of Methodism in America when the United States had secured their independence. Five years before the rebellion Francis Asbury – a gardener's son summoned to be a preacher from the life of an apprentice in a Birmingham ironworks – had been sent out, while still in his mid-twenties, to organize a movement which had sprung up spontaneously among lay people and had been only rather casually visited by itinerant Englishmen. He had won great success and the first American conference had been held in 1773.

John Wesley never suffered from inhibitions about his powers. Setting himself the task of compiling a version of the Book of Common Prayer for the American Methodists, he halved the original. But he knew that it was impossible for him to claim to exercise personal control any longer; not only was America a long way away, but during the war he had written four vehement pamphlets against the Americans' rebellion (while also pleading for more sympathy with their just claims before the war). Thomas Rankin, whom he had sent as special ambassador to impose discipline on the American Methodists (and on Asbury), had met with hostility. Wesley begged Robert Lowth, an able and friendly man who was Bishop of London 1777–87, to ordain Methodists as priests for the American movement, but the request was refused. John Wesley then, in Bristol in September 1784, 'set apart' two men as deacons and presbyters and also Thomas Coke as a 'superintendent'.

He was persuaded of his right to ordain priests or presbyters by his acceptance of the argument that in the New Testament the terms 'presbyter' and 'bishop' covered the same man (an argument which modern biblical scholars accept). He now drew the conclusion that he could in this pastoral emergency act as a bishop himself. What he, by status a priest, thought he was doing when he ordained Coke (already an Anglican priest) as a Methodist 'superintendent' he never fully explained. He presented Coke with a certificate saying simply: 'Know all men that I, John Wesley, think myself providentially called at this time to set apart some persons for the work of the ministry in America.' But when Coke on his arrival in America, together with Asbury, took to using the title 'bishop', John Wesley was indignant: 'How can you, how dare you, suffer yourself to be called Bishop? I shudder, I start at the very thought! Men may call me a knave or a fool, a rascal, a scoundrel, and I am content; but they shall never by my consent call me Bishop!' But Coke was not as willing as John Wesley was to act as a bishop (or archbishop) without being called one.[19]

---

[19] See *The History of American Methodism*, vol. 1, ed. E. S. Bucke (Nashville, Tenn., 1964).

Charles Wesley was 'thunderstruck' and angered by these ordinations, and attributed them to 'age'; John was already in his eighties. But it was not the act of a senile dodderer. John Wesley, undeterred by the protests, proceeded over the years to ordain more than twenty others to work overseas or in Scotland. At first he forbade those ordained for Scotland to appear as clergymen in England, but finally, in 1788, he ordained Alexander Mather to work in England – Mather subsequently claimed, as a bishop.

Another factor which brought about the separation from the Church of England was John Wesley's knowledge that he must die. In earlier days there had been an Anglican clergyman in mind to succeed him – his brother Charles or John Fletcher, by birth a Swiss, since 1760 the saintly vicar of the rough parish of Madeley in Shropshire. But neither man possessed John Wesley's single-mindedness or itch for organization; indeed, Charles settled down first in Bristol and then in London as the pastor of the local congregation and as the proud father of two musical prodigies. (Charles's son, the composer Samuel, was the father of the great Victorian cathedral musician, Samuel Sebastian Wesley.) John Wesley, in contrast, had such a clear vocation, and genius, as the leader of Methodism that he sacrificed marriage to his task. He did not press his suit with Grace Murray who would have made an excellent wife; then in 1751, on the rebound from that disappointment, he impulsively married an unsympathetic widow, Molly Vazeille. He refused to reduce his travels or his preacher's righteousness in letters to her during his many absences, and the marriage broke down completely amid much unpleasantness. Death released her in 1781; the event does not seem to have moved him greatly. It was not to be expected that a man who had sacrificed so much, including marriage, to his work would be content for that work to end with his death.

Eventually it became clear that only the Methodist Preachers' Conference could inherit his rights and responsibilities, and this he settled by a legally executed 'deed poll' in February 1784. It ought to have been clear to him that this arrangement ensured the full emergence of Methodism as a denomination – although three years later he was still saying that when the Methodists left the Church of England God would leave them. The hundred preachers meeting as the legally constituted conference had not the slightest wish to dissolve their movement – or to be placed under bishops, either the Church of England's or their own. After John Wesley's death they pointedly did not elect as their first president either of the two men who nursed ambitions to succeed him as leader (Thomas Coke and Alexander Mather). But the preachers were men for whom it was unthinkable that Methodism, raised up by God through John Wesley, should cease with his earthly life. 'The best of all is, God is with us' – so said their master just before he died. They knew it, and they interpreted it as a mandate to leave the church which had treated their divinely inspired master with so little understanding.

When John Wesley died he left confusion behind him in Methodism's relationship with the Church of England, although he had been such a disciplinarian. Some of his preachers shared his own high doctrine of the Eucharist, celebrated solemnly on a Sunday morning; to others the central activity was the sermon on a Sunday evening, with hymns before and after. Some of his preachers used the Book of Common Prayer; others did not. Some refrained from baptizing, burying and preaching during 'church hours'; others did not. Some believed that only an episcopally ordained priest should celebrate the Eucharist or the Lord's Supper; others did not. Since it was tolerated, this confusion must have been implied in Wesley's own ambiguous position. He had founded a movement which must move. He knew that he had to spread 'scriptural holiness' and to 'save souls' from misery in this life and from hell in the next. But he did not know what would be the future of Methodism. It is a true verdict on his leadership of the people called Methodists that, like a vigorous rower, he looked back while he moved rapidly forward.[20]

---

[20] In addition to the books previously recommended, see Frank Baker, *John Wesley and the Church of England* (London, 1970); Bernard Semmel, *The Methodist Revolution* (London, 1974); and the more hostile E. P. Thompson, *The Making of the English Working Class* (London, 1963). There is valuable material in older books, for example the two by Leslie F. Church, *The Early Methodist People* (London, 1948), and *More about the Early Methodist People* (London, 1949).

EVANGELICALS IN THE PARISHES

The Evangelical awakening within the Church of England did not depend on the Wesleys. Its leaders could be called 'Methodists' – and for a long time they were so called by those who wished to insult them. But from the 1770s onwards the movement was increasingly referred to as 'Evangelical', and fairminded people recognized that it was resolved to remain loyal to the 'Evangel' or Gospel within the Established Church. When, beginning in 1779, the Countess of Hunting-don chose to register her chapels as Dissenting meeting houses rather than have any Anglican authority interfering with them, churchmen were shocked; and in 1782 the Evangelical clergy-men who had been her chaplains resigned in a body. There was a similar, hardening, opposition to John Wesley's insistence on recruiting other priests' parishioners into Methodist societies where the orders were given by him and the hymns written by his brother. When in 1764 he sent out an invitation to some fifty clergymen inviting them to join an 'association', only three replied. Long before the Countess caused ministers trained for the work of her connexion to be ordained without any bishop in 1783, and before Wesley's own ordinations in the following year, Anglicans had shown a refusal to accept the claims of both dictatorial Founders.[21]

The vision of Christ as the believer's Saviour was at the heart of this Evangelical awakening because it retained much of the power which it had had in the days when Calvinism had been the Church of England's predominant theology. It was still available as the answer to many spiritual struggles. And Calvinist theology also retained something of its power as an interpretation of this vision. The sophisticated had long ago abandoned it, but there were still simple believers. The Devon clergyman Augustus Toplady spoke for them when he taught that if God was God, he must be free to choose whom he would save: 'I can discern no medium between absolute predestina-tion and blank atheism.' Regarding Arminianism as 'the great religious evil of this age and country', he indulged in some very

---

[21] The standard study is L. Elliott-Binns, *The Early Evangelicals* (London, 1953).

bitter controversy against this element in Methodism. He was so angry because the Wesleys seemed to deny the towering, supernatural grandeur of the 'Rock of ages, cleft for me'. Approaching that rock, the sinner should not – could not – appeal to anything except God's decree of mercy; and Toplady knew very clearly that the mercy was for the predestined few. His poem entitled 'A Living and Dying Prayer for the Holiest Believer in the World' addressed Christ in 1776:

> Nothing in my hand I bring,
> Simply to thy Cross I cling,
> Naked, come to thee for dress;
> Helpless, look to thee for grace;
> Foul, I to the fountain fly;
> Wash me, Saviour, or I die!

In Rochdale, a quiet market town in Lancashire, William Grimshaw, then a curate, spent almost the whole of one Sunday in 1742 in ecstatic prayer. His rapture was caused by his sudden conviction about the truth of the book he had been reading, a treatise on faith by the old Puritan leader, John Owen. And his experience changed his life. Moved to the village of Haworth on the Yorkshire moors, he was able to transform a bleakly remote and largely pagan parish. He drove stray parishioners into church with a horsewhip, and appeared like an avenging angel when young people were indulging in horseplay rather than assembling for his instruction. His personality had not faded from his awed parishioners' memories when Patrick Brontë arrived to be rector in 1820, and some of the memories may have gone into Emily Brontë's *Wuthering Heights*.[22]

About Christmas in 1757 a similar experience changed the life and work of another clergyman, John Berridge. He had been a witty Cambridge scholar inclined to unconventional opinions. Then, moving to the village of Everton, he had been its devoted but not very convincing pastor. Now, 'as I was sitting in my house one morning, and musing upon a text of Scripture, the following words darted into my mind with a

---

[22] Frank Baker provided a biography of *William Grimshaw* (London, 1963).

wonderful power and seemed indeed like a voice from heaven, *Cease from thine own works*. . . . The tears flowed from my eyes like a torrent. The scales fell from my eyes immediately. . . .' He burned all his old sermons, for in the words carved on his tombstone, he 'fled to Jesus alone for refuge 1756'.

Thus the Evangelical revival first showed its power in quiet country parishes.[23] It was led by clergymen who made their own discoveries and preached to their own parishioners, and sometimes also elsewhere in their neighbourhoods. It took time for the movement to grow from these rural roots into the universities, the bishops' palaces, the homes of the rich and the pulpits of London. When in 1768 six students were expelled from St Edmund Hall, Oxford, for holding Evangelical views, Samuel Johnson commented: 'A cow is a very good animal in a field but we turn her out of a garden.'

No Evangelical was entrusted with a diocese until 1815 when Henry Ryder was made Bishop of Gloucester, perhaps largely because his brother was a prominent Tory peer. Only a few rich laymen were Evangelicals – although one of them was Robert Raikes, who among other business interests owned the local newspaper in Gloucester. In 1780 Raikes began paying four women to teach the children of the poor on a Sunday. On the other days of the week they would be at work. The main purpose was to teach them the Bible, but before they could learn that they had to learn to read and write. This was not the nation's first Sunday school but Raikes was able to secure publicity for it and the idea spread rapidly as a result.

John Thornton, another layman who showed what Evangelicals could do, had made an immense fortune in business, mainly through trade with Russia. His son Henry was equally rich and philanthropic; before his marriage he gave away six-sevenths of his income, and after marriage two-thirds. In 1792 Henry Thornton bought a house in Clapham, then a village at a distance of three pleasantly rural miles from London. Clapham gradually became a centre for Evangelicals of similar affluence and piety; the group was later (in 1844) called the Clapham Sect.. They ate fine food and drank good

---

[23] Examples are in G. C. B. Davies, *The Early Cornish Evangelicals* (London, 1951).

wines at each other's tables, and their families struck up close friendships. In those days before the telephone the ease with which they could communicate as neighbours stimulated and assisted their labours for good causes, and a favourite meeting place was Henry Thornton's house, Battersea Rise, with its thirty-four bedrooms.[24]

E. M. Forster commented that Henry Thornton was, in most of his characteristics, typical of his family and wider circle but that 'what distinguishes him from the rest of them was his outstanding intellect. This appears not only in his public career but in his private letters. He never pens a sentence that is clumsy or feeble, and he knows exactly what he wants to say.' Henry Thornton's children grew up in a home which Forster well described as being full of 'affection, comfort, piety, integrity, intelligence, public activity, private benevolence; and transcending them all an unshaken belief in a future life where the members of the household would meet again and would recognize each other and be happy eternally.'[25]

For long the Evangelical movement had only one spokesman among all the preachers of London: the austere William Romaine. His message was so little appreciated by the gentry that his own churchwardens refused to provide light for his evening services; so he preached holding a candle. Then in 1779 the important church of St Mary Woolnoth in Lombard Street, at the very centre of the City of London's financial operations, was secured by John Thornton's influence for John Newton, the most interesting of all the first generation of the Evangelical clergy.

His Calvinism was implied in his famous hymns 'Amazing grace' and 'How sweet the name of Jesus sounds' – but it was accompanied by an equally firm adherence to the Church, expressed in 'Glorious things of thee are spoken'. Newton, although to the end a clumsy preacher, had a great gift for winning individuals to Christ and to the Church by private talk

---

[24] See E. M. House, *Saints in Politics: The Clapham Sect and the Growth of Freedom* (Toronto, 1952), and Michael Hennell, *John Venn and the Clapham Sect* (London, 1958).

[25] E. M. Forster, *Marianne Thornton* (London, 1956), pp. 23, 29. See also Standish Meacham, *Henry Thornton of Clapham* (Cambridge, Mass., 1964).

and by letter, because he was affectionate and because he could tell them his own story of spiritual rebirth. Ten years of his life had been spent in the slave trade, first as a sailor who became virtually a slave himself and then as the master of a ship. Through many sufferings and adventures he had hardened and coarsened but had not forgotten either his mother, who was a devout Dissenter, or the childhood sweetheart who eventually became his devout wife. At one stage he had picked up a copy of *The Imitation of Christ*, the only book available with which to pass the time, and had asked himself: 'What if these things should be true?' During a shipwreck on the coast of Newfoundland he had sworn to give his life to God if he survived. After his conversion came another spell in the slave trade; 'I never had the least scruple as to its lawfulness', he recalled later, when he became an opponent of it. But his vocation to help white fellow sinners had been insistent. After a shore job in Liverpool (a port growing rich through this infamous trade), he had persuaded a bishop to ordain him, at the age of thirty-nine.

Few clergymen have had a more sensational story to tell – and Newton told it, in *An Authentic Narrative* published soon after his ordination (in 1764). Twenty years later Coleridge was staying with Wordsworth, and Wordsworth was reading this book. It is almost certain that the *Authentic Narrative* was one of the books of travel that fed Coleridge's own *Tale of the Ancient Mariner*. In that poem, the mariner's blessing of the water-snakes lifted the curse off him; 'the self-same moment I could pray'. In the narrative of his life Newton told how he had once exclaimed 'almost without meaning': 'if this will not do, the Lord have mercy on us.' As he recalled, this was 'the first desire I had breathed for mercy for the space of many years'; and the little phrase halted his previously incessant flow of blasphemous oaths. He, too, found that he could pray.

This autobiography in its first draft had an immediate effect on an Evangelical peer, Lord Dartmouth. He invited its author to become the curate in charge of Olney, a tumbledown village in Buckinghamshire. Newton baffled most of his parishioners, but won some response as he went round the homes of the poor in his sailor's blue jacket and as he fumbled in the pulpit for words with which to tell others that they could be saved from slavery to sin as he had been. The centre of his work became the intimately informal Tuesday evening prayer meeting, for which he tried to provide a new hymn every week. Some of these were written by a poet who became his close friend and who rented a house in the village, William Cowper.[26]

Cowper was a minor poet reckoned major because his age was so unpoetical. Although he celebrated *The Ride of John Gilpin* and the delights of nature and of home life, like George III or Samuel Johnson he was the victim of a mental disease which cannot now be diagnosed with certainty. Because he was swept into the Evangelical revival it is possible to blame his madness on his religion. But it seems fair to say that Cowper's tormented fear that he had committed the unpardonable sin and was doomed to everlasting punishment was the symptom, not the cause, of the periods of mental illness which afflicted him long before his Evangelical conversion or his friendship with Newton. A just verdict has been passed by a fellow poet, Norman Nicholson. 'Without the Revival he would never have become a poet, for it gave him a deep emotional experience, a prolonged fervour which for many months lifted him like a love affair above the compromises and consequences of everyday life.'[27]

Some of Cowper's most moving poems are among the sixty-six which he contributed to *Olney Hymns*, a collection edited and largely composed by John Newton (and financed, like so many other projects, by John Thornton). 'Oh! for a closer walk with God' expressed his longing for a 'calm and serene' life and his knowledge that rural peace could not entirely satisfy that longing. 'God moves in a mysterious way' would serve as a commentary on the storms in Newton's life but seems to have been in fact a courageous acceptance of new

---

[26] Biographies include Bernard Martin, *John Newton* (London, 1950), and John Pollock, *Amazing Grace* (London, 1981). A modern selection of Newton's spiritual letters is available in *The Voice of the Heart*, ed. William Culbertson (Chicago, Ill., 1950).

[27] The best studies are Maurice Quinlan, *William Cowper: A Critical Life* (Minneapolis, Minn., 1953), and William Hutchings, *The Poetry of William Cowper* (London, 1983).

storms springing up in Cowper's own mind amid the rural peace. And 'Jesus, where'er thy people meet' was written in 1769 for the opening of a room in Olney for weekly prayer meetings. There, among his fellow villagers, this man of sorrows found comfort.

CHARLES SIMEON
AND HIS DISCIPLES

The time was coming when Lord Melbourne would complain to Queen Victoria: 'Nobody is gay now, they are so religious.'[28] But when Charles Simeon became a 'serious' Christian in 1779 he did not know anyone to whom he could go for help. During his first term at King's College, Cambridge, he was warned that he would be required to receive Holy Communion on Easter Day. His schooldays at Eton had left him in a moral condition which he later recalled: 'Satan himself was as fit to attend as I.' However, he had enough religion left in him to be alarmed by the approach of the compulsory service and turned to 'the only religious book that I had ever heard of', *The Whole Duty of Man*. This anonymous exposition of morality as sustained by the customs of the Church of England had been famous ever since the middle of the seventeenth century. It made him more miserable. But the thought flashed into his mind: 'I can transfer all my guilt to Another!' And by Easter Day he was convinced that this Another 'is risen today' – so that at the once dreaded Communion he found 'the sweetest access to God through my blessed Saviour'.

Although the guilt had been replaced by assurance, Simeon's life remained in many ways a classic example of eighteenth-century privilege. Without passing any examination he became a Fellow of King's College, almost his whole duty being now not to marry. He was ordained – as were most

---

[28] See Muriel Jaeger, *Before Victoria: Changing Standards and Behaviour 1787–1837* (London, 1956); Ford K. Brown, *Fathers of the Victorians: The Age of Wilberforce* (Cambridge, 1961); Ian Bradley, *The Call to Seriousness: The Evangelical Impact on the Victorians* (London, 1976).

of his colleagues, although it did not make their attendance at chapel much more regular. Because his father knew the Bishop of Ely, he was entrusted with the care of Holy Trinity church in Cambridge at the age of twenty-two. All through his life he remained very much the gentleman, fond of horses, well-dressed, elegant in his hospitality, anxious that his guests should wipe their shoes. Many thought him affected and vain, and this did not help him when he faced opposition. His colleagues in King's snubbed him during most of his life there; the churchwardens of Holy Trinity led a prolonged and bitter opposition to his ministry; worldly undergraduates said cruel things about the young 'Sims' he attracted; even fellow Evangelicals sometimes resented his clumsy attempts to win their devoted friendship and complete confidence. He recorded a moment which was typical of much of his life. 'When I was an object of much contempt and derision in the university, I strolled forth one day, buffeted and afflicted, with my little Testament in my hand. . . . The first text which caught my eye was this: *They found a man of Cyrene, Simon by name; him they compelled to bear his cross.*'

Yet his funeral in 1836 was the most impressive Cambridge had ever seen, town and gown uniting to honour 'the old Apostle'. He achieved this influence by staying at his strategic post for half a century. Primarily he was a preacher. On Sunday mornings and evenings he preached in his own church, usually for fifty minutes. During the afternoon it was his practice for many years to ride out to preach in one of the villages; then he changed his habit and taught preaching to ordinands in Cambridge. On Friday evenings he welcomed all undergraduates to 'conversation parties' in his college rooms; the conversation consisted of questions to him about religion and the drink was tea. He published 2,536 sermon outlines and always he tried to combine the Bible-based passion of the earlier Evangelicals with the clear reasonableness of the eighteenth century.

His base continued to be his handsome rooms in King's College, but from this base he made effective expeditions into his parish and into the nation. He did not hurry through the Prayer Book in church; he read it out like a man who relished every word. He did not keep worship coldly formal; he delighted in hymns and formed prayer meetings and societies to provide fellowship between the services. And he knew the importance of visiting parishioners in their homes. In 1796 he was at last able to appoint a full-time assistant curate who was not a substitute during his absence (as curates were then generally regarded) but a partner in the pastoral work which previously he had undertaken single-handed. He needed such a colleague because he had set himself a national task in a style which was rare for any preacher or parish priest.

When the small and innocuously named Eclectic Society, the first national organization for Evangelicals, had been formed around John Newton in 1783, Simeon attended its London meetings whenever he could. He went round to other groups of like-minded clergymen, building up the confidence of a nationwide progress. He bought up the right to present a rector or vicar (the 'advowson') in a considerable number of key parishes. As a biblicist he could not defend the method of making appointments which made this spread of the Evangelical message possible in return for cash – but he cheerfully took advantage of the system. He supported the emergence of great national societies designed to stimulate the parishes and to do on their behalf work which they could not tackle. These societies solicited subscribers, employed itinerant agents and published literature. Simeon was a great believer in the distribution of Bibles to the laity, and took the lead amid much controversy in the foundation of a 'local auxiliary' to support the British and Foreign Bible Society, which had been launched in 1804 and which included Dissenters; his decisive move in this Cambridge drama was to secure a royal duke as chairman.

He was involved in missions overseas. In 1796 at a meeting of the Eclectic Society, he raised the question: 'With what propriety, and in what mode, can a Mission be attempted to the heathen from the Established Church?' In 1799 – the year of Napoleon's campaign in Egypt – a society was formed to attempt just that, although all the bishops stood aloof. At first called 'the Society for Missions to Africa and the East', this bold little group was soon to be known far and wide as the

Church Missionary Society. One of Simeon's disciples, Henry Martyn, translated the New Testament into Urdu, revised the unsatisfactory versions in Arabic and Persian, and by a journal published after his death commended the mission to India.[29]

So the pattern of the Evangelical parish took shape. Its worship was lively, its preaching intense and systematic, its laity were regular readers of the Bible capable of conducting their own family prayers at home, and it supported missions to the heathen. Its loyalty to the Church of England was unquestionable; Simeon may even be said to have sacrificed his life to this, since he caught a fatal chill by insisting on going to Ely to pay his respects to the new bishop. Congratulating his former curate Thomas Thomason over his pastoral work in Calcutta — work which transformed the English community there — he wrote in 1824 that 'the whole world seems to have received somewhat of a new impulse: and glorious times are fast approaching. The sun and moon are scarcely more different from each other than Cambridge is from what it was when I was first Minister of Trinity Church: and the same change has taken place throughout the whole land'.[30]

WILLIAM WILBERFORCE AND THE SLAVES

William Wilberforce was determined to show that an Evangelical could still make a very agreeable member of the governing class and could even be the acceptable guest of the Prince Regent in Brighton. It was not that he was personally ambitious, at least not on the scale of others with his gifts in the House of Commons. What he wanted was support for his schemes. Many of these schemes concerned the 'reformation of manners' in England. To a considerable extent that meant the reformation of the lower orders by their social superiors. Aristocrats were sought as subscribers to good causes; thus the Prince Regent, a notorious debauchee, patronized the London

[29] See Constance Padwick, *Henry Martyn* (London, 1922).
[30] See Charles Smyth, *Simeon and Church Order* (Cambridge, 1940), and Hugh Evan Hopkins, *Charles Simeon of Cambridge* (London, 1977).

Female Penitentiary. However, the attention of the Evangelicals was also turned towards the moral improvement of the upper class by personal evangelism. Wilberforce went to dinner parties with what he called 'launchers', carefully prepared conversational gambits which would launch the talk into the ocean of religion from which souls could be fished. He wanted their support – but he also wanted them.

He had a winning personality. 'There never lived on earth, I am sure, a man of sweeter temper than Mr Wilberforce', wrote Dorothy Wordsworth. Sir James Mackintosh, in politics a radical and in religion a sceptic, reckoned him 'the most "amusable" man I ever met in my life. Instead of having to think of what subjects will interest him, it is perfectly impossible to hit one that does not.' A small and slight man suffering from much ill-health (he took opium every day), his head often dropping forward in a manner which might have been thought grotesque, he seemed to be a threat to no one and a delight to everyone. As a young man he was very willing to sing and to dance. His private conversation was always full of affection, playfulness and cultured knowledge. He made it his business to win friends by hospitality, and for this purpose kept open house in his home a few yards away from the House of Commons. In public debates he could be the equal of any man in his age, the greatest age of English oratory. His melting power as an orator as well as his wealth as the son of a Hull merchant made him one of the Members of Parliament for Yorkshire, the most numerous and most prestigious constituency in all England, and kept him in that position for almost thirty years. But perhaps what attracted them most was his real saintliness. It was characteristic of him that he organized a pension for Charles Wesley's widow (John Wesley did not), and that when his eldest son lost vast sums in business he paid the debt although it meant that for the last few years of his life he had no home. Large numbers of friends flocked round him even when he had married his beautiful and pious Barbara, who took no interest in politics and very little in running his household.

His Evangelical conversion did not withdraw him from Parliament or from popularity. Early in 1785 he read Philip Doddridge's *Rise and Progress of Religion in the Soul* and through that book recovered his boyhood's intellectual acceptance of the Bible's teachings. Later that year, during continental travels, he read the New Testament in Greek. He returned to England profoundly convinced of his sinfulness, but by Easter 1786 this despair had been replaced by a joyful acceptance of Christ. John Newton comforted and guided him in his emotional crisis – and had the sense to see how badly he was needed in public life. The moral standard of the Commons fell below its standard of eloquence. Not until 1812 was a definite Evangelical appointed to high political office (Nicholas Vansittart then became Chancellor of the Exchequer). The bishops of the age, while more moral, were scarcely prophetic, and the Archbishopric of Canterbury had been condemned to a further period of snobbish mediocrity in 1782, when it had been turned down by the two most able bishops, Robert Lowth of London and Richard Hurd of Worcester.

In intervals of this public life he wrote a book of almost five hundred pages, which was published in 1797 under the title *A Practical View of the Prevailing Religious System of Professed Christians in the Higher and Middle Classes in this Country Contrasted with Real Christianity*. It was a disorganized book, and theologically amateurish; but it criticized its readers from within their own world and it was totally free of theological bigotry. 'Real Christianity' was to Wilberforce a straightforwardly biblical religion, to be accepted as the guide and rule of all human life. God's love was for him the essence; and the morality he urged was always loving conduct. So this *Practical View* had an influence both wide and deep in the classes to which it was addressed. Edmund Burke spent the last two days of his life reading it.

Such a religion could easily be associated, as the old Puritanism had been, with repression of the people's vices – and also of the people's political views, for Wilberforce was the intimate friend of the Tory Prime Minister, William Pitt. He voted for all the harshly repressive legislation which Pitt and his successors enacted in order to suppress threats of an English revolution (without a proper police force). In the years 1817–20 civil war in England seemed closer than it had ever been since the 1640s; in those three years 427 people were executed and in their panic gentlemen such as Wilberforce, sorry as they might be, agreed that the severity was essential. What Wilberforce might have become can be seen from the example of Hannah More. An intellectual lady (the term 'blue stocking' was invented to describe her and a little group like her), after her conversion she was self-sacrificing enough to pour her energies into the foundation of schools for the children of her poorest neighbours in Somerset. It was a charity which Wilberforce, like Henry Thornton, helped to finance. Hannah More was not afraid to castigate upper-class vice, as in her booklet on *The Manners of the Great.* But in the eyes of posterity she has made herself ridiculous or odious by the tracts which she wrote for the instruction of the poor – vividly written tracts (three a month appeared in the series of 'Cheap Repository Tracts' launched in 1795), exhorting them to accept the ordering of society as well as the Christian Gospel.[31]

Wilberforce, too, might have been branded as a mere moralizing conservative. Indeed, many attempts have been made to place him as a reactionary by historians willing to forget that like others of the Clapham Sect he pressed for some control over working conditions in factories, the rescue of chimney boys, the abolition of press gangs to force sailors into the Royal Navy, civil rights for Roman Catholics, prison reform, Parliamentary reform, church schools for the poor and some other causes which the future would regard as progressive. However, for one achievement he has always been given credit. He was the chief spokesman in the long campaign against Britain's large share in the shipping of slaves out of Africa and against slavery itself in the sugar-growing islands of the British West Indies.

In 1787 his agreement to speak against the slave trade in the House of Commons was an indispensable encouragement to those who had begun to care less conspicuously – men such as the young Thomas Clarkson (who had been forced to brood over those horrors by being set slavery as the subject for an essay-prize in Cambridge) and Glanville Sharp (who had become involved by meeting in a London street one of the

---

[31] See M. G. Jones, *Hannah More* (Cambridge, 1952), and John McLeish, *Evangelical Religion and Popular Education* (London, 1969).

thousands of ex-slaves then roaming around England). Twenty years later 'Wilberforce' was the name praised amid emotional scenes as the slave trade was made illegal for British ships. He retired from Parliament in 1825, but just before he died in July 1833 he knew that he and his associates had won the emancipation of the West Indian slaves.

Of course he was not alone in the public struggle. The campaign would have found success even harder than it did had it not been for the almost incredible toils of a Scot, Zachary Macaulay, in amassing and analysing the facts, and of James Stephen in presenting them with all the skills of a first-class lawyer. The whole Clapham Sect had to be mobilized – and it was a group with as much talent as any cabinet and as much appetite for factual detail as any civil service. Other men of wealth and talent were enrolled; a brewer, Thomas Fowell Buxton, took over the leadership from Wilberforce for the last ten years of the struggle. Much was also due to the Quakers (the first religious body to forbid its members to have anything to do with the slave trade, in 1758) and Methodists. A Congregationalist missionary, John Smith, who died in prison in 1824 after being falsely accused of stirring up riots among the slaves on Demarara, was the movement's martyr. The Evangelicals even admitted an avowed Unitarian, William Smith, MP, into their counsels and their friendship because he, too, was a friend of the slaves. Nor did they avoid all collaboration with the Whig leader Charles James Fox, whose morals were notorious.

Especially in its later stages the campaign had to become something new in English history – a nationwide, popular agitation, reaching far beyond the religious world. It was in this English fight against slavery that modern propaganda techniques hitherto unknown were developed. Large public rallies were assembled and addressed; great petitions to Parliament were arranged (one contained a million signatures); notes were supplied to feed speakers and preachers on less spectacular occasions; speakers were sent out as paid agents of the Anti-Slavery Society; journals scholarly and popular were distributed; the art of lobbying influential men in private was perfected; and to supplement this barrage of words a Wedgwood cameo was manufactured which depicted an enchained

Negro kneeling in supplication and uttering the plea, 'Am I not a man and a brother?' Thus a swelling chorus from many quarters surrounded Wilberforce's speeches to the Commons.

So did changing economic conditions. The slave trade and slavery itself became less important to Britain during the philanthropists' long campaign against them. The trade in slaves did not decline before it was made illegal, but other industries developed rapidly to absorb capital and promise profits, so that the slave-based sugar colonies no longer had the significance in the British economy which they had possessed twenty years before. The prohibition of the sale of British-shipped slaves to Britain's actual or potential enemies came in 1806, and it ended two-thirds of the trade before the total prohibition the following year. It was also realized that the loss of seamen's lives through disease in the slave ships was larger than the large loss of the lives of slaves; while another non-ethical factor in the ending of slavery was the knowledge that the heavy pioneering work of clearing the ground of the sugar plantations in the British West Indies by slave labour was over. It began to seem possible that 'free' labour could be hired at low wages to do the remaining routine work. After 1807 such labour was easier to handle than slave labour; for the slaves now showed their discontent and in 1832 their impatience boiled over into a rebellion on Jamaica. By the 1830s English consumers knew that other sugar merchants had arisen to break the West Indian monopoly. The East India Company had ventured into production; sugar was being produced in abundance in Cuba and Brazil; sugar beet was now being grown in Europe. Indeed, these new sources were usually able to supply sugar at a lower price than seemed possible in the West Indian plantations, often run inefficiently for absentee owners. In the period 1815–30, the price of sugar in the London market fell from £70 a ton to £30.

Yet when all these other factors have been allowed for, the glory of William Wilberforce's personal achievement remains. For right up to the end the defence put up by the traders and owners of slaves was very powerful in the only assembly which ultimately counted, Parliament; and a fraction of the profits of the slave and sugar trades was enough to finance counterpropaganda on a very large scale. Ports such as Liverpool and Bristol were reminded vigorously that they owed their prosperity to a trade which had probably by now shipped eleven million human beings across the Atlantic (perhaps as many slaves had died during the course of the journey). The profits made out of the slave trade and its immediate consequences had been an indispensable source of finance in the vital early stages of Britain's industrialization. The strength of the economic arguments in favour of shipping slaves could be seen by anyone who meditated on one fact: it had been more profitable for the slave-owners to buy more labour from the slave-shippers than for them to make the elementary arrangements needed to ensure that their existing slaves had plenty of healthy children who could grow up to be useful labourers. Nor were subsidiary arguments lacking. It was argued (by Nelson, for example) that during a great naval war it would be madness to damage British shipping. It was feared – with good reason, as events showed – that when the war against Napoleon was over it would be a hard and thankless task for the Royal Navy to suppress slave-running in the ships of other nations. It was suggested that those who were opposed to slavery were probably in their hearts the enemies of all forms of private property and commerce; and it was urged that a Britain passing through hard times could not afford to compensate the West Indian owners of slaves for this invasion of their sacred property rights. It was also pointed out, with far more truth, that Africans themselves supplied the slaves whom the British shipped – and did not have equally desired products to exchange for the English goods which they coveted. The abolition of the slave-trade and of slavery might, or might not, be desirable in principle; it might, or might not, be less disastrous economically than had recently seemed certain. But of one thing realists were still sure. Its speedy abolition seemed a Utopian dream, as nuclear disarmament was to seem a century and a half later.[32]

---

[32] The best short study is Basil Davidson, *Black Mother* (revised Harmondsworth, Middx., 1980). See also Roger Anstey, *The Atlantic Slave Trade and British Abolition 1760–1810* (London, 1975), and D. B. Davis, *The Problem of Slavery in an Age of Revolution* (Ithaca, N.Y., 1975).

With all these forces and arguments arrayed against them, Wilberforce and his fellow campaigners were often close to despair. Between 1799 and 1804 they had not the heart to introduce into the Commons their private bill for the slave trade's abolition. For many years they had to deny that they sought the end of slavery as well as the trade. Wilberforce was a Christian crusader, and that dimension was needed to end an evil which the more secular philosophy of the eighteenth century had often deplored – but tolerated. Had he not arisen so often from his seat in the House of Commons to plead for justice, and had he not been so systematically hospitable in winning friends to this cause, it is likely that the slaves of the West Indies would have had to wait longer. The difficulties had been enough to wring from John Wesley his prophecy to William Wilberforce, in the last letter he wrote: 'Unless God has raised you up for this very thing, you will be worn out by the opposition of men and devils. But if God be for you, who can be against you? Are all of them together stronger than God?'

In the end, the prestige acquired by these great moral victories helped Wilberforce and his Evangelical companions to open up Africa and India to Christian missionary work, understood as another kind of liberation. They had to concentrate first on Sierra Leone, which they founded in 1787 as a colony on the coast, to enable ex-slaves facing destitution or crime in England to settle in Africa as farmers and traders. The small colony around Freetown suffered many calamities and was virtually destroyed by a French squadron in 1794, to be rebuilt by Zachary Macaulay who was willing to spend five years there as governor. The Evangelicals remained inflexible in their support until at last in 1808 missionary work that proved permanent was established, using a mighty river, the Rio Pongas – and in the same year the colony was taken over by the Crown. Gradually the conviction spread that whites owed something to the 'dark continent' after all the horrors of the slave trade; and that the Christian Gospel was among the white man's blessings which he ought to share with Africans despite the violence often encountered, despite the degradation which the trade in human flesh had left behind, and despite the killer-diseases including malaria. And this mission was planted on African soil during the great war against Napoleon. For many reasons it was a mission which up to the 1840s was one of almost overwhelming difficulty.[33]

Still the eyes of the Evangelicals were on India. Until quite late in the eighteenth century it had been generally assumed that the English were in India simply in order to make money. The East India Company had taken to paying for its purchases in India out of the heavy taxes which it levied on the land – and had allowed many of its servants to make their own fortunes by private trade, by receiving bribes or by straightforward plunder. The English word 'loot' had come from India. But gradually official profits had dwindled until the company had got deep into debt, and private profits had been curbed; the turning point had been the impeachment of Warren Hastings for corruption while Governor General. And at a time when it was obviously incapable of supplying an efficient government, the company had clearly acquired a massive political responsibility.

The decline and fall of the Mogul empire had led to the disintegration of India, to gross corruption and inefficiency in the successor states, and to a growing feeling that the victories won by Englishmen such as Clive over 'native' princes and French rivals were clear signs that the political vacuum must be filled. The spectacle of a commercial company chartered by Queen Elizabeth on the last day of 1600 stumbling into the government of Bengal and most of India's west coast had been too much for the conscience to swallow even in the eighteenth century. The English Crown had been involved to some extent ever since Charles II's Portuguese queen had brought Bombay as a dowry, and in 1773 Parliament established a Governor General resident in India, with a supreme court in Calcutta to hand down English justice to any who appealed to it. Eleven years later the Governor General's powers were enlarged, a small Board of Control was set up in London, and the company's directors were forced to defer to it in all questions of political policy.

The belief that the English were in India to exercise a trusteeship mysteriously placed in their hands by Providence

---

[33] See John Peterson, *Province of Freedom: A History of Sierra Leone* (London, 1969).

now began to prevail. It was much encouraged by the Evangelicals who penetrated India's new government. The most influential of these was Charles Grant, who had gone out to India in 1767 and had undergone an Evangelical conversion in the course of his grief over the deaths of two young daughters. In his later life a leading resident of Clapham, he became chairman of the company's directors. His well-trained son Robert became Governor of Bombay, and the spirit in which Sir Robert Grant governed Indians is shown by his authorship of the hymn 'O worship the Lord all glorious above'. Among Grant's collaborators was John Shore (Lord Teignmouth), who on becoming Governor General in 1793 made no secret of his religious inspiration. He declared: 'I consider every native of India, whatever his situation may be, as having a claim upon me.' A more flamboyantly ambitious Governor General, Lord Wellesley, although without a personal religion, officially attended church. He spoke about England's 'sacred trusteeship' in India – and acted on this principle, ruling, annexing or 'protecting' the sub-continent to such an extent that the East India Company, alarmed about the expense, recalled him in 1805.

Meanwhile horrified Englishmen read reports such as Charles Grant's *Observations on the State of Society among the Asiatic Subjects of Great Britain* (1792). They were told about the temple prostitutes, about the enormous car called the Juggernaut (from the place Jagannath) under which devotees of Krishna allowed themselves to be crushed, about the thugs who strangled travellers as a sacrifice to Kali, about the murder of unwanted daughters and the old or the sick, about widow-burning (*sati*). Not only Evangelicals despised the Hinduism which had produced such customs. Contempt for degrading superstition also inspired a *History of India* published in 1817 by the leading Utilitarian philosopher, James Mill. When the East India Company refused to interfere in such customs, or even to criticize them, on the ground that trade might suffer, England's honour seemed to be diminished.[34]

[34] G. D. Bearce, *British Attitudes towards India 1784–1858* (Oxford, 1961), may be compared with P. J. Marshall, *The British Discovery of Hinduism in the Eighteenth Century* (Cambridge, 1970).

There had for long been a Roman Catholic presence in India. Indeed, the first Englishman known to have set foot on Indian soil had been a Jesuit, Thomas Stevens, who had sailed in 1579 after reading St Francis Xavier's description of the mission; and letters sent home by that Jesuit missionary to his father, a London merchant, had helped to arouse the interest leading to the East India Company's foundation. The company had of course done nothing to encourage Roman Catholic missionary work, but for many years, from 1714 onwards, it had given some assistance to Lutheran missionaries. These were supported by a Church of England society (the Society for Promoting Christian Knowledge) in the Danish colony at Tranqubar near the southern tip of India. The company had given them free passages to India and had often paid salaries for their work as chaplains. It had also turned a blind eye to missionary work by a few English enthusiasts. With such precedents, it was impossible to maintain for ever the official attitude that Englishmen in India must avoid spreading Christianity as if it were a disease.

The company's charter was due for renewal in 1813. Anticipating this, one of the company's own chaplains, Claudius Buchanan, devoted himself to propaganda in favour both of missionary work and of a much enlarged 'Indian Ecclesiastical Establishment' to convert the godless English; and when 1813 came, the Evangelicals seized the opportunity to secure the admission to India not only of merchants who were not members of the company but also of persons wishing to enter it 'for the purpose of enlightening and reforming Indians'. The new charter also instructed the company to devote £7,500 a year to education. To lead the chaplains still to be appointed by the East India Company, and to exercise an undefined influence over any missionaries, there was to be a Bishop of Calcutta on a noble stipend, £5,000 a year, assisted by three archdeacons. The preamble to the East India Company's new charter declared: 'It is the duty of this country to promote the interests and happiness of the native inhabitants of the British Dominions in India; and such means ought to be adopted as may intend to the introduction among them of useful knowledge and of religious and moral improvements.' The connection between the island and the sub-continent was no longer to be predominantly commercial.[35]

Wilberforce's personal following in the Commons should not be exaggerated; the group of MPs known as 'the saints' was seldom more than twenty-five. But the series of achievements associated with his honoured name were a remarkable development in a religious movement which had begun in a few obscure parishes, and were all the more remarkable because they brought benefits to African slaves or to Indians who were not Christians (although of course the Evangelicals hoped for their eventual conversion). 'Christianity', Wilberforce declared during a three-hour speech in the decisive debate of 1813, 'assumes her true character . . . when she takes under protection those poor degraded beings on whom philosophy looks down with disdain.' And he went on to assure the Commons that they need not fear that the missionaries would make Indians into Christians by force. 'Compulsion and Christianity! Why, the very terms are at variance with each other – the ideas are incompatible. In the language of Inspiration itself, Christianity has been called the "law of liberty".'[36]

[35] See P. J. Marshall, *Problems of Empire: Britain and India 1757–1813* (London, 1968). A. T. Embree, *Charles Grant and British Rule in India* (New York, 1962), showed the change from the eighteenth-century background well sketched by Percival Spear, *The Nabobs* (London, 1963). The biographical sketches in Philip Woodruff, *The Men who Ruled India: The Founders* (London, 1953), went from 1600 to 1858.

[36] Biographies include Lord Furneaux, *William Wilberforce* (London, 1974), and John Pollock, *Wilberforce* (London, 1977).

CHAPTER THREE

CHURCHES IN CHANGE

THE NEW POPULATION

The conventional idea of a country parish was expressed by Shelley. One morning early in the summer of 1815 the 'atheist poet' was walking in the country with his friend, Thomas Love Peacock. He was in a restless mood, having recently made final his separation from his wife, Harriet. The two men stood outside a vicarage. According to Peacock, Shelley mused aloud: 'I feel strongly inclined to enter the Church.' When his companion expressed astonishment, Shelley explained that an English clergyman's assent to the supernatural part of Christianity was 'merely technical'. He went on to expound how much good a good clergyman may do 'in his teaching as a scholar and a moralist; in his example as a gentleman and a man of regular life; in the consolation of his personal intercourse and of his charity among the poor. . . . It is an admirable institution that admits the possibility of diffusing such men over the surface of the land. And am I to deprive myself of the advantages of this admirable institution because there are certain technicalities . . . ?'

Although she belonged heart and soul to the 'admirable institution' on which Shelley looked from outside, Jane Austen viewed it more realistically. Born in a rectory, she meekly followed her clerical father to retirement in Bath. Two of her brothers were ordained and another, a naval officer, caused a mild stir by kneeling during church services. She was always pondering moral questions and she conducted her own life in a manner which made her burial in Winchester Cathedral in 1817 entirely appropriate. She acknowledged her need of a Redeemer (her well-lettered tombstone said so), but the lack of sensitivity and reserve with which the Evangelicals pressed the point was entirely against the values of her family and her class. She was suspicious of the Evangelicals' claim that God inspired their many utterances and arranged every detail of their lives to their spiritual advantage. With a sharp eye for humbug she admired not 'zeal' but modesty, tact and prudence; not 'seriousness' but liveliness, irony and wit; not the urge to distribute Bibles but the contentment which produces the wish to be agreeable to others; not the heights of holiness but reasonableness and elegance. She took her share in local good works but observed 'causes' from afar.

So far as we know, she never opened her heart about religion (although some evidence may have been lost because her sister Cassandra, a lady even more discreet than she was, destroyed some passages in her surviving letters). Her novels never seriously consider a religious topic – or a clergyman's soul. They are about how people behave in society, not about their philosophies or yearnings. The conversation in them is confined to the upper middle class in the rural south of England and a few fashionable towns, with only faint echoes of the great war being fought at the time. But occasionally in the remaining letters we are given a glimpse of a faith at once firm and cool. When she received the news that Sir John Moore had spoken of England before dying on the battlefield of Corunna, she wished that he 'had united something of the Christian with the Hero in his death'.

A letter of 1814 reminds us that her sensible tolerance could extend even to Evangelicals – who were, however, still kept at their distance. She had to act as Aunt Jane to motherless Fanny Knight who was having one of her many love problems. This time the young man, John Plumptre, was attractive in many ways; handsome, with good manners and (as Aunt Jane reminded her) 'the eldest son of a man of fortune'. But was he dull? Evidently he was, for he disappeared from Fanny's life – and Aunt Jane (who never married) warned her: 'Anything is to be preferred or endured rather than marrying without affection.' But this broad-minded aunt wrote: 'And as to there being any objection from his *goodness*, from the danger of his becoming even Evangelical, I cannot admit *that*. I am by no means convinced that we ought not all to be Evangelicals, and am at least persuaded that they who are so from reason and feeling, must be happiest and safest. – Do not be frightened from the connection by your brother having most wit. Wisdom is better than wit, and in the long run will certainly have the laugh on her side; and don't be frightened by the idea of his acting more strictly up to the precepts of the New Testament than others.'

Jane Austen did not paint with strong colours or on a broad canvas; she analysed her art as 'the little bit (two inches wide) of ivory on which I work with so fine a brush'. But her unsentimentally happy and quietly optimistic prose (achieved after many revisions) defended her world against internal and external enemies. In her world, the Church of England was unobtrusively dominant; and conduct was judged by a code which, although it fell short of the heights of 'the precepts of the New Testament', was intended to be humanely Christian.[1]

When Charlotte Brontë was urged to write like Jane Austen, she replied that *Pride and Prejudice* was 'a carefully-fenced, highly-cultivated garden, with neat borders and delicate flowers; but . . . no open country, no fresh air. . . .' Her own writing marked a general movement out of the garden into the storm. Her *Shirley* is for our purpose the most illuminating of the novels which she and her sisters wrote. Published in 1849 but set in Jane Austen's time, it begins with a picture of three bachelor curates having dinner together – abusing the dinner, its cook, their parishioners and each other. Jane Austen would have shuddered at their vulgarity. Their pastoral work lies in the industrial villages of a Yorkshire which is miserable because the new machines have reduced employment while the war is reducing exports; so they leave the dinner-table to become the allies of the owners who defend their mills, pistols in their hands. *Shirley* is, however, not an anticlerical novel. Its author was to marry, and later to fall in love with, one of the curates – a man who appears in the novel with the remark that

---

[1] See Mary Lascelles, *Jane Austen and Her Art* (Oxford, 1939), and Marilyn Butler, *Jane Austen and the War of Ideas* (Oxford, 1975). The materials on which any biography – for example, Lord David Cecil's *Portrait of Jane Austen* (London, 1978) – must be based are in *Jane Austen's Letters*, ed. R. W. Chapman (second edition, Oxford, 1952).

'the circumstance of finding himself invited to tea with a Dissenter would unhinge him for a week'. *Shirley* is not even anti-capitalist. Its main theme is the human condition, understood as a storm of suffering. Caroline is told by her mother: 'O child, the human heart *can* suffer. It holds more tears than the ocean holds waters. We never know how wide, how deep it is, until misery begins to unbind her clouds, and fill it with rushing blackness.' In the year before those words were printed; the little-understood disease of tuberculosis had claimed three victims in the author's family, two of them in the very house where *Shirley* was written. Charlotte Brontë had seen her tragic brother die, closely followed by her sisters, Emily and Anne. Each of the sisters left behind an isolated novel to disclose a major author, and each was a poet; Emily was a major poet of the mystic's lonely encounter with God in the midst of an evil world. The same disease that had taken them was soon to kill Charlotte.

A redeeming influence in this world of suffering was compassionate love; and among those who showed such love was the father, Patrick Brontë. An Irishman, he was a snob (he was born in a tiny cottage and his surname was originally Brunty) and a failure as a scholar and poet. In the eyes of many admirers of his brilliantly gifted daughters, he was a half-mad tyrant. But he loved them; in many ways he nurtured their genius, he endured the degradation and death of their brother in whom he had set high hopes – and with all his oddities he was, it seems, appreciated by his parish. In 1861 the whole village went into mourning for his funeral. Mrs Gaskell, whose memoir of Charlotte Brontë first gave a wide circulation to the gossip about him, knew little about his pastoral work in Haworth over forty years. But she recorded that when Patrick Brontë was nearly blind, very tired and lonely, and full of grief after many storms of adversity and bereavement, 'he was out of doors among his parishioners for a good part of each day'.[2]

The most serious moral question for the England of the

---

[2] The voluminous literature includes L. and F. M. Hanson, *The Four Brontës* (Oxford, 1949), and John Lock and W. T. Dixon, *A Man of Sorrow: The Life, Letters and Times of the Rev. Patrick Brontë* (London, 1965).

Brontës was whether the degrading conditions under which millions of men, women and children now suffered were, or were not, essential if the greatly increased population was to be supported. Was it essential that one in every two of the children born in the new industrial towns should die before the age of five, and that agricultural labourers in the Suffolk of John Constable's tranquilly glowing pictures should bring up a family on far less than a pound a week, supplemented by six shillings from the poor-rate?

Later generations have on the whole agreed that the answer is obvious: these conditions were caused by the wickedness of factory owners and landlords, and the Christian Church ought to have been foremost in demanding their abolition. And so it seemed to many radicals at the time. But most Anglicans – and most Dissenters – sincerely believed that the moral question must be answered by saying that the country could not afford higher wages or greater subsidies if the economy was to develop in the interests of all.

In his *Essay on Population* (1798) a Cambridge scholar, Thomas Malthus, first absorbed the fact of a rapidly expanding population into a major – although not large – treatise on economics and ethics. He noted that while the population grew, the means of subsistence did not grow equally. He recognized the absolute necessity to limit population growth and in this necessity he found consolation for the checks on breeding which distressed him as a clergyman – famine, disease, war and vice. He also advocated 'moral restraint': since artificial contraception was wrong, people should postpone marriage and be chaste before it. At first he was explicitly complacent in the belief that this whole set of stern limits to human wishes had been decreed by the divine Providence; but more maturely regretting and suppressing the brutality of some of those early statements, he announced that he relied mainly on moral restraint.

He had raised questions which were to be taken very seriously by all thoughtful people in the second half of the twentieth century – and they were recognized as real questions during the first half of the nineteenth. Apart from moral restraint, the main answer seemed to be the increase of the means of subsistence by the improvement of the techniques used in agriculture and in manufacturing. England was then a developing nation, the very first nation in all the world to have the opportunities presented by modern farming and industry. But at the time the extent of the prosperity ahead, to be helped by birth control, was inconceivable. This was the age of iron, not gold.[3]

In a two-volume work of 1816 a future Archbishop of Canterbury, John Bird Sumner, an Evangelical, based his hope for the country on the Bible. His work was entitled *A Treatise on the Records of the Creation*, but his most interesting argument was on the controverted frontier between economics and ethics in an age considerably later than the creation. He applauded Malthus for his realism about the danger of over-population, but drew from the best economists known to that age (particularly Adam Smith) the optimistic belief that the means of subsistence could be increased if the economy were left to grow by trusting to the incentives to private enterprise and to the disciplines of the free market. Later on Sumner lost much of his faith in the sweat of the brow as the panacea for worldly grievances and fell back on the Evangelical consolation that a heaven awaited those who behaved properly in this vale of tears; and few other churchmen displayed his talents either for economics or for ethics. But a less systematic accept-ance of the iron laws taught by the economists did lie behind what was taught by almost all the leading churchmen. It was the conventional doctrine that men, women and children must work or starve, and in the conditions of the industrial revolu-tion must endure poverty in order that one day there might be plenty. Meanwhile the low prices made possible by low wages afforded some consolation. And allied to this conviction about economic laws there was a sincere belief that God had arranged the order of society just as he had set the stars in their courses. To interfere with the rights of private property seemed to be not only against the law of England and the long-term interests of the poor, but also against the law of God. The rich had their duties – to use their talents to the full, to set good

---

[3] See Patricia James, *Population Malthus* (London, 1979).

examples, to avoid extravagance, to be just and to be charitable. To pay more than standard wages was not among their duties.

The violence of the French Revolution, and of the great war to which it led, deeply frightened the propertied classes and strengthened their belief that the society under their control must be defended as a divinely ordained hierarchy – particularly because the revolutionaries were, or were reckoned to be, atheists. Many English preachers regarded the revolutionaries (and later Napoleon) as Antichrist and turned to the Bible for the interpretation of the dramas of the age as signs of the end of the world. Samuel Horsley, one of the ablest of the conservative bishops, declared that in 1800 mankind was facing the greatest crisis 'since the moment of our Lord's departure from the earth'. This apocalyptic mood continued in the post-war world when it was feared that English agitators might revive the revolution which Nelson and Wellington had crushed in their victories over the French. Amid such alarms reform of modest dimensions could easily be identified with revolution and revolution with the destruction of Christianity. Even Christians who avoided the extremes of reaction felt it a religious duty to preserve the constitution, the social order and the morality now under threat. In 1834 a fifth of the magistrates in the country were Church of England clergymen. They embodied the enormous investment by the Churches in social stability.

But many churchmen saw that the Church of England was not doing enough to influence – and, as it was usually hoped, to quieten – the new England. On Easter Day 1831 out of a total population of just over thirteen million, only about 605,000 received Holy Communion at its altars. All the irrationalities in its system which had been conspicuous in the eighteenth century were even more notable now. One example was the non-residence of their incumbents in thousands of the rural parishes. It was true that many of these parishes were deep in the countryside, with very small populations; but it was still scandalous that pastoral reorganization had not changed the pattern bequeathed by the Middle Ages.

Parliament was persuaded to legislate in 1803, but five years later was informed that some seven thousand priests were still not resident in parishes to which they had been appointed. By

1812 there were still over a thousand parishes where there was
no resident incumbent or curate. One result of this reform was
that a brilliant and deservedly popular talker and writer,
Sydney Smith, found himself exiled from the company of his
fellow wits and Whig patrons in London to his remote Yorkshire parish of Foston. He was miles from the nearest lemon, as
he complained, but he wrote to his friend Lady Holland that he
had given himself quietly up to 'horticulture and the annual
augmentation of my family'. He became in fact the pastor,
magistrate and amateur doctor of the village, for twenty years
from 1809, before his return to London as a canon of St Paul's.[4]
However, even after this tightening up the bishops and parish
priests had still not been redeployed to meet the movement of
population to the industrial towns and villages. Nor had they
been inspired to make a widespread appeal to those remaining
in the countryside. William Cobbett's *Rural Rides*, reporting
about the English people in the 1820s, concluded that 'the
labouring people have in a great measure ceased to go to
church'. It was a situation in which the Established Church
needed more than wit for its defence.

In 1820 a journalist, John Wade, published anonymously a
'Black Book' in which he argued that the Church's wealth was
so immense as to be the source of its immense vices. Three
years earlier Jeremy Bentham's *Church of Englandism*, of almost
seven hundred closely printed pages (although unfinished),
had poured scorn on the chaos of an institution so heavily
endowed. 'The Church of England system is ripe for dissolution', he concluded. 'The *service* provided by it is of a bad sort:
inefficient with respect to the ends or objects professed to be
aimed at by it: efficient with respect to divers effects which,
being pernicious, are too flagrantly so to be professed to be
aimed at.' Such books found a sympathetic readership, and, as
their message was passed on, an indignant audience; and the
criticism exploded when John Wade's polemic reappeared as
The Extraordinary Black Book of 1831. We cannot wonder that
when the reform of the electoral system in 1832 (against the
votes of most of the bishops) was believed to have destroyed the

---

[4] See Alan Bell, *Sydney Smith* (Oxford, 1980).

Church of England's chief support, intelligent men thought that its wealth was about to be confiscated. Three days after the Reform Bill became law, Thomas Arnold, Headmaster of Rugby, wrote: 'The Church as it now stands, no human power can save.'[5]

SAVING THE CHURCH

But was it necessary for the Church to remain unreformed – to fall because its sons left it to perish 'as it now stands'? It is scarcely too much to say that the Church of England was saved because laymen decided that it deserved to be equipped with the means to discharge its mission to the new population. An early leader among them was Joshua Watson. A wine merchant with wider commercial and financial interests, he was one of those who had done well out of the war; but he retired from business in 1814 to devote himself to good works. He had a house conveniently close to Parliament, but his home was in Hackney, still (like Clapham) a village; and there a group of High Churchmen gathered, to be called the Hackney Phalanx in deliberate contrast with the Evangelicals of the Clapham Sect. Their journal was the *British Critic*. They included pastors who represented the best of the Church's steady life in the parishes. However, Watson was influenced most by the example of William Stevens, who had died in 1807 but who for many years before that had been the treasurer of Queen Anne's Bounty (the nearest the Church of England got to a central administration) and the central pillar of many church societies. Watson set himself to do for a new generation what Stevens had done for his.

He succeeded in so many of his aims because, although he was determined to get what he wanted and prepared to work

---

[5] R. A. Soloway has researched into a period little covered in the standard histories, in *Prelates and People: Ecclesiastical Social Thought in England 1783–1852* (London, 1969). E. R. Norman, *Church and Society in England 1770–1970* (Oxford, 1976), was strong on this period. Two short studies have illuminated English popular religion or irreligion in a European context: A. D. Gilbert, *Religion and Society in Industrial England* (London, 1976), and Hugh McLeod, *Religion and the People of Western Europe 1789–1970* (Oxford, 1981).

for it (unlike the archbishops), what he wanted was acceptable to the Tory government. Spencer Perceval, the Prime Minister who was assassinated in 1812, had shared many of the feelings of the Evangelicals since Cambridge days and might have done much for church reform had death not come to him at the age of fifty. Lord Liverpool, his successor for fifteen years, actively encouraged Watson.[6] The central problem was that the Church of England had lacked its own national assembly; nothing could be done except by Parliament. To wait until Parliament was in the mood for radical reform meant waiting until the appointment in June 1832 of a Royal Commission to inquire into church revenues – by when Watson was a tired, backward-looking man, whose caution had become so great that he had advocated a commission composed entirely of clergy and with a very limited mandate. But when at the height of his powers he had done what he could, which was much. 'I remember so well, as a lad', wrote Bishop Selwyn, who heroically founded the Church in New Zealand, 'case-hardening myself against the name of Joshua Watson, which I was continually hearing as a final authority on all Church matters, and I pictured to myself a hard, dry, impenetrable man, who had no sympathies beyond a committee room.' Although there was truth in that picture, it is also revealing that in the 1810s Watson was trusted by the government and the public to administer two large half-public, half-private funds – one to relieve a war-ravaged Germany, the other to benefit the widows and orphans left by the battle of Waterloo.

Two other great charities in which Joshua Watson was prominent were directed to challenges within England.

One was the National Society for Promoting the Education of the Poor in the Principles of the Established Church, of which he was treasurer from its foundation in 1811. Its purpose was to encourage parishes to start their own schools, and the grants which it distributed were enough of a stimulus to ensure the education of a hundred thousand children by 1815 and of

---

[6] The best introduction to the politics is now Norman Gash, *Aristocracy and People: Britain 1815–65* (London, 1979). See also Denis Gray, *Spencer Perceval the Evangelical Prime Minister* (Manchester, 1963).

nearly a million twenty years later. The society was not supported by a government grant until 1833, but in the years before Watson's resignation in 1842 it bore the main burden of responsibility for the primary education of England's children. It also carried the main hope that these children would grow up to be supporters of their parish churches. At the time it seemed unnecessary that the State (or the tax-payer) should shoulder this burden.

State aid in education also seemed wrong, for it would deprive the Established Church of its duty to educate the new generation. The bishops in the House of Lords did not hesitate to wreck any proposal (beginning with the brewer Samuel Whitbread's bill of 1807) that there should be a national system supported out of rates or taxes, and as the years went by even those who had advocated such a system acknowledged that the National Society was achieving a considerable success by evoking private charity. As late as 1839 F. D. Maurice, one of the two most creative theologians of nineteenth-century England, was giving lectures which Joshua Watson welcomed in answer to the question: 'Has the Church or the State the power to educate the nation?' And the success of the National Society seemed so obvious that Watson was encouraged to play a leading part in the foundation in 1828 of a new Anglican institution of higher education, to supplement Oxford and Cambridge – King's College, London.[7]

The other great charitable effort which Watson led was the movement to build new churches. For the children now being educated by the Church must be given the opportunity to grow into regular churchgoers; and Watson and his associates were so optimistic as to suppose that if they were given the opportunity they would take it. Yet it was very difficult for private enterprise to solve the problem, even if the money could be found. To create a new parish required an Act of Parliament until 1818, and to build a new church within an existing parish required the consent of the patron and of the incumbent, either of whom might feel that his rights (including the rights to tithes

---

[7] See John Hurt, *Education in Evolution: Church, State, Society and Popular Education 1800–1870* (London, 1971).

and fees) were being infringed. The result of the neglect could
be seen in the populated but unchurched towns – not only the
new industrial towns in the north such as Sheffield (where
there was seating in church for 6,280 out of 55,000) or Manchester, but also the fashionable towns in the south such as
Bath or Brighton. Richard Yates, a London clergyman, wrote
a pamphlet full of statistics and warnings. Its title was the old
rallying-cry: *The Church in Danger*.

In 1818, however, substantial progress was made. An Incorporated Church Building Society was formed by Watson.
This was widely regarded as an appropriate thanksgiving for
the total victory over Napoleon – and as a sound investment in
the country's own peace. In the same year the government
under Lord Liverpool established an official commission with
a grant of a million pounds. Another half a million was voted in
1824. It was the most solid recognition in English history that
taxpayers had a duty towards the Established Church. The
Parliamentary grants had been used up virtually by 1828 and
were not renewed, but such was the stimulus given to private
subscribers that the commission did not cease work until 1857,
two years after Watson's death. By then it had built 612 new
churches accommodating about 600,000 people.[8]

Side by side with Joshua Watson we may place Reginald
Heber, who did much to rescue the name of the clergy. Well
born, well educated and well endowed with literary talents, he
might have become an English dean or bishop of distinction,
remembered for his hymns, including 'Holy, Holy, Holy, Lord
God Almighty', 'God that madest earth and heaven' and
'Brightest and best of the sons of the morning' – and among
scholars, by his edition of the works of Jeremy Taylor. Instead,
Heber left his delightful Shropshire rectory (designed by himself) and his prospects in England to sail out to India in 1823, to
be the second Bishop of Calcutta at the age of forty. Three
years later he was dead. Neither of his two successors survived
in India for as long as two years.

---

[8] See A. B. Webster, *Joshua Watson* (London, 1954), and M. H. Port, *Six Hundred
New Churches* (London, 1961). E. R. Wickham studied Sheffield in *Church and People in
an Industrial City* (London, 1957).

Most members of the Church of England who supported the new mission in India were delighted when a man so gracious assumed the leadership, although some wondered how hard he would work. In his parish he had been a dedicated pastor – and that he now became to India, regarding himself as the 'Chief Missionary'. He was acceptable both to the Evangelicals of the Church Missionary Society and to the High Churchmen of the rejuvenated Society for the Propagation of the Gospel. He had, indeed, in his more innocent days drawn up a scheme to merge the two societies, and one of his hymns, written rapidly for Whit Sunday 1818, became a missionary classic, 'From Greenland's icy mountains'. He knew how to get on with the civil authorities, so that the Bishop of Calcutta's powers were clarified and enlarged for his benefit, but he did not cling to all the conventions; he shocked an archdeacon by wearing white trousers. He was not full of a sense of his own importance, as the first bishop (T. F. Middleton, formerly an archdeacon) had been. Nor did he believe that all Hindus and Muslims were going to hell; on the contrary, he had a Romantic enthusiasm for the people of the East. As a young man he had made an exciting journey through Russia ending up among the Cossacks. Without hesitation he now ordained a Tamil convert, Christian David, who had been refused the priesthood by Bishop Middleton; David became an evangelist in his native Ceylon. Reginald Heber went to India because he was an English gentleman with a chivalrous sense of duty. He had heard a call to work as a clergyman and to share the quiet joy of his Christian faith. The Church which could breed such a man was not doomed.[9]

THE BIRTH OF NONCONFORMITY

Although the *Nonconformist* was not founded as a weekly magazine until 1841, the great movement which the Victorians knew

<hr>

[9] His vivid journal was edited with an introduction by M. A. Laird as *Bishop Heber in Northern India* (Cambridge, 1971). There has been no biography since George Smith's in 1895.

as Nonconformity had its origins earlier in the nineteenth
century. Both Methodism and the 'Old Dissent' prospered
during the years of war and industrialization, the 1790s and
1800s – so much so that many in the Established Church
became alarmed. Lord Sidmouth, who had been Prime Minister as Henry Addington, instituted an inquiry and then introduced a proposal into the House of Lords in 1811. No one
should be allowed to preach unless vouched for to the magistrates by six 'substantial and reputable householders'. Unless
illiterate preachers ('cobblers, tailors, pig-drovers and chim-
ney-sweepers') were suppressed, he warned, 'we should be in
danger of having a sectarian people'. The snobbish intolerance
of the proposal shocked even the Lords. The outcry against it
first brought Methodism into common action with the Presbyterians, Baptists and Congregationalists (or Independents)
of the 'Old Dissent'.[10]

The key factor was the same spiritual awakening that we
have observed in the response to Whitefield, to the Wesleys
and to the Evangelical clergy who remained in the Church of
England. For the Evangelical revival transformed many Dissenting ministers and their congregations, turning them into
the force which Lord Sidmouth feared. And among the
Evangelical Dissenters the most famous was William Carey,
the son of a village schoolmaster. Young William was appren-
ticed to a shoemaker and married to his master's illiterate
sister-in-law. He was, however, bored by the parish church,
and an act of petty dishonesty troubled his conscience. He
joined a small Dissenting congregation, underwent adult baptism and early in 1785, at the age of twenty-three, was given a
pittance to preach as a Baptist without any formal training.
But this young worker was already reading any books he could
get hold of, and so he absorbed Captain James Cook's narrative of voyages to Australia (1768–76). It was not long before
he was asking a question at a meeting of Baptist ministers in
Northampton. 'Was not the command given to the Apostles, to

---

[10] A good survey, concentrating on the birth of Nonconformity in the industrial
areas, is W. R. Ward, *Religion and Society in England 1790–1850*, while David M.
Thompson, *Nonconformity in the Nineteenth Century*, is an illuminating collection of
documents with a commentary (both London, 1972).

teach all nations, obligatory on all succeeding ministers to the end of the world, seeing that the accompanying promise was of equal extent?'

The question was ruled out of order by the chairman; Carey was only an 'enthusiast' who must be told to 'sit down'. But in 1792 he published a pamphlet, *An Enquiry into the Obligation of Christians to use means for the Conversion of the Heathen*. The 'enquiry' was, in fact, a clear plan. Three weeks later he persuaded another meeting, also in Northampton, to form something unprecedented: the Baptist Missionary Society. He was fortunate in that Andrew Fuller, a neighbouring minister, was an ex-wrestler, eager for spiritual exertions, who was to toil as the Missionary Society's secretary until his death in 1815. Fuller also toiled at preaching and writing, his main theme being that 'it is the duty of every minister of Christ plainly and faithfully to preach the Gospel to all who will hear it'. That was no platitude among these Particular Baptists, who had often interpreted Calvin and the New Testament to mean that the elect were few and were converted already, so that preaching the Gospel to others was a waste of time. Now the urgency of the Gospel for the world could inspire a mission to England – and to India. With Fuller's encouragement, in 1793 Carey determined to go to India, thirty years before Reginald Heber.

His doggedness was extraordinary. He faced destitution until he obtained a position as manager of a small indigo factory; he endured great loneliness until colleagues joined him in 1800; he had to overcome countless difficulties as he struggled to come to terms with the local languages and customs; he had no satisfactory base for his work until he was invited to set up a mission in the Danish settlement of Serampore near Calcutta; his wife became insane; and seven years passed before he baptized an Indian. His faith was tested very severely – although before leaving England his motto had been: 'Expect great things from God; attempt great things for God.'

Carey and his colleagues laid foundations. He went on preaching in India. He married again and much more happily, he became an expert botanist, and he established a prolific printing press. He also turned out to be a brilliant linguist. He and his assistants translated the entire Bible into six Indian languages, and parts of it into many more. All this work was to need revision, but he had shown what could be done. He compiled dictionaries and grammars and translated Hindu classics into English. He founded schools and a college for Indians, and at Fort William College became a professor paid by the government to share his great store of 'oriental' knowledge with young Englishmen. He earned large sums – and kept only a fraction of them for his own needs.

Thus this 'consecrated cobbler' (it was Sydney Smith's gibe) did many of the great things which he had advocated in his *Enquiry* in 1792. And at the end of it all, in 1834, he was buried in Serampore. His grave bore simple words, adapted from a hymn by Isaac Watts, recalling the Evangelical experience of his youth in the far-off English village of Paulersbury: 'A wretched, poor and helpless worm on thy kind arms I fall.'[11]

Many other 'worms' were stirred into new life and action by the touch of the Evangelical revival. Carey's first letter home inspired a group of Congregational ministers in Bristol to work towards the foundation of the London Missionary Society in 1795. The new venture was not denominational; an Evangelical rector in the Church of England, Thomas Haweis, did more than any other man to get it off the ground. A 'fundamental principle' was adopted: 'Our design is not to send Presbyterianism, Independency, Episcopacy or any other form of Church Order and Government . . . but the Glorious Gospel of the blessed God to the Heathen.'

In this spirit they immediately decided to send a little band of missionaries to the Pacific island of Tahiti – a place very much in the imaginations of Englishmen because of Captain Cook's visit there some twenty-five years before. The place was reputed to be a paradise. But Tahiti's promiscuous women often murdered their babies; and since the arrival of the Europeans, the population had been halved by venereal disease. The ship *Duff* had on board four ordained ministers, while the rest of the missionary band of thirty 'understood the mechanic arts'. Not many of them persevered in a paradise full

---

[11] See E. D. Potts, *Baptist Missionaries in India* (Cambridge, 1967), and Mary Drewery, *William Carey* (London, 1978).

of carnal temptations. The mission as a whole yielded to the temptation of using the power of the local king to enforce Christianity – the very contradiction of Dissent. But when a Russian explorer dropped anchor at Tahiti in 1820, he noticed how strict was the observance of the Sabbath. He noticed, too, that the young girls' lascivious dances which had delighted Captain Cook's crew were all now prohibited, and that men and women alike wore European clothes.[12]

Within England the Evangelical impetus quietly transformed Dissenting life in town and village. Under its challenge those Dissenters who denied the divinity of Christ became self-conscious and formed the Unitarian Society in 1791, supplemented by the Unitarian Fund in 1800 and the aggressive British and Foreign Unitarian Association in 1825. Some prominent Dissenters who were in practice Unitarians deplored the separate organization. Thomas Belsham, the most influential preacher with the new message, was now minister of the most distinguished of the Unitarian congregations, in Essex Street in London; and he objected to any suggestion that he was less than a respectable Dissenting minister. William Smith, a rich and cultured gentleman who became a Unitarian under Belsham's influence, was for many years (1805–32) chairman of the Protestant Dissenting Deputies. A leading Whig MP, he persuaded his Parliamentary colleagues to pass the Unitarian Toleration Act in 1813. Although the laws against blasphemy remained, the polite denial of Christ's divinity was no longer to be a crime. Yet by the 1830s Smith seemed a figure out of the past, the contemporary of his more secular fellow Whig, Charles James Fox.[13]

The real progress in Unitarianism was being made by ministers who built it up as one denomination among many, not large but strong in its appeal. It appealed to the more intelligent and benevolent type of employer in the great centres of industry such as Liverpool, Manchester and Birmingham;

---

[12] Niel Gunson studied *Messengers of Grace: Evangelical Missionaries in the South Seas, 1797–1860* (Melbourne, 1978).

[13] See Richard W. Davis, *Dissent in Politics 1780–1830: The Political Life of William Smith, M.P.* (London, 1971).

and it appealed to some of the more intellectually ambitious members of the new industrial working class. Naturally the employers and the workers usually worshipped in separate congregations, but nineteenth-century Unitarianism was as a whole not now so indifferent to the problems of the poor as Joseph Priestley had been. Even the ministers of affluent congregations changed their style. 'Ministers no longer preached only on Sunday and spent the rest of the week in the conduct of a school in order to supplement an inadequate income; in any case, there was by 1850 less opportunity for schoolmastering, now that the great national voluntary societies were at work. Instead the minister was urged to take up a double task: on Sunday mornings to preach to his middle-class congregation and for the rest of Sunday and during the week to conduct a variety of philanthropic activities, centred in the Sunday School, for a quite different body of people, of the poorer classes.'[14]

Among Dissenters who remained Trinitarians, resistance gathered to this Unitarian missionary zeal. Successful legal efforts were made to force some chapels to return to the orthodox Presbyterian faith of their founders – until the Dissenters' Chapels Act of 1844 made such litigation far more difficult. More important was the spiritual revival of orthodox Dissent; and there was growth, on a scale to which the Unitarians never aspired.[15] The inspiration was to be seen in the *Evangelical Magazine* – for 'Ruin, Redemption, Regeneration' was the clear message. With older children teaching the younger, schools for the poor spread according to methods brilliantly advocated by a Quaker, Joseph Lancaster. Much energy was put into the Religious Tract Society (1799) and the British and Foreign Bible Society (1804), managed jointly by Dissenters and by churchmen who agreed on the Evangelical mission to spread the scriptures and to offer simple explanations. And perhaps most influential of all was the Sunday school movement. In its early years it was usually non-

---

[14] H. L. Short in *The English Presbyterians*. p. 263. R. V. Holt presented *The Unitarian Contribution to Social Progress in England* (London, 1938).

[15] A. D. Gilbert, *Religion and Society in Industrial England*, pp. 32–6, 52–68.

denominational, which made many of the clergy and ministers suspicious. It was the only education, indeed almost the only recreation, available to many of the children employed in the new factories – and the rich could wonder uneasily what was being taught. But by 1816 Henry Brougham, after a survey, could estimate that some 420,000 children attended Sunday schools in England and Wales.[16]

By the mid-1820s about a third of the adult population was identified with this movement which was to become Nonconformity. With such a harvest obtainable if mobs and magistrates let them alone, most preachers had no wish to add Revolution to 'Ruin, Redemption, Regeneration'. They did not, however, neglect the duty of charity to relieve individual distress. In 1828 came the reward for their political loyalty. They secured the repeal of the Test and Corporation Acts – an objective which had been just beyond the Dissenters' grasp in the 1780s and plainly impossible during the years of anti-revolutionary reaction. Now the royal Duke of Sussex presided over a celebratory dinner with a sumptuous menu and twenty-four enthusiastic toasts.[17]

Dissenters were convinced that many opportunities must come through the widening of the Parliamentary electorate in 1832 and through the act of 1835 which similarly reformed the government of 178 cities and towns. They objected to paying church rates to repair parish churches which they did not attend, to being excluded from university education, to being married and buried according to the rites of the Church of England, and to being unregistered at birth unless they were baptized in the Church of England.

A response to the last grievance came quickly. Registrars were also authorized to attend Nonconformist marriages, although until 1856 applications for this privilege had to be made to the Poor Law Guardians. In 1836 a royal charter was granted to the new university of London, where University

---

[16] Thomas W. Laquer studied *Religion and Respectability: Sunday Schools and Working Class Culture* (London, 1976).

[17] Studies of the transition include Raymond G. Cowherd, *The Politics of English Dissent 1815–1848* (London, 1959).

College (founded in 1828) was open to Dissenters. But an anticlimax followed when the Whigs failed to deliver further reforms. In 1837 only one Dissenter was elected to Parliament – Edward Baines, the campaigning editor of the *Leeds Mercury*. By now many disillusioned Dissenters or Nonconformists, having at last acquired a taste for politics, were turning away from their Whig patrons towards self-help and radicalism. Partly for this reason, 'that year marks the beginning of the process of substituting for the Whig party and its aristocratic leadership a Liberal party with a middle-class leadership.'[18] The story of Victorian Nonconformity was beginning. But the swing to radicalism was still resisted by many of the preachers, and battles between radicals and conservatives split Methodism, which by the 1830s accounted for two-thirds of the numerical strength of Nonconformity.

CONFLICTS IN METHODISM

Almost all historians are now agreed that Methodism was not an alternative to a revolution. To claim that Methodism stopped England going the way of France is to exaggerate both the popularity of Methodism and the likelihood of a violent upheaval.[19] But for Methodists the struggle to decide their own future was an exciting battle where principles could be invoked on both sides – principles which were basically political, Right against Left. The sixty years after John Wesley's death in 1791 witnessed conflicts in Methodism which would have distressed him greatly by their bitterness resulting in schisms, but part of the explanation is that these conflicts brought to the surface tensions between suppressed political energies.

On the one side were the conservative Wesleyan Methodists, convinced that they were being faithful to John Wesley's principles. Wesley's death left 'Church Methodism' still an option theoretically, and those who advocated it could rightly

---

[18] R. Tudur Jones, *Congregationalism in England*, p. 207. Clyde Binfield studied the Baines family in *So Down to Prayers* (London, 1977), pp. 54–100.

[19] The classic study was Emile Halévy, *The Birth of Methodism*, translated and introduced by Bernard Semmel (Chicago, Ill., 1971).

plead Wesley's refusal to separate himself from the Church of England. But soon that option melted away, and what replaced it was the determination to build a church more strongly organized than the Church of England – a shadow Establishment. The Methodist Conference (of preachers only) was to be the 'living Wesley', entitled to govern as the founding autocrat had governed but delegating its local powers to the superintendent ministers appointed by it. These superintendents were entitled to expel any unsatisfactory Methodist without anyone's consent. Together with this hierarchical conception of church government went a 'no politics' rule which in practice tended to mean no radical politics. The upshot for the Wesleyans, as for John Wesley himself, was the acceptance of a hierarchical society as the work of Providence; and for the poor the political consequence of the Gospel was obedience.

On the other side were rebels – who believed that they were being faithful to John Wesley's own impatience with man-made rules, loyal to his own appeal to the poor over the heads of the king, clergy and gentry. Laymen must be included in church government at every level, from the national conference to the local society. Ministers must be regarded as servants rather than masters, happy to serve at low pay for a limited period. The minister's one essential function was to evangelize, to make new recruits for a Christian family where all were equal. Implied (and sometimes stated) in this alternative vision of Methodism was a revolutionary vision of England.

When their founder or 'father' was taken from them, the Methodists all agreed to follow 'Mr Wesley's plan'. The difficulty lay in agreeing what that was. Four years after John Wesley's death it was already necessary for the Methodist Conference to appoint a committee to draw up a 'plan of pacification'. While insisting that Holy Communion should never be celebrated in a Methodist chapel at the same time as in the parish church, this plan allowed the celebration if the majority of the local leadership desired it, subject to a veto by the conference; and it allowed a certain right to the local leaders to alter the conference's 'stationing' of ministers. Locally the admission and expulsion of members were to be agreed on by ministers and lay officials. On this basis Wesleyan Methodism controlled 631 preachers by 1815, and after 1818 they could use the title 'Reverend'. But the 'new Connexion' did something to assert its slogan, 'liberty and equality', by forming a splinter group. In 1800 it possessed only twenty preachers. By 1815 it had about 275.

The next major split from the Wesleyan Methodists occurred with the formation of the Primitive Methodists around Hugh Bourne in 1811. Bourne was a carpenter erecting windmills and watermills to serve the new industries in Staffordshire. After experiencing an Evangelical conversion ('like Bunyan's pilgrim I had to make my way alone'), he became a wandering preacher, and when the emotionalism of his preaching so alarmed his fellow Methodists that the Burslem society expelled him he simply carried on, dedicated to evangelism in the open air and earning his living as a casual labourer. Under the influence of an American, Lorenzo Dow, Bourne imitated the revivalist 'camp meetings' which were at that time winning thousands of converts for Methodism on the American Frontier.

'Camp meetings' were condemned by the Methodist Conference but won a considerable response. To their fellow workers these evangelists offered not only the rich emotional experience of a religious conversion, and not only a new direction in daily life, but also the support of a hearty fellowship into which no employer would intrude. In sickness or unemployment or old age these Methodists would visit each other; in prosperity they would buy from each other. To protect their family life they would renounce alcohol and be 'sparing in smoking tobacco'. Chapels were to be built not by the gifts of one benefactor, or of a few close neighbours, but by the united efforts of the whole society; 'all the society is considered as one family, the burden is to be borne by the whole.' And the preachers were to stay close to the people. None of them was to earn more than £15 a year (at a time when an Anglican incumbent drawing under £150 a year was reckoned poor), and they were to be appointed or dismissed by a predominantly lay conference. 'O Lord,' ran a prayer, 'bless the work of our servant, thy minister!'

As a representative of many working people who found

fulfilment within Primitive Methodism, Hugh Bourne developed great skills as a leader. He continued to preach until well into his seventies; it was his habit to walk around the country, although he sometimes used the new railways. He visited America, edited a hymn book, conducted a magazine and published and wrote many booklets. He sometimes had disputes with collaborators as rough as himself, but when he died in 1851 large crowds of adults and children sang hymns as his coffin was carried in triumph.

A roughly similar breakaway movement, the Bible Christians, flourished in Devon and Cornwall, with revival meetings which lasted for several days and nights. But all this only added to the conservatism of the main Methodist movement. After a bloody confrontation between a crowd and over-excited soldiers in Manchester – the so-called 'Peterloo Massacre', in 1819 – the workers were urged to rely on Providence, not on 'tumultuous assemblies'. Even after the 1832 Reform Act the Methodist Conference issued another of its warnings against listening to political debates 'with too warm an interest'. 'No politics' remained throughout this stormy period the official policy both of Wesleyan Methodism and of the groups which broke away from it. Many individual Methodists, particularly in the splinter groups, continued to defy such discouraging guidance, however. Of the six Dorset agricultural labourers who were sentenced to transportation to Australia for seven years for attempting to form a trade union in 1834 (the famous 'Tolpuddle Martyrs'), five are known to have been active Methodists. What went on in 'class' meetings could never be controlled by any national conference or full-time preacher.[20]

It was perhaps partly as an alternative to political radicalism that the official leadership provided a fresh outlet for Methodist enthusiasm: foreign missions. But it is certain that the Methodists did catch the infection of a genuine missionary enthusiasm. Work among the slaves in the West Indies captured the restless mind of John Wesley's most able associate,

---

[20] The standard study is still R. F. Wearmouth, *Methodism and the Working-Class Movements of England 1800–50* (London, 1937). See also John T. Wilkinson's biography of *Hugh Bourne* (London, 1952). Thomas Shaw studied *The Bible Christians* (London, 1975), and Joyce Marlow *The Tolpuddle Martyrs* (London, 1971).

Thomas Coke. Then early in 1813, having been disappointed in his hope that the authorities of the Church of England would make him Bishop of Calcutta, Coke formed the plan of a Methodist mission to the east. Local missionary societies were formed in Yorkshire and elsewhere to support him. He died during the voyage out, at the age of seventy-six, but the mission went ahead.[21] And one of the Yorkshire ministers who built up support for Coke's scheme was Jabez Bunting. A man with extraordinary talents, energies and ambitions, Bunting had already been called in to straighten out the mission's accounts, since the visionary and elderly Coke paid little attention to such details.

Jabez Bunting was no doubt sincere in his own support of the Methodist mission at home and abroad, but he was also sincere in believing that he was indispensable to that mission's success. He was often called the 'Pope of Methodism'. John Wesley had been called the same, but it has been said truly that 'Wesley's was the ascendancy of a saint, Bunting's the ascendancy of a masterful ecclesiastic'.[22]

The formal basis of Bunting's power was not large. He was secretary of the Methodist Conference and of the missionary society which now emerged on a nationwide scale; in order to discharge these two posts, he was glad to move to London in 1833. During conference debates and in business between those annual sessions, he was head-and-shoulders above his fellow ministers in administrative and argumentative power, and was also quite unusual in his lack of scruple. He had no hesitation in insisting that others should obey the regulations ('it is no sin for a man to think our discipline wrong, provided that he quits us'). He also had no hesitation in breaking those rules himself. With these qualifications he was elected president of the conference for a second term in 1828, again in 1836 and yet again in 1844. He persuaded the Wesleyans to open a 'theological institution' with himself as the active president; his last surviving letter is a veto of the radical idea that young men intending to be Methodist ministers should learn German. His

---

[21] See John Vickers, *Thomas Coke: An Apostle of Methodism* (London, 1969).

[22] E. R. Taylor, *Methodism and Politics 1791–1851* (Cambridge, 1935), p. 129.

firm hand was also applied to editing the denomination's magazine.

The real secret of Bunting's hold on his colleagues who became his subordinates was that he was known to possess the decisive influence in 'stationing' ministers and to be ruthless in punishing any who dared to criticize him. This was effective since every preacher was frequently moved about the country and no layman was ever admitted to the decision-making conference until 1878. In 1836 he arranged that men should be ordained more solemnly, with the laying-on-of-hands at the Methodist Conference. He also arranged that the leadership should be housed more grandly: a large headquarters, the Mission House, was built for himself and the missionary society.

In any local disputes he upheld the rights of ministers to instruct and to discipline their flocks. In 1827, for example, he insisted that the Brunswick Chapel in Leeds should have an organ, although most of the Methodists there considered this instrument a symbol of clericalism, if not of Popery, and in protest formed their own denomination. In a speech of 'several hours' he warned the conference against the 'insurrection' of the organ's enemies. Using a voice almost as loud as the organ, he proclaimed that disobedience to those ministers of whom he approved was wickedly like disobedience to employers; that 'Methodism agrees as well with democracy as with sin'. His first controversy came in 1812 when he refused to conduct the funeral of a man who had taken part in the Luddite riots against the new machinery. Although in general 'we stand stock still' was his motto, he managed to combine this conservation of discipline with many pleas for support for those who were achieving the economic progress of the nation as well as for those who were making Methodism more efficient. The unifying factor in his philosophy was a belief that the people must obey those appointed to lead – even when the leadership moved forward.

Such a philosophy, backed by an ecclesiastical dictatorship, was at the time hard for Wesleyans to resist. In 1835 one of his opponents, Samuel Warren of Manchester, was expelled from the Methodist Conference – in effect, for being an opponent –

and it was ruled legally that Warren could not change his
church into a Congregational church, with the result that
another splinter group, the Wesleyan Methodist Association,
had to be formed at considerable expense. For those who did
not wish to be thrown out of Wesleyan Methodism, it seemed
safest to let Bunting dominate and define Methodism. During
the 1840s, however, his policy and his personality were attacked furiously in anonymous pamphlets or *Fly Sheets* and by an
opposition newspaper, the *Wesleyan Times*. At a stormy conference in Manchester in 1849 James Everett, a disgruntled
preacher and satirist, was accused of the authorship of the *Fly
Sheets* (almost certainly with justice) and was expelled, along
with two contributors to the *Wesleyan Times*. Public meetings of
protest followed; a union was effected with those who had
walked out after Dr Warren; and in 1857 the United Methodist
Free Churches were formed, Liberal in politics and lay in
ecclesiastical emphasis, with James Everett as the first president and almost forty thousand members. In all, Bunting's
excessively masterful ascendancy is reckoned to have aroused
reactions which meant the loss of about a hundred thousand
members from Wesleyan Methodism, more than a quarter of
the total. It also aroused many feelings of disillusionment and
bitterness. One historian of Methodism writes of 'a spiritual
earthquake that shook the very foundations, undermined the
work of past generations, and threatened the whole structure
with collapse'.[23]

These conflicts, accompanied by much bitterness, certainly
diverted Methodism from evangelism among the unchurched,
and contrasted strangely with the claims made among the
heathen on behalf of Christianity as the Gospel of peace and
love. Yet it is surely also fair to say that the very intensity of
these quarrels within Methodism pointed to its vitality. They
showed how much religion was coming to mean to many
hundreds of thousands of ordinary English people. It is significant that the Methodist 'connexion' left behind by John
Wesley was sufficient to attract and absorb the ambition of a

---

[23] R. F. Wearmouth, *Methodism and the Struggle of the Working Classes 1850–1900*
(Leicester, 1954), p. 91.

man as talented as Jabez Bunting, the son of a radical tailor in Manchester. And when Wesleyan Methodism fell under the control of conservatives among whom Bunting was supreme, these leaders did not lack followers. On the contrary, more than a quarter of a million adult Wesleyan Methodists (full membership was some 260,000 in 1855, at the depth of the reaction against the Bunting regime) accepted his control of their national life, and the local rule of ministers acceptable to him. Basically they wanted the Gospel which they believed had been entrusted by God to these authoritarian pastors. After the impact of Jabez Bunting there was no more talk about returning to the Church of England, because in the Wesleyan Methodism which this man had refashioned many of the English found a spiritual home.

After his census of churchgoers in 1851 Horace Mann estimated that about two million people were in the habit of attending Methodist chapels of one sort or another. In Yorkshire the various brands of Methodism included about a sixth of the population, in Cornwall about a third. In England over twenty thousand laymen were Methodist local preachers.[24]

CATHOLIC EMANCIPATION

Alarmed by the Irish rebellion in 1789, in 1800 William Pitt had secured the union of Ireland with England, Scotland and Wales under one King, in Parliament, and this union still

---

[24] W. R. Ward edited *The Early Correspondence of Jabez Bunting* (London, 1972) and *Early Victorian Methodism: The Correspondence of Jabez Bunting 1830–58* (Oxford, 1976). The fullest account of the often unseemly conference debates remains Benjamin Gregory, *Side Lights on the Conflicts of Methodism 1827–52* (London, 1897). John Kent offered a defence of Bunting as 'the last Wesleyan' in *The Age of Disunity* (London, 1966) and Robert Currie a hostile view in *Methodism Divided* (1968). In *A History of the Methodist Church in Great Britain*, vol. 2 (London, 1978), essays by John Kent and John Wilkinson represented the Wesleyan and Primitive traditions. J. C. Bowmer, *Pastor and People: A Study of Church and People in Wesleyan Methodism* (London, 1975), admitted Bunting's arrogance but regarded him as essentially a defender of the 'classical Wesleyan' church order. Oliver Beckerlegge studied *The United Methodist Free Churches* (London, 1957) and D. A. Gowland *Methodist Secessions* in Manchester, Rochdale and Liverpool (Manchester, 1979).

seemed vital if Britain was to be Great. Yet the Irish peasants, and many in the middle classes, had emerged from the eighteenth-century persecution still loyal to their Catholic faith. Slowly this Irish majority was being allowed to compete with the ruling and exploiting Protestants; Catholics suitably qualified by property ownership had been given votes for the Irish Parliament in 1793. The conviction grew in the largely conservative mind of Pitt, and in the even more conservative minds of his Tory successors a quarter of a century later, that the stability of political union could not be secured unless Irish Catholics could vote for, and be elected to, the United Parliament. Without that, the oppression of the Irish was too naked. It became logical to make the same concession over town councils – and to extend it to the whole of the United Kingdom. Thus 'Catholic emancipation was carried because the Irish were prepared to fight for it, and the English government was not prepared to put down a rebellion'.[25] The main obstacle to be overcome was the prejudice which reigned at every level of English public opinion, from the monarch to the mob. What eventually quietened this prejudice sufficiently was the sheer absence of any evidence that the Roman Catholic community was either able or willing to deprive Protestant Englishmen of their liberties. 'It was an entirely secular settlement; tolerant conviction played no part in the government's purpose', it has been truly said. 'On the other hand, intolerant conviction was not strong enough to defeat this purpose.'[26]

In 1801 all William Pitt's services to his king and country were not sufficient to save him as Prime Minister once he had formed a conviction that Roman Catholics must be given the vote, and in 1807 the same fate befell the coalition government which had taken over after his recall and death. The prejudice against 'Popery' was so strong that the clerical leaders of the Catholic cause – the diocesan bishops in Ireland and the four

---

[25] Ursula Henriques, *Religious Toleration in England 1787–1833* (London, 1961), p. 260.

[26] G. I. T. Machin, *The Catholic Question in English Politics, 1820 to 1830* (Oxford, 1964), p. 178. See also R. B. McDowell, *Public Opinion and Government Policy in Ireland 1801–46* (London, 1952).

vicars apostolic in England – were for long ready to appease it. For instance, they were willing to allow the English government a veto in the appointment of their successors. They did not immediately reject a scheme originating among English Tories to pay the Irish Catholic clergy out of taxes – in other words, to buy their loyalty. Among the leading English gentry who had remained faithful to it, Catholicism was presented as a respectable religion and their private affair. They stressed that it was inconceivable that any pope should absolve them of the allegiance which they owed to the Crown, and in church affairs they were often 'Cisalpine': they did not question the Papal primacy but had no wish to see English affairs controlled from the other side of the Alps. Neither bishops nor laymen were ambitious for political power or for numerous conversions; they simply wanted to make sure that the long persecution of their faith really had ended. It was only in 1808 that the Irish peasants forced their bishops to abandon this fawning attitude to the English government, with the result that the most forceful of the vicars apostolic in England, John Milner, who was also the Irish bishops' agent, joined the refusal to give guarantees. As late as 1815 Pope Pius VII annoyed the Irish by being willing to compromise on this issue.

An Anglo-Irish 'Catholic Association', revived in 1823, began to demand emancipation as of right, without concessions – and began also to threaten, or at least to hint at, disorder. These shows of strength naturally provoked a Protestant reaction. 'Orange' and 'Brunswick' Clubs were formed in England, with the cry that the Hanoverian dynasty was once again in danger from Popish plots, and there were some large public meetings. Had the electoral system been more democratic at this stage, no Parliament meeting in Westminster would have offered any relief to the Papists. However, the system was such that if the King and the leading Tory politicians were ever to be persuaded to concede some relief in order to avoid further trouble, popular English prejudice would be powerless to prevent it.

That was what now happened. The leading members of the Tory government were the Duke of Wellington and Sir Robert Peel. Wellington had been born into one of the 'orange'

Protestant families ruling 'green' Ireland, and Peel's Protestantism had been so outspoken that his nickname was Orange Peel. But they were both at heart pragmatists, priding themselves on their truly patriotic superiority to popular clamours. They became persuaded that Catholic emancipation had to be granted, since the only alternative was the serious risk of civil war; and a tearful George IV found himself unable to think of any political alternative to allowing them to proceed. Many bitter words were still spoken against the betrayal of the 'Protestant' or 'Happy' Constitution, but they remained words and although many of them had been spoken by bishops of the Church of England, in the end ten bishops brought themselves to vote in the Lords with Wellington. In April 1829 Catholic emancipation became a fact.

It did not, however, result in any great increase in the influence of those Roman Catholic gentlemen who were now free to become MPs. In 1830 only five of them were elected by English constituencies. Internally, the Roman Catholic community was no longer deferential to the gentry. It had become a people's church, appealing to much the same class as Primitive Methodism; yet because of 'Catholic principles' lacking in Methodism, the church's leadership was able to be authoritarian in a manner which perhaps Jabez Bunting, stout Protestant as he was, secretly envied. So the decline of the gentry had been to the advantage of the priests, and above all of the bishops and the Pope.

A modern historian of Roman Catholicism in England sums up the period 1771–1830 as 'The Victory over the Laity'.[27] Certainly this period, and even more the period 1830–1860, saw a transformation. In its day a book such as *The State and Behaviour of the English Catholics to the Year 1780*, defending enlightened Catholic laymen and like-minded clergy, had caused a stir. Its author was Joseph Berington, a priest who survived many attacks by more conservative Catholics because he was taken into gentry households as a chaplain. 'I am no Papist', he wrote, explaining that the Pope was only 'the first magistrate in a well-regulated State.' He denounced the super-

---

[27] Hugh Aveling, *The Handle and the Axe* (London, 1976), pp. 322–45.

stition of foreign Catholics and was contemptuous of monks and Jesuits, but hailed the growth in England of a reasonable Catholicism, as simple as the primitive Church's. No other Catholicism, he was sure, would have a future. The Catholic equivalent of Joseph Priestley, he, too, found his voice drowned by the general conservatism which reacted to the French Revolution – but he consoled himself by writing a large *History of the Rise, Progress and Decline of the Papal Power*, never published. Even Bishop Milner, the author of *The Divine Right of Episcopacy* and one who attempted to assert that right in his work as vicar apostolic in the Midland district for twenty-three years from 1803, was no ardent Papist. He advocated worship in English not Latin and took care to keep on cordial terms with neighbouring Protestants. Before making his base in industrial Wolverhampton he had been for twenty-four peaceful years the priest in Winchester. John Lingard, who ministered in a village near Lancaster and whose work as an historian was respected by Protestants, had a similar mind, loyal to two heritages, Catholic and English.

What now happened was the transformation of the laity.[28] In the eighty years after 1770, when it numbered about eighty thousand, the Roman Catholic community in England seems to have increased to some seven hundred thousand. It was the most dramatic religious change seen in the country since the restoration of the Church of England with Charles II.

Some of the increase was due simply to the nation's growth in population, more than doubling between 1770 and 1850. The growth in churchgoing should not be exaggerated, since there were just under 253,000 at Mass on the Sunday in 1851 when a census was taken. But some evidence suggests that the Roman Catholic priests were rather more successful than their opposite numbers in the Church of England in persuading people to attend worship in the new industrial towns and villages. Back in the countryside these people or their parents had probably gone to Mass, if available, more often than

---

[28] The standard account was provided by Bernard Ward in seven volumes on *The Dawn of the Catholic Revival in England, The Eve of Catholic Emancipation* and *The Sequal to Catholic Emancipation* (London, 1909–15). For a more recent analysis see John Bossey, *The English Catholic Community 1570–1850* (London, 1975), pp. 295–363.

many a villager had supported his parish church – and when they moved to the new work the priest might be able to set up a chapel, often also a school, without facing the legal difficulties which encumbered the Established Church, and without feeling any need to make a building expensively handsome.

The main cause of the growth in the community was, however, not recruitment from the English. Just as Catholic Emancipation in 1829 had been due to Ireland, so the later, massive numerical growth was due to the immigration into England of the Irish.

Bishops in England complained that the Irish clergy would not come over to help, and parish priests complained that half the immigrants were scandalously irreligious. Many of these peasants whose faith and life-style had been little changed since the Middle Ages were thoroughly demoralized by life in an English factory, or roaming the countryside as casual labourers, or building the railways in the notorious gangs of 'navvies'. In his account of *The Condition of the Working Class in England* (1845), Friedrich Engels recorded of the Irish in Manchester that their standard of living was the 'lowest conceivable in a civilized country'. But the Irish immigration was bound to change the face of England's industrial cities. From its very beginning the Industrial Revolution in England had drawn labour from Ireland (whose economic development the English had wrecked), but the tide became a flood when the potato crop on which the Irish peasantry depended for survival was ruined by disease in the years 1845–47. During the 1840s about a quarter of a million of the Irish died because of the famine, and about a million fled overseas. By the census of 1851, almost 520,000 people born in Ireland were living in England, three per cent of the whole population, in addition to their children born in England; and ten years later there were eighty thousand more. The great majority of these incoming Irish were, at least nominally, Catholics; Irish Protestants tended to go to Scotland. By the 1820s the Irish Catholics in England seem to have outnumbered the English Catholics. By the end of the 1840s about three-quarters of the Roman Catholics in Liverpool, Manchester and London were of Irish extraction. In some other new industrial areas the proportion was similar.[29]

The leadership of this expanded community fell to men who could offer a faith strong enough to survive its ugly and harsh surroundings – strong enough to attract the Irish back to Mass, to recruit priests, to build churches and schools. The strength did not come from the old Catholic tradition in England, a tradition of inconspicuous reserve (priests were called 'Mr' and dressed as laymen), of a sober piety (churches contained no statues or side altars), of an emphatic English patriotism. The incoming Irish cared for none of these things. A style which had shielded the English Catholics' piety from inquisitive Protestant neighbours made no appeal at all to half a million destitute Irish who, if they were not to sink completely into an animal-like existence in their English exile, needed to be rescued by vigorous pastoral expeditions, hardhitting sermons and dramatically impressive services, preferably not in English. Only in that way could their Catholic religion, which had probably been rather slack in Ireland, become the foundation on which these refugees could rebuild their devastated lives.

Who, then, was to supply spiritual leadership and fill the vacuum? In 1840 there were only about five hundred priests at work in England. The Irish could, and gradually did, produce their own priests but in the emergency other priests came from the continent; the outstanding missionaries of the 1840s were two Italians, Aloysius Gentili and Dominici Barberi, both of whom, worn out, died young. Such men linked England with a wider Catholic revival.

When Napoleon had been compelled to conclude a concordat with the papacy, Christianity in its Catholic form had seemed necessary to provide emotional food for the French and some legitimacy for the new empire. When Napoleon had been toppled the Catholic religion had been patronized by the

---

[29] The chapters on 'The Increase in Population' and 'The Religion of the People' are among the valuable features of G. Kitson Clark, *The Making of Victorian England* (London, 1962). Cecil Woodham-Smith told the story of *The Great Hunger: Ireland 1845–59* (London, 1964).

victorious reactionaries, and the restored altar placed near the restored throne; the Pope's triumphant return to Rome in 1814 had seemed to symbolize all the return of the old days. When the time came for the recovery of a revolutionary (or at least liberal) spirit, many Catholics – for example, the brilliant group around the French paper *L'Avenir* – dreamed of a reconciliation between the Church and democracy under prophetic priests and popes. When the papacy itself reacted by condemning *L'Avenir* and the leader of that group wandered off heartbroken, many did not take his path into the wilderness, being prepared to accept even a Church which declared war on democracy and modern civilization. Not even the identification of the cause of the Church with the maintenance of the temporal power of the popes as the sovereigns of Rome and a considerable part of Italy could end this recovery of the Catholic faith to be seen in nineteenth-century Europe. When the slow rise of modern intellectual scepticism did disturb some believers, the surrender of the mind to the old Catholic faith in its mysterious beauty and supernatural authority could seem all the more of a relief. Many in Europe felt like that; and these thoughts or dreams were in the minds of some Englishmen who during the 1820s and 1830s were like actors, waiting in the wings before the serious drama of the Catholic revival could be performed on stage.[30]

The most important member of this hopeful group was Nicholas Wiseman. Of Irish descent although born in Spain, he was sent to the school and seminary established at Ushaw in County Durham in 1795. The spiritual climate at Ushaw was too dull to do much for him, but the very fact that he received this schooling in England was significant. Previous generations of Catholic gentlemen's sons had been compelled to go to the colleges abroad. Such colleges were now closed thanks to the French Revolution, but that was no disaster since there was now freedom to run Catholic schools in England. There was even some new sympathy with, and respect for, the Catholic

---

[30] See Alec R. Vidler, *Prophecy and Papacy* (London, 1954); W. G. Roe, *Lamennais and England* (Oxford, 1966); Owen Chadwick, *The Popes and European Revolution* (Oxford, 1981).

clergy; thousands of them had been temporarily exiled from the continent into England by the terror of the revolution.

In 1818, at the age of sixteen, Nicholas Wiseman was sent to Rome as one of the first six students to reopen the English College. It had been looted and closed by the revolutionaries twenty years before. He never forgot the first walk in silence through the empty college's halls, through the library with its unused and disordered books, through the chapel with the desecrated graves. Remaining in Rome as a priest, he became an accomplished scholar and ardent preacher.

In 1835 he returned to England. In a large mansion overlooking Bath, Bishop Baines, the vicar apostolic of the Western district, was establishing a school and seminary which he hoped would rival the colleges already in existence at Ushaw, at Oscott near Birmingham and at Ware in Hertfordshire. There was talk of a Catholic university, and of Nicholas Wiseman at its head. The trouble with the grandiose scheme was that so few people trusted Bishop Baines. He was a Benedictine monk, but the monks of Downside Abbey in his district had resisted an earlier scheme which would have made their abbey his headquarters. The monks of his own monastery, Ampleforth Abbey, had resented the fact that so many of their small community had been summoned away from Yorkshire to Bath, where the monk-bishop lived in excessive state. When they met, Baines and Wiseman soon discovered that, charming as they both could be, they did not charm each other. The breach was just as well for Wiseman's career, since the school-cum-palace from which Baines looked down on Bath was soon destroyed by fire, and the obstinately courageous Bishop had to spend the rest of his life trying to raise money to rebuild it. After delivering some highly successful lectures in London, Wiseman was better off back in Rome.

When he finally returned to England in 1840, it was to the Midland district where he assisted old Bishop Walsh. He also took charge of the school and college at Oscott. He still kept in touch with the world of ideas, editing the new *Dublin Review* which was financed by the Irish leader O'Connell but directed towards the literary end of the Catholic market. A lover of food, wine and wit, he moved easily among other gentlemen. He

admired John Talbot, the fabulously rich sixteenth Earl of
Shrewsbury who shared his own romantic illusion that the
English were about to return in very large numbers to the old
religion of the Catholic Church. The heir of the finest tradition
in medieval chivalry, the earl's main interest lay in building
churches for Catholic worship in the new industrial towns. His
favourite architect was Augustus Welby Pugin, who from the
design of fashionable Gothic chairs had moved on to construction of Gothic churches with a consistently Gothic style in the
furnishings and vestments. To Pugin, such a revival of
medievalism was itself an act of Christian worship and witness.
This romanticism aroused Bishop Wiseman's appreciation.
He was, however, willing to incur Pugin's wrath by resisting
the introduction of a rood screen into St Chad's Cathedral,
Birmingham. He opposed it because it would separate the
priests from the people.[31]

[31] See Brian Fothergill, *Nicholas Wiseman* (London, 1963), and for the Romantic
background Denis Gwynn, *The Second Spring 1815–52* (London, 1942), and *Lord
Shrewsbury, Pugin and the Catholic Revival* (London 1946).

CHAPTER FOUR

THREE POETS

BLAKE AND MAN

During these richly formative years English Christianity was, however, not only a religious revival which could be organized into Methodism, Evangelicalism, the quieter High Church recovery, the birth of militant Nonconformity and the transformation of Roman Catholicism. It was also something much harder to pin down: a movement of thought about man and God. And it is the good fortune of the student of pre-Victorian religion that three great poets are available to act as guides to this spiritual movement – William Blake, William Wordsworth and Samuel Taylor Coleridge.

The more conventional Robert Southey failed to think out his religious position thoroughly, or at least failed to make honest and deep thoughts public, because after a radical youth he became a prolific Tory journalist. It is not necessary to condemn him as 'Mr Feathernest', who abandoned the revolutionary cause solely in order to make money out of royalist and patriotic effusions as Poet Laureate and best-sellers such as *The Book of the Church*. As late as 1812 Shelley got the impression from their only meeting that Southey 'tho' far from being a man of great reasoning powers is a great man'. During their talks the older poet apparently agreed with 'my idea of the Deity, a mass of infinite intelligence' – and recommended that Shelley should get in touch with the philosopher William Godwin, a recommendation with fateful consequences. All the evidence suggests that Southey was sincere in his hatred of the excesses of the French Revolution and in his fear that English civilization was about to be brought to an end by mob violence accompanied by economic collapse. He regarded the Church of England as one of the great institutions of the country, so useful that it deserved to be defended from its enemies although he could not accept all its theology. In 1814 he confessed to a friend: 'I am neither enthusiast nor hypocrite, but a man deeply and habitually religious in all my feelings, according to my own views of religion, which views differ from those of the Church which I defend. . . . *Not* believing in the inspiration of the Bible, but believing in the faith which is founded upon it, I hold its general circulation as one of the greatest benefits which can be conferred on mankind. *Not* believing that men are damned for not being Christians, I believe that Christianity is a divine religion, and that it is our duty to diffuse it.'[1]

At the other extreme, the unconventional Shelley failed to exert much influence on English religion because he could so easily be dismissed as an eccentric who was in rebellion for rebellion's sake – or as a very wicked man who did not dare to live in England. This great poet and wide-ranging and courageous thinker, for all the passionate sincerity of his hatred of the oppressors of the English poor, was too much the son of a very rich baronet ever to feel at ease with the actual poor. In much the same way, his lofty conception of a purified new religion was accompanied by such provocative, often adolescent, attacks on Christian doctrines and morals that his notoriety meant that he could never gain a hearing among the religious. Despite his 'simultaneous perception of Power and Love in the absolute, and of Beauty and Good in the concrete' (the tribute was to come from Robert Browning), the reputation with which Shelley went to Oxford – 'the Eton Atheist' – dogged him. It was still his reputation when he died in his twenty-ninth year; and he had done much to earn it.

The pamphlet which brought about his expulsion from Oxford, while itself a perfectly reasonable demonstration that the existence of God could not be proved, was entitled *The Necessity of Atheism* and was mailed to all the bishops and all the heads of colleges. Had he lived to the same age as his father he would have died in 1882 and might have become a mature philosopher. But in a letter dated to Shelley in 1820, Southey

---

[1] Geoffrey Carnall, *Robert Southey and His Age* (Oxford, 1960), pp. 216–17.

expressed respectable England's reaction to the life that had been lived. Shelley had driven his first wife to suicide: 'You robbed her of her moral and religious principles, you debauched her mind. . . . You have reasoned yourself into a state of mind so pernicious that your character, with your "domestic arrangements" as you term it, might furnish the subject for the drama more instructive, and scarcely less painful, than the detestable story of the Cenci. . . . It is the Atheist's Tragedy.'[2]

We shall study William Blake instead, for he rose above the conventions to glory. Born in 1757 in London, he lived mainly there until his death in 1827. His background was middle class; his father, a solid tradesman, was a member of a Dissenting congregation. In youth he read widely, in a number of languages; in old age he learned Italian in order to read and illustrate Dante. No other reading, however, had as much power for him as his delight in the imagery of the Bible. At the age of four he thought he saw God pressing his face against the window, and on another occasion his father almost beat him for claiming to have seen angels in a tree. He learned draughtsmanship by drawing the monuments in Westminster Abbey; he loved that great church (and the Gothic architecture which it represented), and had a vision of Christ and his apostles walking through it. His devotion to Jesus was so clear, and so eloquent, that countless orthodox Christians have loved to pray in his words. His poem 'On Another's Sorrow' may be judged the finest statement in English of the compassion of God expressed in the birth and death of Jesus. All through his life eternity seemed close to him and he claimed that he often talked with the dead. Among all the English poets he felt closest to Milton, about whom he wrote a major poem. There is a story that he and his wife Catherine were once discovered by a bewildered Thomas Butts sitting naked in the garden; they were Adam and Eve, reading *Paradise Lost* aloud. Asked what the poet did when his vision faded, his wife once replied factually: 'he prays.' In 1802 he wrote to Thomas Butts: 'I still and shall to all eternity embrace Christianity and adore him

---

[2] Richard Holmes, *Shelley: The Pursuit* (London, 1974), p. 608.

who is the express image of God; but I have travel'd thro' perils and darkness not unlike a champion.'

But like Shelley, Blake was in total rebellion against all authority in Church and State. His parents, who allowed his formal education to cease at the age of ten, at least had the insight not to try to make him conform. What he really inherited from his family was the Levellers' tradition, radicalism seeking a revolution, and it seems that he concealed the extent of this radicalism beneath a cloud of mythological writing and drawing in order to protect himself in an age when an Englishman flaunting 'anarchism' and 'atheism' would invite imprisonment and probably hanging. He had an argument with a private soldier during the invasion scare in the autumn of 1803, while he was living near the sea at Felpham; he was accused of sedition but no evidence about his connections with dangerous radicals was produced at his trial, and he was acquitted. When Bishop Watson published his *Apology for the Bible* against Tom Paine, Blake wrote on his copy: 'To defend the Bible in this year 1798 would cost a man his life.' But what was the Bible to him? We face a further difficulty as we try to get at his real opinions: in private conversation Blake liked to tease, making a point by exaggerating it with a shocking sense of humour. Henry Crabb Robinson met him in December 1825 and found this 'Artist or Genius – or Mystic or Madman' so fascinating that he recorded his private opinions. Blake 'eagerly concurred' in Robinson's suggestion that the soul existed before the body's birth and after his death. He had, indeed, often conversed with Socrates and with Jesus. But he added: 'we are all coexistent with God, partakers of the divine nature.' On being questioned about the divinity of Christ, 'he said *He is the only God*, but then he added – "And so I am and so are you".'

Many scholars hold that he really was an anarchist and an atheist. 'Blake's visionary universe', writes one commentator, 'began at every point from the experiment of assuming that the supreme reality in the universe was not, as the Jews, Christians and exponents of natural religion seemed to suppose, a distant, holy and affectionate God but man – man conceived in the fuller nature which was revealed to him by the workings of his energies and his imagination.'[3] But we cannot be certain that this is the correct assessment of Blake's basic position, for it is also possible to assemble passages which suggest another conclusion – that he was, as another scholar has said, 'a monotheist; God is the source of all being, the One "who only Is".'[4] Blake wrote that 'I see the face of my Heavenly Father, he lays his hand upon my head and gives a blessing to all my works'; and much else that was compatible with a devout orthodoxy. The truth seems to be that he was a mystic poet, not a philosopher, and that it was enough for him to record his intuition that God was to be adored in the creation, without troubling to be precise in his metaphysics. His working philosophy was summed up in *The Marriage of Heaven and Hell*: 'God only Acts and Is in existing beings or men.'

It is certain that his child's vision of God at the window never left him. But actually the face seen at the window was a man's face; and his vision of Jesus was of a man who was no conformist:

> He scorn'd Earth's parents, scorn'd Earth's God,
> And mock'd the one and the other's rod;
> He seventy disciples sent
> Against Religion and Government.

So Blake hated Protestants as well as priests, holding that they had all joined in the age-old conspiracy to invent a God who is distinct from man. They had attributed to that imaginary God either a cold rationality ('Urizen' was Blake's name for the Deity thus conceived) or else a fiery wrath in upholding the conventions (another name for God was 'Nobodaddy'). Blake's positive creed, the theme of all his attempts to replace the God of the evil imagination, was threefold: 'Man has no body distinct from his soul. . . . Energy is the only life, and is from the body. . . . Energy is eternal delight.' He adored 'the Eternal Great Humanity Divine'.

That sounds like the famous affirmation of Keats: 'I am certain of nothing but of the holiness of the heart's affections

---

[3] John Beer, *Blake's Visionary Universe* (Manchester, 1969), p. 1.

[4] J. G. Davies, *The Theology of William Blake* (Oxford, 1948), p. 85.

and the truth of Imagination. What the Imagination seizes as Beauty must be truth – whether it existed before or not. . . .' But Blake meant by 'eternal' that the spirit of man really was indestructible; when his brother Robert died, he saw his spirit rising through the ceiling, 'clapping its hands for joy'. He sang on his own deathbed. He meant by 'energy' (a great Romantic word) sexual energy but also many lesser forms of delight in the 'minute particulars' of the visible world. Although he advocated a man's right to enjoy many wives or mistresses, in practice he seems to have been satisfied with his patient wife, and his basic message was that the world was full of a glory which could be known as surely as a woman could be known in bed. Even the 'tyger burning bright' was glorious because sublimely energetic in his wrath. His vision was that

> The pride of the peacock is the glory of God.
> The lust of the goat is the bounty of God.
> The wrath of the lion is the wisdom of God.
> The nakedness of woman is the work of God.

He affirmed that 'everything that lives is holy'; that 'if the doors of perception were cleansed everything would appear to man as it is, infinite'; that the sun when it rises is not 'a round disk of fire somewhat like a guinea' but is 'an innumerable company of the heavenly host crying, "Holy, Holy, Holy is the Lord God Almighty"'.

This vision of glory endured despite the sufferings which he saw in the London streets as the symptoms of a desperately diseased age:

> I wander thro' each charter'd street,
> Near where the charter'd Thames does flow,
> And mark in every face I meet
> Marks of weakness, marks of woe . . .
>
> How the chimney-sweeper's cry
> Every black'ning church appalls;
> And the hapless soldier's sigh
> Runs in blood down palace walls.

He took no pride in England's industrialization and foresaw none of the advantages which it was to bring to the people. He was saddened by the wars against the Americans and French, and his paintings of the 'spiritual forms' of Pitt and Nelson, the war heroes, were ironic: he saw them as men of semi-angelic intelligence, guiding great monsters to destruction. He could not take pleasure in battles when

> Each outcry of the hunted hare
> A fibre from the brain does tear.

In the Evangelical revival he found nothing except the condemnation of the pleasures with which the people sought brief escapes from their miseries. In his response he had to be himself, not the convincing analyst but the haunting artist. 'I will not reason and compare', he wrote; 'my business is to create.' *Jerusalem* was the culminating statement of his understanding of the poet's task as being

> To open the eternal worlds, to open the immortal eyes
> Of man inwards into the worlds of thought; into eternity,
> Ever expanding in the bosom of God, the Human Imagination.[5]

WORDSWORTH AND GOD

If William Blake is not inconceivable as a professional preacher of Radical Dissent, William Wordsworth had periods in his life when he was very close to being a clergyman of the Church of England. When his uncles paid for him to proceed from Hawkshead grammar school to Cambridge, it was in the belief that he would obtain a fellowship of a college and then settle down in a parish. As late as 1793 his sister Dorothy, to whom he poured out all his secret thoughts, still dreamed of the time when she and William would be snug together in a 'little parsonage'. In the course of that year his uncles admitted to themselves that William, who had had an illegitimate daughter by a Roman Catholic Frenchwoman, and who even more

[5] There is a large literature on Blake, but the most useful books in this context are Bernard Blackstone, *English Blake* (Cambridge, 1949); David Erdman, *Blake: Prophet against Empire* (revised, Princeton, NJ, 1969); Morton D. Paley, *Energy and Imagination: A Study of the Development of Blake's Thought* (Oxford, 1970); Michael Davis, *William Blake: A New Kind of Man* (London, 1977).

scandalously had fallen in love with the French Republic, was not going to be ordained. Yet within twelve years he had become a fully convinced Christian believer and an upholder of the Church of England. When his long poem about the growth of his mind was eventually published after his death in 1850 and named *The Prelude*, almost all the passages written half a century or so before and hinting at heresy had been adjusted to the sincerely accepted demands of orthodoxy. When his official biography was written by his nephew Christopher (a future bishop), no reference was made to his illegitimate daughter and as little reference as possible to other indiscretions of his youth.

For the historian of English religion, however, the fascination of Wordsworth's life is seeing 'the river' (a favourite image of his) taking its own way to this sea.

His mother's death when he was aged eight left him with a father absorbed in sorrow and business (and the father also died, in 1783). He wrote so much about the happiness of childhood that it comes as a surprise to learn that his 'home' for many holidays was a place of rebellious misery, a flat above the shop owned by an uncongenial uncle in Penrith. His whole world might have been ruined by his parents' deaths had it not been for the joy he found in nature – and had an Elizabethan archbishop (Sandys) not founded an excellent grammar school at Hawkshead, which he attended as a boarder, living in the cottage of kind Ann Tyson. His closest friend was a humble 'packman' or tinker who recited folktales and ballads and took him on long walks.

After Cambridge, nature again had to heal a deep distress. Wordsworth had gone to France as a tourist, not as a womanizer or as a student of revolutionary politics. We are reminded of this by the facts that Annette Vallon, to whom he gave his heart, was a domestic soul four years older than he was – and an ardent Royalist. The liaison was an act of gross folly. He could not earn his living in France and she would be disapproved of in England; so he had to abandon her and their daughter, and it says much about her that she reproached him so little. That experience was so profoundly humiliating that he never wrote about it except obliquely. He was also reduced to despair when he saw his high hopes for the revolution, hopes which he celebrated in fine poems, guillotined by the Jacobins in their reign of terror.

Shattered, Wordsworth crept back to lodge with his brother in London. He later walked over the Salisbury Plain, having seen the fleet in the Solent preparing for battle with the French; and nature did not prevent him having many dreams about the violence of the early Britons who had lived on the same plain. He remained a political radical for some years, but he did not live in the revolutionary underworld of London which Blake inhabited. Instead he gave himself to nature, being enabled by a small legacy to rent very simple accommodation which he could share with his sister. And perhaps that itself became a problem. It is possible (although there is no certain evidence) that he was conscious that his relationship with his sister developed unhealthily, so that it was emotionally (although not physically) incest before his marriage to Mary Hutchinson in 1803.

He now offered to nature not a religious faith but a religious longing. He recalled in *The Excursion* how

> In such access of mind, in such high hour
> Of visitation from the living God,
> He did not feel the God: he felt his works . . .
> Such hour by prayer or praise was unprofaned,
> He neither prayed, nor offered thanks or praise,
> His mind was a thanksgiving to the power
> That made him: it was blessedness and love.

Of course such a spirit could not be satisfied by materialism:

> The world is too much with us; late and soon,
> Getting and spending we lay waste our powers:
> Little we see in Nature that is ours. . . .
> It moves us not. – Great God! I'd rather be
> A Pagan suckled in a creed outworn . . .

Richer than the 'wealth of nations' were the moments when

> we are laid asleep
> In body, and become a living soul;
> While with an eye made quiet by the power

> Of harmony, and the deep power of joy,
> We see into the life of things.

His first poem in which his genius was at full stretch was composed 'a few miles above Tintern Abbey' in 1798. The beauty of nature has been approached through questions

> in lonely rooms, and 'mid the din
> Of towns and cities. . . .

These are questions about human suffering,

> the heavy and the weary weight
> Of all this unintelligible world. . . .

He remembers a time when after 'the coarser pleasures of my boyhood days' he had reached the 'aching joys' and 'dizzy raptures' of a time when 'nature to me was all in all'. But even in that time he had not sought absorption into nature as the complete nature-mystic would. He had been too conscious of his unhappiness,

> more like a man
> Flying from something that he dreads than one
> Who sought the thing he loved.

Now 'that time is past'. But he does not mourn, since he has had an 'abundant recompense': he has deepened the questions which he brings to nature, because he has deepened his understanding of humanity's burdens and powers. He has heard

> The still, sad music of humanity,
> Nor harsh nor grating, though of ample power
> To chasten and subdue.

He has learned, too, that the understanding of nature comes from the creative imagination. He speaks

> of all the mighty world
> Of eye, and ear – both what they half create
> And what perceive.

This creative insight is what has equipped him to find in ambiguous nature

> The anchor of my purest thoughts, the nurse,
> The guide, the guardian of my heart, and soul
> Of all my moral being.

The vision of nature which consoled him in 1798 was not precisely defined in terms of theological or philosophical prose. In so far as it could be so defined, it probably should be classified as pantheism; it was what Coleridge was to call 'the misty rather than mystic confusion of God with nature'. The lack of precision was inevitable because, in the words of a modern critic, 'Wordsworth was not primarily a thinker but a feeler. The determining events of his career and the sources of all that is essential in his poetry were the personal tragedies, the anguished decisions, the half-conscious, half-animal, terrors and ecstasies, and *not* the discoveries of the intellect'.[6] But the unclear answer given by nature to his distress in 1798 was beyond dispute grand:

> I have felt
> A presence that disturbs me with the joy
> Of elevated thoughts; a sense sublime
> Of something far more deeply interfused,
> Whose dwelling is the light of setting suns,
> And the round ocean and living air,
> And the blue sky, and in the mind of man:
> A motion, and a spirit, that impels
> All thinking things, all objects of all thought,
> And rolls through all things.

The next major poem which is sublime is the ode, *Intimations of Immortality*. Most of it was written early in 1804. The first part had been abandoned in 1802, when Wordsworth had only got so far as to record the waning of his ecstasies in the presence of nature:

> Whither is fled the visionary gleam,
> Where is it now, the glory and the dream?

His answer at that stage was that the glory could be recaptured by remembering childhood's 'vision splendid' – and that

---

[6] F. W. Bateson, *Wordsworth: A Reinterpretation* (London, 1954), p. 40.

children had this vision of nature's glory because they were closer to nature's God. The poet was here using the belief, taught to the West by Plato, that the soul existed before birth. The belief appealed to a number of literary-minded people in that time; Blake held it, and Shelley once startled a mother crossing Magdalen Bridge in Oxford by asking her what her baby remembered of heaven. Within the next year, 1805, however, Wordsworth was addressing questions to nature which no half-serious belief could satisfy. For his brother John, whom he regarded as a saint, was drowned at sea when in command of one of the East India Company's great ships. And William Wordsworth then asked with all the passion of his soul whether darkness or light prevailed.

For some days he and Dorothy could do little but weep together. Then he could put his question into words. 'Why have we a choice and a will, with a notion of justice and injustice, enabling us to be moral agents? Why have sympathies which make the best of us so afraid of inflicting pain and sorrow, which yet we see dealt about so lavishly by the Supreme Governor? Why should our notions of right towards each other, and to all sentient beings within our influence, differ so widely from what appears to be his notion and rule, if everything were to end here? Would it not be blasphemy to say that, upon the supposition of the thinking principle being destroyed by death, however inferior we may be to the great Cause and Ruler of things, we have *more of love* in our nature than he has? The thought is monstrous; and yet how to get rid of it, except on the supposition of *another* and a *better world*, I do not see.'

In that tormented letter he did not say that John could not perish utterly because he was a part of nature – although one of the 'Lucy' poems had experimented with that solution,

> Rolled round in earth's diurnal course
> With rocks, and stones, and trees.

Nor did he say that he knew that John was alive because Christ had risen. What he implied was that nature had revealed to him that there was a 'great Cause and Ruler of things' but had left him bewildered about the fate of individuals. Because life was so unjust his own moral sense rebelled against God the 'Cause and Ruler' – unless there was a 'better world' of persons in eternal relationships, upheld by the immortal, personal and loving God. Was there such a world? He could not be a total rebel; the sense of being a creature was fundamental to his sense of being anyone at all. So in the end 'the supposition of *another* and a *better* world' was what he chose. 'Christianity', a modern scholar has concluded, 'reached Wordsworth neither through a sense of sin nor a sense of glory but through wanhope, a colourless despair. . . . Wordsworth does not embrace Christianity: it is forced on him by the exclusion of alternatives. . . . The most certain thing about Wordsworth's religion is its initial poverty.'[7]

His religion did not remain poor. 'Theologians may puzzle their heads about dogmas as they will,' he wrote to an intimate friend (Sir George Beaumont) in 1825, 'the religion of gratitude cannot mislead us. Of that we are sure, and gratitude is the handmaid to hope, and hope the harbinger of faith. I look upon Nature, I think of the best part of our species, I lean upon my friends, and I meditate upon the Scriptures, especially the Gospel of St John; and my creed rises up of itself with the ease of an exhalation yet a fabric of adamant.' He did not mention in that letter that he was a regular churchgoer; but so he was, after his brother's death.

He knew that his faith fell short of knowledge, but as he wrote to Lady Beaumont in 1815, he was undeterred by the scorn of 'London wits and witlings' because he did not regard them as superior thinkers; 'for we have no thought (save thoughts of pain) but as far as we have love and admiration.' By then he knew that he could never complete the major philosophical poem, *The Recluse*, 'containing views on Man, Nature and Society', which Coleridge had urged on him. But he had been entrusted with the power to write poems 'to console the afflicted, to add sunshine to daylight by making the happy happier, to teach the young and the gracious of every age to see, to think and feel, and therefore to become more actively and securely virtuous; this is their office, which I trust

7 John Jones, *The Egotistical Sublime* (London, 1954), pp. 49, 52, 168.

they will faithfully perform long after we (that is, all that is mortal of us) are mouldered in our graves.'

As the years went by, the power of the poetry to 'console' and to make men 'securely virtuous' was subjected to the cruellest of tests. His own children died, and Dorothy became prematurely senile. An eye disease nearly blinded him, and he knew that he was often mocked by his former allies; it was a solid fact that he who had been an ardent radical in the 1790s lived to become an almost complete Tory (and a civil servant). The poetry survived all these tests with its 'healing power' (Matthew Arnold's phrase, which became the standard Victorian tribute). He grew strong as he repeated it with wonder to himself during his walks, or to the many visitors who came on pilgrimage. The recitals usually struck others as egotistical but innocent. It was as if the poet had been given gifts greater than his own personality, to preach and to worship, like a priest.

It was a painting by Sir George Beaumont (John Constable's most important patron) that inspired Wordsworth to record his conversion to Christian belief in a poem written in the decisive year, 1805. The painting was of Peele Castle in a storm. Wordsworth had known the castle during a summer's holiday, when the air around it was 'calm' and the sea near it was 'glassy'. He could then have painted it serenely

> To express what then I saw; and add the gleam,
> The light that never was, on sea or land,
> The consecration, and the Poet's dream.

But as it was, the storm in the picture now matched the storm of his grief for his brother – and the storm had driven him closer to the rest of suffering mankind, with its strange sense of God's control, its suffering which seemed utterly to contradict that control, and its hope.

> So once it would have been – 'tis so no more;
> I have submitted to a new control:
> A power is gone, which nothing can restore;
> A deep distress hath humanized my Soul. . . .
>
> But welcome fortitude, and patient cheer,
> And frequent sights of what is to be borne!

Such sights, or worse, as are before me here. –
Not without hope we suffer and we mourn.[8]

COLERIDGE AND THE VICTORIAN FUTURE

When Samuel Taylor Coleridge moved to the village of High-gate overlooking London in 1816, nothing would have appeared more improbable than his influence on the Victorian future – an influence so formative that in a famous essay John Stuart Mill declared him to be one of the two seminal minds of the nineteenth century, with his insistent question: 'What is the meaning of it?' (The other mind was Jeremy Bentham, with his question: 'Is it true?')[9]

In 1816 Coleridge seemed the opposite of a Victorian sage. He had moved into a home for drug addicts – and while there he continued to buy opium surreptitiously. As a counter-stimulant, he used brandy excessively. For ten years he had been separated from his wife, having endured a marriage in which the happiest moments were, he told a friend, those which he spent alone in his study, crying. He had also lost touch with Sara Hutchinson (the sister of Mary who married Wordsworth), the woman he had come to prefer to his wife. He had quarrelled with the two poets with whom he had formed alliances, collaborations and intimate friendships – Southey and, far more important, Wordsworth. He had seen his powers as a poet drying up while Wordsworth appeared to compose endlessly and effortlessly. He had turned to the metaphysical philosophy of Germany, but deep down he must have known that he was incapable of the highest flights in that realm. He formed the habit of incorporating considerable passages from

---

[8] The best biography is Mary Moorman, *William Wordsworth* in two volumes (Oxford, 1957–65). Among all the criticism, Geoffrey Hartman, *Wordsworth's Poetry 1787–1814* (New Haven, Conn., 1964), and John Beer's two volumes on *Wordsworth and the Human Heart* and *Wordsworth in Time* (London, 1978–79) are of special value. Michael Friedman studied *William Wordsworth: The Making of a Tory Humanist* with sympathy (New York, 1979).

[9] John Stuart Mill's *Bentham and Coleridge* was edited by F. R. Leavis (London, 1950).

German books without acknowledgement. Was he, after all, a journalist? He had done much journalism – partly for his own little radical papers, both of which had disappeared in debts, but mainly where he had written at the editor's command. The verdict is just: 'Coleridge straddled too many fences, was aware of too many contradictory trends, and lacked the profound power of integration necessary to launch a true theological movement.'[10]

He really had only two assets left in 1816 – and he kept them both until he died in 1834. One was the power of his talk.

He was a compulsive talker, probably compensating for a lonely childhood. (His father had been an impractical clergyman who died when the boy was only nine, and he had never got on with his aggressively practical mother.) His 'conversation' could be called 'one-versation', virtually always a pontifical monologue, taking up practically any subject but tending always to philosophy. Schoolfellows such as Charles Lamb remembered from their time at Christ's Hospital how he had been discoursing even then on metaphysics, with 'a hunger for eternity'. To less friendly hearers the monologue could seem like eternity. John Keats said that Coleridge, unlike Shakespeare, lacked '*Negative Capability*, that is, when a man is capable of being in uncertainties, mysteries, doubts, without any irritable reaching after facts and reasons.' Thomas Carlyle, who was himself not a bashful talker, included in his *Life of Sterling* an impression of Coleridge's Thursday evening parties, when he 'sat on the brow of Highgate Hill, in those years, looking down on London and its smoke-tumult, like a sage escaped from the inanity of life's battle. . . . To the rising spirits of the young generation he had this dusky sublime character; and sat there as a kind of *Magus*, girt in mystery and enigma.' The ruined poet held court in this way for eighteen years. Carlyle was among those influenced during the 1820s – although on the whole he was cynical, indignant when the 'Church of England cobwebs' seemed to be ensnaring clever young men.

---

[10] James D. Boulger, *Coleridge as Religious Thinker* (New Haven, N.H., 1961), p. 219.

Coleridge's second great asset remaining from the wreckage of his young manhood was the power of his Christian faith (which Carlyle rejected: he preferred the Infinite).

He dictated on his deathbed his conviction about 'the Absolute Good . . . the eternal reality in itself and the ground and source of all other reality.' And to this faith in God he added a Trinitarian faith in the divine Spirit proceeding from the Father through the Word or *Logos* ('the person of the *Logos* by whom that reality is communicated to all other beings'). But the Trinitarianism was not a lifeless orthodoxy. When he had begun to think for himself in Cambridge, he had become an admirer of Joseph Priestley's brand of Rational Dissent. He had nearly accepted an appointment as a Unitarian minister, until Priestley's friend Josiah Wedgwood had promised him a small annual pension so that he might become a great poet instead. He had reached the Trinitarian faith through much suffering. That was what made its reality communicable, although he spoke or wrote only in aphorisms or in mysterious fragments of the theological system which would never be complete. 'The truth is', Robert Southey once complained, 'that he plays with systems, and any nonsense will serve him for a text from which to deduce something new and surprising.' There was truth in that criticism. But it was not the whole truth about Coleridge's religion.

It was typical of the enthusiasm of his earlier years that the *Ancient Mariner*, first conceived as a popular ballad for a magazine in order to raise some cash for a trip to Germany, ended up as an affirmation of the sacredness of all life, the sin of man who thoughtlessly destroys life, and the redeeming power of the prayerful love of life. It was also typical of him that, when the trip to Germany came off, he used it to learn the language and to begin to study German metaphysical philosophy (whereas Wordsworth spent the winter writing poetry and would later 'thank Heaven' that he had never read a word of German metaphysics). For a time Coleridge, like the young Wordsworth, saw nature as animated by the God of the Unitarians – or was it the God of the pantheists? In the original draft of *The Eolian Harp* he asked:

> And what if All of animated Life
> Be but as Instruments diversely fram'd
> That tremble into thought, while thro' them breathes
> One infinite and intellectual Breeze? . . .
> Thus *God* would be the universal Soul,
> Mechaniz'd matter as th' organic harps
> And each one's Tunes be that, which each calls I.

This was not a self-centred vision; the ego was far less prominent than in the young Wordsworth. Anyone who reads the notebooks which tell the sad story of the young Coleridge's mismanagement of his life must be astonished that, so far from being as conceited as many thought he was, the poet had no ambition except to be a poet serving his vision; and that, so far from being full of self-pity, immediately after noting some personal calamity his mind would move into the observation of nature or into a philosophical speculation. When as an older and sadder man he looked back, he thought that his youthful opinions were 'in many and most important points erroneous' but he accurately recalled that 'in the expansion of my enthusiasms I did not think of *myself* at all'. And in that he had not been completely unique. It was a time when, as Basil Willey observes, 'not Coleridge alone but all speculative Europe was smitten with longing for the Great, the Whole and the Indivisible, hoping to find the One in the Many and the All, and feeling the presence of One Life within us and without'.[11]

What made Coleridge see more in 'the One' than the pantheists did was his exceptionally intense drive to see more because in his growing introspection he felt himself to be a sinner. He had rejected David Hartley's philosophy of the mind as a blank sheet on which sensations were imposed by nature, for the doctrine was contrary to his experience as a poet with a glorious power of imagination. Now he rejected also David Hartley's doctrine that progress to perfection was necessary, for the doctrine was contrary to his own experience of multiple miseries and to his self-condemnation. Rejecting William Paley, he once wrote: '*Evidences* of Christianity! I am

---

[11] Basil Willey, *Samuel Taylor Coleridge* (London, 1972), p. 86. See also T. B. McFarland, *Coleridge and the Pantheist Tradition* (Oxford, 1969).

weary of the word. Make a man feel the *want* of it; rouse him, if you can, to the self-knowledge of his *need* of it; and you may safely trust it to its own Evidence.' He did not believe that it was of any use doing theology in the detached mood of the eighteenth-century intellectuals. 'Christianity is not a Theory, or a Speculation, but a *Life*; – not a *Philosophy* of Life, but a Living Process. . . .TRY IT.' On the other hand, he could not be satisfied by a religion of the emotions alone; he once compared the 'Methodist stove' with the Unitarians' 'moonlight' and concluded that he needed sunshine – the mind's light as well as the heart's heat. 'He who begins by loving Christianity better than Truth', he wrote, 'will proceed by loving his own Sect or Church better than Christianity, and end by loving himself better than all.' Sinner as he was and knew himself to be, he remained a reasoner as he approached the mystery of the One. 'Faith', he observed out of his own experience, 'is a *total* act of the soul; it is the *whole* state of the mind, or it is not at all, and in this consists its power, as well as its exclusive worth.'

For Coleridge, there was a kind of 'reason' which was superior to the mere 'understanding'; and it was supremely this reason – the conscience – that judged one's existence and whispered the meaning of that existence. So Immanuel Kant was teaching at this time in Germany, and Kant's teaching took possession of Coleridge's mind 'as with a giant's hand'. Coleridge gladly echoed the German giant's conclusion that the 'practical reason' demanded the three highest truths: *God* as the source of this moral law, *freedom of the will* because the conscience said that righteousness was possible, and *immortality* because the conscience also said that righteousness must be rewarded. But Coleridge also went further than Kant, in that he believed that this kind of 'reason' actually enabled one to know God, to receive God's self-revelation, to use one's freedom to accept God's gifts and forgiveness leading to immortality. 'Reason' drove him to enter the world of religion which always remained closed to Kant; to do for England, in English, something of what was being done for the German Protestants by a far greater theologian, Schleiermacher, in answer to the challenge of Kant.

He found inspiration in 'the old England, the spiritual

Platonic old England'. By that he meant the England of Shakespeare and Sydney, an England where a spiritual reality was always present in nature and history and where this reality challenged the poet and philosopher; not the England of John Locke and David Hume. He read the seventeenth-century Cambridge Platonists with delight. He admired the teaching of Bishop Berkeley that nature was the 'visible language' of God. He once mused on the Platonic tradition in these words. 'Every man is born an Aristotelian or a Platonist. I do not think it possible that any one born an Aristotelian can become a Platonist; and I am sure no born Platonist can ever change into an Aristotelian. . . . Aristotle was, and still is, the sovereign lord of the understanding; the faculty judging by the senses. He . . . never could raise himself into that higher state which was natural to Plato.'[12] The Christian Platonism in which he came to believe was to him the truth from eternity conveyed to the mind of man by symbols, in much the same way as the symbols in nature conveyed a message to the poet. But to say that religious truth was symbolic was not to belittle it, for a symbol 'always partakes of the Reality which it renders intelligible'. And to teach this truth with power, to spread sunlight, the Christian had the Church and the Bible.

When he had finally abandoned the Unitarians he was insistent that true Christianity was found only within the visible Church, the 'sustaining, correcting, befriending Opposite of the World'. 'My fixed principle is: that a Christianity without a Church exercising spiritual authority is vanity and illusion.' He became proud of the Book of Common Prayer; its imperfections were only 'spots on the sun'. He became proud of the Church of England's comprehensiveness; he saw in 'the Church-Establishment . . . the greatest, if not the sole, bulwark of toleration.' He became proud of the parish system, rejoicing 'that to every parish throughout the kingdom there is transplanted a germ of civilization; that in the remotest villages there is a nucleus round which the capabilities of the place may

---

[12] Recent studies include René Wellek, *Immanuel Kant in England, 1793–1838* (Princeton, N.J., 1931), and David Newsome, *Two Classes of Man: Platonism and English Romantic Thought* (London, 1974).

crystallize and brighten; a model sufficiently superior to excite, but sufficiently near to encourage and facilitate, imitation.' And the Church was more than a civilizing agency. Basically, its authority over the consciences of its members derived from the fact that the Gospel entrusted to it had been revealed by God. Indeed, 'all religion is revealed religion'.

To Christians, therefore, the Bible was indispensable. But Coleridge explicitly attacked 'the belief that every sentence found in a canonical book, rightly interpreted, contains the dictum of an infallible Mind.' Instead, the Christian must examine the purpose of the particular passage and relate it to the whole Bible, 'for it is the spirit of the Bible, and not detached words and sentences, that is infallible and absolute'. In his *Confessions of an Enquiring Spirit* (written 1825–27 although not published until 1840), Coleridge commended this approach which at that time in England, a country almost entirely innocent of biblical criticism, was boldly radical. He wrote as a lover of the Bible. 'Need I say that . . . I have found words for my inmost thoughts, songs for my joy, utterances for my hidden griefs, and pleadings for my shame and feebleness? In short whatever *finds* me bears withness for itself that it has proceeded from a Holy Spirit, even from the same Spirit "which . . . in all ages enters into holy souls and maketh them friends of God and prophets".' If any enemy of fundamentalism could disarm the Evangelicals, Coleridge could. He wrote: 'This I believe by my own dear experience – that the more tranquilly an inquirer takes up the Bible as he would any other body of ancient writings, the livelier and steadier will be his impressions of its superiority to all other books, till at length all other books and all other knowledge will be valuable in his eyes in proportion as they help him to a better understanding of his Bible.' In his notebooks he left behind many fragments of an attempt to write a commentary on the whole of the Bible.

It was supremely in his call to the Church to apply the principles of the Bible to the whole life of England that Coleridge was in the end influential. In the politics of his time (when, he thought, 'the principles are worse than the men'), he had little impact. But the principles which he expounded gradually won influence in the elite which he called the 'clerisy'

– widening that term to include not only the clergy but also doctors, lawyers, musicians, teachers and others in a 'permanent, nationalized learned order' responsible for the civilization of the country, somewhat like the guardians in Plato's *Republic*. It has been well said that 'the most valuable ideas that Coleridge had to communicate were not, in fact, such as would provide simple solutions to specific problems; they were ideas relating to a new kind of political and social consciousness, the development of which would slowly but inevitably lead to the solution of these problems'.[13] His was a gospel, disturbing and suggestive if not complete, for a nation – in an age when the message of the Methodists or the Evangelicals remained largely individualist and Wordsworth's conversion to Christianity was (like Southey's) accompanied by his conversion to a reactionary Toryism. He believed that 'religion, true or false, is and ever has been the centre of gravity in a realm, to which all other things must and will accommodate themselves.'[14]

---

[13] John Colmer, *Coleridge, Critic of Society* (Oxford, 1959), pp. 169–70.

[14] The best introduction is Walter Jackson Bate, *Coleridge* (London, 1969). John Cornwell, *Coleridge: Poet and Revolutionary 1772–1804* (London, 1973), is a critical biography, and *Coleridge's Variety*, ed. John Beer (London, 1974), a collection of scholarly essays. The best study of *Coleridge and Christian Doctrine* is by a Jesuit, J. Robert Barth (Cambridge, Mass., 1974). See also C. R. Sanders, *Coleridge and the Broad Church Movement* (Durham, N.C., 1942); D. P. Calleo, *Coleridge and the Idea of the Modern State* (New Haven, Conn., 1966); Ben Knights, *The Idea of the Clerisy in the Nineteenth Century* (Cambridge, 1978).

Part Two

THE VICTORIAN
CHRISTIANS

CHAPTER FIVE

THE VICTORIAN CHURCH

THE QUEEN'S RELIGION

The Victorian age was given its artificial unity by the fact that the Queen, born in 1819 and reigning from 1837, did not die before 1901. Had death come to her at an age then more normal, Victorianism would have ended in time for the last quarter of the nineteenth century to be associated with the name of her son Edward – and that sign that things had changed would have been illuminating. The last part of the age which we have to call Victorian saw the beginning of the rise to power of the working class, whose members mostly disbelieved that any religious institution had earned the right to influence their behaviour. This period saw, too, an expansion of scientific and technical education. The expansion was an inadequate response to the needs of an industrial nation now facing competitors, but it began to provide a positive alternative to traditional religion among the educated. In sophisticated circles it became the fashion to be openly bored with Puritanism. In the serious arts realism became the mood. With modernization, secularization was conquering in all these ways and in 1882 a Cambridge theologian (F. J. A. Hort) warned a new Archbishop of Canterbury (E. W. Benson) about the Church of England's 'calm and unobtrusive alienation in thought and spirit from the great silent multitude of Englishmen, and again of alienation from fact and love of fact.' The Queen scarcely lived in the same England as the workers, the scientists or the sophisticated. That is quite obvious in her published journals – and would no doubt have been even more obvious had her daughter Beatrice not destroyed many passages thought to be embarrassing. Her survival, however, did not mean that her values survived in the great multitude with their old authority.

Thus after about 1875 much of English life may be reckoned modern or Edwardian. Yet there are ways in which it is right to think of *Victorian* England as entering the twentieth century. Imperialism in India, in Africa and in the empty lands of Canada and Australia became a potent force after 1876, the year when the Queen eagerly assumed the title of Empress of India; and the imperial self-confidence which blazed like the fireworks around her Diamond Jubilee of 1897 still had some basis in the economic realities. Gross national income doubled between the 1840s and the 1880s, and the value of Britain's exports quadrupled. The real value of industrial wages within England rose by two thirds between the 1860s and the 1890s, and began to fall only in the new century – and only that fall brought back the widespread labour unrest of the 1840s. The decline of British agriculture became apparent during the 1870s, when the railways and steamships began to distribute the limitless harvests of North America and the mutton and beef of Australasia and the Argentine, but there was enough strength in the coal, iron, steel and textile industries with their immense exports to postpone the great day of reckoning with industrial competitors. Able to sustain a population which almost doubled in the second half of the century, England was a very powerful nation – by many standards (supremely sea power), more powerful than any other in the world. Waited on by many servants, its governing class felt assured of an imperial destiny despite problems best left to the future. Queen Victoria's last Prime Minister, Lord Salisbury, was descended from the Cecil who had served Queen Elizabeth – and three of his sons were elected to the House of Commons. The Conservative cabinet under Salisbury consisted entirely of rich men.

The last ten years of the Queen's life were, indeed, the most successful in her relations with the public. She had emerged from her youthful indiscretions and tantrums, and from the unpopular seclusion of her bereaved middle years. This little old lady, less than five feet tall, had become the half-legendary mother of the largest empire the world had ever seen, and the grandmother of the emperors of Russia and Germany. And her unyielding resistance to the loose morals and careless religion of the circle around the Prince of Wales reflected the continuing power of Victorian values in the middle classes and among the respectable workers. That part of Victorian England was never Edwardian – or at least was seldom openly so. To widespread admiration, the Queen believed in a close but ordered family life; in hard work including some inventiveness but without the expression of any dangerously unconventional thoughts; in doing one's duty without accepting that the working class had any right to say what one's duty was; in the sacredness of the class system tempered by some compassion for the poor as individuals and a liking for servants who loyally fitted into the system; in patriotism tempered by an eventual willingness to overcome prejudices against the Jews, the Irish and the Indians when such strange people could be useful to England. Despite doubts she also believed in the non-dogmatic kind of Christianity which had been taught to her as a girl.

The young Victoria was influenced by her Lutheran mother and her tutor, George Davys, a mild Evangelical, but mainly her mind was formed by her governess, Baroness Lehzen, a woman of simple piety and morals. Nature meant Victoria (called 'Drina' when young) to be a merry and mischievous girl with an ear for music and languages. It was her misfortune to spend her childhood with her domineering mother; a rogue who in his turn dominated that widowed mother; no brothers or sisters; and the uneasy sense that, although not rich now, she would one day inherit the throne from her wicked uncles. What she absorbed from her early training, and what sustained her during her clashes with adults, was a simple Protestant ethic, untroubled by theology. She expressed it on being told in 1830 how close to the throne she was (since her wicked uncles could not produce legitimate, long-living children): 'I will be good.' On succeeding to the throne she became spoiled and petulant, and the advice which she eventually received from Lord Melbourne, a cynic who sentimentally doted on her, was not so sound as has usually been claimed. She became a partisan and often indiscreet Whig. She was rescued from much of her wilfulness by her marriage to the German prince who was not only a handsome lover but also a very successful substitute for a father. Earnest and efficient, tireless in his dedication to the progress of his adopted country, Albert became (at least in her eyes) a duplicate prime minister. Together, they were not particularly pious but decidely good.[1]

When in 1861 Albert fell a victim to typhus and left her a widow at the age of forty-two, her personality and religion became far more morbid. Her greatest comfort was to pray in his mausoleum at Frogmore, and to scatter many memorials to him around her dominions. Although she insisted on the deference of politicians she refused to play her proper role in public life now that she was 'alone'. Her relationship with her eldest son, whose immorality she illogically blamed for Albert's death, became notorious. She was rescued from this pathological grief by her growing love of the Highlands, to which Albert had taken her for holidays at Balmoral. She approved of the Protestantism which she found there. It was simple; she had a horror of ceremonial in church (and most unwisely persuaded Disraeli to persecute the Anglo-Catholic ritualists in the Church of England). But it was not a denial of the world; she had an almost equal horror of total abstinence from alcohol, preferred whisky to tea, and accepted drunkenness in her favourite servant, John Brown. She first took part in the sacrament of the Lord's Supper in the Church of Scotland (where no bishops had survived) in 1873. Her reply to protests about disloyalty to the Church of England's insistence on bishops was virtually to cease to be an Anglican communicant. Thus when she did reappear in the world, it was with the strength provided by a version of Christianity much the same as the religion she had learned as an innocent girl.

She never became a theologian. She called Oxford 'that monkish old place which I have a horror of'. She probably did not often touch on Calvinism in her talks with her favourite preacher in Scotland, Norman Macleod. In England her favourite clergyman was Dean Stanley of Westminster – and like him, she never achieved certainty about what she believed. When she was an old woman she sometimes exchanged confidences with Randall Davidson, the Dean of Windsor, whom she liked because he was a handsome and sensible young Scot.

---

[1] The best biography is Robert Rhodes James, *Albert Prince Consort* (London, 1983).

'She asked me,' he wrote, 'if there ever came over me (as over her) waves or *flashes* of doubtfulness whether, after all, it might all be untrue.' This confession showed her to be a typical Victorian. Doubt was in her private mind. It was almost as strong as the sense of decorum which prevailed in public. Essentially it was doubt whether goodness really would have its eternal reward. We have, however, no reason to question that she was a sincere Christian who as she lay dying (with her head propped up, hour after hour, by the German Kaiser) was 'earnestly trusting to be reunited to my beloved Husband', just as her will had declared would be the case. Beside her bed in the great house which she and Albert had built at Osborne on the Isle of White – the bed where she died – was a large picture of the dead body of Christ.[2]

REFORM AND THE CHURCH OF ENGLAND

The blind conservatism of the Church of England's leadership was shown in the struggle against Parliamentary reform. The votes of twenty-one bishops in the House of Lords helped to kill the second Reform Bill in October 1831. Infuriated mobs burned the bishop's palace in Bristol (four men were hanged for this) and raged against other bishops, nearly hitting the stately Archbishop Howley in Canterbury with a dead cat as late as August 1832. Even Englishmen who would never throw a cat at an archbishop were indignant that the bishops seemed determined to destroy the old political system altogether rather than adjust it to the demand that the constituencies should reflect the geographical distribution of the middle classes. The first Reform Bill had been introduced, as was said, in order to 'satisfy all reasonable demands, and remove at once, and for ever, all rational grounds for complaint from the minds of the intelligent and independent portion of the community.'

During the winter of 1831–32 civil war was feared, until it became clear that the Tories were unable to form a convincing

---

[2] The best biography is *Victoria RI* by Elizabeth Longford (London, 1964). The American title is *Queen Victoria, Born to Succeed.*

government. William IV was forced not only to summon back the reforming Whigs but also to threaten the Lords that their ranks would be swollen by the creation of new peerages unless reform was passed. So the peers, including most of the bishops, yielded – and found that, after all, reform did not spell revolution. As the result of the Reform Act of 1832 no more than a fifth of adult men in England and Wales, and no women at all, possessed the vote. The Tories usually collected the largest number of votes although they were generally outnumbered in the Commons by the Whigs in coalition with small groups such as the Irish and the radicals. In the unstable political situation thus created, moderate reform was both the minimum and the maximum that could be successful.

Moderate reform had to include church reform. The alternative was obvious in an atmosphere still thick with talk about disestablishing and disendowing the Church of England. In Ireland there was what seemed to many like a rehearsal for drastic action in England: the foundation in 1833 of Ecclesiastical Commissioners with about £150,000 a year derived largely from mergers of underpopulated dioceses and from an income tax on the richer incumbents. In a clause dropped in response to the hostility of the Lords, the authors of this Church Temporalities Act had originally provided that any surplus in the funds of the new commissioners was 'to be applied to such purposes as Parliament shall hereafter appoint and direct'. Philip Pusey, a brother of the more famous theologian Edward, translated a German hymn dating from the terrible period of the Thirty Years' War. It expressed what many sons and daughters of the United Church of England and Ireland were feeling in 1834:

> See round thine ark the hungry billows curling;
> See how thy foes their banners are unfurling;
> Lord, while their darts envenomed they are hurling,
>   Thou canst preserve us.

Of crucial importance in re-establishing the Church of England's popular position was the need to meet financial grievances. Most Englishmen resented the collection in the parishes of compulsory tithes to support the parson, and of compulsory rates to repair the church. Until 1868 Parliament was unwilling to abolish compulsory church rates in England, and disputes continued; but this grievance declined in practical importance. Legal judgements made it clear that the rates could not be collected unless authorized by the churchwardens and the majority of the council known as the 'vestry'. Dissenters were entitled to vote in the election of both authorities, and thus church rates lapsed in many towns and cities – in Birmingham, for example. At least this was better for the Nonconformists than a scheme which the House of Commons accepted at one stage, to repair all the parish churches out of taxes.

Over tithes, Parliament did something. The Tithe Commutation Act of 1836 ended the quarrels between tithe-owners and the local farmers over the interpretation of the ancient law that a tenth of all the produce must be sacrificed to the Lord, to his priests or to the laymen who had over the centuries acquired this privilege. In future local bargains were to be struck – as they already had been in about a thousand parishes – commuting payment in kind for cash. The sum of money was to be based on the average of the prices of corn, oats and barley over seven years. Special arrangements were to be made for market-gardeners and for the growers of fruit and hops, and disputes were to be decided by Tithe Commissioners. In 1891 all responsibility for tithes was fixed on the shoulders of landlords not tenants. It was an additional easing of the relationship between a county parson and his less wealthy parishioners.

The disadvantages to the clergy were considerable, although largely unexpected. They could not profit, as they had previously done, from improvements in land values and, because agricultural prices fell disastrously during the last quarter of the nineteenth century, £100 worth of tithes in 1835 was to be worth less than £67 in 1901. It was 'the Church's worst financial crisis since the middle of the sixteenth century.'[3] In the 1880s and 1890s the incomes of many parish priests in the

---

[3] G. F. A. Best, *Temporal Pillars* (Cambridge, 1964), p. 471. This is the standard history of Queen Anne's Bounty and the Ecclesiastical Commissioners.

countryside fell by about a third. In 1893 a report to the Convocation of Canterbury observed 'that this clerical distress is not only very severe but also widespread, and that it has been borne with the noble spirit of patient endurance.' It was in response to this financial crisis that the custom began (and continued until the 1970s) of giving to the parson the collection on Easter Day. But the new custom showed how much the atmosphere had improved since the old days of quarrels over compulsory tithes. The clergy were both poorer and more popular.

In their financial problems they looked for help to a central authority. They did not now look in vain, for the Ecclesiastical Commissioners created by Sir Robert Peel brought about the overdue administrative reformation which had hitherto seemed impossible. Peel deserves to be remembered for the feat. A distinguished historian of the Victorian age remarked that 'it is an arguable proposition that if any one man saved the Church of England, it was Sir Robert Peel.'[4]

The son of a rich Lancashire cotton-spinner, Peel could seem to various eyes at various times a coldly efficient administrator, a coldly obstinate conservative, and a coldly cynical traitor to the Tory cause. But his letters show that he was a churchman no less devout than was his brother, a clergyman. He was eager to discuss the moral aspects of politics with his former tutor, Bishop Lloyd of Oxford, and warm feelings inspired those changes in his policies which brought him the hatred of more extreme conservatives. He grew to be convinced that some reforms were essential – Catholic emancipation, Parliamentary and ecclesiastical reform, the highly controversial grant out of taxes to the Roman Catholic seminary at Maynooth in Ireland in 1845, and eventually the repeal in 1846 of the corn laws which had kept the industrial workers' food dear by protecting the prices charged for grain by English farmers against foreign competition. With a rare courage Peel was perfectly ready to sacrifice his popularity with his own party, and his career, to his new convictions about his duty; and in the end, he was also prepared to sacrifice his party's prospects of

---

[4] George Kitson Clark, *The Making of Victorian England*, p. 156.

power. It has been said with justice that this unemotional man invented the Victorian idea of politics as morality.[5]

Commissioners appointed by Parliament to inquire into the Church of England's 'revenues and duties' met for the first time in Peel's home in February 1835. Next year they were converted into an executive by an Act of Parliament sponsored by Peel's Whig successors. The explanation of this procedure is that during the 1830s, and for a considerable period later, it was thought acceptable that the government, as it hesitantly extended its interests in the welfare of the public, should operate through boards or committees containing a strong voluntary element, rather than through a civil service still very small. The Ecclesiastical Commissioners were conceived in this context. They were expected to prepare 'orders' for endorsement by the Privy Council and where necessary bills for Parliament, and at first it was thought that a few bishops and a few lay nominees of the government would be adequate to supervise the secretary and his assistants in this limited programme. By 1850 it was apparent that all the diocesan bishops must be commissioners, at least in name, and that three Church Estates Commissioners must be appointed, two of them salaried, to take the lead in the business which grew more complicated year after year. The Earl of Chichester served (or domineered) as First Church Estates Commissioner 1850–78, and Lord Stanhope then filled this seat until 1905.

Because there was never any radical change after the withdrawal of Peel's innovating hand, the Ecclesiastical Commissioners never became a government department answerable to Parliament through a minister. They retained a degree of independence thought necessary in the 1830s if reform was ever to triumph over the opposition of vested interests in the House of Lords and in the Church at large. Inevitably, however, the initiative at the most vital points in the development of this powerful office had to come from the government, for the Church of England possessed no effective assembly of its own. Nor did it possess courts of its own with effective powers. The

---

[5] Norman Gash wrote the best biography of Peel (London, 1976) and W. J. Baker an account of Charles Lloyd, *Beyond Port and Prejudice* (Orono, Maine, 1981).

highest ecclesiastical court, the Court of Delegates established in 1534, was quietly abolished in 1833; its functions were vested in the Judicial Committee of the Privy Council. A more comprehensive scheme to reform the church courts was abandoned, as being (as one exasperated reformer put it) 'of second-rate importance and of first-rate difficulty'. This was not a period when the Established Church seemed capable of reforming itself.[6]

The respectable way for clergymen to resist the Ecclesiastical Commissioners was to complain not about the government's initiative but about the Church's centralization.[7] There was some substance in such complaints. The leading commissioners, whether bishops or laymen, always knew how to look after themselves, and their staff were paid at civil service rates to deal with clergymen often much poorer. The meetings had to be in London – suggestions of decentralization were made, but defeated easily – and in practice that meant that the control was exercised by a small number of men, effectively controlled by nothing except their consciences. Nor were the staff exempt from human frailty. C. K. Murray, who shaped the work of the office as the commissioners' secretary 1836–49, had to flee to Australia having used some of their funds for his own speculations in railway shares. The suspicion which surrounded the Ecclesiastical Commissioners resulted in an unwillingness to insist that their work should be merged with that of a much smaller but older-established office dealing with the clergy, Queen Anne's Bounty. In 1830 when John Paterson could not continue as Treasurer of Queen Anne's Bounty after applying £30,000 of its funds to his own purposes, or in 1871 when his successor was persuaded to retire at the age of eighty-seven, it might have seemed that the case for reform and a merger was overwhelming; but it did not overwhelm until 1948.

Fortunately one of the bishops, C. J. Blomfield of London,

---

[6] The background was studied by Olive Brose, *Church and Parliament: The Reshaping of the Church of England 1828–1860* (Oxford, 1959), and David Roberts, *Victorian Origins of the Welfare State* (New Haven, Conn., 1960).

[7] Kenneth A. Thompson explored *Bureaucracy and Church Reform: A Study of the Church of England 1800–1965* (Oxford, 1970).

was both willing and able to be the mastermind among the commissioners when Peel had lost office. Blomfield was himself not entirely a reformed churchman; he had been a non-resident incumbent and a tutor to young aristocrats. He was unwilling to sacrifice any of the income which he had taken over on becoming Bishop of London in 1828, and when he retired in 1856 it was only after insisting on a very large pension. His cure for the poverty of so many other Englishmen was to take a lead in the movement which produced the Poor Law of 1834 and so created the hated workhouses which Dickens portrayed in *Oliver Twist*. All this made Blomfield the most unpopular of all the bishops. But he was a bold, tireless and very capable administrator both in his own diocese and on the new commission. The Archbishop of York confessed that 'till Blomfield comes, we all sit and mend our pens, and talk about the weather.'

For long many in the Church refused to believe that the commissioners would prove permanent or powerful. Church finance was a field where by tradition the diocesan bishops were theoretically supreme, although in practice almost powerless. But gradually it was seen that there was no alternative to extending and prolonging the commissioners' mandate; for the need was undeniable.

In 1832 Peel's Evangelical brother-in-law, Lord Henley, had issued a *Plan of Church Reform* which had fastened on two necessities: there must be more equality in the incomes of the bishops, and some of the endowments of the cathedrals must be used to sustain pastoral work in the parishes. Loud were the protests of bishops and cathedrals, but gradually action was taken – although not nearly such radical action as Henley had wanted. Most of the bishops were now paid £4,000 a year (but had to meet heavy expenses out of their own pockets), and the deans of the cathedrals £1,000. The money thus released was used to bring the stipends of parish priests looking after more than two thousand people to £200 (and proportionately for smaller numbers). Many new parishes were created; too many, for the number doubled between 1850 and 1900 and had to be reduced in the next century. In 1888 grants for curates in the poorest areas were added, although it was not until 1907 that some arrangements were made for the clergy's pensions, encouraging them to retire.

In all these reforms, the rights of the parishes' private patrons were safeguarded – but with the authority of Parliament, these commissioners had the will and the power to treat the wealth of the mightiest cathedral as belonging to the Church as a whole. It was the decisive move away from the medieval idea of the Church as a collection of corporations and office-holders with inviolable rights. In its own way it mattered as much as the suppression of the monasteries under Henry VIII.

THE EVANGELICALS

'Victorian England was religious.' So Professor Owen Chadwick's masterly two-volume study of *The Victorian Church*, published in 1966–70, began. A similar assessment was made in Sir Robert Ensor's volume in the *Oxford History of England*. 'No one will ever understand Victorian England', he wrote, 'who does not appreciate that among highly civilized, in contradistinction to more primitive, countries it was one of the most religious that the world has known. Moreover its particular type of Christianity laid a peculiarly direct emphasis upon conduct; for, though it recognized both grace and faith as essential to salvation, it was in practice also very largely a doctrine of salvation by works. This type, which had come to dominate churchmen and Nonconformists alike, may be called, using the term in its broad sense, Evangelicalism.'[8]

What, then, was Victorian Evangelicalism?

The attack on desolate Sabbaths in the third chapter of *Little Dorrit* was not the only occasion on which Dickens expressed contempt for the Evangelicals. In *Bleak House*, for example, we meet Mrs Jellyby, who cares so much for the natives of Borrioboola-Gha that she neglects her own children. Many

---

[8] R. K. A. Ensor, *England 1870–1914* (Oxford, 1936), p. 137. A similar verdict was reached in G. M. Young's *Victorian England: Portrait of an Age* (annotated by George Kitson Clark, Oxford, 1977).

other Victorian novels provide satirical or hostile portraits; Anthony Trollope's sketch of Obadiah Slope the oily chaplain in *Barchester Towers* was somewhat more benevolent than the portraiture in his mother's novel, *The Vicar of Wexhill*.[9] And some famous exposures of Evangelical homes were published by writers outside the realm of fiction.

Two books, Samuel Butler's *The Way of All Flesh* and Sir Edmund Gosse's *Father and Son*, have, indeed, often been taken as accounts of typical childhoods stifled by Evangelicalism. Published in 1903 and 1907, they were greeted as key documents in the reaction against Victorianism and they have certainly deserved their status as modern classics about the artist as a frustrated, misunderstood, cruelly ill-treated young man. But it is improbable that the childhoods which they described were typical of Evangelical homes. Samuel Butler frankly disliked his parents. His portraits of Theobald and Christina Pontifex corresponded with the reality of his actual parents in patches, and other rectories contained parents like them – the father without the power of independent thought or the capacity to communicate at any deep level with the new generation, exhorting his parishioners and chastising his children as a matter of duty; the mother frightened of the father and of life in general. But there is no evidence that Canon and Mrs Butler were as cruel to their son as he was to be to their memories. Edmund Gosse was far more affectionate when painting his portrait of his father. It may be taken as a largely accurate account of that unhappy man and of the congregation to which he was the unpaid preacher. But Philip Gosse and that congregation belonged to a group of extreme Puritans known as the Brethren. And he was a recluse even before he became a widower, his main work being the writing of books on marine zoology based on solitary study.

Both *The Way of All Flesh* and *Father and Son* were poisoned by the bitterness of the debate aroused by Charles Darwin's science. Samuel Butler while an undergraduate expected to be

---

[9] There was a chapter on 'The Low Church Contribution' in Margaret Maison, *Search Your Soul, Eustace: A Survey of the Religious Novel in the Victorian Age* (London, 1961), but Elisabeth Jay, *The Religion of the Heart* (Oxford, 1979), was a more thorough treatment of the Evangelicals in Victorian fiction.

ordained. When he had discovered that he was no longer a Christian, his central interests became those of an amateur scientist, arguing that evolution was not so purposeless as the Darwinians tended to believe. He despised men such as his father, whose faith seemed untroubled. Edmund Gosse knew that his father's most heartfelt book had been a religious response to the new science. Pathetically, old Philip Gosse had attempted to argue that God had made the world just as Genesis said – but with the fossils already in the rocks, as a test for the faith of the Victorians. This did not destroy all the value of Philip Gosse's research (indeed, Edmund Gosse wrote a conventional biography which praised him), but it was hard for a son to take such a father with intellectual seriousness.[10]

The group to which Philip Gosse belonged was part of a much wider stirring of interest in the idea of the perfect Christian, often coupled with the idea of the perfect world. Another such group was the Catholic Apostolic Church, the name taken by the followers of Edward Irving. As a young minister of the Church of Scotland Irving was equally effective among the poor in Glasgow and (from 1822) among the fashionable in London, but he became more and more fascinated by the traditional faith in the Second Coming of Christ to reign for a thousand years. *The Coming of Christ in Glory and Majesty* (the title of a book by a Spanish Jesuit, which he translated in 1827) now seemed to Irving to be the one hope of sinful mankind; and for the Church his main hope was that the tongue-speaking and charismatic excitements which broke out around his preaching in 1831 were signs that the end, the millennium, was near. He came to believe that the Lord's Supper must be restored to be the central act of Christian worship every Sunday, as part of a general restoration of practices recorded in the Acts of the Apostles. He also became fascinated by the theological question about Christ, arguing that God the Son had assumed human nature including its sinfulness. For these indiscretions and heresies he was deprived of his ministry by the Church of Scotland and he died in

[10] See Philip Henderson, *Samuel Butler: The Incarnate Bachelor* (London, 1953), and Edmund Gosse, *Father and Son*, ed. James Hepburn (Oxford, 1974).

1834 soon after the start of the Catholic Apostolic Church. His most effective ally, and virtual successor, was a rich banker, Henry Drummond, who inspired and subsidized the new Church until his own death in 1860. Under his influence the Catholic Apostolics developed a strong attachment to High Church ritual. Many of them worshipped in Anglican churches when they could not sustain a congregation of their own.[11]

In contrast, the 'Brethren' enjoyed neither the delights of ecclesiastical ritual (to them mere relics of paganism) nor the blessings of an undivided leadership. It was their misfortune to be led by more than one man with too strong a personality and too long a life. J. N. Darby was a young Irish clergyman, eccentric in appearance and theology but charismatic in his influence on a disciple and never afraid to tackle an enemy. Not for nothing was his middle name Nelson. His disputes with the Anglican authorities were inevitable; he was indignant when the 'Established Church Home Mission' was closed down as being too enthusiastic, and proceeded to write an article entitled 'Parochial arrangements destructive of order in the Church' and a pamphlet called *The notion of a clergyman the sin against the Holy Ghost*. But his enthusiasm attracted some remarkable brethren into a movement which, because it was launched in Plymouth in 1831, was called by the public 'the Plymouth Brethren'. It usually called a chapel 'the Room' and it did its best to be completely cut off from the vanities of the world. Several adherents were well-off and highly educated, but they gave away their wealth and accepted a thorough fundamentalism. The Brethren gathered every Sunday to 'break bread' together in the Lord's Supper, and any one was entitled to preside or to preach if he could persuade others that this was the will of the Lord. However, Darby's leadership did not always commend itself as being divinely inspired, so that this small perfectionist movement was split by bitter disputes.[12]

---

[11] A. L. Drummond studied *Edward Irving and His Circle* (London, 1938), and J. F. C. Harrison *Popular Millenarianism 1780–1850* (London, 1979).

[12] See Harold Rowdon, *The Origins of the Brethren* (London, 1967), and F. Roy Coad, *A History of the Brethren Movement* (London, 1968).

If we want to understand the Victorian Evangelicals, it is far more relevant to see how with their quiet and steady leadership they absorbed the fruits of powerful spiritual revivals.

The revival beginning in the USA in 1857, and reaching England two years later, has been called the 'Second Evangelical Awakening'. To some extent it deserves that grand title. Many of its gatherings on both sides of the Atlantic were as full of excitement as the congregations of Whitefield and the Wesleys, and its leaders could travel around and address evening meetings far more easily than the pioneers could, thanks to the steamship, the railway and gas light. Some striking characters became famous in this way – Richard Weaver the English miner who had previously been Undaunted Dick the boxer, converted to Christ when he saw blood streaming down the face of his opponent; Reginald Radcliffe, formerly a solicitor, who sent out assistants on to the streets of Liverpool urging men to come to the services conducted with shock tactics every half hour in the mission hall; and Mrs Phoebe Palmer as the pioneer of the women preachers, now at last beginning to be acceptable to male sinners. The hymn 'Stand up, stand up for Jesus' is a lingering echo of the enthusiasm, although it seems that in general the Evangelicals of the Church of England held aloof, worried by the emotionalism. They put their trust in quieter methods of evangelism leading to church membership and practical social work. And the churches where this sober Gospel was preached became the spiritual homes of many of those converted by revivalist preachers.

The most effective of all those who were converted was Dwight L. Moody. A rough but energetic businessman who was never ordained, he accepted the Evangelical Gospel in 1857, in Chicago. Three years later he felt called to full-time leadership in Christian work, particularly in the Young Men's Christian Association, and in 1875 the revival which he led reached London. Another event of 1875 was the holding of the first Keswick Convention, a rallying point for Evangelicals seeking commitment and inspiration in a definitely English version of American revivalism. Seven years later Moody made a great impact on the young men of Cambridge, transforming some privileged undergraduates into missionaries. The Cambridge Intercollegiate Christian Union, like the annual Keswick Convention, became a powerful spiritual force.[13]

Definitely Evangelical teaching was now legitimate in the Church of England. That was established in 1850, when an attempt by the Bishop of Exeter to resist the appointment of George Gorham to a parish in his diocese was ended by the Judicial Committee of the Privy Council.[14] In 1865 the Church Association was formed to assert the merits of such teaching more militantly, and under the editorship of Alexander Haldane the Evangelical and Tory *Record* was positively vituperative in its commentary on events and personalities. By and large, however, the Evangelicals were on the defensive theologically, first against the Oxford Movement in the Church with its revival of Catholicism, then against the Darwinian movement in science with its revival of unbelief; and they produced no very significant theologian. Their intellectual weapons were already outdated when they used them, for they assumed the validity of their interpretation of the authority of the Bible and of the Reformation (seldom of Calvinism in particular). That ought not to have been taken for granted. They had the post-Reformation tradition of the Church of England on their side, and proved it; but the nineteenth-century question could not be settled by any appeal to the past. It was about truth.[15]

More impressive than the Evangelical defences of an old theology were the practical activities of men such as J. C. Miller, vicar of St Martin's in the heart of Birmingham for twenty years from 1846 and the inventor of children's services. Hundreds of vicars or rectors were as dedicated to pastoral

---

[13] See J. E. Orr, *The Second Evangelical Awakening* (London, 1949), and for a more critical study John Kent, *Holding the Fort* (London, 1978). J. C. Pollock, *Moody without Sankey* and *The Keswick Story* (London, 1963–64), presented the facts simply and sympathetically.

[14] J. C. S. Nias studied *Gorham and the Bishop of Exeter* (London, 1951).

[15] The case to the contrary was argued by Peter Toon, *Evangelical Theology: The Response to Tractarianism* (London, 1979). But documents illustrating *Religious Controversies of the Nineteenth Century* were edited by A. O. J. Cockshut (London, 1966), and by their very silence about contributions from this school they provided one more proof of the sad intellectual isolation of the Evangelicals.

work as he was, and by the 1860s the Church Pastoral Aid Society, one of the Evangelicals' favourite charities, was supporting five hundred curates. The highest placed Evangelical (but not extreme) clergyman was John Bird Sumner, appointed Archbishop of Canterbury in 1848 after working for twenty years as bishop of the very large diocese of Chester. While archbishop he made his mark chiefly by his simplicity; in contrast with the previous prince-archbishops, he would pick up his umbrella and walk from Lambeth Palace to the House of Lords. His brother Charles was another moderately Evangelical bishop, appointed to the see of Winchester at the age of thirty-seven on the recommendation of Lady Conygham (one of George IV's mistresses), but thoroughly justifying the strange appointment by his charm and pastoral energy. More Evangelical appointments were made in the years when Lord Palmerston was Prime Minister (1855–65, with an interval of fifteen months). Palmerston was bored by clergymen, but he was advised by Lord Shaftesbury; Lady Shaftesbury was almost certainly his illegitimate daughter. And the Evangelical peer produced for him nineteen hard-working, if dull, pastors.[16]

Shaftesbury himself possessed a character more interesting than any Evangelical clergyman's – and far more complex. He often wrote in his egotistical journal, which foolishly he did not destroy, that people wanted him only for his title – together with many other uncomplimentary remarks about his contemporaries in Church and State. The truth was that he had become too hard a fighter to arouse love in those closest to him. Although as a young man he had shown a considerable interest in science, he developed into an intolerant fundamentalist who held that 'Satan reigns in the intellect, God in the heart of man'. As he moved from the chair of a committee to the chair of a public meeting, he tried to make up for his lack of fresh thought by being pompously garrulous. And he was quick to reply by coldness to what he thought to be a personal slight. Yet few suspected that he was quite so bitter and depressed as

---

[16] Michael Hennell introduced some leading Victorian Evangelicals in *Sons of the Prophets* (London, 1979).

he told his journal night after night, and what they knew was that his experience of human suffering had made him determined to relieve it. To know about the suffering of his childhood is to be ready to forgive him the sourness of his adult relationships – and to learn about his manhood is to admire him for the self-discipline which he maintained when not writing up his journal.

His father, who was chairman of the committee work of the House of Lords for forty years, presumably transmitted an appetite for public work. The fact that his father was a large landowner enabled him to borrow money – as he had to, until he was fifty – so that he could devote his life to public service; and the constituency which first elected him to the House of Commons was controlled by his mother's father, the Duke of Marlborough. But more deeply important for his character was the fact that his parents were loveless and grossly neglectful, so that his childhood would have been utterly miserable without his nurse. She introduced him to the Evangelical message, but he does not seem to have undergone any dramatic crisis of religious conversion. His conversion to the duty to care about the poor was not too profound to prevent his first years in Parliament taking the pattern normal for a young, handsome and ambitious Tory aristocrat. Probably he would never have become a great man had the misery of his own childhood not given him a motive to help the wretched – a motive which gradually become his predominant characteristic.

He agreed in 1833 to take over the Parliamentary sponsorship of the Ten Hours Bill from a Tory MP (Michael Sadler) who had lost his seat in the recent election. At that stage he had never visited a factory, and the approach from the factory reformers filled him with 'astonishment and doubt and terror'. His chief, Sir Robert Peel, who as we have observed was courageous in other directions, was convinced that the restriction of working hours by Parliament would so damage the economy that unemployment would increase disastrously. Even John Wesley had approved of the employment of children in factories. When the use of children was restricted to six and a half hours a day in 1833, the reform was accompanied by gloomy prophecies of economic disaster. The factory owners were able to embarrass the young MP by proving that his father's labourers in Dorset were much worse off than their own employees, and his discomfiture was completed when he lost his seat as part of Peel's defeat. When the Ten Hours Act was passed in 1847 he was therefore not able to sponsor it. And when the factory owners got round that legislation by working 'relays' or a shift system, he was denounced by the workers' leaders for suggesting as a compromise the change of the maximum of ten hours a day to the maximum of sixty hours a week.[17]

The destruction of Shaftesbury's career meant, however, that he concentrated entirely on religious and charitable work, earning his eventual reputation as the Working Man's Friend and his inappropriate commemoration by the statue of the Greek god of love in Piccadilly Circus. He became president of innumerable Evangelical societies (including the Bible Society and the Parker Society to reprint the works of the divines of the English Reformation). He became the architect of the humane Lunacy Act of 1845 and gave countless hours to his work as one of the commissioners supervising the new lunatic asylums. He was also a mainstay of the Public Health Commission formed in 1848 to force sanitation into one town after another – although until 1872 one death in three was still to be caused by infectious diseases. He did more than any other man to regulate the lodging houses where so many working-class people had to live. He befriended the blind, the cripples, the destitute incurables; the women and children wearing their bodies out in factories or underground in the mines or as 'gangs' at work on the farms; the exploited flower-girls and millinery workers; the boys made to climb chimneys as sweeps; the children beaten into being acrobats; the vagrant boys or adult thieves whose only hope of escape from a life of crime was the scarcely believable luxury of emigration or training; even the cabmen who needed cheap and respectable clubs. He insisted on denouncing the British profit from the opium trade imposed on China; he probed into the conditions of work in Indian factories; he defended the liberties of Italians and Poles;

---

[17] See J. T. Ward, *The Factory Movement 1830–55* (London, 1962).

he fought to restrict the vivisection of animals in laboratories. His chief pleasure became his visits to the 'ragged school' run by volunteers for very poor boys and girls, but much of his time was given to the personal inspection of scenes of work and poverty in London and the industrial towns, scenes that made him weep.[18]

When we seek to understand the strength of the Victorian Evangelicals, we ought to see Shaftesbury finding a ragged boy asleep in the roller used in Regent's Park. We ought to think of Elizabeth Gilbert, the blind daughter of a bishop, opening the first workshop for blind men in her home in 1853. We ought to remember the missions to workers in jobs which most of the country was happy to ignore. Evangelicals noticed the navvies who built the Crystal Palace which was the marvel of London; and Catherine Marsh made them seem marvellous in the book she wrote about her work among them, *English Hearts and English Hands*. They cared for the deepsea fishermen who found cheap alcohol the best way of forgetting the cruel conditions on their little boats in the North Sea. The Victorian Evangelicals did not merely condemn. Nor did they live only among the respectable. They followed their Master in seeking out the lost. And without intending to do this, they laid the foundations of the twentieth-century Welfare State by putting into practice their acknowledgement of a duty to interfere in the results of the working of the laws of capitalist economics.[19]

Such lives impressed Mary Anne Evans, who used the pen-name George Eliot and whose mind had travelled far from an Evangelical youth. Her first poem had been pious enough to merit publication in the *Christian Observer* in 1840. But she read Sir Walter Scott's novels and her imagination was stretched; she noticed that miners nearby, while Methodist, were certainly not moral; and she made unorthodox friends. Early in 1842 she told her father that she could no longer go to church.

---

[18] There are modern biographies by G. F. A. Best (London, 1964), Georgina Battiscombe (London, 1974), and Geoffrey Finlayson (London, 1981).

[19] See David Roberts, *Victorian Origins of the Welfare State* (New Haven, Conn., 1960); Kathleen Heasman, *Evangelicals in Action* (London, 1962); Ian Bradley, *The Call to Seriousness* (London, 1976).

Already a widower, he was heartbroken. As she wrote to him during this crisis: 'While I admire and cherish much of what I believe to have been the moral teaching of Jesus himself, I consider the system of doctrines built upon the facts of his life and drawn as to its notions from Jewish materials to be most dishonourable to God and most pernicious in its influence on individual and social happiness.' Yet she never forgot. 'What she brought from her Evangelical background,' the far from pious F. R. Leavis wrote, 'was a radically reverent attitude towards life, a profound seriousness of the kind that is a first condition of any real intelligence, and an interest in human nature that made her a great psychologist.'[20]

THE OXFORD MOVEMENT

The Oxford Movement arose in circumstances scarcely favouring its growth as a spiritual renewal which was in the end to transform the Church of England and to influence both the worldwide Anglican Communion and the Roman Catholic Church. For it was originally a protest against the reform of Anglicanism in Ireland – a protest made by clergymen in Oxford University and applauded by clergymen in English country parishes.

It could not be plausibly argued that the apparatus of Anglicanism in Ireland did not need reform. When he moved to hew it down in 1868, Gladstone compared it with 'some tall tree of noxious growth, lifting its head to heaven and poisoning the atmosphere of the land so far as its shadow can extend'. In the 1830s a government census showed that just over eighty per cent of the Irish population was Roman Catholic and about eight per cent Presbyterian. Yet the Church of Ireland, united with the Church of England by Act of Parliament in 1801, was more notorious than the Church of England itself for the combination of wealth and inefficiency in its leadership and for the non-residence of many of its parish clergy. A considerable

---

[20] F. R. Leavis, *The Great Tradition* (London, 1948), p. 24. The standard biography is Gordon Haight, *George Eliot* (Oxford, 1968).

number of its parishes did not even have churches in use. Particular reasons why it was hated included the restriction of government grants for education to the schools of this Established Church, and the obligation imposed on the peasants to pay tithes and church-rates to Protestant clergymen, often non-resident and usually regarded as heretical intruders. The extravagance of this colonial Church's finances was paraded in Dublin by the existence of two Anglican cathedrals (St Patrick's where Swift had been dean and Christ Church). The cynical attitude to Irish ecclesiastial affairs traditionally taken by English politicians was shown once again when in 1831 Earl Grey, the Whig Prime Minister, casually offered the archbishopric of Dublin first to the most faithfully Whig bishop in England, Henry Bathurst of Norwich, aged eighty-seven, and then to an Oxford tutor, Richard Whateley, of whom he had not previously heard but who was recommended as clever and liberal if eccentric. The Archbishop of Dublin had an income larger than all but six of the English bishops – although three Irish Anglican bishops were richer, the Archbishop of Armagh being almost twice as rich.

The Church Temporalities Act of 1833 provided that when vacancies occurred two of the four Irish archbishoprics should be demoted into bishoprics, and there should be ten mergers between dioceses. The estates previously managed or mismanaged by the agents of the bishops were to be reduced gradually, the bishops being increasingly paid by new Ecclesiastical Commissioners – and paid at levels more uniform and more adjusted to the levels on which lesser clergymen had to live. Underpopulated parishes were also to be merged (together with the two Deaneries in Dublin), and the richer incumbents were to be taxed for the benefit of the poorer. The Anglican parishes were no longer to have the power to levy rates for church repair or other purposes, but were for the first time to be supervised by archdeacons with power. Tithes remained a source of grievance, but in fairly recent years more than half the parishes had already commuted their tithes for cash payments, and the process was to continue until in 1838 a new system was enforced by Parliament, turning all tithes at three-quarters of their former value into a rent-charge payable by landlords not tenants, and granting a million pounds to the Anglican clergy in lieu of unpaid tithes.[21]

All this surely constituted the minimum of reform necessary to satisfy for the time being the grievances of Roman Catholics and the consciences of Anglicans. It certainly did not spell disaster to Irish Anglicanism; when the next religious census was taken, in 1861, the numerical relationship of Anglicans and Roman Catholics in the total population was virtually unchanged. Yet in the 1830s many Anglicans were outraged by these reforms, for they were enforced by a Parliament for which Roman Catholics and Protestant Dissenters had just been permitted to vote. The Irish Anglican bishops, whose views were confused, had not been consulted formally and the Irish clergy had no means of making their opinions known. It was the imminent likelihood that the Westminster Parliament would accept these reforms that caused John Keble to preach his sermon on 'National Apostasy'. John Henry Newman always remembered that date, Sunday, 14 July 1833 as 'the start of the religious movement' of which he became the greatest leader.

It was the 'Oxford Movement' and the sermon was preached in St Mary's, the university church; appropriately, for the university was a very rich institution monopolized by Anglicans, teeming with irrationalities and remote from most contemporary realities. All its members had been compelled to declare their acceptance of the Thirty-nine Articles. Many of its graduates became clergymen without any further training, yet no instruction in pastoral work was available. The wealth lay in the hands of the colleges and most of the power was exercised by the heads of these houses who were clergymen, as were all on the teaching staff above a certain seniority. To call most of the fellows of the colleges teachers would, however, be an exaggeration, since they were young men waiting for appointment to a parish (often a parish where the college was the appointing patron), largely in order to be able to marry. The 'tutors' among the fellows delivered lectures but under-

---

[21] D. H. Akenson studied *The Church of Ireland: Ecclesiastical Reform and Revolution 1800–1885* (New Haven, Conn., 1971).

graduates had to pay extra for any private tuition, and for most of them university life was neither intellectually nor morally challenging. A young man reading for a pass (not honours) degree could afford to drink considerably more than he read. Chapel attendance, although compulsory, was lethargic. The situation at Cambridge was roughly similar, except that Dissenters were allowed in as undergraduates (they were not permitted to take degrees), and the position given to mathematics had kept alive a tradition of harder thinking, at least in the intellectual elite of the undergraduate body.[22]

The lives of Pusey and Keble show the real but limited kind of sanctity that was possible for the leaders of a movement with these origins.

When Edward Bouverie Pusey, then a young Fellow of Oriel College, went to Germany to learn the language and the new biblical scholarship in 1825, he believed that only two men in Oxford already knew German. When he had heard a few lectures analysing the Bible, the thought struck him: 'This will all come upon us in England and how utterly unprepared for it we are!' On his return home he found that a Cambridge man, H. J. Rose, had issued some lectures claiming that German theology amounted to no more than rationalism; so he published a reply, admitting that there was some pernicious rationalism but blaming it on the dead orthodoxy of Lutheranism, not on the contemporary scholars.

On the strength of this unusually thorough preparation Pusey was appointed Regius Professor of Hebrew in 1828, when he was not yet thirty. Wrapped in his studies, he did not read Keble's sermon on 'National Apostasy' – and his studies were of a technical rather than philosophical kind, so that his own writing tended to be a string of quotations. But the three *Tracts for the Times* which he contributed to the series edited by Newman were, as Richard Church later reckoned, 'like the

---

[22] The hothouse atmosphere was caught in Sir Geoffrey Faber's *Oxford Apostles* (London, 1933). The story of reform was told by W. R. Ward, *Victorian Oxford* (London, 1965), by A. J. Engel, *From Clergyman to Don* (Oxford, 1983), and by Sheldon Rothblatt on Cambridge, *A Revolution of the Dons* (London, 1968). On the wider needs, see Michael Sanderson, *The Universities in the Nineteenth Century* (London, 1975).

advance of a battery of heavy artillery on a field when the battle has been hitherto carried on by skirmishing and artillery'; and soon afterwards he launched a *Library of the Fathers* in translation (to be completed in almost fifty volumes over almost fifty years) and made such a generous gift to building new churches in London that he had to reduce his standard of living. He seemed all set to become the learned and devout, but aware and relevant, leader that Oxford University and the Church of England needed.

Then in 1839 his deeply loved wife, Maria, died. Already his relationship with her had brought him severe emotional problems. Forbidden by his overbearing father to marry when he had fallen deeply in love as a student, he had absorbed himself in overwork and self-denial during the years of waiting. By the time that marriage proved possible he had become as inflexible as his father – inflexible in a regime of austerity which fatally damaged his wife's health. Now he was convinced that his previous self-discipline had not been severe enough to deflect the wrath of God which had thundered in the infliction of this overwhelming tragedy. The bereavement which lasted until his own death made him a recluse, refusing to dine with his colleagues or to enter his own drawing room. Often he worked all through the night as well as all through the day. To his surprise he was eventually able to smile again, but the smiles were to be very few. He also became a more extreme conservative, believing that God had punished him for his youthful liberalism, that an inflexible orthodoxy must now be part of a life of penitence. His isolation and general unpopularity increased when the Oxford Movement seemed to have become a nursery of converts to Rome.

He was revered as a holy man by those who knew him. The sermon for which he was condemned by the vice-chancellor of the university in 1843 was a devout exposition of the Holy Eucharist in line with the teachings of the Fathers, and at the time of Newman's sensational submission to Rome his own main preoccupation was the building of St Saviour's, a new church for the poor in Leeds, entirely at his own expense although anonymously. And he aroused holiness in others. He heard many private confessions and gave counsel. He it was who heard the vow of celibacy taken in 1841 by a young woman, Marian Hughes, who after further years of waiting became the superior of an Anglican religious order. He it was who guided the foundation of a small sisterhood in London in 1845, the first 'nunnery' to be set up in the Church of England since the Reformation. Three years later he was similarly the godfather at the birth of another sisterhood under the formidable Priscilla Lydia Sellon, an admiral's daughter. This second sisterhood became larger, and eventually popular, because of its work among the diseased poor of Plymouth and Devonport – work which Victorians could not deny was honourable work for Christian women, whatever they made of Pusey's appeals to precedents in ancient years. The first stable religious community for men was founded in Cowley, a suburb of Oxford, in 1866, by R. M. Benson, who had been deeply influenced by Pusey while an undergraduate. It was the Society of St John the Evangelist.[23]

He hated the word 'Puseyism', but his own answer to a correspondent's question, 'What is Puseyism?', was to define the holiness being sought in these six points:

1. High thoughts of the two sacraments.

2. High estimate of episcopacy as God's ordinance.

3. High estimate of the visible Church as the body where we are made and continue to be members of Christ.

4. Regard for ordinances, as directing our devotion and disciplining us, such as daily public prayers, fasts and feasts etc.

5. Regard for the visible part of devotion, such as the decoration of the house of God, which acts insensibly on the mind.

6. Reverence for and defence of the ancient Church, of which our own Church is looked upon as the representative to us, and by whose views and doctrines we interpret our own Church when her meaning is questioned or doubtful; in a word, reference to the ancient Church, instead of the Refor-

---

[23] Studies of this revival of the religious life include A. M. Allchin, *The Silent Rebellion* (London, 1958); T. J. Williams, *Priscilla Lydia Sellon* (revised, London, 1965); Michael Hill, *The Religious Order* (London, 1973). *Benson of Cowley* was edited by M. L. Smith (Oxford, 1980).

mers, as the ultimate expounder of the meaning of our Church.

Pusey never became a complete conservative. He granted that the universe had not been made in six days, and when he defended the accuracy of other passages of the Bible he did so with arguments which he genuinely reckoned to be scholarly. His advocacy of the Holy Communion as the central weekly act of worship in the parishes, and his decision to defend the 'ritualists' who revived medieval ceremonies dignifying this service, made him the enemy of those Conservatives such as Disraeli who linked ritualists with rationalists, 'rits' with 'rats', as disturbers of the peace. He was not sorry. Politically, as he wrote in a letter of 1865, 'I could not be a Conservative, i.e. I could not bind myself, nor risk the future of the Church, on the fidelity or wisdom of persons whose principle it is to keep what they think they can, and part with the rest. I believe that we are in the course of an inevitable revolution; that the days of Establishments are numbered, and that the Church has to look to her purity, liberty, faithfulness to Catholicism.'

But in his loyalty to the ancient Church he had abandoned the kind of intellectual development which could have been predicted before his wife's death and the isolation of the 1840s. In 1852, when a government commission was bent on making Oxford professorships more important and on opening college fellowships to life-long laymen, he wrote an hysterical pamphlet arguing that 'the aim of a university is not simply or mainly to cultivate the intellect'; a university existed to form minds 'which shall discharge aright whatever duties God, in his providence, shall appoint them' and because of this in a university 'all things must speak of God, refer to God, or they are atheistic.' When he was defeated, he wrote that 'Oxford is lost to the Church of England . . . there is nothing more to fight for.' But he fought on. He published a vast book completely rejecting other scholars' work on the Book of Daniel. In 1865 he assured a cheering Church Congress that 'faith lives above the clouds of human doubt, in the serene sunshine of the Eternal Light'; and he showed what that light had come to mean to him by opposing plans to revise the Authorized Version of the Bible

– perhaps forgetting that as a young man he had begun work on
his own revision of the seventeenth-century English of the Old
Testament. When for a time he was optimistic that the Vatican
Council of 1870 might bring Anglicans and Roman Catholics
nearer, the basis he recommended was one that left little room
for development since 'the English Church preserves the entire
faith, such as our Lord left it with the Apostles, to evangelize
the world.' The decision of 1873 that the Athanasian Creed
must still be recited in church at Christmas, Easter and other
great festivals was due in no small measure to his insistence on
the preservation of the ancient faith in its entirety. Here was a
long, technical document full of curses against the unorthodox;
but he had announced that he would resign his position in the
Church of England were its use to be made optional.

His last substantial book appeared in his eightieth year:
What is of Faith as to Everlasting Punishment? It showed the
intelligence, grandeur and intense moral seriousness of the
man. Hell fire need not be understood as material fire; God
does not predestine anyone to it; 'none will be lost whom God
can save without destroying in them his own gift of freewill';
after death there is a 'vestibule' for those who long for the
Beatific Vision but are not yet ready for it. But the everlasting
punishment of the obstinately wicked was to him a fact and he
had a rule, on getting to bed, to confess every night that he was
unworthy to lie down except in hell. In comparison, no other
fact mattered. That was the context in which this holy man
believed in the Holy Catholic Church and in the Holy Communion. However, after all Pusey was a professor until his
death – and he deserves to be judged on intellectual grounds.
There it must be said that his conservatism in responding to
the challenges of the nineteenth century became tragically
extreme during the last forty years or so of his influential life.
He was intransigent at the many – too many – points where he
thought Christianity was under threat. Because of his moral
prestige, his failure at this point played no small part in holding
up the reception of biblical scholarship in England and the
necessary reinstatement of Christian theology. He set an example to the Victorians of a clergyman's duty to renounce independent thought on religious topics unless he was prepared to

go through the agony of resigning his Holy Orders. The Germans complained that too much English theology was written within the sound of church bells.[24]

Until he won a scholarship to Oxford at the age of fourteen, John Keble's education was entirely in his home; and as his best-loved hymn, 'New every morning is the love', reminds us, his heart never left home. Home was a house in the small Gloucestershire town of Fairford. His father, born in that house in 1745, died there in 1834, and it was not until 1835 that John Keble felt free to become vicar of Hursley in Hampshire, a village almost entirely owned by a squire who had been an admiring pupil in Oxford. There he remained until his death in 1866. The squire would allow no Dissenter, let alone an atheist, among his tenants. The vicar would thwack boys slow to raise their caps to him, and would refuse to discuss 'infidelity', saying briefly to a young inquirer in 1851 that most of the men who had difficulties with Holy Scripture were 'too wicked to be reasoned with'. He denounced the State's provision of facilities for divorce in 1857. He was, however, powerless to make sure that brides entered his church as virgins; 'a village wedding is in general the most melancholy of all ceremonies to me'. Lamenting the lapse of the practice of confession of sins to a priest, he recorded 'how blindly I go about the parish, not knowing what men are really doing; and whenever I do make discoveries, they disclose a fearful state of things.'

Keble, although in the eyes of Oxford men a practical parish priest, lacked worldly wisdom and this accounted for three disastrous pieces of advice which he gave to Newman. He urged the publication of the journal (or *Remains*) left by a close friend of theirs, Hurrell Froude, who had died in his early thirties, a journal full of indiscreet remarks about the hatefully Protestant character of the Church of England.[25] His contribution to the series of *Tracts for the Times* drew from the mysticism of some of the Eastern Fathers the apparently dishonest doc-

---

[24] No modern study has replaced *The Life of E. B. Pusey* by his disciple, H. P. Liddon, and others in 4 volumes (London, 1893–97) and his *Spiritual Letters* (1898), but the essays in *Pusey Rediscovered*, ed. Perry Butler (London, 1983), are of high value.

[25] Piers Brendon studied *Hurrell Froude and the Oxford Movement* (London, 1974).

trine that some religious truth was so sacred that there must be 'reserve' when communicating it. And he urged the publication of Newman's Tract Ninety, which brought the series to a crashing end by arguing for a large measure of agreement between the Thirty-nine Articles and Roman Catholicism. Those three publications largely accounted for the reputation of the Oxford Movement (or 'Tractarians') as a movement where young men became morbidly self-absorbed or wrapped in mystic nonsense, and were deprived of any manly sense of the difference between truth and falsehood.

Why, then, was Keble College founded in Oxford as a national monument to this escapist country priest? And why did *The Christian Year*, Keble's book of poems published in 1827, run into almost a hundred printings in his lifetime, being more of a monument than the college, as Pusey declared at the college's opening? The explanation is that he gave an example of contentment by ministering to an obscure parish and by writing verses based on the Book of Common Prayer in an age when so many (including Newman) thought that, whether the Established Church was right or wrong, it could never be poetic. In country or town parishes many thousands of Anglicans, ordained or lay, whose religious opinions or sentiments might otherwise have led them towards Rome, felt a pride in belonging to and serving the Church of England because it was the Church to which John Keble had given his heart. Often they looked to such an example because their own bishop was too Protestant or too worldly; the first bishop to identify himself with the ideals of the Tractarians was W. K. Hamilton, who in 1854 took over the diocese of Salisbury. Gradually the heirs of the Tractarians became more confidently militant, organizing themselves into the English Church Union (1859) and enjoying the often vitriolic propaganda of the weekly *Church Times* (1863). But in his sermon of 1833 Keble had announced that the victory of the Church would be 'complete, universal, eternal' – and had implied that it would be not at all vulgar or loud. It showed his confidence in this victory that he was willing to take such trouble over daily services in his church, visiting the cottages, and preparing the young people for Confirmation. His poem 'Blest are the pure in heart' made both a hymn and a self-portrait. He was the priest to whom Pusey confessed. Thanks to the Oxford Movement, the Catholic religion as believed in, and practised by, Anglicans could seem assured, beautiful and a school of saints.[26]

NEWMAN

It was supremely through the life of John Henry Newman that the Oxford Movement first stirred the consciences of young men and then moved and renewed more than one Church, winning a greater influence in the twentieth century than in the nineteenth. Partly because he had been an Evangelical while young, Newman broke decisively away from the tradition that those Anglicans who emphasized their Catholicism must be 'high and dry', formal in manner, legalist in argument, backward looking in theology, wedded to the social order of the old England. The 'high and dry' tradition was embodied among the Victorians by Henry Phillpotts, who was appointed Bishop of Exeter by the Duke of Wellington's last act as Prime Minister in 1830. He survived in that diocese until 1869, having been engaged while bishop in more than fifty lawsuits and in even more fierce attacks in the House of Lords on proposals to change the old order in Church and State.[27]

The motto which Newman took as a cardinal was (in Latin) 'heart speaks to heart'. He fascinated many by his preaching and writing as an Anglican priest, and when he had been despised and rejected showed that he could revive that fascination by a classic among autobiographies, *Apologia pro Vita Sua* (1864). The book was sparked off by two casual and monstrously unjust sentences in an article by the novelist, Charles

---

[26] See Georgina Battiscombe, *John Keble: A Study in Limitations* (London, 1963), and Brian Martin, *John Keble: Priest, Professor, Poet* (London, 1976). Two useful collections of documents are *The Mind of the Oxford Movement*, ed. Owen Chadwick (London, 1960), and *The Oxford Movement*, ed. E. R. Fairweather (New York, 1964). Geoffrey Rowell assessed the movement's influence in *The Vision Glorious* (Oxford, 1983).
[27] G. C. B. Davies provided a biography of *Henry Phillpotts, Bishop of Exeter* (London, 1954).

Kingsley. 'Truth for its own sake has never been a virtue with the Roman clergy. Father Newman informs us that it need not, and on the whole ought not, to be; that cunning is the weapon which heaven has given to the saints wherewith to withstand the brute male force of the wicked world which marries and is given in marriage.'[28] So Kingsley wrote. What he had in mind in addition to Newman's failure to marry was his habit of recommending 'reserve'. As an Anglican, that often meant in practice a reticence in saying how Roman Catholic his restlessly changing convictions already were. There was a certain lack of integrity in this position. But when Newman had became a Roman Catholic the continuing 'reserve' in his conduct amounted to no more than loyalty to his superiors in public. It has rightly been suggested that 'Catholicism improved his character'.[29] His private criticisms could not be kept secret, and they wrecked his ambitions; for when he had made his submission and therefore in theory had 'no further history of my religious opinions to relate' (so he ended the *Apologia*), in practice he distanced himself from the Roman Catholic authorities by retaining many Anglican attitudes. When he defended papal infallibility on the ground that all Catholics believed it, he did not wish to see it defined, and wrote that if he had to give a religious toast after dinner 'I shall drink to the Pope, if you please – still to Conscience first, and to the Pope afterwards.' Illuminated by that very English remark, Newman's spiritually may be seen to rise above the controversies of his time. It continued to appeal to Anglicans when they had forgiven his desertion of their Church. He has also appealed deeply to some Lutherans.[30] When the Second Vatican Council met a hundred years after the publication of his *Apologia*, the growth of his influence on that time of brave renewal was such that he could be called the Council's 'invisible father'.

---

[28] Newman's *Apologia* was edited by Martin Svaglic (Oxford, 1967). See also G. Egner, *Apologia pro Charles Kingsley* (London, 1969).

[29] Robin Selby, *The Principle of Reserve in the Writings of John Henry, Cardinal Newman* (Oxford, 1975), p. 42.

[30] The Swedish scholar, Yngve Brilioth, contributed what remains the most profound theological study of *The Anglican Revival* (London, 1925), and gave *Three Lectures on the Oxford Movement and Evangelicalism* (London, 1934).

In his *Apologia* he recalled how as a boy he had already formed the habit of resting his mind 'in the thought of two, and two only, absolute and self-evident beings, myself and my Creator'; and as an old man he would say that there had never been a period when he had not known God in his conscience ('I know that I know'). At every stage in his adult life he sought men friends who would be disciples, but the only women who meant much to him were his mother and sisters, particularly Mary, after whose premature death he wrote: 'What a veil and curtain this world of sense is.' The material world and its improvement he always reckoned unimportant; he recalled how in childhood 'I thought life might be a dream, or I an angel, and all this world a deception, my fellow angels by a playful device concealing themselves from me, and deceiving me with the semblance of a material world.'

His father was a banker who was ruined in 1816 and who subsequently failed in attempts to manage a brewery. That seemed to be the end of the world for the boy; and in that sad year of 1816, at the age of fifteen, when left behind at school in the holidays, he fell under the influence of an Evangelical schoolmaster. However, he never underwent a full Evangelical conversion producing an assurance about the Saviour greater than his childhood sense of God in the conscience – as readers of his *Apologia* pointed out to him. The Evangelical book that most impressed him was Joseph Milner's *History of the Church of Christ*, for it was the Church that seemed able to assure him when God seemed remote. Later he expounded the Evangelical doctrine of justification by faith with the emphasis on the Church's sacraments, since the human heart by itself was unstable, deceitful, and wicked, cut off from God by sin. His own brothers, who trusted in their hearts, showed the dangers. Francis – whom we met in connection with the Brethren – became a very unorthodox Christian and a very eccentric man, and Charles an atheist and a recluse. Of Hurrell Froude's brothers, Richard the historian wrote a novel about *The Nemesis of Faith* and a history of England celebrating Protestant anti-clericalism, and William the scientist became an agnostic. These Newman and Froude brothers were liberals in religion – and that in John Henry Newman's view was their fatal mistake. 'Now by liberalism', he explained in his *Apologia*, 'I mean false liberty of thought, or the exercise of thought upon matters, in which from the constitution of the human mind, thought cannot be brought to any successful issue, and therefore is out of place. Among such matters are first principles of whatever kind; and among these the most sacred and momentous are especially to be reckoned the truths of Revelation.'

He became a Fellow of Oriel College, the vicar of the university church, and the learned author of *The Arians of the Fourth Century*. He ceased to be a Calvinist but never abandoned the belief in God's predestinating care of him. During a holiday in Italy to recover from overwork he nearly died of a fever but pulled himself together with the conviction that he still had work to do in England. While convalescing on the voyage home, he wrote the poem that became the famous hymn 'Lead, kindly light'. He reached home five days before Keble's attack on 'National Apostasy' shone a closer light on his eager face. A born journalist, he enjoyed editing sixty-six short *Tracts for the Times* in two years. It was apostolic activity, for 'I am sure the apostles did not stay still'. More deeply he enjoyed preaching, although he was no actor; he read his sermons monotonously, leaving pauses between the long sentences. His most frequent theme to parochial congregations was the holiness of the Christ of the gospels, demanding the hearer's moral obedience. To a university audience he would expound the differences between reason and faith, rebuking his own past tendency 'to prefer intellectual excellence to moral'.[31]

He saw that his fellow clergy might soon cease to enjoy the 'secular advantages' of 'your birth, your education, your wealth, your connections', as he told them in Tract One, urging them to remember instead 'our apostolic descent' since priests were 'assistants, and in some sense representatives', of bishops. But the Bishop of Oxford was not in full agreement with him, so that Newman turned to dead bishops such as Andrewes and Laud, to the Fathers on whose works he was

---

[31] See *Newman's University Sermons*, ed. D. M. MacKinnon and J. D. Holmes (London, 1970), and Roderick Strange, *Newman and the Gospel of Christ* (Oxford, 1981).

already England's leading authority, to the English saints whose lives he caused to be rewritten in a new series of volumes. 'It still remains to be seen', as he wrote at this stage, 'whether what is called Anglo-Catholicism . . . is capable of being professed, acted on, and maintained on a large sphere of action and through a sufficient period, or whether it be a mere modification or transition-state either of Romanism or of popular Protestantism.' Or was it a mere 'paper religion', incapable of leading living men to the living God? In 1839 he felt that the Anglican appeal to 'Antiquity' was 'absolutely pulverized' by an article by a Roman Catholic (Wiseman), who presented the Papacy as the guardian of Catholicism against the Donatists, fifth-century schismatics in North Africa. In 1841, in Tract Ninety, he announced (or implied) that at the Reformation the Church of England had become a modification of Romanism. It is surprising not that his university and the bishops united to condemn that, but that Newman was 'quite unprepared for the outbreak'.

However, he did not become a Roman Catholic until 9 October 1845, when he was received into the Church by an Italian missionary, Fr Dominic Barberi. He spent the intervening years largely in the historical study which lay behind his book on *The Development of Christian Doctrine*, 'one of those works of genius in which a man's whole store of learning is mobilized under great existential pressure'.[32] He did not inquire into the contemporary reality of Roman Catholicism; he used to say that he had never met a Roman Catholic until he became one. His driving concern was to find and to show that there must be development, since the authority of the dead past would make only a 'paper religion'; yet the development must be legitimate, the 'notes' of legitimacy being listed – preservation of type, continuity of principle, power of assimilation, logical sequence, anticipation of its future, conservative action on its past, chronic vigour. The councils of the undivided Church could legitimately develop the doctrine to be found in the New

---

[32] Paul Misner, *Papacy and Development* (Leiden, 1976), p. 61. See also Owen Chadwick, *From Bossuet to Newman: The Idea of Doctrinal Development* (Cambridge, 1975), and Nicholas Lash, *Newman on Development* (London, 1975).

Testament and because development was necessary ('in a higher world it is otherwise, but here below to live is to be changed, and to be perfect is to have changed often'), uncertainty was possible. Consequently holiness was very difficult, unless there was an 'infallible expounder'. But was the Roman Catholic Church that infallible expounder of developing doctrine? All that Newman had thought so far could be regarded as no more than the working out of two proverbs he had learned as a schoolboy from the writings of Thomas Scott, the Evangelical whose works had taught him Trinitarianism. These proverbs were: 'Holiness rather than peace' and 'Growth the only evidence of life'. But he now saw that only the Papacy made universal claims about itself, claims which surely agreed with the universal nature of Catholicism. And the integrity in his character, more basic than any of the tactical devices he had employed as an Anglican, now came out as he followed his conscience and asked to be received into the Catholic Church.

When he reached Rome as a humble student in 1846, taking his theory of development with him, no theologian in the Eternal City could understand it. They were content with second-rate manuals of conventional doctrine. In fact Newman never found a sphere worthy of his gifts. Because the bishops were too suspicious of the liberalism remaining in him, he had to abandon the editorship of a magazine and schemes to found a great school in Birmingham, a chaplaincy in Oxford, a university in Dublin. He grew to love the 'Oratory' in Birmingham which he made his headquarters, but was not completely fulfilled. Usually he recognized that it was his vocation to be a solitary thinker, communicating by letter rather than conversation, at his best when at prayer; his greatest achievement was to be *The Dream of Gerontius* (1865), a poem about the soul's approach to God through death. But at times he felt too solitary. He once wrote in his journal: 'I have no friend at Rome, I have laboured in England to be misrepresented, backbitten and scorned. . . . O my God, I seem to have wasted these years that I have been a Catholic.' He criticized or pitied his own failures like this while feeling that the religion he wished to advocate was in retreat. As he wrote in a letter of

1877: 'My apprehensions are not new, but above fifty years' standing. I have all this time thought that a time of widespread infidelity was coming, and through all those years the waters have in fact been rising as a deluge. I look for the time, after my life, when only the tops of the mountains will be seen like islands in the waste of waters.'[33]

Despite the intensity of his determination never to rebel against the Church to which he had so dramatically surrendered, his heart was with much that was said by the bolder critics of the prevailing trends. An article in which he urged that 'the faithful' – he meant chiefly educated Roman Catholic laity – should be consulted by the bishops was reported to Rome for heresy. Fiercer criticisms of the bishops' regime came from a few laymen such as the rich and learned Sir John Acton. Acton's mind possessed a true historian's penetration and it had been trained by another great historian, Professor Döllinger of Munich, who openly rebelled against the definition of papal infallibility in 1870 and was excommunicated. Acton had no wish to suffer Döllinger's fate – and escaped it.[34] Newman was usually still more submissive in public. But the publication of their private papers has shown how close in many of their questionings the two men were – and how isolated they often felt as reaction seemed triumphant.

Over twenty years he struggled to write a philosophical defence of religious belief, and his *Essay in Aid of a Grammar of Assent* appeared in 1870. It was a subtle analysis of 'real assent' to doctrines – an assent which was neither shallow nor yet a simple matter of logical inference. This assent resulted in 'certitude'. But the book made no great impact. On the one hand, Protestants and sceptics marvelled that a man so intelli-

---

[33] Studies of these sad episodes include Joseph Altholz, *The Liberal Catholic Movement in England: the 'Rambler' and its Contributors 1848–64* (London, 1962); Francis McGrath, *Newman's University: Idea and Reality* (London, 1951); Dwight Culler, *The Imperial Intellect: A Study of Cardinal Newman's Educational Ideal* (New Haven, Conn., 1955).

[34] See David Matthew, *Lord Acton and His Times* (London, 1968), supplemented by Hugh McDougall, *The Acton-Newman Relations* (London, 1962); D. McElrath, *Lord Acton: The Decisive Decade 1864–74* (London, 1970); Peter Gunn, *The Actons* (London, 1978).

gent had given his assent to dogmas and miracles which they regarded as nonsensical. It was often felt, and sometimes said, that he had sacrificed his intellect to his imagination in order to avoid the atheism to which he felt the argument was moving. On the other hand, most of Newman's fellow Catholics could make little of his 'illative sense' which yielded 'certitude' about doctrines which the book did not specify. To them, what they wanted was logic to prove the doctrines actually taught by the Holy Roman Church. Their attitude was expressed perfectly by Pope Pius IX, who in 1864 issued a *Syllabus of Errors*, one of the errors being the suggestion that the Roman Pontiff should accommodate himself to liberalism or to 'progress' in any other nineteenth-century form. Newman had submitted to an authoritarian Church and his remaining sympathy with theological liberalism, even with the age's scepticism, won no sympathy for him until the official atmosphere was somewhat changed under Leo XIII, an aristocratic pope more benevolent towards modern civilization. In 1879 he was made a cardinal and assured his friends that 'the cloud is lifted from me for ever'. He did not die until he was almost ninety, and during his last years he knew that he was honoured in the Church he had joined as well as in the Church he had left. But it was now far too late to achieve the work which had never been entrusted to him when he was at the height of his powers. The wide influence which was denied him during his lifetime (although he always had devoted disciples and was always admired for his style as a preacher) was to come during the twentieth century.

By 1964 Pope Paul VI could declare that Newman, 'guided solely by love of the truth and fidelity to Christ, traced an itinerary the most toilsome but also the greatest, the most meaningful, the most conclusive, that human thought ever travelled during the last century, indeed one might say during the modern era, to arrive at the fulness of wisdom and of peace.'[35] Gradually Christians in many countries and in many

---

[35] Christopher Hollis, *Newman and the Modern World* (London, 1967), p. 215. See also *The Rediscovery of Newman: An Oxford Symposium*, ed. John Coulson and A. M. Allchin (London, 1967), and John Coulson, *Newman and the Common Tradition* (Oxford, 1970).

Churches have appreciated Newman's direct intuition into the reality of God, and his courageous dismissal of the reality of this world; his power so to read the gospels that the holy Christ walked out of them to command discipleship; the patient determination of his search for fuller religious truth. They have come to share his understanding of faith as a movement by the whole person, not a mere assent to a doctrine, not a decision into which one could be either argued or tortured. The truth to be discerned by faith with 'certitude' must be much more than any 'paper religion' – a criticism of the Anglican appeal to history but also (at least potentially) of Roman dogmatism. Although he never worked out a modern theology, Newman left behind him a feeling that a modern theology was needed. He wrote in 1839: 'We cannot, if we would, move ourselves back into the times of the Fathers; we must, in spite of ourselves, be Churchmen of our own era, not of any other, were it only for this reason, that we are born in the nineteenth century, not the fourth.'[36]

MAURICE AND CHRISTIAN SOCIALISM

Chartism, the first great working-class political movement in the history of the world, was a movement born out of anger about the failure of more peaceful popular movements which had respected the Reform Act of 1832. All the protests against the harsh new Poor Law did not secure its repeal, and the 'Ten Hours' movement to reduce the exploitation of factory workers also seemed to be defeated. Most of the leaders of those movements were Tories and churchmen whose consciences

---

[36] There are many—too many—books on Newman. There is even a book about his political thought, by Terence Kenny (London, 1957). Meriol Trevor's *Newman's Journey* (London, 1974), was based on her biography in 2 vols. (London, 1962). The short studies by C. S. Dessain (3rd ed., London, 1980) and Owen Chadwick (Oxford, 1983) took account of Newman's *Letters and Diaries*, ed. C. S. Dessain and others in 31 vols. (London, 1961, onwards). His *Autobiographical Writings* were edited by Henry Tristram (New York, 1957). Studies of his theology include David Pailin, *The Way to Faith* (London, 1969), and Thomas Vargish, *Newman: The Contemplation of Mind* (Oxford, 1970). On his spirituality, see H. C. Graef, *God and Myself* (London, 1967).

had been stirred by conditions in the industrial north. There were laymen such as Michael Sadler, the MP who realized what was happening to the children when they fell asleep in his Sunday school; or Richard Oastler, who put his money as well as his mouth into the 'Ten Hours' agitation. There were parish priests such as George Bull, an Evangelical Tory who was moved by the helplessness of the poor in an industrial village near Bradford. The fact struck them that in Yorkshire, which William Wilberforce had represented in Parliament, there was slavery as bad as anything to be found in the West Indies. There had been poverty in England for many centuries, but the poor now crowded into factories and disease-ridden hovels, their misery apparent to each other and to sensitive people who saw them.[37]

The Chartists, however, no longer trusted either Tories or parsons to provide effective leadership. That must come from men who stood closer to the workers and who were not afraid of advocating violence if the workers' demands were not met. The demands were varied, but the theme of 'the People's Charter' for which signatures were collected was that every adult man in England should be entitled to vote in secret in the election of a new Parliament each year, with equal constituencies and salaried MPs.

At a meeting in 1848, when this agitation was at its height, Charles Kingsley stammered out sensationally that he was a 'Church of England parson – and a Chartist'. But he exaggerated. He drew up a placard after the failure of the largest Chartist demonstration: 'The Almighty God, and Jesus Christ the poor Man who died for poor men, will bring freedom for you. . . . Workers of England, be wise, and then you *must* be free, for you will be *fit* to be free.' It was not a demand for the vote now. From 1844 until he died there in 1875, his beloved home was the large and lovely, if damp, rectory of Eversley in Hampshire. Moved by the poverty of the agricultural labour-

---

[37] Cecil Driver wrote a biography of Oastler entitled *Tory Radical* (New York, 1946), and J. C. Gill one of *Parson Bull of Byerley* (London, 1963). See also *Popular Movements c. 1830–1850*, ed. J. T. Ward (London, 1970); J. T. Ward, *Chartism* (London, 1973); David Jones, *Chartism and the Chartists* (London, 1975).

ers he produced journalism under the name of 'Parson Lot' and a novel, *Yeast*, in 1850 to stir up the heirs of landlords if not the landlords themselves; and in that aim he was successful. The novel had sequels – *Alton Locke* about the sweat shops in the tailoring trade, *Two Years Ago* about the importance of sanitation, *The Water Babies* to popularize the cause of the chimney sweeps. These novels were sufficiently radical to mean that he was not offered promotion until Prince Albert made him tutor to the Prince of Wales and persuaded Lord Palmerston to make him a part-time professor. But social reform was not his only interest. He wrote much else, partly for pleasure and partly for the money – including his best books, *The Heroes* to re-tell the myths of Ancient Greece to children, and the patriotic novel for boys, *Westward Ho!* He was an amateur scientist, a devoted fisherman, a preacher and practiser of 'muscular Christianity' (in order to cure his own tendency to introspective melancholy). So many were his interests that Dean Stanley aptly called him 'a layman in the guise or disguise of a clergyman'.[38]

In contrast, Frederick Denison Maurice used to insist that his only vocation was theology. Men without sympathetic patience would dismiss his thought as merely muddled; listening to him was, Aubrey de Vere thought, 'like eating pea soup with a fork'. But he inspired colleagues and disciples, including some who did not fully grasp his theology – men such as Thomas Hughes who wrote *Tom Brown's Schooldays* and did much else; John Ludlow, the intensely practical Christian who became legal adviser to the first of the modern trade unions (the Amalgamated Society of Engineers), and Chief Registrar of Friendly Societies, and who lived to plead that 'Christianity must be applied to the economic system' at the Pan-Anglican Congress of 1908; or the more heretical Edward Vansittat Neale, a rich barrister who sacrified his fortune and himself to a philanthropic life as a founder and general secretary of the British Co-operative Union. Because of the influence of his principles on such disciples and on a wider public, Maurice has, indeed, usually been reckoned the greatest moral and

---

[38] Two biographies marked the centenary of his death: Brenda Colloms, *Charles Kingsley*, and Susan Chitty, *The Beast and the Monk* (London, 1975).

social prophet to arise within the Victorian Churches. The Working Men's College which he founded in London in 1854 has not been the only place to keep his memory green.[39]

In 1848 he nervously allowed Ludlow to edit a short-lived magazine called the *Christian Socialist*; but to him 'Socialism' was merely the opposite of individualism. He was certainly no Chartist; he deplored the extension of the electorate in 1867, as he deplored trade unionism. It is fair to say that he was, 'in plain language, a Tory paternalist with the unusual desire to theorize his acceptance of the traditional obligation to help the poor.'[40] None of these idealists had any sympathy with Karl Marx's demand that the State must own the means of production; Marx denounced Christian Socialism as 'holy water'. They saw much more glory in the application to economic life of the Christian idea of co-operation (preferring producers' co-operatives to the consumers' 'co-op' shop which eventually emerged as the substance of the Co-operative Movement). But the experiments came to very little. It was difficult to secure orders since the products were often clumsy and their distribution was another problem; and it was difficult to secure brotherhood since wages had to be paid at commercial rates. As conceived by these Christian Socialists, co-operation was a gallant gesture in defiance of the capitalist system, a gesture comparable with the utopian agricultural communities which were another doomed creation of nineteenth-century idealism. What remained was the haunting idea of a decentralized, power-free, humanly fulfilling 'Guild Socialism' which was to attract later generations of Christian social pioneers.[41] And for students of Christian thought, Maurice's theology also remained, its most powerful expression being in 'Letters to a Quaker' published as *The Kingdom of Christ* (1838), when he was a hospital chaplain amid the slums of Southwark.

---

[39] Recent studies include E. C. Mack and W. H. G. Armytage, *Thomas Hughes* (London, 1952); N. C. Masterman, *John Malcolm Ludlow* (Cambridge, 1963); P. N. Buckstrom, *Christian Socialism and Co-operation in Victorian England* (London, 1974); Brenda Colloms, *Victorian Visionaries* (London, 1982).

[40] Edward Norman, *Church and Society in England 1770–1970*, pp. 171–2.

[41] W. H. G. Armytage studied utopian communities and their fates in *Heavens Below* (London, 1961).

This prophet's vision of God as the very foundation of all unity in the family of man resulted from his experiences as a boy. He was the son of a Unitarian minister and of a mother who became a Calvinist in the Church of England without believing that she was numbered among God's elect. One sister became a Baptist, the other an Anglican; and this theologically divided family made a practice of writing letters of religious exhortation to each other while living under the same roof. The boy was fond of them all and distressed by the divisiveness of their Christianity or Christianities. In 1831, at the age of twenty-six, he was baptized into the Church of England, but he was never willing to exclude from the communion of the Church anyone who claimed to be a Christian. He valued the Church not as an institution confronting the world but as the supreme sign of the 'Kingdom of Christ' already established in the world. And he went further than that. In lectures on *The Religions of the World* published in the 1840s he claimed that non-Christians were sincerely seeking God (then an original suggestion) and twenty years later he published a similar claim about the philosophers of the West. He was deprived of his professorship at King's College, London, for daring to hope for the 'salvation of all'. Christianity was to him not merely one religion; 'we have been dosing our people with religion, when what they want is not this but the living God.' It was not the rescue of the individual sinner, as in Evangelicalism. Nor was it the imposition on the individual of a discipline derived from the past, as in the Oxford Movement. It was not the encouragement of any 'sect' or 'party' or 'system' or 'notion' outside or inside the Church. It was a message about the unity of England and of all mankind under Christ as 'Head and King' and under the Father.

The key to Christianity was that 'God has claimed us all in Christ as his sons'. 'I tremble to think', he wrote, 'what a crushing of all systems, religious and political, there must be, before we really do feel our gathering together in Christ to be the hope of the universe.' Baptism was the sacrament which asserted the 'constant union' between God and his children; the Church's worship was 'the speech and music of humanity'; the Christian ministry was a sign of the universality of the

Church; church buildings were hints that 'the city and the men in it are holy'; the whole life of the Church was a sign of what the world could become and, deep down, already was. The Atonement did not change God's will, as the Evangelicals then usually asserted; it declared that will and thus declared also the true character of humanity – something far more important than any individual conversion. It showed that the Father is love, that we are most fully ourselves when loving, that sacrifice is 'the law of our being'.

This theology, accepting both the Church and the world, could be interpreted in a way that encouraged the worldly complacency which has often accompanied the privileges of the Church of England. John Stuart Mill complained with some justification about Maurice's belief 'that the Church of England had known everything from the first, and that all truths on the ground of which the Church and orthodoxy have been attacked (many of which he saw as clearly as anyone) are not only consistent with the Thirty-nine Articles, but are better understood and expressed in those articles than by anyone who rejects them.' In his own day Catholics and Evangelicals, believers and unbelievers, found his synthesis of their positions confused and unsatisfactory. They agreed in complaining about his muddled mind, and in 1971 an American scholar, Olive Brose, summed up the enigma of his personality in the title of her study, *Rebellious Conformist*. Such a man was bound to make all the conventional, including the conventional rebels, uneasy.

Certainly he wrote far too much and too rhetorically to be precisely authoritative; it was his custom to dictate his books, which read too much like sermons. A crucial weakness was that he never seems to have become calm enough to think out clearly what was the authority of the Bible and the creeds. He would leap to their defence without really listening to their critics. But in an age when religious vitality was usually expressed in a narrowminded and intolerant enthusiasm for some neat creed narrower than the Bible, for some small system of belief and church life, he was a reconciler. He bequeathed to thoughtful Anglicans a hunger for a more comprehensive Catholicism on a firmly scriptural basis, and a

Roman Catholic commentator has rightly observed that among Anglicans the theological victory has been won by the theory of a Catholic-Church-in-becoming, to the development of which all who aspire to Catholicity may contribute.[42] This turning to the future has largely replaced earlier Anglican dependence on the claim to be at least a branch of the pure Catholicism of the past. Such was the influence of Maurice's vision of Christian unity. He also deserves to be remembered as a man who did what he could to end the class war which Karl Marx was sure would intensify. Before his death in 1872, he talked much with his son Frederick about his failures, but he added: 'The desire for unity and the search for unity both in the nation and in the Church has haunted me all my days.'

THE CHURCH AT WORK

When Bishop George Selwyn returned from New Zealand, the manly hero of the hour, to preach at Cambridge in 1854, he declared that 'a great and visible change has taken place in the thirteen years since I left England. It is now a very rare thing to see a careless clergyman, a neglected parish or a desecrated church.' That assessment may have been too rhetorical, but the evidence of parish registers, newspapers and novels supports the impression of a revival. A modern student of the transformation which overtook the Victorian Church selected this quotation from journalism in 1857: 'True theology has revived, pluralities have been abolished, residence enforced, services multiplied, schools built; while the clergy as a body have displayed a zeal, a diligence and a liberality which will bear comparison with the brightest periods of ecclesiastical

---

[42] George H. Tavard, *The Quest for Catholicity* (London, 1963) p. 200. Other recent studies include M. B. Reckitt, *Maurice to Temple: A Century of the Social Movement in the Church of England* (London, 1947); A. M. Ramsey, *F. D. Maurice and the Conflicts of Modern Theology* (Cambridge, 1951); Torben Christensen, *The Origin and History of Christian Socialism, 1848–54* (Aarhus, 1962), and *The Divine Order: A Study of F. D. Maurice's Theology* (Leiden, 1973); A. R. Vidler, *F. D. Maurice and Company* (London, 1966); F. M. McClain, *Maurice Man and Moralist* (London, 1972). In *The Integrity of Anglicanism* (London, 1978), Stephen Sykes questioned the merits of Maurice's influence.

history'.[43] In the fifty years 1830–80, the number of Easter communicants doubled.

Part of the reason for the greater efficiency was the increase in the number and morale of the clergy. In 1831 there were 10,718: twenty years later, 17,621. The priest was now expected to be devout, and a growing number of churches actually had Morning and Evening Prayer daily, as the Prayer Book directed. He was expected to consult with brother priests; from 1835 onwards the post of rural dean was revived in order to draw the clergy together. The clergyman was expected to be an educated man (in 1878, 16,297 of the 23,612 clergymen had been to Oxford or Cambridge), yet a father to the children and the poor; to be, as Archbishop Tait put it in 1873, 'the accredited minister of the National Church, resident in the midst of every community with incomparable advantages for gathering the people round him, and organizing them for any good purpose which may subserve the kingdom of Christ.' He was expected to show that he was on duty by dressing in black, although the cut of his coat could disclose whether he was an Evangelical or a Tractarian. He was usually not expected to hunt with the gentry, or to labour on his glebe land, or to drink in a public house. He was different from his neighbours – and, because he was sacred, different from much in his own profession's past.[44]

The clergyman's training also became more professional than it had been since the arrival of Christianity in England. In 1869 a board of theological professors at Oxford began to build up a faculty of theology capable of teaching and examining. At Cambridge, where the theologians had been less suspicious of each other, such a board already existed and the 'tripos' or examination in theology was begun in 1874. Durham University and King's College, London, also taught theology at the undergraduate level. Diocesan theological colleges hesitantly modelled on the Roman Catholic system provided extra training for graduates preparing to be priests; the earliest were at Chichester and Wells (1839–40). Other colleges still more

---

[43] Brian Heeney, *A Different Kind of Gentleman* (Hampden, Conn., 1976), p. 91.
[44] Anthony Russell traced the development of *The Clerical Profession* (London, 1980).

hesitantly catered for non-graduates. Although no central
body to supervise this training for the ministry existed until
1912 (and then it was only a 'central advisory council'), the
Victorian bishops became able to be far more thorough than
their predecessors in examining candidates.[45]

These mid-Victorian clergy left a very large legacy behind
them in the shape of new or restored churches. The new
churches were almost always in the 'Gothic style' which put
into stone the yearning to recover the Faith and the Christendom of the Middle Ages – although the partly mechanized
nineteenth century contributed its rapid (sometimes too rapid)
building methods. In 1876 Parliament was told that 7,144
churches had been restored in the parishes of the Church of
England since 1840, and 1,727 new churches had been built.
The achievement was a spectacular fulfilment of the dreams
nursed by a small group of young churchmen in the Camden
Society at Cambridge. Led by John Mason Neale they founded
a national Ecclesiological Society in 1845, and up and down
the country clergy and laity became enthusiastic for the new
pattern – pews which were modest and free, unobtrusive
heating, a stone font near the entrance, on opposite sides of the
church a brass lectern for the Bible and a pulpit for biblical
preaching, an organ replacing the little band of often clumsy
instrumentalists, a long sanctuary with a robed and surpliced
choir, the altar as the climax beneath the stained glass in the
east window. 'Few undergraduate societies have exercised
such an influence', it has been observed.[46]

John Mason Neale, the warden of a little community of nuns
in Sussex and dead before he was fifty, revolutionized what
went on in church by translating hymns. From a past hitherto
unknown to Protestant England came majestic hymns such as
'Come thou Redeemer of the earth' or 'The royal banners

---

[45] F. W. B. Bullock provided *A History of Training for the Ministry, 1800–74* (St
Leonards-on-Sea, Sussex, 1955).

[46] G. W. O. Addleshaw and Frederick Etchells, *The Architectural Setting of Anglican
Worship* (London, 1959), p. 203. Basil Clarke studied *Church Builders of the Nineteenth
Century* (London, 1938), and J. F. Whyte *The Cambridge Movement* (Cambridge,
1962). J. Stanley Leatherbarrow described the building of a fairly typical church in
Lancashire in *Victorian Period Piece* (London, 1954).

forward go' or 'The strife is o'er' or 'The Day of Resurrection!' or 'Come, thou holy Paraclete' or 'Of the glorious Body telling' or 'O what their joy and their glory must be' or 'Jerusalem the golden' – although he was on occasion not ashamed to be popular, as in 'Good King Wenceslas'. When the *English Hymnal* was compiled forty years after his death, seventy-two of its 656 hymns were his. He was said to speak twenty languages, but his great gift to the Church of England was to assure it that hymns, previously composed mainly by Dissenters, Methodists or Evangelicals, were fit to be the language of a 'happy band of pilgrims' (his best loved hymn other than his translations). The pilgrims sang – accompanied by the organ. During Neale's lifetime (in 1864), the Royal College of Organists was founded, marking the now widespread distribution of what was becoming the Church's favourite musical instrument, replacing the village band.[47]

John Ellerton, like Neale, made some Latin hymns famous by translating them. These included 'Sing alleluia forth in duteous praise' and 'O strength and stay upholding all creation'. But his best-known hymns were both of his own composition, and both about evening – 'Saviour, again to thy dear name we raise' was meant to be the last hymn of the Sunday in the gaslit parish church of Crewe, and 'The day thou gavest, Lord, is ended' was to remind his parishioners that now the Christian Church was worldwide, so that as Crewe went to bed 'our brethren 'neath the western sky' began their praise. When *Hymns Ancient and Modern*, which had begun life as a small book of 1861, entered one of its many new editions in 1889, it contained twenty-six Ellerton hymns. Even better loved as an evening hymn was Henry Lyte's 'Abide with me' (1847), the prayer of a priest facing premature death. It was as simple in its faith as Mrs Alexander's 'There is a green hill', written by the bedside of a sick child; but it became the favourite both of football crowds and of F. D. Maurice.[48]

---

[47] A. G. Lough studied *The Influence of John Mason Neale* (London, 1962), and *J. M. Neale: Priest Extraordinary* (London, 1975).

[48] Ellerton was for a time rector of Barnes near London and appears in John Whale's history of the parish, *One Church, One Lord* (London, 1979), pp. 130–49. B. G. Skinner wrote about *Henry Lyte* (Exeter, 1974).

Other favourite Victorian hymns were more robustly cheerful. Henry Lyte's most enduring hymn turned out to be 'Praise,
my soul, the King of heaven', and the Christian life was
compared with a military march as often as with a lonely
pilgrimage. Sabine Baring-Gould, a handsome young Yorkshire curate who at about the same time insisted on marrying
an illiterate mill girl, wrote 'Onward Christian soldiers' for the
children of the Sunday school in 1864. Later he translated from
the Danish 'Through the night of doubt and sorrow', fathered
fifteen children and wrote 160 books.[49]

Victorian country parsons often took the lead which landowners ought to have taken in the relief of distress and
ignorance. Because only efficient farming thrived and it required capital, the class of 'yeoman' or independent small-
holder famous in English life and literature declined miserably,
and just over three-quarters of the land in Victorian England
came to be owned by only seven thousand families. The
farmers who were the tenants of these landlords could get as
much labour as they wanted with low wages and often poor
housing, since for most of the century the countryside remained overpopulated. When the decline of British agriculture
had begun in the 1870s, not even employment at this low level
was readily available. The charitable relief of the sick and poor
was needed – and it often came in daily visits from churchgoers when the parson and his wife led by exhortation and
example.

Many parishes ran savings banks with clothing, boot and
coal 'clubs' to encourage saving – and many distributed these
necessities free to those without the required pennies. Much of
the clergy's work was educational and was not confined to the
Sunday school or the private tutorial establishment. J. S.
Henslow, who had taught botany to Charles Darwin at Cambridge, built a school and paid for it out of his own pocket in his
remote parish. John Keble's parish had a school, where he
taught every day; Charles Kingsley's did not, but he could
spend six evenings a week during the winter supervising classes

---

[49] William Purcell's biography was called *Onward Christian Soldier* (London,
1957).

for adults. A lending library encouraged reading, and for the majority who still found reading difficult 'penny readings' were an entertainment. In the vast drawing room of the rectory in Old Alresford in Hampshire, in 1876, Mrs Mary Sumner founded the Mothers' Union which was to become worldwide. It gave advice both spiritual and practical to 'cottage mothers', and proved to be a vastly successful exercise in adult education. Nor were the husbands neglected. Many of the clergy included the improvement of agriculture in their amazingly wide range of studies, badgered the landlords into building better cottages, and provided allotments on their own 'glebe' land. Church halls were built to provide recreation, and involvement in church life became itself an education. Towards the end of the century voluntary church councils were replacing the old 'vestries' which had mixed secular with ecclesiastical business, and 'lay readers' – first recruited for London and other great towns in the 1860s – were beginning to take services in the country parson's absence. Such developments mostly heralded the twentieth century, where rural religion was going to depend increasingly on the laity.

Although there was much activity, it should not be exaggerated. A realistic portrait of the laity in a stagnant area of the mid-Victorian countryside has been provided by a modern examination of part of Lincolnshire. In 1851 it had 237 parishes served by 154 clergy, although half of these parishes contained under five hundred souls, and the standard of pastoral duty was higher than ever before. But church attendance was 'low to middling' and mainly female, and the numbers of communicants were usually small. Most of the young people confirmed seem to have made their communions once, if at all. The churches were usually locked on weekdays. The clergy's basic problem was, it seems, that their churches were not really regarded as the people's spiritual homes. Some of those who did attend probably did so in order to establish their respectability or in order to please the squire, who might well be also the employer and the landlord. The religion which really involved, and even excited, the people was Methodism, often charismatic and boisterous in its enthusiasm. At least the chapel was a scene of democracy and a source of entertainment in dull lives.[50]

Lives in early Victorian towns were often worse than dull. Many town parsons, knowing the problems because they visited the homes and also chaired the 'vestries' which were largely responsible for local government in its early stages, were acutely worried about the diseased slums which had been spewed out by industrialism. They became active in the whole mid-Victorian movement to make urban sanitation less barbaric, the movement which had as its banner the Public Health Act of 1848. With the removal of the filth came the decline of the two killer-epidemics, cholera and typhoid, and although other diseases continued to claim many victims because the towns were overcrowded and dirtied by coal, progress came. Hard work, together with the advantages possessed by industrial and colonial Britain in world trade, enabled a predominantly urban population which doubled in the second half of the century to pay for its food and for much else. Praised by his superiors for his self-discipline, the urban worker was awarded the parliamentary vote in 1867.

This was the background to the labours of town priests such as Walter Hook, vicar of Leeds 1837–59, who raised the money to build twenty-two churches, twenty-three vicarages and twenty-seven schools. His ecclesiastical position was conservative (so he clashed with Pusey) but his religious energy was new in the Church of England's urban mission, and he more than anyone else established the pattern of the devoted and inexhausible vicar, like an admiral commanding a squadron of curates in the battle for a city's souls. Later on the most admired pioneers were the 'slum priests' of the Anglo-Catholic movement – men who believed that the poor deserved not only

---

[50] James Obelkevich examined *Religion and Rural Society: South Lindsey 1825–75* (Oxford, 1976). Other studies include A. Tindal Hart and Edward Carpenter, *The Nineteenth Century Country Parson* (Shrewsbury, 1954); G. Kitson Clark, *Churchmen and the Condition of England 1832–85* (London, 1973); Brenda Colloms, *Victorian Country Parsons* (London, 1977); Peter Hammond, *The Parson and the Victorian Parish* (London, 1977). Joyce Coombes studied the origins of the Mothers' Union in *George and Mary Sumner* (London, 1965). For the background, see G. E. Mingay, *Rural Life in Victorian England* (London, 1977).

devoted love and the Evangelical call for definite conversions, but also all the drama, colour and consolation of 'advanced' religious ceremonies. Typical of them was Charles Lowder of St Peter's, London Docks. He won the love of the people by his heroism in the cholera epidemic of 1866, and his funeral in 1880 was a triumph. Such 'Anglo-Catholics' were the heirs of the Tractarians, but broke right away from academic privilege.

In lectures published as *The Parish Priest of the Town* in 1880, John Gott talked to young men in Cambridge about his ideal of the priesthood as one of Hook's successors in pastoral work among the people of Leeds. 'The first day of my diaconate I was given charge over a district of eight thousand souls and that day was the true sample of my life till today.' He was intensely proud of his profession; 'every word spoken at present by a leading clergyman is a deed, and every deed is a force.' But his pride was based on the willing acceptance of very hard work. The town priest should systematically teach the children in church and school, should appoint district visitors to cover the whole parish, should visit people's homes every afternoon. 'The true pastor discovers sickness almost by instinct; through his visitors, Sunday or day teachers, and kind-hearted neighbours, his eye is everywhere, and he is often on the spot before the doctor.' Each Sunday evening he should mark on a list all the present and absent communicants, with a view to visiting during the week. There should be a personal interview with every communicant every Lent.

While so many hard-working pastors and churchgoers are forgotten, one man, Richard Church, can be remembered as a figurehead of the rural and urban mission of the Church of England in the Victorian age. Gladstone wrote in 1878 that 'there is no one whose ultimate judgement would carry more weight with one.' He wanted to make him a bishop, perhaps

---

[51] See C. J. Stranks, *Dean Hook* (London, 1954), and Lida Ellsworth, *Charles Lowder and the Ritualist Movement* (London, 1982). K. S. Inglis surveyed *The Churches and the Working Classes in Victorian England* (London, 1963), and the background was presented by J. F. C. Harrison, *Early Victorian Britain*, and G. F. A. Best, *Mid-Victorian Britain* (London, 1979). John Kent contributed a suggestive essay on 'Feelings and Festivals' to *Victorian City: Images and Realities*, ed. H. J. Dyos and Michael Wolff (London, 1973), vol. 2, pp. 855–71.

even Archbishop of Canterbury, and did succeed in dragging him from eighteen years in a parish with two hundred inhabitants (Whatley in Somerset) to London as Dean of St Paul's in 1871. Walter Hook had declined the post; he was too old.

Richard Church was one of Newman's closest friends, but when Newman ceased to be an Anglican, Church's reply was to be found with other friends in the *Guardian*, a weekly paper where a moderately High Church theology was to be combined with a sensitive commentary on social and cultural events. His own writing was wide-ranging and of great distinction, and he was no enemy of scientists; he had a small laboratory in his rectory. No man did more to reassure Anglicans that they belonged to a tradition Catholic both in the sense of being loyal to ancient church order and also in the sense of embracing the best in the contemporary world. At St Paul's until his death in 1890 he remained literary and shy but was deeply respected for his wisdom and saintliness. Fortunately the cathedral had H. P. Liddon as a canon. A professor at Oxford and in London, a preacher of great eloquence and force, Liddon was in effect the spokesman of his master, Pusey. A similarly gifted, but rather more flowery and liberal preacher, Henry Scott Holland, was appointed a canon in 1884. Sir John Stainer was a great church musician. There were others, too, who worked to make St Paul's more beautiful, and much more used as a church, than it had ever been. So Dean Church lived to see new life all around him. In 1877 he referred to 'the victories which the revived English Church has achieved and which, in spite of disasters and menacing troubles, make it the most glorious Church in Christendom'.[52]

---

[52] B. A. Smith studied *Dean Church: The Anglican Response to Newman* (London, 1958), and G. L. Prestige *St Paul's in Its Glory* (London, 1955).

BISHOPS IN THE CHURCH

Many of the Victorian bishops were decisive leaders. They were not elected by their dioceses and did not feel answerable to them: they belonged to the governing class. On the other hand, when they were nominated by the Prime Minister of the day for appointment by the Queen (subject to a formal election by the cathedral chapter), it was seldom for mainly political reasons. They were chosen on their records as outstanding parish priests or university scholars in order that they might lead the Church vigorously in the direction of which the Prime Minister approved. It was seldom an extremist direction. Opinionated as they were in their own territories, they often saw each other in London; they had to learn to work together; and their general tendency was to plead for loyalty to the Church.

Several of the bishops were highly effective organizers, but supreme among them was Samuel Wilberforce, Bishop of Oxford 1843–69 and of Winchester 1869–73. Had Gladstone become Prime Minister in October instead of December 1868, Wilberforce would have become Archbishop of Canterbury – although Gladstone had warned him that his reputation among politicians was 'that of a most able prelate, getting all you can for the Church, asking more, giving nothing'. Disraeli, who refused to promote him in 1868, referred to him in his novel *Lothair* (1870): 'He was fond of society, and justified his taste in this respect by the flattering belief that he was extending the power of the Church; certainly he was favouring an ambition which could not be described as moderate.'

His ambition had been encouraged by his father, William Wilberforce, and by Sir Robert Peel. Peel made him a bishop at the age of forty, only seven months after making him Dean of Westminster. Already he was widely known as a public speaker with his father's magic, and to the end of his life he held forth on platforms up and down the country, or in the House of Lords, on what he reckoned to be the good causes of the day. But it was unjust to think of him as being a climber like, say, Disraeli. He was truly convinced about certain High Church principles, and when he compiled his father's *Life and Letters* (in seven volumes, with his brother Robert) he never made it quite clear how much of an Evangelical his father had been. His convictions, he reckoned, damaged his career. He burst out privately in 1857: 'You do not suppose that I am so blind as not to see perfectly that I might have headed the Evangelical party and been seated by them at Lambeth.' But he was responding to a new spirit in the Church, to be seen in the fact that his three brothers, his daughter Ella, his sister-in-law Mary, and two other Anglican clergymen who married the beautiful sisters of his beautiful wife, Emily Sargent, all became Roman Catholics. He remained a convinced Anglican, and his convictions became inflexible when he mourned his Emily's premature death in 1841 – as he did all the rest of his life.

His remedy for grief was work; he was afraid to be alone or at leisure, and one result was that his theology was frozen in the 1830s. His work was to be seen at its enduring best in his own diocese, which included three counties in addition to the university which was the flashpoint of theological controversy. 'It is the bishop who must be the main instrument in encouraging the zealous,' he wrote to Lord Shaftesbury, 'in stirring up the faint-hearted, in animating the despondent.' He made ordinations intensely devotional occasions; he used horses or the railways to be all over his diocese for confirmations or for inspections of the six hundred parishes; he consecrated more than a hundred new churches and approved of more than seventy new parsonages and more than 270 church restorations; he received regular reports on the parish priests from the rural deans, and wrote many letters of praise or blame in his own hand; he addressed the clergy in spiritual retreats and the laity in parochial missions; he founded a college to train priests and another for schoolmasters. And from this diocesan achievement went on to become, in Walter Hook's phrase, the 'Lord Bishop of England'. He was the leading advocate of the revival of the Convocations of the clergy which in the period 1851–61 began to transact business as they had not done since 1717. In the 1860s Church Congresses began to gather the laity more informally. It was not unreasonable for S. C. Carpenter, in his history of *Church and People 1789–1889*, to see Bishop Wilberforce's work as the turning point, saying about the

Oxford Movement: 'The Church accepted it in the same modified sense as that in which he accepted it.'[53]

Samuel Wilberforce's great rival, Archibald Campbell Tait, was the Queen's successful candidate for Canterbury in 1868. He was everything that she liked best in a clergyman – a Scot, a Protestant, earnest about the work of the Church without being fanatical about its rights, liberal in taking account of contemporary laymen's feelings without being controversially theological. But his preparation for becoming Bishop of London in 1856 on his way to Lambeth Palace was, as he noted in his journal after being offered the appointment, 'deep affliction'. As Dean of Carlisle he had faced bitter opposition to his new ideas from the canons of the cathedral – and had also seen five of his daughters die of scarlet fever within a month.

Tait (like Wilberforce) found the work of a diocese a consolation for grief, but his religion differed from his rival's. In childhood his soul had been fed by a beloved Evangelical nurse and her influence was never obliterated. While Bishop of London he preached in the open air, encouraged services in theatres, and persuaded Westminster Abbey and St Paul's to hold Sunday evening services for the poor. He also set his firmly Protestant face against Anglo-Catholic ritualism ('this childish mimicry of antiquated garments'). But Tait was never a straightforward Evangelical. Disraeli described his complexity to the Queen in 1868: 'an ecclesiastical statesman obscure in purpose, fitful and inconsistent in action, and evidently, though earnest and conscientious, a prey to constantly conflicting convictions.' Tait regretted that 'Broad Churchmen' sometimes treated sacred subjects with a lack of earnestness: that was why he signed the bishops' declaration reacting against the manifesto of liberal scholars in 1860, *Essays and Reviews*. But he also had a keen sense that most laymen were

---

[53] Standish Meacham supplied a modern biography: *Lord Bishop* (Cambridge, Mass., 1970). See also Owen Chadwick, *The Founding of Cuddesdon* (Oxford, 1954); Diana McClatchey, *Oxfordshire Clergy 1777–1869* (Oxford, 1960); David Newsome, *The Parting of Friends* (London, 1966). Dieter Voll, *Catholic Evangelicalism* (London, 1963), studied some of the Victorians who used the Wilberforce approach in urban churches.

now reluctant to see liberal scholars driven out of the Church; that was why he supported the Judicial Committee of the Privy Council when it decided that clergymen holding such views could also keep their appointments. He was undeterred when eleven thousand clergymen – the majority – signed a manifesto reaffirming the everlasting punishment of the wicked in hell and the divine inspiration of the Bible 'without reserve or qualification'.

As Archbishop of Canterbury he was far more decisive than his predecessor (C. T. Longley, a hard-working bishop for more than thirty years but scarcely a constructive ecclesiastical statesman). His supreme purpose was to preserve and strengthen the establishment of the Church of England, because the Church was to him the guardian of the simple Christian truths which the nation had adopted as its faith. He contrasted England with the continent, where 'either you have atheistical philosophers or you have superstitious devotees'. He urged the clergy to remember that England was still at heart Christian England; that sceptics would feel differently 'in hours of sickness and approaching death, and when friends are taken from them; then we may find their consciences awake and their hearts open, ready to return to the faith of their childhood and to believe in the great Redeemer.' In the year before he died, he claimed that 'on the faithfulness of the Church of England in the discharge of its highest duties rests the future welfare of this English nation and not of the English nation only, but I may also say, of the Christian Church throughout the world'.

Tait gave his reasons for devoting so much attention to the battle against ritualism. 'I have great sympathy with earnestness, and I have great sympathy with liberty, but I have no sympathy with persons who make the Church of England something quite different from that which it was made at the Reformation.' He feared 'lest the foolish conduct of a few might so shake the confidence of the people in their National Established Church, that they would consider it no longer worth preserving.' The explanation, entirely subordinating the alleged requirements of Christian worship to the alleged requirements of national life, was one more reminder that his values were those of a Protestant, patriotic layman. Such values led him into the blunder of supporting the Public Worship Regulation Act, under which parish priests who had revived medieval practices could be, and were, sent to prison. Accordingly, most of the Anglo-Catholic clergy hated him. Their organ, the *Church Times*, declared: 'What music is to a man with no ear, that religion is to Archbishop Tait.'[54]

Tait's two successors in the archbishopric of Canterbury repeated the contrast which had existed between him and Wilberforce. Edward White Benson held High Church and Conservative convictions, and had put them into practice as the first Bishop of Truro; but he was out of touch with lay thought, including the psychological oddities and religious doubts of his own wife and children. Frederick Temple, on the other hand, was cautiously liberal like Tait, in theology as in politics. His real work had been done as a headmaster and bishop before he went to Canterbury in his old age. Indeed, despite all his labours, probably his most lasting contribution to church history was to demonstrate that a headmaster who had contributed to the liberal volume of *Essays and Reviews* could become a bishop and archbishop. When Gladstone appointed him to the see of Exeter there was an outbreak of indignation, although his contribution had been no more than the reworking of a sermon comparing the progress of humanity with the maturing of an individual. The ablest of Temple's fellow contributors, Mark Pattison and Benjamin Jowett, were ruined as theologians by the reception of their essays; the orthodox never forgave them, and they became increasingly more embittered, sceptical and cynical in Oxford. But while he was a bishop Frederick Temple's clergy forgot that he had ever been branded as a heretic. Although they feared him because they found him gruffly authoritarian, he could set them on fire

---

[54] Randall Davidson and William Benham compiled Tait's *Life* in 2 vols. (London, 1890). Despite its unjustified title, P. T. Marsh's study of *The Victorian Church in Decline: Archbishop Tait and the Church of England, 1868–82* (London, 1968), was well researched. M. A. Crowther studied theological controversies in *The Church Embattled* (Newton Abbot, Devon, 1970), and James Bentley studied legal battles in *Ritualism and Politics in Victorian Britain* (Oxford, 1978).

when he preached about national righteousness and the English mission to the world.[55]

Other Victorian bishops had a national standing while being mainly absorbed in diocesan work. One became known as the saintly pastor of agricultural labourers – Edward King of Lincoln; another as the champion of working men – James Fraser of Manchester. A third was famous as a writer of Evangelical tracts – J. C. Ryle, the first Bishop of Liverpool (who rebuked Fraser for his support of an agricultural workers' strike: both men spent many years as country parsons before moving to great industrial cities). A modern biography of Ryle assesses him in terms which could be applied to many of these bishops. 'Respect is perhaps the key word in describing the mutual relations of Ryle, the father, presbyter and bishop, and his family and flock. His undoubted ability, his strong convictions, his commanding appearance, his faithfulness and his sincerity created respect.' Edward King, however, was loved.[56]

Several of the Victorian bishops possessed international reputations as scholars. There were two great historians: William Stubbs, Bishop of Chester and Oxford, and Mandell Creighton, Bishop of Peterborough and London. Like Fraser and Ryle, these two also had spent happy years as country parsons. It was the boast of Stubbs that 'I knew every toe of every baby in the parish'. While in that parish and while a professor at Oxford, he did more than any other man of his generation to put English history before the Reformation on a new basis – the study of original documents (even if, being a good Victorian, he did tend to interpret the politics of the past

[55] A. C. Benson compiled *The Life and Letters of E. W. Benson* (2 vols., London, 1899). More informal material is to be found in A. C. Benson, *The Trefoil* (London, 1923), and E. F. Benson, *As We Were* (London, 1932). Books about the family include Betty Askwith, *Two Victorian Families* (London, 1971), and David Williams, *Genesis and Exodus: A Portrait of the Benson Family* (London, 1979). Braving his prohibition of a biography, E. G. Sandford compiled *Memoirs of Arshbishop Temple by Seven Friends* (2 vols., London, 1906). Geoffrey Faber wrote about *Jowett* (London, 1957) and Ieuan Ellis about *Seven against Christ: A Study of Essays and Reviews* (Leiden, 1980).

[56] Peter Toon and Michael Smout, *John Charles Ryle* (Cambridge, 1976), p. 103. See also John Newton, *Search for a Saint: Edward King* (London, 1977).

in terms of statesmen defending or developing a parliamentary democracy associated with the Anglo-Saxons). Creighton dared to put the history of the Renaissance Papacy on a solid foundation in books which he wrote in a vicarage in Northumberland. Partly because of his tolerance towards the sins of the popes the Victorians often suspected Creighton of cynicism – but they were unjust. He believed in generosity towards the dead and the living as a part of his Anglican faith. 'Current morality, philanthropy, high aims in politics, ideas of progress, of liberty, of brotherhood – what you will – owe their position to Christianity', he once claimed.[57]

Two Cambridge theologians, J. B. Lightfoot and B. F. Westcott, were successively Bishops of Durham. They had both been schoolfellows with the future Archbishop Benson at King Edward's School, Birmingham, in the 1840s. Jointly they did much to justify Bishop Creighton's claim about Christianity's influence in Victorian England.

Lightfoot was a matter-of-fact man. Apart from a part-time canonry at St Paul's he lived in the academic peace of Cambridge until he went to Durham at the age of fifty-one, and he was immensely learned. 'Does it not sometimes happen to you', he once innocently asked a young clergyman, 'that when you have read a book you forget in what language it was written?' While a bishop he continued these scholarly labours, but gave his main energies to his diocese. He preached about the local saints; but he was also practical with an unexpected vigour. The over-large diocese was divided by the creation of the diocese of Newcastle, and in what remained, the administration and finances were reorganized. Forty-five new churches were built in ten years, and lay people were encouraged to assist the clergy in preaching and visiting. The Bishop had young men who wanted to be priests to live with him in Auckland Castle, and was often in the villages and towns – as a pastor, not a prince.[58]

---

[57] See W. H. Hutton, *William Stubbs* (London, 1906). His widow Louise compiled *The Life and Letters of Mandell Creighton* in 2 vols. (London, 1905), and W. G. Fallows considered *Mandell Creighton and the English Church* (Oxford, 1964).

[58] See *Lightfoot of Durham*, ed. G. R. Eden and F. C. Macdonald (Cambridge, 1932).

When Lightfoot had worn himself out by this work, he was succeeded by the slightly older Professor Westcott. The term 'mystic' was often applied to Westcott, a man who was unworldly but not vague. He worked with another Cambridge scholar, F. J. A. Hort, on a revised Greek text of the New Testament, using manuscript sources superior to those available to previous generations of scholars. This text was published in 1881, just before the Revised Version of the New Testament in English which it had assisted. He encouraged the beginnings of the Cambridge degree course in theology, of the 'university extension' movement for adult education, of the Cambridge Mission to Delhi – believing that 'no nation, no church . . . was ever called to fulfil a greater work than that to which the English nation and the English Church are now summoned'. And he wrote much, his constant theme being that all men had been taken by the humanity of Jesus the Consecrator into the life of God. The Resurrection and Ascension were to him pledges that the long process of evolution, so far from being merely a struggle for existence governed by accident, was progressing to the final unity and transfiguration of the universe which God had created in his love; so that Christ was 'Consummator' as well as Consecrator. And he plainly believed that the Victorian age had brought the consummation somewhat nearer. It was Westcott's belief that 'the Church educates and inspires society, which moulds the State'.

The Conservative Prime Minister scotched the Queen's suggestion in 1890 that Westcott should be made Archbishop of York, by drawing her attention to 'the Socialist tendencies of the speeches which he has made since becoming a bishop'. By 1892 he was sufficiently trusted by the (mostly Methodist) miners of County Durham to be asked to mediate between them and their employers during a strike by about 10,000 men which had reduced most of their families to destitution. Westcott negotiated a compromise which lessened the reduction in wages proposed by the employers. It was an achievement unusual in the history of mysticism.[59]

---

[59] His son Arthur compiled *The Life and Letters of Brooke Foss Westcott* in 2 vols. (London, 1903). See also A. C. Benson, *Leaves of the Tree* (London, 1911), and

The Christian Social Union of which he was president can be criticized as a middle-class, predominantly clerical, effort to form study groups which talked about brotherhood instead of joining the necessary revolution. It can also be said to have been too vague about questions such as how St John's gospel was related to miners' wages. A recent historian has commented about this and other manifestations of the revival of Christian Socialism towards the end of their century, that 'their "Socialism" was an intellectual ragbag, and most of them never faced up to the dominant question: "What is specifically Christian about Christian Socialism?"'[60] George Bernard Shaw presented the Christian Socialist as an overconfident orator in his play *Candida* (1898), and there was always an amateurish flavour to the movement. For example, Stuart Headlam who founded the Guild of St Matthew in 1877, and was its leading spirit until its dissolution in 1909, was an Etonian who had become a ritualist while serving as a curate in the East End of London. He had a sincere belief that the Eucharist was meant to be a rehearsal for a drama in which justice would be distributed far more evenly among the poor. And he had courage; he met Oscar Wilde, who had been imprisoned for homosexual practices amid great unpopularity, on the morning of his release from prison, and looked after him until he went into exile. But he always kept up the tastes of a gentleman. He loved cigars, he was a devotee of the ballet, he had little taste for economics.[61]

Even the more practical northerners of the Church Socialist League founded in 1909, or individualists such as Conrad Noel who was appointed vicar of the lovely Essex church at

Geoffrey Best, *Bishop Westcott and the Miners* (Cambridge, 1967). A Swedish scholar, Folke Olofsson, wrote a study of Westcott's theology: *Christus Redemptor et Consummator* (Uppsala, 1979).

[60] Peter d'A. Jones, *The Christian Socialist Revival 1877-1914* (Princeton, N.J., 1968), p. 449.

[61] Reginald Groves, *Conrad Noel and the Thaxted Movement* (London, 1967), may be compared with Walter Kendall, *The Revolutionary Movement in Great Britain 1900-21* (London, 1969). Late Victorian social idealism was studied by Melvin Richter, *The Politics of Conscience* (Cambridge, Mass., 1964). Studies of Headlam, Noel and other Christian Socialists were edited by M. B. Beckitt as *For Christ and the People* (London, 1968).

Thaxted in 1911, advocated a decentralized 'Guild Socialism' on a medieval pattern. They could be (and were) dismissed as sentimentalists by those who looked forward to the great take-over by the State or who simply demanded higher wages. G. K. Chesterton commented about the Christian Social Union:

> And so they sang a lot of hymns
> To help the Unemployed.

Yet Chesterton himself wrote a much used hymn about social righteousness ('O God of earth and altar'), while Scott Holland's hymn 'Judge eternal, throned in splendour' found echoes in many hearts with its plea for the cleansing of a great empire, in 1902. In 1909 William Cunningham, who in addition to being an archdeacon was an economist very critical of inexpert idealism, noted that 'in any gathering of clergy and ministers, there are sure to be many who take a pride in declaring that they are Christian Socialists. It may be doubted whether any such change in public opinion occurred even at the Reformation itself.'[62]

It was the natural tendency of the Church of England throughout the nineteenth century to be 'the Conservative party at prayer' (a much-repeated gibe of uncertain authorship). The appeal of Christian Socialism to some of the best of the Anglicans was therefore a remarkable tribute to the influence of intellectual leaders such as Maurice in the middle of the century and Westcott towards its end. Their teaching inspired idealism. Still more remarkable was the evolution of the conscience of the devout Anglican layman who was the century's most fascinating and creative force in English public life.

THE GREATEST VICTORIAN

It was Disraeli who made the most famous of the announcements that Victorian England was divided into two nations,

---

[62] George Kitson Clark, *Churchmen and the Condition of England*, p. 312.

the rich and the poor. This was in his novel *Sybil* (1848), where a Chartist's daughter was loved by an enlightened young aristocrat. And Disraeli did much for the working class. He secured votes in future elections for workers who occupied their own houses – in 1867, the year when the first volume of Karl Marx's *Das Capital* was published obscurely in London. When he had made sure of the leadership of the Conservative party by the skill of that feat, he proceeded to make the Conservatives popular by a programme of limited social reforms at home and unlimited imperialism abroad, asserting that others could rise as he had done. The man who emerged as his successor in the Conservative leadership after his death in 1881, Lord Salisbury, also wooed the people by social reforms and imperialism. However, being more of a philosopher than Disraeli, he was also more of a pessimist. The most that the Conservatives could do, in his honest conviction, was to postpone the day when his whole world would lie in ruins.[63]

But it was William Ewart Gladstone, the greatest of all the Victorians, who contributed most to the union of the rich and poor. In the final analysis he did not do it in order to win political victories for himself or his party; had his motivation been entirely selfish, he would probably have led the Conservatives not the Liberals, and would have retired from politics to bask in scholarly leisure and a prestige above controversy long before he got himself and his party bogged down in the insoluble problems of Ireland. When he died in 1892, he was assessed by Lord Salisbury in the House of Lords (an institution which had narrowly escaped from his wrath) in words which were more than funeral flattery. Salisbury declared that 'what he sought were the attainments of great ideals' which 'could have issued from nothing but the greatest and purest moral aspirations'. To Salisbury and to others who had recently been his embattled opponents Gladstone was an example,

[63] Recent studies include Robert Blake, *Disraeli* (London, 1966) and *The Conservative Party from Peel to Churchill* (London, 1970); Paul Smith, *Disraelian Conservatism and Social Reform* (London, 1967); A. L. Kennedy, *Salisbury 1830–1903* (London, 1953); M. Pinto-Duschinsky, *The Political Thought of Lord Salisbury 1854–68* (London, 1967); C. H. D. Howard, *Splendid Isolation* (London, 1967).

'to which history hardly furnishes a parallel, of a great Christian'.

This tribute to Gladstone was more accurate than the more famous verdict of Disraeli: 'a sophisticated rhetorician inebriated with the exuberance of his own verbosity, and gifted with an egotistical imagination that can at all times command an interminable and inconsistent series of arguments to malign an opponent and to glorify himself.' From adolescence to death, Christianity was his deepest interest and most powerful inspiration – which was also true of Salisbury.

Gladstone received this faith in an Evangelical shape, from an intensely religious mother. His father, a Liverpool merchant involved in many highly profitable projects including the ownership of slaves in the West Indies, for some time associated with the Whig Unitarians dominating his prosperous city but, when he grew rich himself, became an Anglican and a Tory.[64] He had social and political ambitions which he could only fulfil by handsomely subsidizing the early career of the most brilliant of his children. The son of such parents was, not surprisingly, a prig while at Oxford after Eton. When not yet twenty he wrote an immense document beginning: 'The state of religion in Oxford is the most painful spectacle it ever befell my lot to behold.' When his attraction to the 'sublime duty' of a clergyman had been discouraged by his father, he entered the House of Commons (in 1833) in a missionary frame of mind, improving his delivery as an orator by reading other men's sermons aloud to himself. As late as 1844 he still saw himself primarily as a member of the Church of England whose vocation happened to be political leadership. As he then wrote to his intimate friend, James Hope: 'The purpose of Parliamentary life resolves itself with me simply and wholly into one question, Will it ever afford the means under God of rectifying the relations between the Church and the State and give one an opportunity of setting forward such a work?'

His first speech in the House was a defence of his father as a slave-owner. His very heavy election expenses, which at a later date would have been considered corrupt, had been met partly

---

[64] S. E. Checkland studied *The Gladstones* (Cambridge, 1971).

by his father and partly by the reactionary duke who in effect dictated to the small electorate. He proceeded to delight the duke by opposing almost all social reforms under debate. His devout eloquence pleading for no change would probably have won for him a devoted congregation, a bishopric and an archbishopric had he become the priest he always was in half his heart; and in the political life which he had accepted as his destiny he now spoke and wrote copiously in defence of the Church.

His book on *The State in its Relations with the Church* (1838) expounded his political creed. Macaulay reviewed it as a nonsensical utterance from 'the rising hope of those stern and unbending Tories', and the Tory leader Peel, who was a realist, despaired of Gladstone's future when he distastefully dipped into it. The book did indeed seem naïve. Gladstone ardently supported the establishment of the Church of England, but not because Church and State were one people (as Hooker had argued in the sixteenth century) or because it was useful to ally them for the benefit of society (as Warburton had argued in the eighteenth). There was now a plurality of Churches, but the State was a corporate 'person' with a conscience, and its sacred duty was to support the Church which taught the truth. The alternative was a nightmare: 'social atheism'. The chapter which caused most surprise was one in which Gladstone surveyed the relations of Church and State in the colonies over which Victoria had begun to rule, everywhere urging the benefits of establishing the Church of England because of its true faith. The experience of the rebellious colonies which had become the United States was dismissed. It seemed to be implied that since Anglican endowments and other privileges in Ireland could be justified on this basis although it meant favouring a minority, a similar establishment would have to be erected in India were that sub-continent ever to be brought under the direct government of Westminster.[65]

Gladstone was, however, rescued from the fate of being

---

[65] Gladstone's teaching on Church and State was examined by A. R. Vidler, *The Orb and the Cross* (London, 1947). Perry Butler, *Gladstone: Church, State and Tractarianism* (Oxford, 1982), went from 1809 to 1859.

remembered in history as 'the last man on a sinking ship' (his own phrase in 1867). He developed a theology which upheld his real convictions about the Church better than any establishment and endowment by the State – and which could continue to give strength and power to the Church after the removal of the State's support.

In the year before he went up to Oxford, he had many talks about religion with his sister Anne, his godmother and 'a perfect saint', who was ill and dying. She persuaded him to enlarge his Evangelicalism, as she had enlarged hers, by accepting 'one Baptism for the remission of sins' and by studying Richard Hooker's theory of the Church as a visible society fed by sacraments and needing beauty and order. After his graduation at Oxford in 1831 (with high honours, but without coming under the influence of the men who were to become the Tractarians), he went on a long holiday to Italy. He was not impressed by the Italian Protestants, but in St Peter's, Rome, he had a vision of the unity of Christendom as the historic body of Christ. In Naples six weeks later he examined the Book of Common Prayer closely, having no other English books to read. The study brought home to him the truth in the Catholicism which his sister had propounded – and, with that, the fact that the Church of England maintained that truth. 'It presented to me Christianity under an aspect in which I had not yet known it: its ministry of symbols, its channels of grace, its unending line of teachers joining from the Head.' So he became sure that the Evangelical acceptance of Christ was likely to lead to the Catholic acceptance of the Church. Gladstone recalled with pride meeting Charles Simeon in 1815, but twenty years later recorded an unshakeable conviction that 'in substance the movement termed Evangelical and that falsely termed Popish are parts of one great and beneficent design of God, and that in their substance they will harmonize and co-operate.'

His book *Church Principles Considered in Their Results* (1840), worked out this belief in terms of the Anglican insistence on a sacramental system authorized by bishops in 'the Apostolical Succession' – and in terms of the Anglican denial of the claims of the nineteenth-century Papacy. And these convictions stayed with him through the 'terrible time' of the early 1850s, when to his anxiety about the future of the Church of England after the Gorham Judgement were added personal sorrows including the agonized death of a daughter and the conversion to Rome of James Hope and Henry Manning, his friends who had helped him revise his books for publication.

Another factor in Gladstone's rescue from the fate awaiting eccentric ultra-Tories was the extraordinary ability which he showed in mastering the problems accompanying high political office. This work was, in his eyes, his duty as a Christian. Here, as people observed, the 'Liverpool' in his heritage showed itself beneath the 'Oxford'. Peel believed in this practical ability despite his bafflement about the operations of the young man's religious conscience. (What could Peel or anyone else in politics make of a conscience which forced him to resign while he was greatly enjoying the Presidency of the Board of Trade, merely because Peel proposed to make a grant to the Roman Catholic seminary at Maynooth in Ireland – a grant which Gladstone thought wise, but which contradicted his book of 1838?) Until old age Gladstone was respected by all MPs, and feared by his political enemies, because on suitable occasions he could give such a superb performance as a statesman. He could discern a moral issue which would appeal to the people, as no other administrator could; he could draft a long bill and steer it to triumph as an Act of Parliament, as no other visionary could; and above all he could make speeches, in the House of Commons and far outside it – speeches which stunned by the authoritative assembly of a mass of details, and which elevated by the equally authoritative announcement of a crusade in the cause of righteousness. Nor did he shirk the drudgery. Sir James Graham said of the young Gladstone that he could do in four hours what it took anyone else sixteen to do – and he worked sixteen hours a day.

Such a statesman, however puzzling his religion might be, could not be dismissed as a naïve idealist. When Disraeli had unscrupulously destroyed Peel's leadership of the old Tories, there was an attempt to enlist Gladstone for a senior position among the new Conservatives. This attempt was renewed by Disraeli in 1858 despite his own intense dislike of the man.

When Gladstone chose instead to serve as Chancellor of the Exchequer under the Whig Lord Aberdeen, the Queen was one of the many who admired his work. When Lord Palmerston had emerged as the leader of the new Liberal Party, a coalition of Whigs and Radicals, he gave Gladstone much freedom as Chancellor of the Exchequer although he, too, disliked him. Ten years of success as Chancellor of the Exchequer, laying important foundations for the mid-Victorian prosperity, were what made him 'the People's William'. It also made his identification with the Liberals so complete that he went into opposition with them in 1866. His disciple and biographer, John Morley, truthfully remarked that 'in other matters he followed, as it was his business and necessity to follow, the governing forces of the public mind; in finance he was a strenuous leader.' The direction of his leadership was towards limited although efficient government, curbing public expenditure, keeping taxation light although just, and freeing trade from control or protection. All these policies he advocated as a moralist and executed as an administrator of genius.

This career was still going strong and making history half a century after the publication of *The State in its Relations with the Church*. His contemporaries – themselves no idlers – marvelled at the sheer energy which helped him to form fresh convictions and to push through fresh programmes when almost all men would have felt that they had contributed enough. The energy derived in part from his physical fitness and toughness; tree-felling really was one of his favourite relaxations in old age. It also derived in part from his confidence about his social position. He was a handsome young man known to be a millionaire's favourite son, and after frightening off two young women with whom he was in love, he married Caroline Glynne. She was related to many of the leading Whigs and brought with her the large estate around the castle at Hawarden in North Wales. Gladstone had to put much of his own time and money into the estate in order to rescue it from mismanagement, but it assured his status. Although too aristocratic to be conventional or competent, Caroline Glynne was in many ways an excellent wife for him. Certainly he liked to have aristocrats around him in public life, but there is no evidence that he felt inferior to any of them.

Probably the most important source of his energy was, however, a rare combination of religion and sex. His religion instructed him, and helped him, to sublimate his passions by putting them into charitable and political work; but when his diaries began to be published in 1968, readers were surprised to see how fierce were his temptations and self-reproaches. It is clear that he was highly sexed, although we have no reason to doubt the truth of his statement to his son Stephen (a priest) in 1896 that he had 'not been guilty of the act which is known as that of infidelity to the marriage bed'. Throughout his adult life until 1886 (when he at last yielded to entreaties from his political associates) he devoted countless evenings and a vast sum of his own money to rescuing prostitutes.

It was Christian charity, which his wife approved of and assisted; he maintained that this form of lay work had become his when a small group of Christian young men in Oxford cast lots in seeking divine guidance about their duties. But his diaries show repeatedly that he needed the stimulus of the company of these young women; that he greatly enjoyed discussing their lives with them; and that he never pretended to himself that his motives were wholly virtuous. He refused to give up this work, even when he was blackmailed, even when he was Prime Minister. He thought it possible that reports about it helped to poison the Queen's mind against him. And even when he ceased to accost prostitutes in the street (in his mid-seventies), he still kept up correspondence with women from this background and still held private conversations with society beauties and actresses whose morals were not 'Victorian'. Nothing could show more clearly how tireless was the drive resulting from a sexual energy which had been christened.

Thus superbly equipped as a Christian statesman, Gladstone felt driven into the leadership of radical causes. It was not a rapid or complete conversion. As early as 1848 he caused a sensation by voting for the admission of Jews to the Commons; but as late as 1862 he caused another by foolishly announcing that in the American civil war the slave-owners of the southern states had 'made a nation'. When he had at last succeeded Palmerston and Lord John Russell in the leadership of the Liberals, he was still so conscious of the remaining Whig element in Liberalism – and in his own mind – that he allowed Disraeli to outmanoeuvre him by introducing a more radical proposal, so that in the end it was the Conservative party that could claim the credit for the doubling of the electorate by the Reform Act of 1867. With his divided mind Gladstone so often was an enigma. In all his governments it was again and again difficult for his colleagues to tell in advance where he would be more radical than they were, and where more conservative, and where simply bored.

Above all, he remained conservative in his loyalty to the Church of England and its historic institutions. When he was defeated in his attempt to continue to represent Oxford University in Parliament (in 1865), he wrote in his diary: 'A dear dream is dispelled.' But it never was totally dispelled. When he lay dying in great pain from cancer, he dictated his thanks for one message. 'There is no expression of Christian sympathy which I value more than that of the ancient university of Oxford, the God-fearing and God-sustaining university of Oxford. I served her, perhaps mistakenly, but to the best of my ability. My most earnest prayers are hers to the uttermost and the last.' He remained sure that there was no electoral mandate for the disestablishment of the Church of England, although he expected that to come after his death and he wished the Church to be prepared for it. He admitted that the Anglican case was weaker in Wales, but he privately described his own party's proposals for disestablishment there as 'plunder'. As the squire of a village in North Wales he saw no need to supplement the education provided by the church school. Although in 1870 his own government had created the Board Schools where religious education according to a denominational document such as the Book of Common Prayer was forbidden, in 1894 he was still asserting to his son Stephen that 'an undenominational system of religion, framed by or under the authority of the State, is a moral monster. . . . Whether the Act of 1870 requires or permits anything of the kind, I cannot say; but if it did, its provisions would involve a gross error.'

Yet he came to see that almost all the causes which he had defended as a young man were wrong. Fundamental to his development was a broadening of his religion. He never ceased to be a devout Anglican; he attended morning and evening services every day while at Hawarden, and wrote many prayers for use at Holy Communion. He was always, as he wrote to a Unitarian friend in 1865, 'one altogether attached to Christian dogma, which I believe to be the skeleton that carries the flesh, the blood, the life of the blessed thing we call the Christian religion.' But he added: 'I do not believe that God's mercies are restricted to a small portion of the human family. ... I was myself brought up ... to believe that salvation depended absolutely upon the reception of a particular and very narrow creed. But long, long have I cast those weeds behind me.'

He now repudiated the notion that the State always had a duty to support a Church – or to support that religion on which all the Churches might agree. The letter of 1894 just quoted expressed his opinion that 'the State has no charter from heaven such as may belong to the Church or to the individual conscience. It would, as I think, be better for the State to limit itself to giving secular instruction (which of course is no complete education). . . .' And he believed that if refounded on the basis of the voluntary support of its own members, an Established Church which had served only a minority of the citizens would find that it was more effective in its spiritual mission because less open to the charge of worldliness. He gave 30,000 of his own books and an endowment to St Deiniol's Library which he built in Hawarden; there the clergy of the future would equip themselves for a mission which would continue and flourish when their present privileges had been withdrawn.

His boldest demonstration of his new beliefs about Church and State was the disestablishment and partial disendowment of the Irish dioceses in the United Church of England and Ireland. When he received the Queen's summons to power in 1868, he declared: 'My mission is to pacify Ireland.'

To those who later looked back, the step seemed inevitable. Of a population of about 5,800,000 in Ireland in the 1860s, fewer than 700,000 were Anglicans. When the Irish National Association was founded in 1864, it agreed to 'demand the disendowment of the Established Church in Ireland as a condition without which peace and stability, general respect for laws, and unity of sentiment and action for national objects, can never prevail in Ireland.' So in March 1868, before the general election, Gladstone secured a majority of sixty-five in the House of Commons for motions endorsing this policy. Yet credit is due to him for his courage in seizing the initiative. Many others reckoned that the problem was too explosive to handle. That was why handling it had been postponed for so long. One question among many which had deterred British politicians was whether some of the Anglican endowments should be given to the Roman Catholics and Presbyterians – a suggestion which seemed equitable to many, but which was denounced by Anglicans as theft and by Roman Catholics and Presbyterians as a bribe. It was also very difficult to decide how much of the endowments should be left with the Anglicans (in the end the decision was: almost two-thirds the financial assets and all the buildings, with nothing going to the Roman Catholics or to the Presbyterians). The complicated and controversial Irish Church Bill needed all Gladstone's advocacy – and thus made him eat many of his own previous words; the publication of *A Chapter of Autobiography* was thought essential. His desertion of what he called 'Church Principles' was deeply resented by many of his fellow Anglicans.[66] When disestablishment came into effect on the first day of 1871, Mrs Alexander's new hymn was sung in Londonderry Cathedral:

> Look down, O Lord of heaven, on our desolation!
>   Fallen, fallen is our Country's crown,
> Dimly dawns the New Year on a churchless nation. . . .

Gladstone's reforming government was defeated in the general election of 1874 mainly because its treatment of education had alienated the Nonconformists. At sixty-five Gladstone announced his withdrawal from the Liberal leadership; he later claimed that he had 'deeply desired an interval between

---

[66] P. M. H. Bell studied *Disestablishment in Ireland and Wales* (London, 1969).

parliament and the grave'. In fact, however, he was active for another twenty years – believing, as he told a young audience, that 'life is a great and noble calling; not a mean and grovelling thing, which we are to shuffle through as we can, but an elevated and lofty destiny.' He wrote extensively on the poetry of Homer. But was he not himself born to be a hero? He edited the works of Bishop Joseph Butler. But was not life for moral action?

It was typical of his religion that his one departure from orthodoxy was to suggest that after death the wicked would simply cease to live. For him, life was righteous or it was nothing. It was also typical of his approach to ecclesiastical affairs that when he denounced 'Vaticanism' in long pamphlets after the First Vatican Council he made the mistake of concentrating his fire on the alleged Roman Catholic threat to civil obedience and political loyalty, when what happened in Rome in 1870 was the claim to a spiritual empire by the proclamation of papal infallibility at the very time when the papacy's temporal power was ended by the Italian nationalists' occupation of Rome. He thus laid himself open to devastating replies, but religion to him was politically involved or it was nothing. Examining himself in his diary during 1878, Gladstone noted: 'I am still under the painful sense that my public life is and has the best of me . . .'

His politics became the politics of liberty. 'I was brought up to distrust and dislike liberty', he told John Morley in 1891; 'I learned to believe in it. That is the key to all my changes.' And in 1876 liberty for the Bulgarians brought him back into political leadership. A revolt in Bulgaria, then a part of the Turkish empire, was brutally suppressed, and Disraeli ordered a British fleet to the Dardenelles as a warning to Russia not to interfere. In British upper-class circles these actions were generally accepted, and Disraeli had so little idea that a storm would break that he accepted an earldom from an admiring Queen and began to enjoy being Prime Minister in the tranquillity of the House of Lords. But Gladstone published his pamphlet on *The Bulgarian Horrors and the Question of the East*; and impressed an initially hostile House of Commons by the greatest speech of his whole parliamentary career, pleading for the Bulgarians as fellow Christians and fellow Europeans. After a sensational victory in a rural, Conservative constituency (Midlothian), he was inescapable as the next Liberal Prime Minister. Within his previous experience of government Britain had entered the Crimean War believing that it could forcibly support a corrupt government in Muslim Turkey without interrupting its own life as a Christian democracy interested in manufacturing and commerce. But he had been one of those who had absorbed that bitter experience of a war that brought only shame. Always after that he was for peace. He urged 'the pursuit of objects which are European by means which are European, in concert with the mind of the rest of Europe and supported by its authority.' He meant a moral authority – for when he spoke about Europe he had in mind the continent of the Christian conscience, the Europe of Dante.[67]

In domestic affairs, the Reform Act of 1884 which gave the vote to the agricultural labourers was the climax of a mental evolution which he had first made public twenty years previously, shocking Palmerston. In 1866 he had replied to the Liberal anti-democrat, Robert Lowe, that the men whose qualifications to become electors were being disparaged were 'our fellow subjects, our fellow Christians, our own flesh and blood.' He then concluded: 'You cannot fight against the future.' His failure to unite the Liberals sufficiently to obtain the credit for the enlargement of the electorate in 1867 showed that Palmerston and Lowe were by no means alone. But Gladstone's conviction could not accept defeat. 'All the world over,' he declared in 1886, 'I will back the masses against the classes. . . . The heart, the root, the beginning and ending of my trust, is in the wise and generous justice of the nation.'

The most courageous crusade of his life was his fight to win more liberty for the Irish. He came to see his moral duty to curb the profits of Ireland's landlords, most of whom lived in England, so that by the Irish Land Act of 1881 he created

---

[67] Olive Anderson studied the psychological impact of the Crimean War in *A Liberal State at War* (London, 1967). C. C. Eldridge, *England's Mission: the Imperial Idea in the Age of Gladstone and Disraeli* (London, 1973), was a study in reluctant imperialism.

tribunals to establish fair rents for tenants. He also became convinced that it was his duty to create a parliament in Dublin capable of dealing with almost all Ireland's internal affairs, and he introduced his first Home Rule Bill in 1886. It was not easy to work out a plan acceptable to the Irish, since there were two enormous problems – how to make rule from Dublin in the predominantly Roman Catholic south acceptable to the Protestants in Ulster, and how to retain an Irish element in the Westminster Parliament, where the Irish Nationalist MPs were often able to trade their votes in political deals since as a large minority they often held the balance of power between the Liberals and the Conservatives. And if such problems were difficult, the problem of how to make any plan acceptable to the majority of the British electorate seemed utterly insoluble. The 1880s and 1890s were the heyday of British imperialism – a cause promising both glory and profits, with an appeal so powerful that even Gladstone had to go along with it. Yet here was a proposal to dismember the British empire by abandoning the large island next door to Britain after an imperial connection dating back to the reign of Henry II. The emotional and economic investment of the British in Ireland was so great that by adopting Home Rule Gladstone in effect condemned his party to division (Joseph Chamberlain, his natural successor, was a Unionist) and to twenty years of paralysis.[68]

When in 1892 the Liberals were returned to power, he was still at their head, and still determined on Irish Home Rule despite bitter disagreements in his cabinet, violent storms in the Commons and rejection by the Lords. The setback only encouraged Gladstone to seek another general election with a programme of restricting the power of the Lords to block the people's path to justice and liberty. This time, however, the cabinet refused to follow him. His colleagues also refused to support him against demands for greater expenditure on the navy. Seeing that his magic was gone, he did at last retire – but even in his last few years he could not refrain from controversy. In June 1896 he sent a public letter to Rome about the

---

[68] J. L. Hammond's classic *Gladstone and the Irish Nation* was reissued with an introduction by M. R. D. Foot (London, 1964).

'ineffable emptiness' of the papal condemnation of Anglican orders. A few months later he spoke for an hour and a half at a great public meeting in Liverpool, passionately condemning the latest Turkish massacre of Armenian Christians.

He died on Ascension Day 1898. His son Stephen gave him the Church of England's last blessing just before his heart stopped beating.[69]

---

[69] Many biographies were published before Gladstone's *Diaries* began to be printed in 1968. *The Life of William Ewart Gladstone* was compiled by John, later Viscount, Morley (3 vols., 1903), and deserved its great popularity, but as an agnostic Morley was handicapped and D. C. Lathbury filled a gap by his *Correspondence on Church and Religion of William Ewart Gladstone* (2 vols., London, 1910). Of the later biographies, the best were by Sir Philip Magnus (London, 1954), E. J. Feuchtwanger (London, 1975), and Richard Shannon (vol. 1, London, 1982). D. A. Hamer was down-to-earth in *Liberal Politics in the Age of Gladstone and Rosebery* (Oxford, 1972).

CHAPTER SIX

NONCONFORMITY

A POLITICAL FAILURE

In various crises Victorian Nonconformity offered a real political threat to the Church of England. In 1847 the Protestant Dissenting Deputies sponsored committees all over the country to secure the return of MPs known to favour 'those ecclesiastical principles which constitute the sole basis of religious freedom and equality'. The Deputies' eagerness to influence general elections then dwindled, but the gap which they left was filled from 1853 onwards by the Liberation Society and its long struggle for the Church of England's disestablishment. That campaign had much to do with Palmerston's defeat in the Commons in 1857, with subsequent elections including the return of almost ninety Nonconformists in 1865, and with the triumph of the righteous Gladstone as the worldly Palmerston's successor at the head of the Liberal Party. The Liberation Society employed agents to influence the constituencies before either of the political parties did.

Nonconformity made its weight felt in the much wider pressure which led to the creation of state schools (or, to be more accurate, of locally-controlled, rate-supported 'Board Schools') under the Education Act of 1870. The State had given grants to church schools since 1833, but its direct intervention in education had been delayed partly because Nonconformity had previously been so negative. Many Nonconformists, over-optimistic about their own resources, had fought for the 'Voluntaryist' principle, campaigning against all state aid to schools. Later there had been an agitation to exclude all religious teaching from any school which was supported by public money. Still in 1870 there was intense resentment against church schools. Only slowly had Noncon-

formists admitted that they would never be able to match the
Church of England's network, so that local School Boards were
essential if education was to be made compulsory between the
ages of five and thirteen. Even slower had been the agreement
that the local board could arrange non-denominational religious education – so deep and embittering had been the
suspicion of Anglican influence.[1]

Other pressures persuaded Parliament to allow Nonconformist ministers to conduct funerals in parish churchyards, and
to create parish councils, elected by all, which would take over
the responsibility for village administration which had been
the monopoly of the Anglican incumbent, churchwardens and
vestry. These two reforms were postponed until 1880 and 1894.
The comment is fair that 'there was not a single issue on which
the Anglican Church met them with generosity. It yielded its
privileges only when it was compelled to do so.'[2] Almost
three-quarters of the Anglican clergy signed protests against
the admission of Nonconformist funerals.

Nothing, however, was done to remedy the Liberation
Society's main grievance: the Church of England's establishment. Indeed, in this crusade even the Liberation Society lost
heart – and lost subscribers. Queen Victoria's successor took
exactly the same oath to defend the Established Church that
Queen Anne had taken, and as the twentieth century dawned
bishops maintained their medieval positions in the House of
Lords. At this central point, all the Nonconformist pressures
failed – and we must ask why.

Some of the explanation is to be found in the recovery of
morale in the Church of England, giving some slight excuse for
Anglican arrogance. In 1859 the Church Institution was
founded 'for defensive and general purposes', and by the 1880s

---

[1] Recent studies include A. B. Bishop, *The Rise of a Central Authority for English
Education* (Cambridge, 1971), and, for local battles, Derek Fraser, *Urban Politics in
Victorian England* (Leicester, 1976).

[2] R. Tudor Jones, *Congregationalism in England*, p. 276. W. H. Mackintosh told the
story of the Liberation Society in *Disestablishment and Liberation* (London, 1972), and
G. I. T. Machin studied *Politics and the Churches in Great Britain 1832–68*. A
particularly notorious case after the death of a child aged two was reconstructed by
Ronald Fletcher, *The Akenham Burial Case* (London, 1974).

it was printing half a million tracts a year. But even before the Anglican recovery could make itself felt in politics, the Church of England was in a position stronger than appeared. The Whig statesmen on whom the Nonconformists had to rely before the 1860s simply assumed in their hearts that the Church always would remain established; it was part of the country they loved, part of the constitution which needed only improvement. Lord Melbourne despised the Nonconformists, as did Lord Palmerston. Lord John Russell owed more to them, but he was himself firmly a Protestant layman of the Church of England, and when denouncing the new Roman Catholic dioceses in 1850 he spoke with enthusiasm about the rights of the bishops whom the Queen nominated. As a modern authority on the period has written: 'The Whigs were at no time prepared to lead a central attack on the Church of England, and without Whig parliamentary leadership organized Dissent could do very little. They were formidable in agitation; they were effective in obstruction. . . . What they could not do was to formulate and impose a policy of their own. They lacked the unity, the positive organization and still more the human material for parliamentary strength.'[3]

Essentially the same problem remained when the Whig Party gradually became the Liberal Party, guided by a slightly more popular leadership and supported by a much more popular press. Naturally this party attracted many votes from Nonconformists since it was the only alternative to the Conservatives. Indeed, some wealthy, confident and well-known Nonconformists, mainly from Yorkshire and Lancashire, now sat as Liberals in Parliament and one of them, John Bright, joined the cabinet in 1868. But some equally prominent Liberals with more conservative instincts went against Nonconformity in two test-cases of public morality in the 1860s, supporting the more aristocratic south in the American civil war and applauding Governor Eyre when he returned from Jamaica accused of excessive cruelty to the negroes. Many Wesleyan Methodists in Yorkshire and Lancashire continued

---

[3] Norman Gash, *Reaction and Reconstruction in English Politics 1832–52* (Oxford, 1965), p. 108.

to vote Conservative, and the Liberation Society itself opposed
unsatisfactory Liberal candidates in elections even when this
meant letting in a Conservative.[4]

John Bright's own life illustrates the difficulty of applying
Nonconformity to mid-Victorian politics. He was born (in
1811) and he died (in 1889) in the Lancashire town of Rochdale, and was brought up in a Quaker home. His powers as an
orator were discovered through the agitation against the landowners' corn laws, and he was often ready to attack the Church
of England; as late as 1883 he spoke on 'The National Church
and National Righteousness', contrasting the two. Since he
was also a man of independent means (his father was a
successful mill-owner), he seemed the natural political leader
of Nonconformity. Yet he was unhappy as an MP – and not
only because his wife refused to join him so far south as
London. A series of nervous breakdowns forced him to resign
from office under Gladstone and to curtail his political activities during the rest of his life. The tension was probably due to
his failure to reconcile his Quaker heritage with the facts of
power as he experienced them. Although he advocated peace
and resigned from Gladstone's government when it bom-
barded the Egyptians in Alexandria in 1882, he did not
concentrate on the international vision as did his fellow crusader against the corn laws, Richard Cobden. Although he advocated the vote for all, he disapproved of the Public Health Act
of 1848 (which launched the struggle to clean up England's
cities); of Lord Shaftesbury's crusade to improve factory traditions; and of later trade unionism. He refused to join the
anti-slavery agitation and the pressure to have alcohol prohibited locally; and he was no more than a 'looker-on' when the
Nonconformists demanded popular education free of Anglican
interference. As firmly as any Whig grandee in former times,
John Bright declined a call to become the preachers' tame
spokesman in Westminster.[5]

---

[4] See John Vincent, *The Formation of the British Liberal Party 1857–68* (London,
1966), and P. F. Clarke, *Lancashire and the New Liberalism* (Cambridge, 1971).

[5] Keith Robbins supplied a biography of *John Bright* (London, 1979). Donald
Read explored an often uneasy partnership in *Cobden and Bright* (London, 1967).

It comes as no surprise that although the Liberal Party emerging in 1859 relied heavily on the votes of Nonconformists, its refusal to cut off all aid to the Church of England's schools and to disestablish the Church killed off the enthusiasm. In 1877 Gladstone cannot have felt able to take the future for granted when he declared that 'Nonconformity supplies the backbone of English Liberalism'. The alliance survived this coolness partly because Disraeli was even more suspect. Lloyd George was to recall from his childhood the Welsh minister's prayer: 'Kill him, O Lord, kill him. We cannot kill him without being hanged ourselves, but thou canst kill him.' It was, however, also a factor that Nonconformity itself, in its disillusionment, was becoming discouraged about the prospects of disestablishment in England. Although the Liberation Society resolved in 1874 that 'the now shattered Liberal Party' needed the cause of disestablishment for its own reconstruction, a number of Nonconformist leaders voiced doubts about the wisdom of aggression, and after 1874 the loudest spokesmen for the cause were John Morley, who as an agnostic wanted a secular state, and Joseph Chamberlain, who was a Unitarian but above all a modernizer. Chamberlain's 'Alternative Programme' of 1885 incorporated Morley's proposal that all churches and cathedrals built before 1818 should be shared between the denominations or turned over to secular uses – a proposal which further alarmed many Nonconformists as being needlessly provocative.

It is conceivable that Chamberlain's radicalism, had he persisted in it, might have gradually won over many of these Nonconformists who hesitated, since they or their successors accepted Gladstone's more cautious movement to 'trust the people'. It seems possible to speculate that had the Liberal Party backed by the Nonconformists championed working-class interests earlier, it might have been able to resist more successfully the argument that an Independent Labour Party was needed in the 1890s. There might have been many more Liberals such as Joseph Arch, the farm-worker and Primitive Methodist lay preacher in Warwickshire, who led the sensational strike of 1872; or the miner Thomas Burt (the first working man to enter the House of Commons, in 1874); or the

stonemason Henry Broadhurst, secretary of the Parliamentary
Committee of the Trades Union Congress for many years from
1875, and briefly a junior minister under Gladstone (the first
working man to serve in a British government); or the engineering apprentice John Burns, President of the Local Government Board in 1905 (the first working man to enter a British
cabinet). Even if one judges that the birth of the Labour Party
was inevitable, one can see that a stronger involvement of the
Nonconformist–Liberal alliance to encourage working-class
progress would have strengthened the 'Lib–Lab' element in
politics at the beginning of the new century and thus would
have grown a larger crop of Christian, and definitely non-
Marxist, Socialism. Later on there would have been more
Labour leaders like Arthur Henderson, Philip Snowden and
Ellen Wilkinson. All were among the chief architects of the
twentieth-century Labour Party and all were deeply convinced
Methodists. Blake's poem about Christ in England, 'And did
those feet . . . ?', was often sung at Labour Party meetings. It
might have meant more than it usually did.

However, most Nonconformists seem to have had little
interest in Socialism.[6] The decision of the Trades Union
Council in 1894 to support 'the nationalization of the land and
of the whole means of production, distribution and exchange'
aroused the scorn of the *Primitive Methodist Magazine*. Liberal
leaders left it to the Conservatives in 1875 to change the law
which had exposed strikers to prosecution and imprisonment
as conspirators to 'restrain trade'. Their lethargy in the matter
was ominous. Gladstone championed Home Rule for Ireland
rather than any of the causes dearer to the Nonconformists. His
successor was an immensely rich landlord, the Earl of Rosebery. The Liberal programme in the 1895 election was heavily
indebted to the Nonconformists, but Rosebery made a thoroughly incongruous champion of it and the electorate's verdict
reduced the number of Liberal MPs to the lowest point since
the 1860s. 'Down goes the middle-class Radicalism and the

---

[6] Robert F. Wearmouth rejoiced in *Methodism and the Struggle of the Working Classes
1850–1900* (Leicester, 1954) and *The Social and Political Influence of Methodism in the
Twentieth Century* (London, 1957). But Robert Moore, *Pit-Men, Preachers and Politics*
(Cambridge, 1974), corrected some exaggerated claims.

Nonconformist conscience', wrote Canon Scott Holland; but these old causes had already gone down in the minds of the Liberal leaders in the twilight of the age of Gladstone.[7]

Rosebery resigned as leader (although his sadly isolated life did not end until 1929), and was free to attack social radicalism openly when the Liberals next returned to power. But the Boer War then brought a fresh division. It was applauded by many Liberals but in 1901 just over half the Nonconformist ministers in England signed a protest against it. Agitated efforts were now made to bind Nonconformity more tightly to Liberalism; R. W. Perks, an MP who was a Wesleyan Methodist and a Liberal imperialist, formed the Nonconformist Parliamentary Committee for this purpose in 1898. But not many Nonconformists could stomach efficiency and imperialism as Liberalism's new creed, and it was only the increased support for church schools in the Conservatives' Education Act of 1902 that revived the old spirit of battle. Anger about education helped to ensure the election of about two hundred MPs from a Nonconformist background in 1906, in a landslide victory for the Liberals. A modern scholar reckons that this anger 'transformed – seemingly overnight – the Nonconformist commitment to Liberalism from a vague sentiment to an active electoral alliance.'[8]

All the hesitations and controversies over radicalism at home and imperialism abroad were forgotten in 1906. For a few years Liberalism and Nonconformity marched hand in hand as in the golden days of Gladstonian crusading, to rescue the ratepayer from captivity in that den of privileged Anglicanism or Roman Catholicism, the church school. But the fervour of the alliance did not last, as we shall see. In general the lesson of this story of ups and downs seems to be that Nonconformity was effective on religious or moral, not political, territory. Its political aim was usually negative, opposing the Established Church but having no clear vision of an alternative society. It never won the total allegiance of a major statesman, or formed

---

[7] See R. R. James, *Rosebery* (London, 1963), and H. C. G. Matthew, *The Liberal Imperialists* (Oxford, 1973). Ian Bradley provided a good overview of Victorian Liberalism in *The Optimists* (London, 1980).

[8] Stephen Koss, *Nonconformity in Modern British Politics* (London, 1975), p. 38.

a strongly coherent and inflexibly determined group in Parliament.

Part of the reason was that it never developed a sophisticated culture as soil in which effective political activity – about education, for example – might grow. Politics often seemed to the Nonconformists a dirty business, to be redeemed only for a time when some prophet arose to lead a moral crusade against a flagrant iniquity; and when the crusade ran out of energy, the previous feeling that saints ought not to be troubled about the world reasserted itself, coupled with the feeling that the saints would be rewarded for their virtuous private lives by financial prosperity. Victorian novels abound in conflicts between enlightened but isolated Nonconformists and the armies of their narrow-minded co-religionists who were in full retreat from the world, apart from the need and the duty to make money. The tradition was still going strong in 1901 when Arnold Bennett's *Anna of the Five Towns* portrayed the sensitive women surrounded by money-minded Methodists in Staffordshire. Mrs Oliphant's *Salem Chapel* (1865) is the story of a young minister who resigns, disgusted with the gossip and backbiting in his congregation; her own brother William had a similar experience. Mrs Gaskell's *Ruth* (1853) is the story of another minister who supports an unmarried mother against the Pharisaical condemnation of laymen in the chapel; the novel outraged the congregation to which her husband ministered in Manchester. Mrs Gaskell's *Cousin Phillis* (1864) is mainly an idyll of innocent rural Nonconformity, with hymns rising as the sun sets, but it does include a scene where the saintly minister is rebuked for his sins by his fellow ministers; he must be a sinner, because God has sent 'brain fever' to his child Phillis.[9]

The protest against Nonconformity's narrow-mindedness was made with a clumsy sincerity in the work of William Hale White, the most extensive treatment of chapel life in nineteenth-century fiction.

His forefathers had belonged to the chapel in Bedford named after John Bunyan, but he was disgusted when simple and sensible inquiries about the Bible which he made when in

---

[9] The best study is Angus Easson, *Elizabeth Gaskell* (London, 1979).

training to be a minister were silenced with anger by his ultra-orthodox teachers; his own father defended him on this occasion in a pamphlet entitled *To Think or not to Think*. He was even more disgusted by what he saw of everyday Nonconformist narrowness and humbug once his eyes were adult and open. So his pilgrimage led him from Bunyan's chapel into the wilderness of a civil service job and journalism in London, just as it led the hero of his most famous novels, Mark Rutherford, to seek deliverance from chapel life. The poems of Wordsworth, the books of Thomas Carlyle, his own cruelly honest thinking about himself and his contemporaries – all these made him radically dissatisfied with the debased Puritanism which he had encountered, although he was never able to find any alternative to make his brooding, self-torturing, soul happy. In vain did he tell himself and his readers that it was his duty to be happy. 'The highest form of martyrdom', he wrote, '. . . is not living for the sake of a cause, but living without one, merely because it is your duty to live.'[10]

In his *Culture and Anarchy* (1869), Matthew Arnold summed up the impression which this political and cultural failure left on many sensitive Victorians. 'Look at the life imaged in such a newspaper as the *Nonconformist* – a life of jealousy of the Establishment, disputes, tea meetings, openings of chapels, sermons; and then think of it as an ideal of human life completing itself on all sides, and aspiring with all its organs after sweetness, light and perfection!'

A RELIGIOUS STRENGTH

Victorian Nonconformity inherited a powerful position in English religion. The official census of churchgoing taken on Sunday 30 March 1851 suggested that there were about 4,500,000 attendances at the principal Nonconformist chapels, only some 800,000 fewer than attendances in all the Church of

---

[10] Wilfred Stone studied *The Religion and Art of W. Hale White* (Stanford, Cal., 1954), and Irvin Stock, *William Hale White: Mark Rutherford* (London, 1956). A comprehensive study of Nonconformity in the nineteenth-century novel by Valentine Cunningham was entitled *Everywhere Spoken Against* (Oxford, 1975).

England's churches. In Wales, where Anglicanism had been established since Tudor times, more than eighty per cent of worshippers were non-Anglicans. But this inherited position needed to be renewed by a constant supply of personal commitment, and particularly in the 1850s anxious Nonconformists asked whether the supply was still flowing. The scandal of the schisms in Methodism coincided with a national mood of militarism responding to the Crimean War and the Indian mutiny. In the towns there were cholera epidemics and in the countryside there was distress. In 1854 the Primitive Methodist Conference recorded that 'provisions have risen, to the humbler classes of society, to almost starving price. The result is that thousands who were cheerful supporters of the Connexional Funds, and creditable members of society, have fainted beneath the pressure of poverty, and withdrawn from Church fellowship'.[11] Declining zeal, it was observed, explained the malaise among Nonconformists able to contribute to funds and to play their parts in chapel life. In 1846 the *Baptist Record* had reckoned that the Evangelical revival was exhausted. 'There are many indubitable signs of spiritual depression, of diminished vitality and power. Nor is this state of things confined to ourselves; wherever the results of close observation have been made known, we are called to notice the same melancholy fact.'

However, Victorian Nonconformity's religious progress was soon resumed. The *Christian World*, founded in 1857 as an organ for Nonconformity, soon achieved the largest circulation of the serious religious weeklies (over a hundred thousand). The revivalist meetings at the end of the 1850s spread enthusiasm, and the celebration in 1862 of the departure of the Dissenters from the Church of England was no occasion either for nostalgia or for reconciliation with the Anglicans; it inspired a spurt of chapel-building. And the forty years after 1862 saw much continuous vitality. In 1897 a Methodist leader, Hugh Price Hughes, boasted that a council of the Free Churches would represent 'a majority of the Christian people of England'. Obviously this boast depended on not reckoning either the Roman

---

[11] H. B. Kendall compiled *A History of the Primitive Methodist Church* (London, 1919).

Catholics or the Church of England's occasional church-goers among the 'Christian people', but the statistics quoted by Hughes were undeniably impressive. The Free Churches had, it was claimed, 1,807,723 communicants, almost 30,000 more than the Church of England. They had 327,685 Sunday School teachers, about 173,000 more; and 3,103,285 pupils, about 774,000 more. They could seat just over 7,600,000 people in their churches, about 832,000 more. And other figures which Hughes did not quote were also to the credit of the Free Churches. They had under 9,000 full-time ministers as compared with over 21,000 clergy in the Church of England. Healthily, they relied on the support of their own lay members to lead the life of some 20,000 chapels. Of particular importance were some 48,000 lay preachers. More than 1,750,000 English people were full members of these congregations, only about a quarter of a million fewer than those who at Easter presented themselves at the altars of the Church of England. Since the population of England grew immensely in the second half of the nineteenth century, Nonconformity never escaped the haunting sense of the unconverted masses; yet in each denomination the growth of full membership during that period gave encouragement. In round figures the Wesleyan Methodists grew to 435,000 from 240,000; the Primitive Methodists to 200,000 from 100,000; the Congregationalists to 258,000 from 165,000; the Baptists to 243,000 from 140,000.[12]

The 'temperance' campaign was an important example of mainly Nonconformist activity, for alcoholism was a major social problem. When the Victorian age opened alcohol had come to dominate daily life, to an extent which was disastrous for health, for thrift and for a rational expenditure on food, housing, clothing, culture and other goods. Spirits were the ruin of rich and poor alike, combined with too many bottles of

---

[12] Ian Sellers, *Nineteenth-Century Nonconformity*, and David Thompson, *Nonconformity in the Nineteenth Century*, are helpful about the Victorians as well as about their predecessors. John Briggs and Ian Sellers have collected documents illustrating *Victorian Nonconformity* (London, 1973). Kenneth Young collected more personal memories in his *Chapel* (London, 1972). *Chapels and Meeting Places* as architecture were studied by Kenneth Lindley (London, 1969). For the distribution of Nonconformity, see John D. Gay, *The Geography of Religion in England* (London, 1971).

port for rich men and too many gallons of beer for poor men (and women and children). Heavy drinking seemed essential because water and milk were both too dangerous, because cooking was often primitive, because homes were often squalid, and because social gatherings without this aid seemed intolerably dull. Because there was no alternative accommodation, committees and societies tended to meet in public houses – and to refresh themselves. And it was by no means easy to find an answer appropriate to a free people. In order to reduce the consumption of spirits, the trade in beer was freed from almost all taxes and restrictions in 1830, but now that a pint of beer was as cheap as a cup of tea naturally the consumption of beer increased dramatically without harming the sale of spirits. A similar effect was achieved when the wine trade was encouraged in 1860.

The result of these disappointments was the growth of the self-denying 'total abstinence' movement, the United Kingdom Alliance for this purpose being founded by a Baptist and a Quaker in 1853. At the end of the 1870s the 'blue ribbon' for those who had taken 'the pledge' spread to England from America, again with Nonconformist support. There was an accompanying agitation to discipline those unable to take such vows for themselves, leading to the re-imposition of firm licensing restrictions on the drink trade as a whole. In 1876 no fewer than 23,000 people were sent to prison for drunk and disorderly behaviour. 'Bands of Hope' were formed for young people who had taken the pledge against alcohol and were urging their elders to be brave; by the end of the century there were three million such children. 'Coffee palaces' and similar establishments were opened to assist these elders. The People's Café Company, directed by the great Congregationalist and philanthropist Samuel Morley, began its work in 1874, using the French name because that word was so strange to England. The first non-alcoholic music hall, the Old Vic, was opened in 1880. But 'the trade' hit back in alliance with the Conservative Party (heavily funded by brewers), and the enemies of alcohol were divided on key questions – should the restrictions be national or should local restrictions be merely permitted by national legislation? And should the aim be total prohibition?

A bill to permit local prohibition was introduced by a Nonconformist MP, Sir Wilfrid Lawson, each year between 1864 and
1880. It was never passed, but during the 1880s the customs of
using public houses to pay wages and to hold committee
meetings at election time were prohibited, and during the
1890s Sir William Harcourt revived Lawson's campaign, con-
tributing to the Liberal disaster in 1895. The battle continued
until the 1920s, when it became clear that the 'pleasures of the
poor' could now be varied and satisfactory enough to reduce
the temptation of drunkenness, while the problems of the poor
were clearly no longer attributable mainly to drink. It seems
fair to conclude that although total abstinence arose as a
working-class movement in the 1830s outside all the Churches,
a fight so prolonged and so confused could never have been
sustained without the religious determination put into it by
the Nonconformists. They had as allies some Church of
England people (usually Evangelicals) and a few Roman
Catholics.[13]

The moral fervour which attempted to dry up this ocean of
alcohol also encouraged many thousands of Nonconformists to
take part in the campaign led by Cobden and Bright in the
1840s to get cheaper food for industrial workers by repealing
the protectionist corn laws.[14] And they responded eagerly to
some later calls such as Gladstone's denunciation of the mas-
sacres of the Bulgarians – when, as Gladstone wrote privately,
'there is now, the first time for a good many years, a virtuous
passion'. Where the Nonconformists were united in such a
passion they could make their strength felt decisively, and
shrewd politicians made their calculations accordingly. At the
end of Victoria's reign Joseph Chamberlain begged the Conservative party managers to remember this strength, and when
to his horror he saw it massing against the Conservatives he
produced 'tariff reform' in an effort to attract votes in the

---

[13] See Brian Harrison, *Drink and the Victorians* (London, 1971), with more details
in Kathleen Heasman's chapter on 'Gospel Temperance' in her *Evangelicals in
Action*. For a parallel movement, see John Wigley, *The Rise and Fall of the Victorian
Sunday* (Manchester, 1980).

[14] Norman McCord studied *The Anti-Corn Law League 1838–46* (London, 1958).

Midlands and the north by the promise of protection against American and German industrial competition. Chamberlain's revival of protectionism did not, however, get many of those votes. Vote-getting crusades could not be manufactured to order. Gladstone himself discovered this when he failed to arouse Nonconformist enthusiasm for Home Rule in Ireland since it seemed too like Rome Rule.

The life of the mind was not entirely neglected, but no major theologian left behind a literary monument to Victorian Nonconformity. On the contrary, the concentration on preaching seemed to be so important and so satisfactory that there was little energy left for quiet and independent wrestling with the new questions posed by science or by historical research into the Bible. The great men were not professors but preachers – for example, R. F. Horton who fascinated the Hampstead intellectuals but also drew some working men because he was so clearly honest, or Alexander Maclaren, whose steady preaching from the Bible filled Union Chapel, Manchester, with businessmen for forty-five years from 1858.[15] And most of the preachers remained conservatively Evangelical until the 1870s or 1880s. A storm was aroused among Congregationalists by the publication of a liberal (and sentimental) collection of *Hymns for Heart and Voice* edited by T. T. Lynch in 1855. In 1857 Samuel Davidson was forced to resign as a professor at the Lancashire Independent College in Manchester because he had thrown doubt on the Mosaic authorship of the first books in the Bible. As late as 1884 the editor of a magazine for preachers, the *Expositor*, was dismissed by its publishers because he had shown too much willingness to expound the results of German biblical criticism. From the 1870s onwards there was widespread acceptance of the critical approach to the Bible among ministers, but even in 1888 a fairly mild presentation of this approach, R. F. Horton's *Inspiration and the Bible*, was still able to produce a shock. Up to the end of the century, Nonconformist preachers who wanted to be 'progressive' had to rely mainly on the stimulus of intellectual imports from Germany, from Scotland and even from the Church of Eng-

---

[15] See Albert Peel and J. A. R. Marriott, *Robert Forman Horton* (London, 1937).

land; and there was a tendency to reduce the suggestiveness of those imports before passing them on to the laity.[16]

The most effective reply to Matthew Arnold's strictures on Nonconformist culture eventually came in the shape of two adjacent colleges in Oxford – Mansfield College, a Congregational foundation, and Manchester College, sponsored by the Unitarians.

˜ These colleges were in effect the creation of two notable theologians, Andrew Fairbairn and James Martineau. Fairbairn, a Scot with Evangelical convictions, fell under the influence of German theological liberalism without ceasing to be a devout believer in the unique saviourhood of Christ. A scholar whose reading was wider than theirs, he was well able to hold his own with the Anglicans when Mansfield College was established under him in 1886. He wrote a series of books on current religious problems without ceasing to be at the service of Congregational churches all over England.

The Unitarian leader James Martineau was even more distinguished. After a long preaching ministry to an intelligent and affluent congregation in Liverpool, he became a part-time professor and then principal at the Unitarian college first in Manchester and then in London, combining this with pastoral work. He, too, was a prolific author. He opposed the idea of a further move to Oxford, but when he had retired the foundation stone of Manchester College was laid (in 1891) and his own thought provided the new college's main inspiration. When he died aged ninety-five in 1900 it was said of him by an ex-Anglican, Stopford Brooke: 'The victory that the ideas of God and Immortality are now beginning to secure over their enemies is largely due to Martineau's stern and quiet leadership, under the banners of the intellect and the conscience, of the soldiers of religion.' It was always his contention that religion need not be either dogmatic or 'rational' (conceding almost everything to intellectual criticism) in order to be real. He discounted miracles; 'miraculous events cannot be regarded as adequately attested, in the presence of natural

---

[16] Willis B. Glover studied *Evangelical Nonconformists and Higher Criticism in the Nineteenth Century* (London, 1954).

causes accounting for belief in their occurrence.' His main concern was to defend belief in God as the basis of ethics. In *Loss and Gain in Recent Theology* (1881) he claimed that, in relation to that supreme purpose, the loss of 'External Authority' in religious belief was sheer gain. In reply to Anglican dogmatism, he wrote as early as 1839: 'We believe, no less than you, in an infallible Revelation . . . you in a Revelation of an unintelligible Creed to the understanding; we in a Revelation of moral perfection, and the spirit of duty in the heart; you in a Revelation of the metaphysics of Deity; we in a Revelation of the character and providence of the infinite Father; you in a Redemption which saves the few, and leaves with Hell the triumph after all; we in a Redemption which shall restore to all at the length the image and immortality of God.'

Fairbairn and Martineau held different views about Christ's divinity, but the quality of their thought was a quietly devastating reply to Matthew Arnold's charge that Nonconformists were uncultured 'Philistines'. Surely there would have been more thinkers of this quality, had Nonconformists been allowed more access to higher education.[17]

FORWARD INTO THE CITIES

'Almost every village of any size has two distinct sets of apparatus for doing good', Edward Miall reminded the House of Commons in 1871 '– the one worked by Churchmen, the second by Dissenters. Every town has its exclusive circles of social intercourse – the one appropriated to Churchmen, the other to Dissenters.' And the strategic decision of Victorian Nonconformity was to throw this strength to be seen in the villages into the battle for souls in the new cities and their suburbs. The measure of success achieved in this battle perhaps explained why on the whole Nonconformity did not display a consistent and implacable anger against the estab-

---

[17] W. B. Selbie provided *The Life of Andrew Martin Fairbairn* (London, 1915), and James Drummond and C. B. Upton, *The Life and Letters of James Martineau* (2 vols., London, 1902), supplemented by J. E. Carpenter, *James Martineau* (London, 1905).

lishment of the Church of England. Joseph Chamberlain, who believed that Gladstone had 'suddenly sprung his Irish policy upon the country . . . to prevent one from placing the disestablishment of the Church of England in the forefront of the Liberal programme', was impatient with Nonconformity's political caution. He once burst out that because they had refused to follow him against Gladstone 'you Nonconformists have got nothing – nothing'. It was not true. In the cities and towns of Victorian England, the Free Churches could win many victories without Chamberlain's help. They were religious victories.

In 1843 a widely discussed book by a Congregational Minister, Robert Vaughan, announced the arrival of *The Age of the Great Cities*. The importance of the new urban age became a constant theme of the Nonconformists' publications and conferences, and thousands of ministers resolved either to draw crowds into the existing inner-city chapels or to build new 'churches' (a more respectable word increasingly preferred) in the suburbs to which the middle classes retreated. In the last quarter of the nineteenth century the Congregationalists, for instance, built some five hundred new churches. Success in Birmingham or Manchester or the industrial towns of Yorkshire was encouraging, and London remained the Jerusalem of the new crusade. 'Our watchword should now be "London and the large towns!" ' declared the secretary of the Home Missionary Society of the Congregationalists in 1861. In 1885 the Wesleyan Methodist Conference agreed that 'this great centre of national, imperial world-life is the prize, the citadel, for which the powers of light and darkness must contend.' There was a special significance in this ambition to storm London, in that the 1851 religious census had shown that Methodism was fairly strong in England's cities and large towns – apart from London.

This battle for the city was seen to be urgent since it was fully appreciated that Nonconformity was suffering from the decline of British agriculture towards the end of the century. The Baptist Union Council commented in 1893: 'Many years ago . . . the tenant farmers of this country were the backbone of religious Nonconformity. That class of supporters may today

be looked for almost in vain among our village churches.' The
Primitive Methodists found in 1896 that three-quarters of their
chapels were in villages but that 516 'societies' had been closed
during the last twenty-five years and only 236 begun. Both the
Baptists and the Primitive Methodists might have yielded to
the temptation to accept decline; because the population in the
villages was decreasing, it could have been assumed that these
denominations must decrease. Instead, both bodies were active in the fight to plant Nonconformity in towns and cities.[18]

Considerable success rewarded the Nonconformist urban
mission, even in London. Although the Nonconformists failed
to draw either the rich or the really poor, a census of churchgoing in London published in 1904 showed that they had
slightly more success than any other religious body with the
lower middle and working classes. The numbers of working
people's children in their Sunday schools were very large,
although the common working-class attitude was that only
children needed to go to church or chapel Sunday by Sunday.
The Nonconformist share of the total population of London
had declined since a census organized by the *British Weekly* in
1886–7, but not so badly as the Church of England's share.[19]

Basically, what the Nonconformists were now providing for
a minority in the cities was what they had provided in many
villages (for Methodists, more in the north and the south and
for Congregationalists and Baptists more in the east and the
west than in either the north or the south). Studies of rural
Nonconformity have shown how difficult it is to make true
generalizations since the villages differed greatly, but one
constant factor was that the chapel flourished most easily in
villages where there was no resident landowner in league with
a resident parson. Like flowers growing on a wall wherever
they could find a little soil, in these villages Nonconformity
had offered intense fellowships where there was no rival
centre, and the exploration of the inner world of mind and
spirit where there was no rival teacher. And that was what

---

[18] Some useful studies were collected in *The Church in Town and Countryside*, ed.
Derek Baker (Oxford, 1979).

[19] Hugh McLeod analysed the social background in London in *Class and Religion
in the Late Victorian City* (London, 1974).

was offered to the inhabitants of the unchurched new cities.[20]

Naturally biblical language was used in the new urban mission, but as a rule the tone of Nonconformity was not hostile to the more respectable pleasures of mankind. 'Hell fire' preaching was less frequent than later generations have tended to suppose.

We can take the life of a small body, the Quakers, as an illustration of some wider tendencies in Nonconformity. At the beginning of the Victorian age the Quakers were strongly under the influence of the Evangelical revival. In 1835 a Manchester businessman, Isaac Crewdon, published *A Beacon to the Society of Friends*, in which he urged the supremacy of the Bible over the tradition which extolled the 'inner light' in every man. He also urged that worship should be Bible-based rather than a silence leading to individual testimonies. Later he advocated the use of the two sacraments, Baptism and Holy Communion. This Evangelical influence persisted. It meant that almost all the Victorian Quakers resisted suggestions that they should join the Unitarians, and it meant an emphasis on benevolent activity rather than on passive quiet. But the Evangelical influence was limited. In England the Quakers consistently refused to accept a paid preaching ministry (accepted by the American Quakers); they refused to adopt any creed or doctrinal declaration; and they refused to be guided by Isaac Crewdon's beacon, so that he left to found his own small sect.

The changes which did secure the approval of the Victorian Quakers were all designed to bridge the very gap which separated their heritage from the society around them. In 1860 it was agreed that they need no longer wear distinctive dress or face expulsion if they married outside the Society of Friends – two traditional features of Quaker life which had been the main causes of the society's numerical decline from about twenty thousand full members in 1800 to about fourteen thousand in 1860. A feature of the history of the Victorian Quakers is their outstanding leadership in business life; from this small society came household names such as the Lloyds and Barclays

---

[20] Alan Everitt studied *The Pattern of Rural Dissent: The Nineteenth Century* (Leicester, 1972).

in banking, the Rowntrees, Cadburys and Frys in cocoa and other food, Clarks in shoes, Bryant and May in matches, Allen and Hanbury in pharmacy, Reckitts in starch. But the record in philanthropy was not quite so bold. Although the Quakers continued to be active in many good works such as prison reform, adult education, the defence of peace and the suppression of prostitution, they mostly failed to support the movement to improve the conditions of industrial workers while that 'factory movement' was battling; they were too closely identified with the vested interests of the manufacturers. Later in the century, however, Joseph Rowntree of York and George Cadbury of Birmingham thoroughly earned their national reputations as model employers, and Rowntree closely studied the workers' problems.[21]

The story of the Unitarians is somewhat similar. At the beginning of the Victorian age the energy of the Evangelical insistence on Christ's divinity provoked many Unitarians into a more eager denial of that divinity. No longer fearing the blasphemy laws, this aggressive Unitarianism remained a force throughout the century, with its own training college for ministers and its own denomination, the Unitarian Association. Unitarians of this sort could be found among the ranks of secularists and the Socialists. But the congregations gathered by this militant message were mainly working-class. Unitarians who were socially superior liked to think of themselves as heirs of the English Presbyterian tradition, and opposed any new denominational identity. They set themselves to be moderate and generous, keeping something of the old belief that God was incarnate in Christ but adding that he was also incarnate in every other member of the human race. Mrs Adams, who wrote the universally acceptable hymn 'Nearer my God to thee' for a Unitarian chapel in 1840, briefly acknowledged the need to be raised by 'a cross' but also implied a high estimate of the Victorian worshipper's own ability to get nearer.

The Unitarian belief in the dignity of everyman did not

---

[21] Elizabeth Isichei, *Victorian Quakers* (Oxford, 1970), is the best study of any denomination in this period.

remain mere rhetoric; it produced some memorable pioneers in uplifting humanity. William Rathbone and Charles Booth were rich Liverpool businessmen, distressed because good deeds were done so inefficiently; the one organized district and workhouse nursing and was the main founder of the Charity Organization Society, the other studied London's social problems with a thoroughness without precedent. Mary Carpenter created 'reformatories' to keep juvenile delinquents out of prisons; Henry Solly 'working men's clubs' to keep their fathers out of public houses; Mary Beard 'nursery schools' to give some help to their overburdened mothers. The 'domestic missions' run by Unitarian congregations in many towns were originally 'domestic' in that the poor were visited and advised in their own homes, but special Sunday evening services and other activities on church premises developed, inaugurating the 'institutional church' which many other Nonconformists copied. Much of all this activity was inspired by the example of philanthropic Unitarianism in New England, then at its height in energy and prestige.

The richer Unitarians delighted to build churches in a medieval or Gothic style; for, whatever a pope might say, they found no difficulty in thinking of their creed as liberal Catholicism. James Martineau wrote that 'for nearly fifty years I have been a most unwilling Nonconformist'. The magazine conducted by the moderates who shared Martineau's feeling of affinity with all other Christians (and with all other believers in God) was called the *Inquirer*, in contrast with the more militant section's *Christian Life*. In 1907 J. M. Lloyd Thomas, the minister of the historic Unitarian congregation in Birmingham, was to take this tendency to its extreme by advocating sacramentalism and even ritualism in *A Free Catholic Church* – and by practising what he preached, with a few others. It was not until 1928 that the militant and moderate traditions were brought together to form the General Assembly of the Unitarian and Free Christian Churches.[22]

---

[22] D. G. Wigmore-Beddoes, *Yesterday's Radicals* (Cambridge, 1971), explored the affinities of these Free Christians with the Anglican Broad Churchmen. See also H. L. Short in *The English Presbyterians*, pp. 252–86.

Generally speaking, Victorian Nonconformity as it moved into the cities took the same path as these Quaker or Unitarian moderates. It conformed to the spirit of the age, which included a strong streak of practical philanthropy. Before 1850 the tradition remained strong that Dissenters should live rather like monks, returning to the chapel on many weekdays for prayer meetings, Bible classes or other definitely religious acts. But in the second half of the century a broader understanding of Nonconformity prevailed and many of the chapels housed a great variety of semi-secular activities: education for the young and the adults, youth organizations galore, a football team, a choral society, a literary society, a 'provident' or 'friendly' society as insurance, a savings bank, a maternity club, and 'temperance' societies including the Band of Hope for the children. Many were the laments that the new activities did not lead to the commitment of the old-style membership – that in Methodism the class meeting often went dead and became optional, or that in Congregational churches there was no pressure to experience a conversion which could be told to the congregation.

H. W. Clark's second volume in a large *History of Nonconformity*, published in 1913, had the theme that Nonconformity had lost its old Puritan ideals by its worldly eagerness to provide entertainment and to flatter the people it wanted to attract. Even a sympathetic historian of the nineteenth century is liable to be even more severe on the compromises involved, painting a portrait of the Free Churches at the end of the century with these words: 'Free souls, having encapsulated God within themselves, surveyed majestically a world ripe for Utopian experiment.'[23] Whatever we make of such criticisms, we must observe that in the next century much of the role of Victorian Nonconformity in these social activities was taken over by better-financed and definitely secular activities – the improved school and public house, the cinema, radio, television, the Bingo hall, with the bicycle or the motor car offering yet another alternative for Sunday. Thus the churches' popu-

---

[23] Ian Sellers, *Nineteenth-Century Nonconformity*, p. 23. J. W. Grant, *Free Churchmanship in England, 1870–1940* (London, 1955), also denounced declericalized Congregationalism.

larity in the second half of the nineteenth century proved
ephemeral. Yet probably at the time no other course was open
to a religious movement aspiring to be popular. Entertainment
was what the people wanted, to counteract the drabness and
loneliness of life. And it is fair to remember that with the
entertainment went a great deal of care for often desperate
needs. It would not be right to forget ventures such as England's first school for mentally defective children, opened by a
Congregational minister, Andrew Reed, in London in 1848. In
1849 Edward Miall, himself the son of a poor man, argued in
The British Churches in Relation to the British People that Nonconformity had become too much the religion of manufacturers
and traders. 'I have endeavoured to put myself in the position
of the humbler classes, and have asked myself, "What is there
here to interest them?" I have been at a loss for a reply.' That
could not be said half a century later.

'We are living in the midst of a great reaction from Puritanism', the Wesleyan Methodist Conference declared in 1890. An
anonymous but semi-official book, *Methodism in 1879*, had taken
a pride in measuring the advance of the denomination by
worldly standards – the educated eloquence of its preachers,
the wealth of its leading laymen, the money collected, the
churches built. This mid-Victorian period in Methodist history became known as the 'mahogany age', referring not only
to the wood used for many pulpits but also to the dining tables
of many laymen. The *Methodist Recorder* had voiced the younger
element's impatience when founded in 1861, but gradually it
became the organ of a sedately established denomination. In
local Wesleyan churches pews were rented by the well-to-do,
although the custom would have horrified John Wesley. In
their national conference, the Wesleyan Methodists admitted
laymen for the first time in 1878, and eleven years later also
admitted that it was not necessary for a Methodist to belong to
a 'class'. These concessions, too, would have dismayed the
Founder, and they led up to the replacement in the 1890s of the
title 'Wesleyan Methodist Society' by 'Wesleyan Methodist
Church'.[24]

---

[24] *A History of the Methodist Church in Great Britain*, vol. 3 (London, 1983), included
valuable essays pointing to the need for a thorough history.

Even the Primitive Methodist Conference noted in 1892 that 'intelligence, wealth and respectability are becoming increasingly characteristic of us as a community.'

The Congregationalists also took the attitude that successful laymen were to be admired and consulted deferentially; in the words of Thomas Binney, 'it is not wrong to be rich'. Binney's book of advice to young men had the title *How to Make the Best of Both Worlds*. In 1894 the chairman of the Congregational Union delivered an address on 'The Secularization of the Church', remarking that 'Christian parents no longer forbid their children to read novels or to learn dancing; some of them accompany their sons and daughters to the theatre and the concert; in many Christian homes billiards and cards are allowed, and both in occupation and amusement the line that once divided the world from the Church is tending to disappear.'

Victorian Nonconformity eventually came to believe that the first step in its approach to the urban working class was to offer some of these pleasures which the middle classes were now taking for granted. The most sustained effort in this direction, the Pleasant Sunday Afternoon, was invented in West Bromwich in 1875. Its motto was 'Brief, Bright and Brotherly'. This meant a meeting with short addresses (not all of them religious) broken up by non-dogmatic hymns and solos; a hymnal, *Worship Song*, was edited for this purpose in 1907. The PSA was organized with a definite membership by an elected committee and took a pride in being non-sectarian. The motive of many of its backers was the hope that working people would return to the normal evening services, and the PSA did produce many thousands of new faces on church premises, particularly in the Midlands; but that hope was not fulfilled on any larger scale, and one disadvantage to the long-term prospects of Nonconformity was that almost all the ministers failed to attach enough importance to the meetings of working people in the trade unions now becoming a major force in non-ecclesiastical surroundings.

The success in the cities was, however, enough to inspire some optimistic dreams. John Wilson, in his Presidential address to the Baptist Union in 1904, asserted that a hundred years previously the Nonconformists had been only one in thirty in the population. Now they were one in two, and in fifty years' time they would, he trusted, be two to one. To give substance to such hopes John Shakespeare, who took over as the Union's secretary in 1898, raised a Twentieth Century Fund. The Baptists soon had an elaborate headquarters, a publications department, a new hymnal, a good newspaper (the *Baptist Times*) and a stronger agreed statement about their beliefs. Another appeal was successful in raising the stipends of ministers to a decent level, and a similar fund was raised for local purposes within the Congregational Union. There, the old tradition that each congregation was independent had already been eroded by the need to subsidise weaker churches if they employed 'authorized' ministers. In the 1870s and 1880s an able secretary, Alexander Hannay, had begun to build what had once seemed inconceivable: Congregationalism as a national organization.[25]

PREACHERS TO LONDON

Among the Nonconformists who preached to Victorian London, two were similar in a remarkable number of ways. Both the Baptist, Charles Haddon Spurgeon, and the Congregationalist, Joseph Parker, came from working-class homes and never went to any university or college. Both accepted a conservative theology. Both attracted such crowds that new churches had to be built around their pulpits, and both taught by the printed as well as the spoken word; yet both failed to impose their views on their denominations. This failure is a reminder that Victorian Nonconformity contained many ministers who were almost as sure as Spurgeon or Parker about what they believed – and almost as much admired by their own people in their own pulpits. It is worth studying the personal history of Spurgeon and Parker because through that history we can explore how it felt to be a Nonconformist – in an age

[25] The official histories, well documented, are E. A. Payne, *The Baptist Union* (London, 1959), and Albert Peel, *These Hundred Years: A History of the Congregational Union of England and Wales 1831–1931* (London, 1931).

whose historians have too often been stunned by the biographies of bishops.

Spurgeon's father was a clerk in a coal yard who was also a part-time Congregational pastor. The home in Essex was so poor that until he was seven the boy was brought up by his grandfather, a full-time minister. Through the books which were still kept by such Dissenters the boy became acquainted with John Bunyan and other Puritans of the sixteenth and seventeenth centuries. He was to collect some seven thousand of their books in his own library, and was often called the last of the Puritans. But he had to undergo his personal conversion (on a snowy Sunday morning in January 1850, when in a little chapel he heard a Primitive Methodist lay preacher expound the text 'Look unto me and be ye saved'). This was followed by baptism in a river. He had become convinced, simply by reading the Bible, that baptism was for adult converts only.

When not yet twenty years old he was called to preach in a famous but run-down Baptist church in London, and he soon accepted an invitation to become its permanent minister, although he always refused to be ordained formally. He later recalled that on his first night in London he had been mocked for his countryman's clothes, a huge black smock and a very large blue handkerchief with white spots, before he crept off to bed in a London boarding house. 'On the narrow bed I tossed in solitary misery, and found no pity. Pitiless was the grind of the cabs in the street . . . pitiless even the gas-lamps which seemed to wink at me as they flickered amid the December darkness. I had no friend in all that city full of human beings. . . .' And next morning when he saw the small, gloomy congregation in the big, gloomy chapel he was not much comforted.[26]

That was in 1853. On a typical Sunday in October 1886 a count of worshippers in London's churches organized by the *British Weekly* recorded that about ten thousand people heard Spurgeon preach. The country lad with the blue handkerchief had established himself as the biggest crowd-puller in the

---

[26] C. H. Spurgeon, *The Early Years 1834–59* (new edition, London, 1962), p. 248.

history of English religion. Soon after his arrival the crowds coming had been so great that he had had to preach in public halls. Finally he had his own church built – the Metropolitan Tabernacle, opened in 1861, in South London in order to be accessible to the teeming population there. There were few really poor people in his congregation, and even fewer professional men or fashionable women, but Spurgeon addressed himself to thousands upon thousands in families struggling to be respectable.

Why did they come? At first he became known because he was a 'boy preacher', like his hero George Whitefield. Then further publicity came just because of the crowds. But he did not remain a boy wonder. Actually, he became overweight because he took no exercise, and chesty because he smoked heavily – and since he was afflicted by gout, he had to use a stick to walk. And the novelty wore off. He preached twice on almost every Sunday until his death in 1892, and most of his sermons were printed. A monthly magazine and many books, lectures and weekday sermons added to the output. Yet still the crowds came.

He was never 'popular' in the sense of entertaining his audience. There was no organ in the Metropolitan Tabernacle in his time, and the sermon usually occupied three-quarters of an hour. He preached a modified Calvinism; he was a kind man who could not believe that any baby who died went to hell, and he was an evangelist who could not believe that anyone who listened to him was doomed to reject his message. ('Lord,' he prayed, 'hasten to bring in all thy elect, and then elect some more.') But he always regarded himself as a Calvinist. When the Tabernacle was opened, he got visiting preachers to expound the five points of classical Calvinism – human depravity; the election by God of those to be saved; 'particular redemption'; 'effectual calling'; 'final perseverance'. Although he did some visiting of families in his early years (his courage when visiting the victims of cholera was not forgotten), before long he had to admit that he could not carry six thousand names in his head, so much pastoral work as was done for the congregation had to be delegated to elders, each in charge of a district. Yet still the people came, each feeling that the sermon was addressed personally – and when his coffin was brought to the Tabernacle, some sixty thousand filed past it. So personal was his people's loyalty that they called his son Thomas to be their minister after his death, although numbers declined.

Once when asked by an American for the secret of his success, he replied: 'My people pray for me.' It was not a sham modesty. He was loved. He founded an orphanage with funds provided by his admirers, an evening school free to all, and a college to train boys without educational advantages to be preachers; and he gave much of his time and income to these and other charities. Another way of showing his love for the people was to preach in a style they loved. 'The histrionics and sentimentalism of Spurgeon in the pulpit are hard to credit', in the view of a distinguished scholar.[27] But J. C. Carlile, a shrewd man who himself became a leading Baptist minister, maintained that Spurgeon's preaching 'revealed to me the magic of the human voice and the stupendous power of sincerity. . . . Spurgeon was to religion what Shakespeare was to drama.'[28] The power came in part from the preacher's confidence in the authority of the Bible, which he regarded as the Word of God from cover to cover.

The tragedy of this marvellous pastor and preacher was that, while his congregation never left him, he felt increasingly isolated from his fellow Baptists because they were infected by the liberal ideas in the air of the nineteenth century. In 1887 his impatience boiled over and he accused them of betraying fundamental doctrines: 'The Atonement is scouted, the inspiration of Scripture is derided, the Holy Spirit is degraded into a fiction, and the resurrection into a myth, and yet these enemies of our faith expect us to call them brethren and maintain a confederacy with them.' In particular he was indignant at the lack of belief in the eternal punishment of the wicked in hell. His resignation from the Baptist Union caused consternation for a time, but the council of the Union refused to be browbeaten and passed a resolution affirming that charges against 'men who love the truth as dearly as he does' without

---

[27] Donald Davie, *A Gathered Church*, p. 89.

[28] J. C. Carlile, *My Life's Little Day* (London, 1935), pp. 56–8.

giving names 'ought not to have been made'. To this it added a Declaratory Statement of the essentials of belief.

Spurgeon continued to complain, but not very effectively. There were four hundred churches where men trained in his Pastors' College were in the pulpit, but no new denomination was formed around him. As has been observed, 'he was one of the few men of his generation who really felt more certain of the truth of the Bible than of the truth of contemporary science.'[29]

Among other princes of the Victorian pulpit, the most princely was Joseph Parker who reigned for a quarter of a century in London, north of the Thames at the City Temple.

The son of a stonemason, he left school at the age of fourteen and never had any formal training for the ministry; yet such became his reputation that in 1869, he was invited to become the minister of the oldest Congregational church in the city of London. One reason why he accepted the call to London was that the congregation was about to sell its present chapel and to buy a larger and more central site. The new 'City Temple' was opened in 1874 – was opened, and was filled morning and evening every Sunday. On Thursdays a lunch-hour service attracted a thousand. In the 1902–03 survey of churchgoing in London it was found that the average Sunday attendance was just over seven thousand, three times the numbers in St Paul's Cathedral.

Until he died in 1902 they went to hear Joseph Parker. A style that may seem to us dictatorial was then magnetic. He prayed aloud as the spirit moved him, and he gradually changed his preaching style from the more formal, written sermon expounding a long text to a much more personal, rambling and extempore discourse based on a few words of Scripture. Although he always reckoned himself an Evangelical, he did not stress the old Puritan doctrines and morals as did Spurgeon. Indeed, he published an open letter to Spurgeon in 1890: 'I accuse you of a bluntness which can only be accounted for by the worst kind of spiritual ignorance. The universe is not

---

[29] W. B. Glover, *Evangelical Nonconformity and Higher Criticism in the Nineteenth Century*, pp. 163–83. Biographies include J. C. Carlile, *Spurgeon* (London, 1934), and E. W. Bacon, *Spurgeon, Heir of the Puritans* (London, 1967).

divided into plain black and white, as you suppose. . . . Believe
me you really are not infallible.' He tried to present what he
believed to be the modern message of the Bible to the young
men (many of them clerks in city offices) and women (many of
them maids in the West End houses of the rich) who sat under
him in large numbers. He kept them awake by explosions; his
'God damn the Sultan!' echoed throughout England in 1899, a
year of indignation against the Turks. Many other preachers
came to listen in the hope of learning the secret of his popularity, only to discover that what he did all the time was to
expound the Bible dramatically; at one stage he took seven
years to work his way through it, Sunday by Sunday. He
published a *People's Bible* including a commentary by him, in
twenty-five volumes.

Explaining why he would not accept an invitation to move to
New York, he declared: 'There is only one London, and it is to
all intents and purposes the centre of the commerce, the
literature and the religion of the world.' In that London, he was
Spurgeon's rival.[30]

PREACHERS AND POLITICIANS

Intellectually abler than Spurgeon or Parker, R. W. Dale
found his life's work in the pulpit of the Congregational chapel
in Carr's Lane, Birmingham, and in the politics of that boom-
ing industrial city. He had no ambition to be a popular
preacher; although the leaders of Birmingham's life came in
considerable numbers to hear his austerely theological sermons, it has been justly remarked that 'no man made fewer
concessions to his hearers'.[31] He did have an ambition to write
books that would last, and to a large extent that ambition was
fulfilled by his authorship of *The Atonement* (1875). There he
rejected both the Calvinist idea that Christ died in order to
save a limited number of the elect from hell and the liberal idea

---

[30] William Adamson compiled *The Life of the Rev. Joseph Parker* (Glasgow, 1902).
[31] Horton Davies, *Worship and Theology in England from Newman to Martineau*, p. 331.
The whole of Chapter X, on 'The Power of the Victorian Pulpit', is valuable.

that Christ died in order to make an appeal to every man's conscience. He affirmed that anyone who repented was saved from the punishment incurred by sin, while after death the souls of the impenitent were annihilated. Certainly Christ's death made a moral appeal, but it provided more than a mere example. It was something *done* for man; it was something objective, not depending for its effectiveness on man's response; it was what made man's penitent response to God possible. Christ, declared Dale, 'endured the penalties of sin, and so made an actual submission to the authority and righteousness of the principle which those penalties express. What we had no force to do, He has done; and through our union with Him, His submission renders our submission possible.'

Born in London in 1829, Dale found his work in Birmingham because after a spell as a schoolmaster he went there to be trained as a Congregational minister and was invited by the distinguished but elderly John Angell James to remain as his colleague at Carr's Lane. He was called in 1859 to be the sole pastor. In Birmingham he would provide models for Church and State – and from Birmingham he would move out to spread his vision over the nation. In order to serve these causes, he was ready to let the great theology of which he was capable remain unwritten.

For Dale, any idea of the priesthood as a separate caste providing the Church with sacraments was hateful because contrary to the Bible. He always dressed as a layman and announced that he had an invincible objection to the title 'Reverend'. He denounced the argument that the National Church needed to be supported and controlled by the State. To argue that was to deny the power and the rights of the living Christ over the congregation of the faithful. When he died he left incomplete a large *History of English Congregationalism* which was published in 1907 and which traced this ideal of the congregation of the faithful back 'through century after century of corruption, superstition and spiritual tyranny' to the 'religious societies to which the New Testament attributes an extraordinary dignity and sanctity'. Yet he taught a high doctrine about the whole gathered congregation as a microcosm of the Catholic Church. His *Manual of Congregational*

Principles (1884) seemed so High Church that it was attacked
by Spurgeon, and an edition had to be printed without the
section on the sacraments. A prominent theme of his preaching
was that Christ was alive, reigning over the Church, and he
chose an Easter hymn for most Sundays in the year. With this
theme he justified the baptism of infants, baptism being the
offer of salvation made by the living Christ before the baby
could respond; and he argued for the central importance of
Holy Communion. Both sacraments were, he insisted, primarily acts of God, creating and feeding the Church; they were
not primarily acts of the minister or the congregation.[32]

He was too much of a theologian ever to think that a
'Municipal Gospel' was enough. Indeed, he constantly emphasized the difference between religion and politics, between
Church and State. Pursuing the logic of this difference, he was
prepared to shock men such as Spurgeon who supported
everything that made England more Christian. Dale urged
that no religious teaching should be given in the State's schools
(although he conceded that the Bible might be read as a
masterpiece of literature); that the House of Commons should
be open to the atheist, Charles Bradlaugh; that the Town Hall
should be open on a Sunday for lectures on secular subjects. In
church preaching the Gospel always had for him the top
priority – and his was a theology almost as conservative as
Parker's, as may be seen by comparing it with the far less
doctrinal message of two other Birmingham preachers influen-
tially involved in radical politics, George Dawson of the independent 'Church of the Saviour' and H. W. Crosskey of the
Unitarian 'Church of the Messiah'.

It was as a citizen who was also a Christian that he felt
impelled to be active in the great reforms of his time. When the
Reform Act of 1867 made Parliament more democratic he
would have been ashamed had he not already campaigned for
it; and he was delighted when his friend Joseph Chamberlain,
then a Unitarian businessman who had made a fortune by
mass-producing screws, became Mayor of Birmingham (1873

---

[32] Dale's teaching about the Church was studied by J. W. Grant, *Free Churchmanship in England*, pp. 1–123.

-78) and led the crusade to turn Birmingham into a fine modern city. Dale never doubted that it was his duty to speak at many Town Hall meetings and to spend evening after evening exhorting the wards of the Chamberlain-controlled Liberal Party. His son recalled that 'he threw himself into the struggle with exultant energy. . . . During those years a succession of serious questions came before the burgesses – the acquisition of the gas- and the water-supply by the community, the provision of public parks and public buildings, a more efficient system of sanitary measures, a costly sewage scheme, the establishment of free libraries and an art gallery, a plan for sweeping away the slums in the heart of the town – great measures conceived and advocated on broad lines of municipal statesmanship, but of a kind to provoke prejudice and to call forth a false cry of economy. In dealing with such questions, Dale spoke with full and exact knowledge. He, too, could see visions and dream dreams. . . . But he was ready to meet critics and opponents on the ground of solid fact. . . .' Above all he was an enthusiastic advocate of the building and maintenance of 'Board Schools' with high standards. He took endless trouble as the chairman of the committee responsible for Birmingham's schools under the Act of 1870, and in the 1880s was an active member of the Royal Commission on elementary education.[33]

Gradually, however, he became disillusioned with Gladstone, who failed to meet the Nonconformists' demands over education and disestablishment; and when in 1886 Joseph Chamberlain broke with Gladstone over Home Rule for Ireland, he followed Chamberlain although with many reservations. Consequently he found himself so unhappy in the atmosphere of the Congregational Union that he ceased to attend its meetings. In his private life he experienced bereavements which greatly saddened him; and although he was still in his fifties, his health broke down. He never regretted that he had been one of the leaders of progress in the city to which he had

---

[33] There is a fine chapter on 'Birmingham: the Making of a Civic Gospel' in Asa Briggs, *Victorian Cities* (London, 1963). See also E. P. Hennock, *Fit and Proper Persons* (London, 1973), pp. 61–176.

given his heart; in 1892 he recalled with pride that 'the men who took part in the great and successful movement for reforming our administration and ennobling it had learnt the principles on which they acted and caught the spirit by which they were inspired very largely in the Nonconformist churches of Birmingham.' But after his death in 1895 an unfinished sermon was found on his desk. It was on unworldliness. It spoke of the vision of God; of 'constant fellowship' with God; of a 'personal and vivid experience of the greatness of the Christian redemption'. The last, incomplete, sentence proclaimed the 'full assurance that, after our mortal years are spent, there is a larger, fuller, richer life in . . . .'

Towards the end of his life Dale encouraged a young admirer, Charles Silvester Horne. When the great man had died, Horne recalled how he had been a boy dreaming of becoming a preacher when he had first met him. 'My lad,' Dale said then, 'remember *our* temptation is not as a rule money.' Then he pointed through the open door of the vestry to the crowded church: '*That* is our temptation.'

In that warning Dale was a prophet, for Horne went on to become immensely popular – by means which Dale would have suspected. He was called to be a preacher in the most fashionable part of London, at Kensington Chapel. Well-informed on many topics, light and lively, very happy in his family life and with a host of friends, patently sincere as he talked in a non-dogmatic way about Jesus, he charmed laymen wherever he went. He was a spiritually minded man, but his most obvious enthusiasm was for the contribution which the Free Churches could make to the progress of the nation. He wrote popular histories of the Free Churches and encouraged the conviction that their greatest days were just beginning.

In 1903 he accepted a call to move from Kensington in order to put new life into a famous church, Whitefield's Tabernacle in Tottenham Court Road, because he was fascinated by the opportunities awaiting in a district full of shops, business houses, smart flats and slums with a cosmopolitan population. To the distressed he offered a tender sympathy; to the successful, a vibrant optimism. In addition to the normal services which became crowded he developed many varied activities, most notably the Sunday afternoon lecture on a topical subject. There was even a room for billiards. The church became an 'institutional' church, attracting thousands to the Whitefields Institute who might, or might not, stay on for the preaching service. Similar churches were associated in the 'Brotherhood movement', defined by the Labour leader Keir Hardie as 'an association for the promotion of fellowship among those who love Jesus' – a category which included other Labour leaders (Crooks, Henderson, Lansbury, Snowden). This movement was formally organized at a national conference in 1906 and soon spread overseas.[34] He returned from a very cheerful visit to Germany in 1909 full of hopes for peace and progress. While chairman of the Congregational Union next year he spoke eloquently about the value of the Free Church tradition which combined freedom and brotherhood and was now flourishing in many countries. Elected to Parliament for Ipswich in 1910, he claimed that 'there is no church meeting held in this country that is more constantly and practically concerned with living religious problems than the House of Commons'. In the spring of 1914 he went to America to lecture on *The Romance of Preaching*. He was received with enthusiasm, and went on to address a great Brotherhood meeting in Toronto. As the boat entered the harbour he was on deck with his wife, eagerly admiring the Canadian city – and suddenly fell down dead, fortunate to the last.[35]

FORWARD TOGETHER?

The most powerful movement to take the English Free Churches into the twentieth century emerged out of Wesleyan Methodism. It was associated with the controversial personality of a Welshman with a Jewish mother, Hugh Price Hughes. When in 1898 he was elected President of the Wesleyan Methodist Conference he declared in his first speech from the chair, 'I am not afraid of any one of you'. He went on to point

---

[34] See J. W. Tuffley, *Grain from Galilee* (London, 1935).
[35] W. B. Selbie compiled *The Life of Charles Silvester Horne* (London, 1920).

out that it was the first honour that his Church had ever paid to him.

Hughes knew that the old style of Wesleyan Methodism could sometimes be effective; his own father was a much loved preacher and pastor. He also knew that in practice the old style of preaching had usually meant conservatism in politics; when he began his own preaching, he was himself an ardent Tory. But gradually he found himself driven by experience to support radicalism, and always his support was active. While a student he became an active supporter of the Liberation Society; while a minister in Dover he became an active supporter of the temperance movement; while a minister in Oxford he became an active supporter of the enrichment of Methodist worship even if it partly meant copying the Church of England; and while a minister in London he became an active supporter of 'Christian imperialism', believing the British empire to be making a major contribution to the coming of the kingdom of God.

On all these issues he was in tension or conflict with the caution, the 'deadly respectability', which had prevailed in Wesleyan Methodism. He was not daunted, for he was sure that God was the greatest radical. In 1885 he founded his own weekly paper, the *Methodist Times*, to 'ventilate' new ideas. This it did very successfully, much to the annoyance of the supporters of the official *Methodist Recorder* – who spoke contemptuously about the 'Hughesful' new paper. Determined to outvote the conservatives, Hughes rallied his supporters in a pressure group which took the provocative name: the Forward Movement.

Experience convinced him that the traditional Methodist chapel would never move forward in a modern city. He advocated, and eventually secured, 'central halls' at strategic points – large buildings not looking like churches, the centres of many social activities in addition to worship. It was typical that those who built these halls (beginning in Manchester in 1887) preferred an orchestra to an organ, chairs to pews. The minister in charge was not to be moved every three years, as was the Methodist custom in all the normal 'circuits'; he was to have the chance to make an impact as a powerful local personality. The whole 'mission' was to be adequately financed out of special funds, and was to be supervised by the national conference not by the local chapels. The building of a Central Hall in Westminster, close to the Abbey and to Parliament, particularly delighted him. On these conditions he was himself appointed to lead the West London Mission, from 1887 to his death. His assistants in the social work included Methodist 'sisters' – and they survived the inevitable protests that they looked suspiciously like nuns. The work had its prominent centre in St James's Hall, Piccadilly, and into it Hughes threw all his energy as an evangelist and pastor, all his inventiveness (one Harvest Festival brought a live sheep to bleat in a pen beneath his pulpit), all his facility as a lecturer on current topics and personalities, and all his courage as a prophet of social righteousness.

He claimed to be the spokesman of a body of opinion which no politician could ignore. In particular he claimed to be able to set the terms of Methodism's alliance with the Gladstonian Liberals. When his children asked who Mr Gladstone was, he replied: 'A man who says his prayers every morning.' But when Gladstone died, he observed that 'on this side of the Tweed his following was strong only where Methodism was strong: that is, in the West, in the great Northern Counties and among the peasants.' And no politician was too eminent to be subjected to a moral scrutiny if he wanted Methodist votes. When the Irish leader Parnell was cited as an adulterer in a divorce case, a denunciation was delivered by Hughes on a Sunday afternoon in 1890. 'We love Ireland. We passionately desire her well-being; but our first obedience and our highest devotion must be to God. We have sacrificed much for Ireland. She is entitled to many sacrifices at our hands. But there is one thing we will never sacrifice, and that is our religion. We stand immovably on this eternal rock; what is morally wrong can never be politically right.' That last sentence echoed all over England – and Ireland. The Irish Catholic bishops joined in the denunciation, as did most of the Irish MPs. By the end of 1890 Parnell was broken, and by the end of 1891 he was dead.[36]

---

[36] The tragedy was set in its context by F. S. L. Lyons, *Charles Stuart Parnell* (London, 1977).

One result of this confident new style was to draw Methodism closer to other morally clear missionaries. This was a
major development; in 1834 Jabez Bunting had declared
openly that 'we cannot be friendly to Dissent. One of its first
principles is – Every man shall choose his own minister. Can
you be friendly to that?' Now the successors to Bunting were
answering yes to that question. As part of that answer, they
were abandoning the defence of wine and beer. In contrast
with 1840, when two young candidates for the Wesleyan
Methodist ministry had been compelled to promise to give up
the heresy of teetotalism, forty years later it was proudly
reported that eight hundred ministers had pledged total abstinence from alcohol. By 1908, when the House of Lords threw
out the Liberal government's Licensing Bill, the whole of
Methodism was united with the rest of Nonconformity against
the brewers.

In November 1892 Hughes made the opening speech at the
first Free Church Congress, in Manchester. When the National Council of Evangelical Free Churches met for the first time
in 1896, he was elected President. Encouraged by generous
financial backing by the Quaker, George Cadbury, he declared: 'Representing the majority of the Christian people at
home, we represent an immense majority in the British empire,
and an overwhelming majority in the English-speaking world.
If the failures and humiliations of the past, as well as the bright
hopes of the present, have at last taught us their Divinely-
appointed lessons, the future of British Christianity and of the
British Empire is in our hands.' For the true idea of the Church
was to be found in the Free Churches and nowhere else. 'We
are "High Churchmen" ', he claimed in 1897, 'so High that we
can no more tolerate the interference of the secular power than
could the Popes of the Middle Ages. . . . We are "Catholic
High Churchmen", for we do not hold ourselves in schismatic
separation from our fellow Christians. . . . We do not boycott
or excommunicate. . . .'

The growing unity in the Free Churches was sufficient to
support a new penny paper, the *British Weekly*, edited from the
start in 1886 to 1923 by a brilliant journalist, William Robertson Nicoll, who had been a minister in the Free Church of

Scotland. The opening article began: 'The creed we shall seek to expound in this journal will be that of progress, and while independent of any sect or party we shall aim at the ends of what is known as Advanced Liberalism. We are believers in progress because we are believers in the advancing reign of Christ.' By 1906 it had a circulation over a hundred thousand, with such a status that Liberal politicians took care to win the approval of its editor.[37] Other activities included Free Church Missions in London and the other main cities.

In order to awaken some seven hundred local Free Church Councils into activity, Hughes now set himself a gruelling programme of visits and addresses in city, town and village, nationwide, disregarding warnings that his health had already suffered from overwork in London. As a result, he had a fatal heart attack in a London street in 1902. It was the crusader's death for which he would have wished. In his eyes the 'Nonconformist conscience' had ceased to be mere dissent from the Established Church. It had become the main carrier of the religion of a prospering nation and an expanding empire. So complete did the contrast seem between 1800 and 1900.[38] Yet questions remained which, in his enthusiasm and eloquence, he had neglected. Was Nonconformity really prepared to take over the leading role from the Church of England? Had it ever been willing to do so? The identification of 'Free Church' unity with the Liberal Party alarmed many, and in 1909 an influential although anonymous book on *Nonconformity and Politics* issued warnings about worldliness which were widely discussed. In the discussion many Free Churchmen clung to the militant alliance with Liberalism, but no great new campaign was launched when the education controversy had to be allowed to die down. Even in the 1890s, when the phrase 'the Nonconformist conscience' had come into general use, the emphasis had still been on preparing the moral ground for a better kind of politics – not on the business of day-to-day politics as experienced by Liberal politicians.

---

[37] T. H. Darlow gave some account of *William Robertson Nicoll* (London, 1925).

[38] His daughter Dorothy compiled *The Life of Hugh Price Hughes* (London, 1904), and E. K. H. Jordan told the story of *Free Church Unity* down to 1941 (London, 1951).

Looking back, an historian of the Victorian Nonconformist conscience found in it three essential features. He drew attention to 'a conviction that there is no complete boundary between religion and politics; an insistence that politicians should be men of the highest character; and a belief that the State should promote the moral welfare of its citizens.' That did not amount to a political programme – and indeed, at its deepest level Nonconformity always knew that it was not a political movement, that its origins lay in a spiritual hunger which the Church of England could not satisfy, as well as in the protests of social groups excluded by the privileges of the Establishment. This scholar has concluded that the euphoria of 1906 was shortlived, that the old distaste for politics soon returned, and that by 1910 'the period of the Nonconformist conscience had come to an end.' Such a verdict may be exaggerated, but it usefully stresses that the real strength of Victorian and post-Victorian Nonconformity was always not political or cultural but religious.[39]

---

[39] See D. W. Bebbington, *The Nonconformist Conscience* (London, 1982).

CHAPTER SEVEN

ROMAN CATHOLICISM

THE SECOND SPRING

Newman's most famous sermon was on 'the Second Spring'. It was preached in 1852, in the chapel designed by Pugin at Oscott near Birmingham, celebrating the restoration of twelve Roman Catholic dioceses in England two years previously. Cardinal Wiseman openly sobbed during it. It was a master-piece of religious emotion in chastely beautiful English. But it showed that the preacher was out of touch with the realities.

It suited Newman's religion, both supernatural and nostalgic, to consider the centuries since the Reformation as a long decline fit to be compared with autumn and winter, so that the bishops could be welcomed like daffodils appearing by a miracle to herald the return of the Middle Ages. 'The past *has* returned,' he exulted, 'the dead live.' It also suited his purpose to prophesy greatness on the medieval scale for the bishops of the future; about the present, he was discreetly vague. 'Canterbury has gone its way, and York is gone, and Durham is gone, and Winchester is gone. . . . Westminster and Nottingham, Beverley, Hexham, Northampton and Shrewsbury, if the world lasts, shall be names as musical to the ear, as stirring to the heart, as the glories we have lost; and saints shall rise out of them, if God so will, and doctors once again shall give the law to Israel, and preachers call to penance and to justice, as at the beginning.' So Newman said.

In reality, however, the task confronting the bishops in the 1850s was to build churches and schools where the priests could teach the Irish and any others willing to be taught. There were never enough priests – only just over a thousand in 1860 (when the Church of England had 19,000 clergy), still under three thousand in 1900 (when the Church of England had almost 25,000 clergy). But these priests worked; some 440 new churches were built in the quarter-century, 1850–75, and many more arose before 1900. In the annual *Catholic Directory* lay numbers grew to one and a half million by the end of the century, although it was never claimed that all these were present at Mass every Sunday.

The ban on contraceptives contributed to growth not only in numbers but also in the sense that this community was separate, even holy. Celebrating the centenary of the political emancipation in 1829, Professor Denis Gwyn could take pride in the refusal of the community to be emancipated in sex. 'It is not only the moral discipline of Catholicism,' he wrote, 'but the whole Catholic outlook upon life that prevents modern birth control propaganda from making headway even among the poorest Catholics, upon whom the burden of large families falls most heavily. A different sense of values, which attaches more importance to the fundamental realities of life than to its material comforts, produces an attitude towards family life which remains steadfast'. In contrast, 'the more sophisticated and pleasure-loving drift inevitably towards race suicide'.[1]

The ban on contraceptives would not have been effective had there not been a strong religious faith within this community. This faith influenced the numerous children born to Roman Catholic parents – and also many converts.

Obviously it is impossible for any historian to write in full detail the story of Roman Catholic religion in the everyday life of Victorian England.[2] Much of the story never escaped from the strict secrecy of the confessional, where the penitent was expected to bare his life and thoughts regularly to the judgement of the parish priest; or from the privacy of the home, where any family known to be Catholic was liable to be visited by the priest if any of its members seemed to be either

---

[1] Denis Gwyn, *A Hundred Years of Catholic Emancipation* (London, 1929), p. xxvii.

[2] The impossibility was fully acknowledged in *The English Catholics 1850–1950*, ed. G. A. Beck (London, 1959), but that volume is indispensable. J. Derek Holmes, *More Roman than Rome: English Catholicism in the Nineteenth Century* (London, 1978), was more independent and Edward Norman, *The English Catholic Church in the Nineteenth Century* (Oxford, 1984), fuller. Maisie Ward's two volumes on *The Wilfred Wards and the Transition* (London, 1934–38) abounded in memories.

dangerously sick or dangerously sinful; or from the obscurity of the classroom, where the Faith was taught as a child's most precious inheritance. Such contacts not only kept the individual's piety going at some heat in a cold world, but also exercised a profound influence on the whole pattern of his life.

Despite their poverty and their well-known temptations to drink, rowdiness, crime and general fecklessness, the Irish often went from their weekly Mass to live as exemplary parents and workers; and the effect can be seen clearly in the history of their assimilation into English life.[3] In the 1840s and 1850s Irish immigrants were often regarded as disease-carriers, and there was great resentment about their open willingness to accept lower pay than the already low average of the English labourer. They militantly opposed Chartist activity, allowed themselves to be used as strike-breakers, and engaged in bitter and bloody battles with the native workmen in many parts of Britain. But by the 1910s prejudice against 'Paddy' had greatly diminished. Catholics of Irish descent were struggling alongside the English in the trade unions – and fighting alongside them in the British army. They and their fellow Catholics never formed a distinct group in English politics, for although the Liberals were applauded for their sympathy with Irish grievances the two leading Catholic weeklies, the *Universe* and the more sophisticated *Tablet*, were Conservative in their political tendency, one of the reasons being the Liberals' dislike of church schools. On the whole the community was, like Nonconformity, non-political. But in his history of *Catholicism in England* Archbishop David Mathew was surely right to emphasize the quiet impressiveness of 'the great mass of the Catholics of the working class. . . . As the families sat in the kitchen at the hot Sunday dinner, with the girls in their print dresses and the boys talking of the new League Football and the first boxing successes of Jim Driscoll, they would always have the money ready for the collector coming Sunday after Sunday for the school building. This generation among the workers had a

---

[3] L. P. Curtis, Jr., studied anti-Irish prejudice in Victorian England in *Anglo-Saxons and Celts* (Bridgeport, Conn., 1968) and *Apes and Angels* (Newton Abbot, Devon, 1979).

profound reverence for the Mass; broad constant humour; vitality; a virile faith'.[4] And the rest of England noticed the regular giving of the pennies of the poor, just as it noticed the pious munificence of the Duke of Norfolk or the religious courage of the Marquis of Ripon, who despite his conversion became Viceroy of India in 1880.

The best loved teachers of Roman Catholicism were the nuns, who brought grace to so many parishes and schools. It would be tedious to compile a catalogue of all the Orders, old or new, to which these sisters belonged. It is, however, the opposite of tedious to notice the extraordinary talents of women such as Cornelia Connelly, formerly an Anglican clergyman's wife and now foundress of the Society of the Holy Child Jesus, an order which has had to its credit a chain of schools conducted on enlightened lines; of Margaret Hallahan, who founded five convents for Dominican Tertiaries with an extensive work of evangelism and education in the Midlands; and of Laura Jerningham, a widow who expanded the work of the Sisters of Notre Dame in many schools and in the great Catholic Training College in Liverpool.[5]

Most of the members of the religious orders for men were more highly educated than the average parish priest. The Jesuits' school at Stonyhurst, tracing its ancestry back to the college at St Omer for boys from Elizabethan England, had flourished since its move to that great house in Lancashire in 1794. The Jesuits' chief church in London (in Farm Street) was served by an eminent succession of preachers, and the quality of the Jesuits' literary work was to be seen in their journal, the *Month*. The Benedictines established famous schools at their abbeys at Downside and Ampleforth. At a more popular level, Roman Catholics in Victorian England were served magnificently by the energy of the English branches of the newer Italian orders – Rosminians, Redemptorists, Passionists and Oratorians. Before Westminster Cathedral was consecrated the Brompton Oratory in Kensington, founded in 1853, was Catholic London's grandest church, dominated by the ex-

[4] David Mathew, *Catholicism in England* pp. 234–7.
[5] See Julia Wadham, *The Case of Cornelia Connelly* (London, 1956).

travagantly sentimental personality of F. W. Faber, an ex-Anglican convert. Ordinary parish priests disliked its flamboyance, and the Baroque architecture and Italianate practices seemed calculated to outrage Victorian Protestants. Votive candles were kept shining before an image of Our Lady ('Mamma' to Faber); the reserved sacrament was talked about as if Our Lord were there as a man, waiting to be visited or to be moved about; unguarded invitations to confess to a priest indicated how to give 'all for Jesus' or 'all for Mary'. Yet Faber also had a totally genuine and lifelong sense of God; his best-known hymn began 'My God, how wonderful thou art'. This communion with the All-Holy communicated itself to men and women, and with that burning light at the centre Faber was able to make the spirituality of the Counter-Reformation a part of the public life of Victorian London.[6]

The parish priests were less glamorous but they thoroughly earned the title 'Father' which now became customary for the first time. The 'Roman collar' which they wore acquired such prestige as a uniform that it was gradually adopted in the Church of England and even in Nonconformity. Naturally their pastoral work became more effective as it became possible to establish in the relevant centres of population a network of small parishes with schools attached – as in Liverpool under the two very formidable bishops, O'Reilly and Whiteside, who devoted their energies to this steady expansion from 1872 to 1921.[7] However, these priests were managed by their bishops in many details of their work, the explanation being that when the dioceses were restored in 1850 the parishes were not restored. Until the revision of canon law was completed in 1918, parish priests in England had the status merely of rectors or assistants in 'missions' under the direct control of the diocesan bishop or his vicar general. The bishop owned the buildings, appointed the priests, authorized their payment according to his estimate of their value, and had detailed reports and accounts submitted to his office.

---

[6] See Ronald Chapman, *Father Faber* (London, 1961).

[7] Conor K. Ward studied the sociological results in *Priests and People* (Liverpool, 1961).

Three of the vicars apostolic who became diocesan bishops in the 1850s were stout northerners with long experience of pastoral work – Briggs at Beverley, Hogarth at Hexham, Brown at Liverpool – and only two of the rest were nonentities. Five new bishops were needed. Among them were two who had come from the same background as Wiseman: Thomas Grant, the young rector of the English College in Rome, and the older George Errington, who had served as Wiseman's assistant both there and at the Oscott seminary. But neither of these remained on good terms with Wiseman. Grant as Bishop of Southwark was a thorn in the flesh of successive Archbishops of Westminster. Errington, first made Bishop of Plymouth, was soon called to act as Wiseman's colleague with the right of succession at Westminster. A strict disciplinarian and a highly competent businessman, Errington angered Wiseman by criticizing his slackness. After much unpleasantness he was dismissed by the personal intervention of the Pope, but it says much for him that the leading parish priests of the diocese nominated him as successor to Wiseman on the Cardinal's death, braving the Pope's fury. It says even more for him that after his fall Errington lived quietly as a parish priest and professor.

Grant and Errington were among the bishops who publicly criticized the 1870 definition of the Pope's infallibility.[8] So was the formidable Yorkshireman, Bernard Ullathorne, Bishop of Birmingham 1850–88, although in the end he voted for it. After a brief spell at sea as a cabin boy, and another spell as a novice and monk with the Benedictines, he had gone to Australia in 1833 while still in his mid-twenties, the senior priest in a vast area; nominally he was vicar-general to a bishop in far-distant Mauritius. He had bravely ministered to the convicts and pioneer settlers – and with equal courage on his return home had spoken and written freely about the harsh conditions of their lives. This man who on the other side of the world had often ministered to convicts before execution was well able to

---

[8] Cuthbert Butler's account of *The Vatican Council* (London, 1930) has been supplemented by F. J. Cwiekowski, *The English Bishops and the First Vatican Council* (Louvain, 1971). See also *Lord Acton and the First Vatican Council*, ed. Edmund Campion (Sydney, 1975). The reasoning behind the opposition was illuminated by Damian McElrath, *The Syllabus of Pius IX: Some Reactions in England* (Louvain, 1964).

keep the over-subtle Newman's deepest respect, to comfort
him when he tormented himself, and to rebuke Westminster's
two cardinals, Wiseman and Manning, for arrogance in the
one case and for duplicity in the other. Noting that his achievements included the opening of more than a hundred new
schools, the historian Philip Hughes judged that Ullathorne,
'despite his subordinate rank, was to be the real centre of
English Catholic activities . . . all in all, surely the greatest of
the ninety bishops whose lives make up the first century of the
restored hierarchy.'[9]

THREE CARDINALS IN
WESTMINSTER

When Nicholas Wiseman arrived in Rome early in September
1850, it was in the belief that the Pope intended him to reside
there permanently as a cardinal. To him, this was a bitter
disappointment. During the previous ten years he, who
formerly had taken such delight in Rome, had been in England, absorbed in the hope of restoring his nation to the
Catholic Church. He had received many converts into the
Church and had confirmed Newman in a service when ten
former Anglican clergymen had been together in the chapel.
He had seen churches, religious communities and schools
springing up, and many thousands of the Irish returning to the
sacraments. He had acted as vicar apostolic of the London
district since 1847 and had frankly hoped to be archbishop – 'to
stand at the helm in the capital of this empire', as he had
written to a friend, 'while the Church is bearing all before it.'
When he had taken leave of Bishop Ullathorne in Birmingham, he had been in tears.

But before the end of September Pius IX not only proclaimed the restoration of the English hierarchy but also

---

[9] *The English Catholics 1850–1950*, pp. 74–5. Ullathorne was honoured by a titular
archbishopric on his retirement. In 1941 Sir Shane Leslie edited his autobiography
as *From Cabin-boy to Archbishop*, based on the original draft completed in the last
months of his life but not going beyond 1852. Cuthbert Butler compiled *The Life and
Times of Bishop Ullathorne* (2 vols., London, 1926).

announced Cardinal Wiseman's appointment as the first Archbishop of Westminster. The news and the consequent ceremonies left Wiseman (who by temperament alternated between depression and euphoria) elated, and in this almost intoxicated condition he dashed off a pastoral letter to be read in the churches of his new diocese, before beginning a triumphant journey home. Entitling this epistle 'From out of the Flaminian Gate', he wrote: 'Till such time as the Holy See shall think fit otherwise to provide, we govern, and shall continue to govern, the counties of Middlesex, Hertford and Essex as ordinary thereof, and those of Surrey, Sussex, Kent, Berkshire and Hampshire, with the islands annexed, as administrator with ordinary jurisdiction. . . . The great work, then, is complete; what you have long desired and prayed for is granted. Your beloved country has received a place among the fair Churches, which, normally constituted, form the splendid aggregate of Catholic Communion; Catholic England has been restored to its orbit in the ecclesiastical firmament, from which its light had long vanished, and begins now anew its course of regularly adjusted action round the centre of unity, the source of jurisdiction, of light, and of vigour.'

It was in his carriage in Vienna, 'full of satisfaction at the events of the past month and reading my *Times*', that the new cardinal found that his appointment had been the subject of the leading article in that newspaper. 'If this appointment be not intended as a clumsy joke,' the editor had thundered, 'we confess that we can only regard it as one of the grossest acts of folly and impertinence which the Court of Rome has ventured to commit since the Crown and people of England threw off its yoke.' Before long the Prime Minister, Lord John Russell, assured the Bishop of Durham that 'there is an assumption of power in all the documents which have come from Rome . . . which is inconsistent with the Queen's supremacy, with the rights of our bishops and clergy, and with the spiritual independence of the nation.' And he translated his indignation into the Ecclesiastical Titles Act.[10]

---

[10] Relevant documents were collected by E. R. Norman, *Anti-Catholicism in Victorian England* (London, 1968).

The penalties announced in that act for any invasion of the rights of the Church of England were never imposed. Many soon felt ashamed of this outburst of intolerance, and within a week of his arrival in London Wiseman had a pamphlet ready for the printer, *An Appeal to the Reason and Good Feeling of the English People*. It was as clever as his letter from the Flaminian Gate had been foolish. First he appealed to 'that love of honourable dealing and fair play which, in joke or in earnest, is equally the instinct of an Englishman.' Next he pointed out that if Catholics did not recognize the spiritual authority of 'the bishops appointed by our gracious Queen' neither did the Church of Scotland or the Protestant Nonconformists of England. Then he assured the bishops of the Establishment that they would be deprived of none of their 'worldly advantages'. Finally he defended the use of Westminster in his new title. 'Close under the Abbey of Westminster there lie concealed labyrinths of lanes and courts, and alleys and slums, nests of ignorance, vice, depravity, and crime, as well as of squalor, wretchedness, and disease; whose atmosphere is typhus, whose ventilation is cholera; in which swarms of huge and almost countless population, in great measure, nominally at least, Catholic; haunts of filth, which no sewage committee can reach – dark corners which no lighting-board can brighten. This is the part of Westminster which alone I covet. . . .'

By the end of the year the cardinal was seen to be morally vindicated. He followed up his success with brilliant lectures and with a novel about fourth-century Rome, *Fabiola*. But the success did not last. He neglected routine business, alienated Newman and many others by a combination of grandeur with clumsiness and inefficiency, and relied in his dealings with Rome on a monsignor who went mad. He grew very fat and very depressed. His death in 1865 was a release not only for him but also for those who had tried to share the work with him. As he lay dying, he said with truth: 'I have never cared for anything but the Church. . . .' Newman wrote *The Dream of Gerontius* while Wiseman was on his deathbed, and his funeral was the largest in London since the Duke of Wellington's, showing that despite everything many Englishmen acknowledged the talents and ideals which had made this man the spokesman of a great tradition now revived.[11]

Under Wiseman the provost of the chapter of Westminster had been Henry Manning, the former Anglican Archdeacon of Chichester who had thrown away brilliant prospects in the Established Church and Gladstone's intimate friendship. He would never have been elected as Wiseman's successor, being far too unpopular, but the Pope appointed him – and his rule was, just as other priests had feared, uncomfortable.

Once enthroned, the new archbishop vetoed any political activity on behalf of the English Catholics unless it was under his control, and he even stopped the informal religious discussions of a London group known as the 'Academy of the Catholic Religion', brought together by Wiseman. By his self-confident ability and by his command of Pius IX's support, Manning was able to impose his policies on this large and growing community right up to his death in 1892, although his grip slackened somewhat when Pope Pius died in 1878.

The symbol of his supremacy was the prohibition of any Roman Catholic enrolment for higher education at Oxford and Cambridge. Some of the richer Roman Catholics defied the prohibition, but not many. Manning's own 'university college' in Kensington collapsed amid debts and scandals, but his policy was inflexible for Oxford and Cambridge represented the Anglicanism from which he had escaped. His loyalty to Pius IX was so extreme that the cardinals managed to delay his promotion to join their number until the Pope finally had his way in 1875. But when papal infallibility had been defined despite the hesitations of most of his fellow bishops in England, Manning had the satisfaction of seeing them all accept the decree, along with Newman. Out of his own experience as a convert he knew well that there was no coherent spiritual and

[11] Brian Fothergill's 1963 study of *Nicholas Wiseman* was more psychological than Wilfrid Ward's *Life and Times of Cardinal Wiseman* (2 vols., London, 1900). E. E. Reynolds portrayed Wiseman with Newman and Manning in *Three Cardinals* (London, 1958), and S. W. Jackman studied his writings in *Nicholas, Cardinal Wiseman* (Gerrards Cross, Bucks, 1977).

intellectual alternative to the confident dogmatism now centred on Rome. It seems a fair comment by an historian (admittedly an Anglican) that among Roman Catholics in England to the end of the century 'the atmosphere of simplicity was not of the credulous but of the childlike. And a sophisticated leader like Manning preferred to have it so. He saw the strength of simple faith . . . in order that the values inherited from the past could be preserved.'[12]

The last years of Cardinal Manning had their sadnesses. The new pope, Leo XIII, responded to the Duke of Norfolk's petition that Newman should be made a cardinal. It would be a sign of his policy of taking the arts and sciences under his patronage, bridging the gap which Pius IX had deliberately widened between the Church and modern civilization. Manning chose to interpret a private letter from Newman, who was suitably modest, as a refusal, and made this public – only to find that Newman made clear his determination to accept the honour. Bishop Ullathorne interpreted Manning's role in this incident in the worst possible light, probably rightly. Rebuffed in this and in other ways by the new regime in the Vatican, Manning never visited Rome during the last nine years of his life.

His true glory was his sympathy with the poor. He bravely championed the agricultural labourers; in the 1880s he issued two pastoral letters in defence of the urban poor; and in 1889 he had his biggest chance to befriend the low-paid in London, when he successfully mediated in the dockers' strike. So Manning was 'the lonely pioneer of Social Catholicism in England'.[13] His successor attributed it to senile decay, and his first biographer, E. S. Purcell, was more dismayed by this involvement in 'Socialism' than by any other aspect of his life. But many others respected him as a brave prophet – and he certainly had a prophet's face. In the words of a Nonconformist journalist, 'it was as if wrinkled parchment was stretched across a fleshless skull, out of which, however, blue eyes

---

[12] Owen Chadwick, *The Victorian Church*, vol. ii, p. 408.
[13] A. R. Vidler, *A Century of Social Catholicism 1820–1920* (London, 1964), p. 71.

gleamed brightly, while a pleasant smile gave life and human fervour to the features of an ascetic.'[14]

His successor in 1892, Herbert Vaughan, shared all his dedication to the triumph of the 'Roman spirit' and all his contempt for Anglicanism. Alarmed by Anglo-Catholic efforts led by the Earl of Halifax to secure some recognition of the Church of England in Rome, he was delighted when in 1896 Pope Leo issued the enclyclical *Apostolicae Curae*, making clear the invalidity of Anglican ordinations: they were 'absolutely null and utterly void'. Vaughan then wrote to Halifax, urging 'the necessity of submission to the Church – the Church of which the Pope is the legitimate Head.'[15] In a pastoral letter which he and other bishops issued in 1900, he expressed his own faith – the faith which his family had kept since the days of Elizabeth I, and which had made five of his brothers priests. 'When our Lord Jesus Christ was upon earth, God spoke through the lips of His Sacred Humanity', they declared. 'After He had ascended into Heaven the Divine Teacher spoke through the mouth of Peter and the Apostles, and He now teaches and will continue to teach through their legitimate successors, "until the consummation of the ages".'

But in other ways Vaughan was more smoothly businesslike than Manning. Not for nothing had he been liked by the businessmen of Manchester as the very active Bishop of Salford, concentrating on the multiplication of schools under his own firm control. He now obtained permission for Roman Catholics to study at Oxford and Cambridge, with careful arrangements for their spiritual care; and he allied himself with the Conservatives who championed church schools for the poor. From him there were no indiscretions about Christian Socialism.[16]

---

[14] E. S. Purcell, *Life of Cardinal Manning* (2 vols., London, 1896), has been supplemented by Sir Shane Leslie, *Henry Edward Manning: His Life and Labours* (London, 1921); *Manning: Anglican and Catholic*, ed. John Fitzsimons (London, 1951); and V. A. McClelland, *Cardinal Manning: His Public Life and Influence* (London, 1962).

[15] See J. J. Hughes, *Absolutely Null and Utterly Void* (London, 1968).

[16] See V. A. McClelland, *English Roman Catholics and Higher Education 1830–1903* (London, 1973).

He told a cousin who met him at the railway station on his arrival as archbishop-elect that his biggest project would be to build a cathedral; and so it was. Early in 1894 he was assured of the support of wealthy men such as the Duke of Norfolk. Next year the design by John Bentley – massive, brick and basically Byzantine, so as to avoid comparisons with Westminster Abbey – was accepted and the work was begun. By the middle of 1902 the domes and campanile were almost complete, although the exhausted architect was dead. Most of the decoration in mosaics had to be left to later generations, but a greater frustration was that the idea of bringing Benedictine monks back to Westminster for the daily singing of the Divine Office came to nothing. The abbeys consulted refused to release monks unless they could also do pastoral work in the area; and Vaughan refused to entrust them with this responsibility. But provision was made for a 'secular' establishment of priests and musicians who would be clearly under the archbishop's control. The whole bold and rapid construction expressed, in brick and in worship, what the word 'triumphalism' means.

On a June day in 1903 the cardinal's body was brought to Westminster Cathedral for a Requiem Mass. It was the first public service held in the great church. But he was buried in his own college for training missionaries at Mill Hill, where he had always remained the Superior General. Knowing that the triumph depended on the mission, he had chosen to die there.[17]

---

[17] Arthur McCormack, *Cardinal Vaughan* (London, 1966), supplemented J. G. Snead-Cox, *Cardinal Vaughan* (2 vols., London, 1911). See also *Letters of Herbert Cardinal Vaughan to Lady Herbert of Lea*, ed. Shane Leslie (London, 1942).

CHAPTER EIGHT

UNCONVENTIONAL VICTORIANS

WOMEN AS CRUSADERS

It is quite wrong to think that all Victorian Christians were smugly comfortable.

Three women astonished the public because as Christian crusaders they dared to learn about, to enter and to transform prisons, hospitals and the lives of prostitutes. After much hesitation, their own nineteenth century applauded what they did. The next century was to be no less interested in who they were; for these were women of indomitable personality who dared to carve out their own beliefs and lives in defiance of long-established conventions. Thus they liberated not only the victims of sordid evils, but also themselves. And by their example they helped to liberate their sex.[1]

Elizabeth Fry is revealed in her journals (too indiscreet for use in the early biographies) as a portly matron with many anxieties, depressions and nervous illnesses, needing the plentiful use of wine and opium. Her emotional problems arose out of her position in society, enviable as that might seem to almost all other women in her age. Herself one of twelve children, she had eleven of her own. Her father was a wealthy merchant and banker in Norwich, John Gurney, her husband a dealer in tea, Joseph Fry. Her position was complicated by the fact that both of them were Quakers. On the one hand, this provided an outlet for her religious energies: she became a 'plain' Quaker, accepting the dress and speech of the little Puritan community, and was recognized as a minister. On the

---

[1] E. K. Prochaska studied *Women and Philanthropy in Nineteenth-century England* (Oxford, 1980).

other hand she was repelled by the emphasis now being given to quiet but steady money-making, and was indignant when the Quakers disowned and expelled her husband after the failure of a bank which he had started over-ambitiously. She was herself ambitious. She wanted to speak in public, to control others; and she wanted fame. She was ashamed of enjoying her work away from home, but she did enjoy it.

Thus mixed motives impelled her to lead a revolution within England's prisons. Prison reform had been frequently debated since the enquiries made by another Quaker, John Howard, in the 1770s; but remarkably little had been done. In January 1813, at the age of thirty-two, Elizabeth Fry was asked by a fellow Quaker to make some clothing for the babies of the women in a London prison, Newgate. The request led her to visit the prison, which was horrifying. Not only were the babies starving and disease-ridden, but the adult women were brutalized by subhuman conditions. She conducted services and a school there, and reorganized the whole of the women's side of the prison under a matron and monitors, with the co-operation or bemused assent of the men in charge. And the logic seemed inescapable – if women were to be cleaned up like that, why not men? And if Newgate was to be reformed, why not every other prison in the land? And if the fate of English prisoners was to be eased, what about the convicts being transported in their thousands to Australia? Elizabeth Fry had found her life's work. When she began this crusade, prisons were under no kind of national control. Everything depended on the local magistrates and on ill-paid and unsupervised gaol-keepers. In theory some two hundred crimes were to be punished by death, but in practice most criminals were imprisoned, in gaols which became more and more overcrowded. In 1823 Parliament intervened to establish some minimum standards of decency, but more was due to Elizabeth Fry. Tirelessly travelling and protesting, by the time of her death in 1843 she had made the Christian Gospel once more what it had been at the beginning: good news for prisoners.[2]

---

[2] The most candid biography is June Rose, *Elizabeth Fry* (London, 1980). Kathleen Heasman summarized the work of Victorian successors in her *Evangelicals in Action*, pp. 169–88.

Florence Nightingale's personality was in many ways similar. She, too, was born into a rich family, although her parents
were dedicated entirely to the pursuit of pleasure; she owed her
Christian name to the fact that she was born (in 1820) in
Florence. She refused all the proposals of marriage made to
her, with the result that the conventions of her class decreed
that she should devote her life to these parents. It was only in
1851 that she was allowed to stay for a time in Kaiserswerth, a
hospital with schools attached run by the Lutheran
deaconesses in Germany; 'Now I know what it is to live and to
love life.' It was only in 1853 that she finally broke away from
her family to become the superintendent of a small Institution
for the Care of Sick Gentlewomen in Distressed Circumstances.

There was then no training for nurses, the pay was very low,
and most nurses were sluts who drank heavily. Not a few were,
or had been, prostitutes. Even Miss Nightingale could never
have done much to change such traditions had she not been
commissioned by her friend Sidney Herbert, then in charge of
the relevant department of the War Office, to lead a party of
nurses out to the Crimean War in the autumn of 1854. She
walked into two years of hell – and into fame as 'the lady with
the lamp'. Her inflexible aims were now to secure a Royal
Commission on hygiene and hospitals in the army, to feed it
with facts, to make sure that it recommended the right reforms,
and to see that its recommendations were carried out – all in
the teeth of opposition. After the strain of the war she collapsed
into invalidism, but always exploited her status as an invalid;
she summoned eminent men to console her in her helplessness
and when they arrived told them in detail what they must do
for the army's hygiene. Nor was this the limit of her slow
triumph. The standards forced on the army must also apply to
the general public, and she founded Britain's first schools to
train nurses and midwives. Her emphasis on character was,
however, such that she resisted the registration of nurses who
had merely passed an examination. And the same standards
must apply to the far-off British army in India. From her
invalid's room in London she corresponded on such a large
scale that although she never saw the places she discussed she

made herself the leading authority on all matters of hygiene in India. In 1870, during the war between Germany and France, she began directing the activities of the new society which later became the British Red Cross.

When asked for the secret of her success she would reply 'hard work' – that, and never denying God anything. She sometimes relaxed a little from her toils to write down thoughts on religion, some of which were published. They show that she had a burning sense of personal mission, fuelled by an intense experience of God the Father (not of Christ). That was her inspiration, although she wrote: 'I must remember God is not my private secretary.'[3]

Prostitution was a thriving trade – as was shown by the number of efforts to 'rescue' prostitutes. Men of the world accepted it as the necessary consequence of the facts – middle-class men did not marry until they were able to support a wife and family; they did not then expect their 'pure' wives to take any pleasure in sex; but, once married, they did not get divorced. At the same time sex between men and women in the working class was often free and easy, the 'age of consent' being twelve. Women with this experience behind them were easily tempted to offer sex to men who could pay for it. Few jobs were open to them apart from factory work (often in brutal conditions), and humiliating and ill-paid domestic service. There were 3,228,000 unmarried adult women in England in 1871. Everything seemed to conspire to make them sell their bodies – often for sixpence, of which they kept twopence. Many thousands of prostitutes roamed the streets of London and all the cities including Liverpool, then one of the largest ports in the world.[4]

There, in the late 1860s, Josephine Butler discovered the problem in human terms. Parliament had recently passed Contagious Diseases Acts intended to protect soldiers from venereal diseases. Prostitutes working in towns where there

---

[3] The best biography is Cecil Woodham-Smith, *Florence Nightingale* (revised, London, 1955).

[4] Recent studies include Judith Walkowitz, *Prostitution and Victorian Society* (Cambridge, 1980), and Paul McHugh, *Prostitution and Victorian Social Reform* (London, 1980).

were many soldiers had to register and to be inspected regularly. Women suspected of belonging to this profession could be apprehended by plain-clothes policemen, subjected to a medical examination, and ordered to report back regularly. Those who did not co-operate could be imprisoned. Roughly similar laws existed in most European countries, and before the spread of clinics to treat venereal diseases this control could be defended as protection. Most gentlemen preferred not to notice; the legislation had received very little comment in Parliament.

Josephine Butler, although the wife of the headmaster of Liverpool College, noticed. She noticed that the State tolerated and regulated vice. She noticed the indignities to which women were subjected, including innocent women, and she noticed the lofty or amused indifference shown by men. She noticed a departure from the English tradition of justice, which assumes a person to be innocent until proved guilty. And her crusading zeal would not be quenched until she had charmed, bullied, persuaded or simply exhausted men into seeing the need to extend English justice to women. First the compulsory medical examination without proof of prostitution was abolished. She went on campaigning when threatened by the brothel-keepers, when rebuked by people whose opinions she greatly valued, when supported by sensation-loving journalists, when moved to Winchester Cathedral Close where her husband was now a canon, and when widowed. Eventually in 1886 the Contagious Diseases Acts were repealed and her victory was complete, although prostitution remained a major phenomenon of English life into the 1910s. And the indefatigable Josephine Butler took 'the Cause' to stir Paris, Geneva and other centres of 'the Trade'.[5]

---

[5] Modern biographies are by E. Moberly Bell, *Josephine Butler: Flame of Fire* (London, 1962), and Glen Petrie, *A Singular Iniquity: The Campaigns of Josephine Butler* (London, 1971). A more personal *Portrait of Josephine Butler* was provided by her grandson, A. S. G. Butler (London, 1954).

SOLDIERS OF SALVATION

In 1883 a pamphlet issued by the London Congregational Union described a city which to the comfortable was still almost another continent. 'Whilst we have been building our churches and solacing ourselves with our religion and dreaming that the millennium was coming, the poor have been growing poorer, and the wretched more miserable, and the immoral more corrupt. The gulf has been daily widening which separates the lowest classes of the community from our churches and chapels, and from all decency and civilization. . . . *This terrible flood of sin and misery is growing upon us.*'

This pamphlet asked of the homes of many of London's poor, in 'rotten and reeking tenements': 'how can those places be called homes, compared with which the lair of a wild beast would be a comfortable and healthy spot?' It gave some shocking details about the unemployment, about the 'sweated' trades where work was little better than unemployment (a shilling for a seventeen-hour day sewing trousers), about the cruelly excessive rents, about the misery of children. 'Who can wonder that every evil flourishes in such hotbeds of vice and disease?' The pamphlet acknowledged the work of a 'noble army of men and women who penetrate the vilest haunts, carrying with them the blessings of the Gospel'. It praised 'Missions, Reformatories, Refuges, Temperance Societies . . . theatre services, midnight meetings and special missions.' It concluded as a result of 'long, patient and sober enquiry' that 'we are simply living in a fool's paradise if we suppose that all those agencies combined are doing a thousandth part of what needs to be done.'[6]

Movements which became internationally famous were included among these agencies battling with the social problems of Victorian London. At the more respectable end of the spectrum were the YMCA and YWCA, responding to the fact that London needed the ill-paid, unexciting but still 'respect-

---

[6] *The Bitter Cry of Outcast London* has been reprinted together with Octavia Hill's 1875 pamphlet on *Homes of the London Poor* (London, 1970). Recent research was summarized by Gareth Stedman Jones, *Outcast London* (Oxford, 1971).

able' work of tens of thousands of young men and women, clerks in offices or assistants in shops. Some had their accommodation provided by their employers, as had been the old custom with apprentices; but most were condemned to find cheap and cheerless lodgings. They could not marry since they aimed to be reckoned middle-class and the convention was strong that a man did not marry until he could support his wife and children. The innumerable prostitutes presented the most obvious temptation both to the young men to relieve their frustrations and to the young women to make more money. But probably most young men and women in this class went to church on a Sunday; there was little else to do. If the church was Evangelical, they would hear great promises and ideals proclaimed by the preacher – but after the thrills they would go their own ways back to shabbiness, isolation and boredom.

In 1844 about a dozen young men with such a background founded the Young Men's Christian Association in the bedroom of George Williams, then a young apprentice in a drapery business. The first international conference of YMCAs was held in Paris in 1855, and the YMCA held its first big meeting in London in 1878. [7]

A similar pattern, of Evangelical origins broadening out, may be seen in work for London's destitute children.

Dr Barnardo's Homes were only one of a number of similar efforts. For example, a civil servant, Edward Rudolf, the superintendent of the teachers in a Sunday school in Lambeth, was disturbed by the daily spectacle of tens of thousands of destitute children on the streets of central London. His own childhood had been poverty-stricken – but nothing like that. So in 1881 he founded the Waifs and Strays Society, later called the Church of England Children's Society, and administered it until retirement in 1919.

Thomas Barnardo's name has survived because he was a forceful, often controversial individualist. Born in 1845 to a German father and Irish mother and brought up in Dublin, he experienced an Evangelical conversion in 1862 and immediately threw himself into religious work among the Dublin

---

[7] See Clyde Binfield, *George Williams and the YMCA* (London, 1973).

poor; naturally he joined the YMCA. Moving to London in order to train as a medical missionary, in 1868 he converted two cottages as the first base of the East End Juvenile Mission. Later he raised funds to purchase a large public house, banning alcohol but welcoming large numbers to enjoy the Coffee Palace. A little lad called Jim Harvis showed him some of the places where he and hundreds of other boys slept in the open air of a winter's night. Barnardo became passionately determined to search for such boys (and girls) and to provide a home for them. And he encouraged others to come; 'No destitute child is ever refused admittance' became his motto. With a flair for publicity, he poured out pamphlets and articles; he habitually worked for seventeen hours a day; and with great self-confidence he personally obtained and administered large funds, scornful of many charges that his financial methods were so personal as to disregard the conventions. In one sense he did well for himself out of the great charity which was always to be linked with his name: he found fulfilment. Before his death in 1905 he had assumed the entire responsibility for rebuilding almost 60,000 young lives.[8]

William Booth was even more of an autocrat. Given a pound a week by a benefactor in order to turn from the hated work of a pawnbroker's assistant to revivalist preaching, he had rejected the Methodist splinter group ('the New Connexion') which had tried to sponsor and control him, and had founded his own 'Christian Mission' in London's East End in 1865. In 1878, when he was almost fifty, he renamed it the 'Salvation Army'. The name was a stroke of genius. The mission halls were now called 'barracks', prayer was called 'knee-drill', and the magazine was renamed the *War Cry*. Banners were paraded, with brass bands to enliven the marches, drown any opposition and accompany the 'songs' (usually very simple hymns, sung to tunes already popular in the music halls). Showmanship to attract audiences was encouraged, but the army did not have to rely on individual eccentrics; it created a stir by being itself in its military uniforms. And it developed practices which

---

[8] The best biography is Gillian Wagner, *Barnardo* (London, 1979). The story of the Waifs and Strays was told by John Stroud in *Thirteen Penny Stamps* (London, 1971).

distinguished it still more from the churches, for it abandoned the sacraments of Baptism and Holy Communion and gave equal status to men and women – all under General Booth, who owned all the property.

The opposition was often violent; to break up meetings, a 'Skeleton Army' was hired by men who saw that the drink trade was threatened. In one year alone, 1882, 669 Salvation Army officers were knocked down or assaulted, about a third of them being women, and some sixty of their buildings were damaged. But 1882 was also the year when the Church of England paid them the compliment of imitation, founding the Church Army; for these soldiers without weapons seemed not to heed their wounds. 'Blood and fire' was one of their mottoes. William Booth's daughter Kate led the army into France; his very able private secretary, George Railton, organized it in America; a former civil servant, Frederick Tucker, outraged the English rulers of India by leading a group which used Indian names and which looked, lived, begged and preached in the style of the Hindu holy men.

Gradually this evangelism was accompanied by more and more social work. In Australia the Salvation Army opened a home for discharged prisoners; in Sweden a home for the deaf and dumb; in London a legal aid scheme for the poor, night shelters for the homeless, 'farthing breakfasts' for hungry children, the country's first labour exchange, and a missing persons bureau. By the end of 1890, often working beside the bed where his deeply loved wife and collaborator, Catherine, lay dying of cancer, William Booth had collected material for an explosive book about the social problems of London and other English cities: *In Darkest England and the Way Out*. He asked for an emergency fund of a million pounds and for a City Colony of linked institutions to relieve distress, a Farm Colony to make sober farmers out of the poor, and great emigration schemes. He was disappointed in these unrealistic hopes, but his vision had many practical results in England – and by now the international army under his command was winning victories which were very widely reported and respected. In Tokyo it fought prostitution, in New York alcoholism, with dramatic public marches. It was heroic in bringing relief after the great San Francisco earthquake, in founding a leper colony in Java, in many other tasks which no other body in all the world could tackle so well. Its social work commended it to rich and poor alike, although the novelty of its military-style revivalism had worn off.

In 1912 the General of this unique army was 'promoted to glory', as Salvationists phrased it; and the streets of central London were silent for four hours to honour his funeral procession.[9]

THE RELIGIOUS UNSETTLEMENT

Social problems were, however, not the only challenge to Victorian religion. It was also an age when the unsettlement of 'unbelief' spread – and could not be stopped by any religiously orthodox revivalism. The first man to use the word 'secular' in its modern meaning was George Jacob Holyoake, who in 1842 had been imprisoned for blasphemy. He was not committed to atheism, preferring the more ambiguous terms 'free thinking' and 'rationalism', but he lived to see the more loud-mouthed Charles Bradlaugh founding the National Secular Society in 1866 and taking his seat in Parliament. He himself founded the Rationalist Press Association in 1899 and continued to organize propaganda for secularism until his death seven years later.[10]

The greatest name in the more intellectual movement in secularization was that of Charles Darwin, whose disciple T. H. Huxley coined the word 'agnostic'. Darwin, too, never liked to be classified as an outright atheist, but during his voyage on HMS *Beagle* (1831–36) lost the complacent Christianity which he had imbibed from the *Evidences* of William Paley. It could

[9] The best biographies are Richard Collier, *The General Next to God* (London, 1965), and Catherine Bramwell-Booth, *Catherine Booth* (London, 1970). Robert Sandall wrote the official *History of the Salvation Army* in three volumes (London, 1947–55), followed by two volumes by Arch Wiggins (London, 1964–68).

[10] The best survey is Susan Budd, *Varieties of Unbelief* (London, 1977). More detail is in Edward Royle, *Victorian Infidels* and *Radicals, Secularists and Republicans* (Manchester, 1974–81).

not survive when he had glimpsed the real world with its many religions. He drew three lessons – first that the Old Testament 'was no more to be trusted than the sacred books of the Hindoos, or the beliefs of any barbarian', second that clearer evidence than was available 'would be requisite to make any sane man believe in the miracles by which Christianity is supported', and third that God had never given an authoritative revelation of himself. Then the amount of suffering inflicted by nature on animals in the interests of the 'survival of the fittest' gripped his imagination and his conscience, making it impossible – or, as in some moods he preferred to say, very difficult – for him to believe any longer that a good and loving Creator, revealed or unrevealed, could have ordained and foreseen the whole bloodbath.

His key idea of 'natural selection' by the 'struggle for existence' became plain to him when, two years after returning home from the *Beagle*, he read the *Essay on Population* by Thomas Malthus. His *Origin of Species* (1859) was sensational not because it propounded a complete explanation of the evolution of man from lower animals, but because men who had open eyes concluded that the Bible could not be literally true in its accounts of creation – and became inclined to suspect that the Bible was not true in any sense. Leslie Stephen, for example, was the son of a great Evangelical and a conspicuously clever and industrious clergyman; but in 1862 he resigned as a Cambridge college tutor because his mind could find 'no real stopping-place' in religion once he had abandoned belief in the infallibility of the Bible. It is curious that in England the main challenge to the old authority of 'revelation' came from the new science, whereas in Germany much more interest was taken in detailed historical criticism of the Old and New Testaments.[11]

'Nothing is more remarkable', Darwin recorded in his old age, 'than the spread of scepticism or rationalism during the latter part of my life.' Although conventional in his own domesticity, he thought that a morality independent of the discredited Christian religion was necessary. Sometimes

---

[11] L. E. Elliott-Binns made this a theme in *English Thought 1860–1900: The Theological Aspect* (London, 1956).

Christianity appeared to him to be actively immoral. 'I can indeed hardly see how anyone ought to wish Christianity to be true; for if so, the plain language of the text seems to show that men who do not believe, and this would include my father, brother, and almost all my best friends, will be everlastingly punished. And this is a damnable doctrine.' What a man needed was a rule of life 'only to follow those impulses and instincts which are strongest or which seem to him the best ones.'

These were disturbing thoughts. Disraeli put his finger on what people were feeling in his famous speech to the Oxford Diocesan Society in 1864. 'What is the question now placed before society with a glib assurance the most astounding? The question is this – Is man an ape or an angel? My Lord, I am on the side of the angels.' Four years previously at a meeting of the British Association for the Advancement of Science in Oxford Bishop Samuel Wilberforce had tried to ridicule Darwin's newly published *Origin*; he added his own wit and self-assurance to information or misinformation largely supplied by a leading anatomist, Sir Richard Owen. He teased T. H. Huxley, who was present and who had been reported as saying that it did not matter to him personally whether or not his grandfather was an ape. Would Huxley be content to trace his descent through an ape as his grandmother? Huxley, having muttered a biblical text to his neighbour ('The Lord hath delivered him into mine hands'), rose and with a deliberate coolness replied in words that burned. A later account of these words was that he would 'unhesitatingly affirm my preference for the ape' rather than have as grandfather 'a man highly endowed by nature and possessed of great means of influence and yet who employs these faculties and that influence for the mere purpose of introducing ridicule into a grave scientific discussion.'

Many of the clergymen and Christian ladies present applauded Huxley (then and afterwards) – and Bishop Wilberforce has been universally condemned for his folly although he tried to make light of the incident. But behind the flippancy of Disraeli and of the bishop who was his ally, we ought to see something more serious. It was a grave question for many intelligent mid-Victorians whether the dignity of mankind (especially the respect given to 'pure' women such as Bishop Wilberforce's grandmothers) could be maintained after the revelation of truth by Charles Darwin. As Professor Sedgwick of Cambridge warned Darwin after the publication of his *Origin*, if the 'moral or metaphysical part of nature' were to be ignored 'humanity would suffer a damage which might brutal-ize it, and sink the human race into a lower grade of degrada-tion than any into which it has fallen since its written records tell us of its history.' Darwin privately asked about belief in God: 'Can the mind of man, which has, as I fully believe, been developed from a mind as low as that possessed by the lowest animal, be trusted when it draws such grand conclusions?' Perhaps the power of the belief in God was caused solely by children being taught it? His was a questioning position very far removed from the centuries of trust in man's godlike reason – and from the 'will to believe' of the Victorians. Whether or not they were fundamentalists in their religion, many of the great Victorian scientists – Michael Faraday, Lord Kelvin, Joseph Lister, Clerk Maxwell, the leading medical men – always remained devout Christians. And when T. H. Huxley died in 1895 three lines from a poem by his wife were inscribed on his tombstone by his wish:

> Be not afraid, ye waiting hearts that weep;
> For still He giveth His beloved sleep,
> And if an endless sleep He wills, so best.

It was not the last testament of a consistent secularist.[12]

The lives of many Victorian laymen illustrate this confusion or conflict between opposed tendencies: the nostalgia for the religious foundations of family life and other agreeable features of the old England, and the awareness that a time had come for which there might be no over-ruling God, no ever-living Christ, no realistic morality other than self-interest.

---

[12] The *Autobiographies* of Charles Darwin and T. H. Huxley were edited by Gavin de Beer (Oxford, 1974). Studies include William Irvine, *Apes, Angels and Victorians* (London, 1955); David Lack, *Evolutionary Theory and Christian Belief: The Unresolved Conflict* (London, 1957); Gertrude Himmelfarb, *Darwin and the Darwinian Revolution* (London, 1959), and *Victorian Minds* (London, 1968); James R. Moore, *The Post-Darwinian Controversies* (Cambridge, 1979).

Matthew Arnold's poetry is full of the tension. He was a son of the great Thomas Arnold whose headmastership of Rugby School did so much to make the public schools more earnestly Christian (and more humane and scholarly), and he was himself an educationist and a kind of lay preacher. He devoted many years to his work as an Inspector of Education and many essays to his battle for the enlightenment and enlargement of the Victorian mind. The two Arnolds, father and son, may be recalled when we read the verdict of a Canadian scholar: 'This was the great accomplishment of the Church in Victorian England. Through the writing, teaching and preaching of its creative minority, it gave to the powerful new middle classes an ethic of service, based upon Christian principles.'[13]

Matthew Arnold, however, had to strain language to its most ambiguous limits when he paid his loyal tributes to his father's faith. His own belief was that 'the peace of God' was 'the Christian phrase for civilization', and 'the kingdom of God' was 'the ideal society of the future'. 'Christian principles' now needed a non-dogmatic basis since truly religion was 'morality touched by emotion'. 'To one who knows what conduct is, it is a joy to be alive; the *not ourselves*, which by revealing to us righteousness makes our happiness, adds to the boon this glorious world to be righteous in. That is the notion at the bottom of the Hebrew's praise of the Creator.' Or at least, that was the creed at the bottom of Matthew Arnold's attempt in a number of books or essays to reconstruct Christianity after the virtual disappearance of God.

Intellectually, it was all that seemed possible if a mid-Victorian who was highly educated in the terms of his own day was to be honest. But emotionally, he knew it was not enough – and his poetry revealed his distress. In 'The Scholar-Gipsy' he addressed a wanderer:

---

[13] Desmond Bowen, *The Idea of the Victorian Church* (Toronto, 1968), p. 258. See T. W. Bamford, *Thomas Arnold* and *The Rise of the Public Schools* (London, 1960–67). Other studies include Frances Woodward, *The Doctor's Disciples* (London, 1954); David Newsome, *Godliness and Good Learning* (London, 1961); Meriol Trevor, *The Arnolds* (London, 1973); J. R. de S. Honey, *Tom Brown's Universe* (London, 1977). The best biography of Matthew Arnold is by Patrick Honan (London, 1981).

> Thou waitest for the spark from heaven! and we,
>   Light half-believers of our casual creeds,
>   Who never deeply felt, nor clearly will'd,
>   Whose insight never has borne fruit in deeds,
>   Whose vague resolves never have been fulfill'd. . . .
>   Ah! do not we, wanderer! await it too?

In 'Dover Beach' he addressed the conventionally minded wife he was marrying:

> Ah, love, let us be true
> To one another! for the world, which seems
> To lie before us like a land of dreams,
> So various, so beautiful, so new,
> Hath really neither joy, nor love, nor light,
> Nor certitude, nor peace, nor help for pain. . . .

For his father's world had been left empty by the retreat of religious confidence from the minds of honest thinkers:

> The Sea of Faith
> Was once, too, at the full, and round earth's shore
> Lay like the folds of a bright girdle furl'd.
> But now I only hear
> Its melancholy, long, withdrawing roar,
> Retreating, to the breath
> Of the night-wind, down the vast-edges drear
> And naked shingles of the world.

The result for Matthew Arnold's heart as shown in his poems was a scene of confusion and terror. It was a world very different from the 'glorious world to be righteous in' of his lay preacher's prose – and from the strongly moral discharge of duties in his daily life. This was his vision:

> And we are here as on a darkling plain
> Swept with confused alarm of struggle and flight,
> Where ignorant armies clash by night.

Thomas Hardy was a novelist and a poet who became an example of a secularization more decisive than the battle going on in Matthew Arnold's mind between belief and unbelief. As late as 1865, when he was twenty-five, Hardy was still considering the possibility of being ordained. His chief interest as

an architect was in the restoration of churches, and his first
wife distributed Evangelical tracts. But the clergyman who
had given him his real education committed suicide, various
love affairs came to desolation, faith died, and by 1912 he could
make his mature position clear in a deeply melancholy poem
on 'God's Funeral'. Although it became his habit to speak
nostalgically or obliquely about religion, a critic of his work has
observed that almost everywhere the driving force was a belief
'that the universe was non-sentient, a kind of machine; that
consciousness was an accident and a misfortune as well. Most
of the quirks, obsessions and insights for which Hardy is
famous, the mechanical imagery, the peculiar home-made
mythology, the trivial incidents, the fascination with the workings of "Chance", and much else besides, could be logically
derived from this "core". . . .'[14]

A very public example of what the Victorian confusion of
spiritual crosscurrents meant to a sensitive spirit is to be found
in the novels and life of Charles Dickens.

Born in 1812, Dickens came from the lower middle class and
his central achievement was to put the life of that class into
print. He knew how to depict it as a good life. Indeed, it has
been said that 'no novel could move further than *Pickwick
Papers* toward asserting not only that the kingdom of God is
within each man but that it is possible to establish something
that resembles the kingdom of God on earth – and this, as
much as anything, accounts for its enduring, universal
popularity'.[15] But the central vision of Dickens was very
different. It was a nightmare vision of English life being
poisoned by the Victorian age – by its exploitation of those
forced to labour in factories or offices, but also by the psychological damage which the dominant materialism inflicted on the
successful.

No institutional form of religion played much of a part in his
thought or life. He wrote to a friend in 1843 about his disgust
with 'our Established Church, and its Puseyisms and daily

---

[14] Kenneth Marsden, *The Poems of Thomas Hardy* (London, 1969), p. 15. Robert
Gittings, *Young Thomas Hardy* and *The Older Hardy* (London, 1975–76), and Michael
Millgate, *Thomas Hardy* (Oxford, 1982), are the best biographies.

[15] Steven Marcus, *Dickens: From Pickwick to Dombey* (London, 1965), p. 51.

outrages on common sense and humanity'. This was not an isolated outburst, but in his novels his hostility was directed against Evangelicals, almost always portrayed as oily, canting and fatuous. Only in his deathbed scenes, when Victorian convention decreed that the angels must be on hand to take away innocent girls, did he begin to write like an Evangelical novelist. In his accounts of his travels he was as contemptuous of Catholicism in Italy as of Protestantism in America; only in his account of the Gordon Riots in *Barnaby Rudge* did he begin to show sympathy with Roman Catholics. Many members of the class from which he came were happily absorbed in the life of English Nonconformity, but all that he noted about the chapels in the 'Coketown' of *Hard Times* was that there were eighteen denominations and it was puzzling to know where their adherents all came from. The nearest he came to being involved in church life seems to have been in 1842–43, when he and his family became members of a Unitarian chapel in London, and towards the end of his life he subscribed to his parish church as a local squire. He was never more deeply committed because he shared the assumption of (for example) Hogarth that in comparison with the honest life of English streets and homes any religious enthusiasm, in the pulpit or on a layman's lips, must be humbug.

However, scholars have usually agreed that Dickens was non-ecclesiastically and non-dogmatically religious. Angus Wilson, indeed, claimed that 'he thought of himself as centrally a Christian' and that he was right, for in profound ways the Christian religion makes sense of his work.[16] The intensity of his hatred of cruelty was totally sincere; and so was his belief that love was blessed by the God who in the mysterious background presided over human affairs. It seems clear that he prayed twice a day and read the Bible regularly. He often assured correspondents that his novels were intended to support the teaching of the Saviour. In his last will – no conventional document, for the first of his legacies was a comparatively small sum left to the young actress who was his mistress – he wrote: 'I exhort my dear children humbly to try to guide

---

[16] *The English Novel*, ed. Angus Wilson and A. E. Dyson (London, 1976), p. 55.

themselves by the teaching of the New Testament in its broad
spirit, and to put no faith in any man's narrow construction of
its letter here and there.' He wrote a *Life of Christ* for these
children of his; it was not published until 1934. Many Christians loved and admired him. They believed that he had been
one of them when they buried him in Westminster Abbey, near
Handel.

His glimpse of hell came in the months of 1824 when he was
put to work in a London factory making blacking polish, while
his parents were imprisoned as debtors. The boy who introduced him to the work was named Fagin. The humiliation
made him inflexibly determined to succeed – and gave him the
raw material for his genius, since one of his assets was his
knowledge of the lights and shadows of London life at most
levels below the top. Despite his extraordinary vitality and his
supreme gift for comedy, the dominant theme of his work
became his hatred of the institutions which had, he believed,
ruined his class and his time; he began writing *Oliver Twist*
before he had finished *Pickwick Papers*. Thus Mr Pickwick,
although he benevolently shared with the twenty-four-year old
author a fame which became immortality as the years passed,
was not fully Dickensian. He was the man at the sunlit door
inviting the public to enter an exhibition hall showing the evils
of industrialism and commercialism. The hall grew darker as
the greatness of the literary achievement grew. In the last
novel, the unfinished *Edwin Drood*, Rochester, the enchanted
cathedral city of childhood and of *Pickwick*, had become a city
of night and death.

In his war against the institutions which had stunted the life
of his England, Dickens was more than a prophet. He was a
story-teller whose characters and dramas – at first melodrama-
tic, then far more subtle – fascinated a public which would
never have opened books full of coldly stated ethical propositions. The propositions can be listed, however. *Martin Chuzzle-
wit* added to its fun the exposure of a society of the selfish made
worse by Pecksniff's hypocrisy. *Nicholas Nickleby* attacked
schools and jobs which tormented or corrupted the young.
Bleak House denounced a legal system which was part of a social
system where, in a fog-like confusion of justice, parasites had

power. The story of *Oliver Twist*, so far from romanticizing the underworld as had become the convention, expounded the thesis that poverty, when treated as a crime, breeds criminals because it supplies pupils for the Fagins of this world; and the story of *Dombey and Son*, so far from romanticizing the captains of commerce, contained the thesis that the dominance of money-making destroys the true life of the heart even for those who prosper. *Hard Times* was a horrifying picture of a factory town, but *Our Mutual Friend* saw a horror in the very success of Victorian England, with a fortune founded on 'dust', a Victorian euphemism for garbage and dung. *Little Dorrit*, perhaps the greatest of his novels, was certainly the most profoundly Christian. It showed in how many ways adults could allow themselves to be imprisoned in situations which crippled their own humanity, and it contained one more not very convincing sketch of the good woman who was the liberator.

In his own life Dickens never found that woman (which helps to explain why in the novels the women are often too good to be true). *David Copperfield* and *Great Expectations* contained strong elements of autobiography and show how the ups and downs of his own life made him understand an age when greed prevailed over innocence, ambition over integrity, snobbery over compassion – and when marriage was often loveless. But this great revealer of the human heart never came to terms with his own tragedy, and this great communicator never told his own story. He gave *Great Expectations* a happy ending because he took the advice that a tragedy would not sell so well. He never told his own wife or children about the most significant event in his life (often returning in his dreams) – the fall from the paradise of his childhood into the blacking factory, total disaster when he had been a precociously bright and sensitive boy scarcely twelve years old. His lifelong pain was that fame and fortune could not convince him that he was loved or lovable. As his intimate friend and first biographer John Forster wrote with reticence, he 'believed himself to be entitled to a higher tribute than he was always in the habit of receiving.' In his own family he longed for a complete appreciation, obedience and devotion, with the result that he became separated bitterly from his wife – and did not find the understanding he had looked for from his mistress. In the end he was not close to most of his ten children, although he had been a merry enough father when they were little. He added to his follies by publishing a fatuous public statement about his domestic crisis. His favourite daughter, Katey, paid the tribute which is often regarded as the excuse: 'He was not a good man . . . he was wonderful.' But his public destruction of his marriage was a terrifying reminder of the failure of the kind of religion in which he sincerely believed to heal his own deep hurt. It has been well said that in the novels 'delight in the pleasures of home, in food and drink and children's games . . . is expressed with an intensity of feeling far beyond the normal. And yet, in spite of all, the marriage, the home, the children, the festivities, all after twenty years are flung violently away, as though the discrepancy between what he had and what he *meant* to have, the lack of that "one happiness I have missed in life, and one friend and companion I never made", had become finally unbearable.'[17]

His chosen form of death has raised very disturbing questions. For long he had been pathologically restless. In order to maintain lavish households and to entertain his friends, he needed to earn more and more of the money he attacked in his books; and although he could still have earned a great deal as a writer, he now chose to give public readings of passages from the novels, with a harrowing double climax in the murder of Nancy and the hanging of Sikes from *Oliver Twist*. He persisted in these readings even when he always ended them prostrated. The pleas of doctors and friends were rejected. For what he really needed, more than all the money, was a substitute for the lost home of his boyhood. And since even a living audience could not be sympathetic enough, what he finally needed most of all was the nearest approach to suicide which Victorian England could allow to a man who wished his reputation to survive. It was to be a reputation flawed by the centrality of his unresolved personal problems.

Essentially he was a dramatist. Had the Victorian theatre offered as much scope for genius as the Elizabethan theatre,

---

[17] Margaret Lane in *Dickens 1970*, ed. Michael Slater (London, 1970), p. 171.

presumably he would have written more, and more serious, plays. But since his novels were dramas personifying social evils, and since as a magazine editor and journalist he was responsible for much non-fictional comment on the problems of his time, he has not escaped assessment as a social thinker. In the cold light of analysis an element of confusion in his ideas is obvious, and it is also obvious that his enthusiasms for particular reforms changed. Angus Wilson has observed that 'the young Dickens aspired to a respectable middle-class radicalism attacking particular social evils and ended as a middle-aged revolutionary with a particular hostility to the middle classes.'[18] This undeniably compassionate man was too wounded in his own spirit, and too preoccupied by those wounds, to be quite the reformer believed in by many of his most fervent admirers. There was in him a pouting child and a sneering adolescent, a bitter cynic and even an isolated criminal, as well as the Dickens who was, as *The Times* said when he died, the world's 'unassailable and enduring favourite'.[19]

POETS OF PAIN AND FAITH

Such an age was for religious poetry the 'bleak midwinter'. But the fact that this phrase comes from the most famous poem of Christina Rosetti, who was a technically accomplished and often impressive poet, shows that it was possible to make something of the doubt with its mental pain: to make a faith which was not at all complacent. Christina Rosetti belonged to a family thoroughly unsettled in religion and life; and in her own life she knew failure, loneliness and very painful illnesses. Yet she could write much poetry of which this was the epitome:

---

[18] In *Charles Dickens: A Critical Anthology*, ed. Stephen Wall (Harmondsworth, Middx, 1970), p. 436.

[19] Denis Walder studied *Dickens and Religion* (London, 1981), Philip Collins *Dickens and Crime* and *Dickens and Education* (London, 1962–63), Norris Pope *Dickens and Charity* (London, 1978), and Michael Slater, *Dickens and Women* (London, 1983). On the fiction see F. R. and Q. R. Leavis, *Dickens the Novelist* (London, 1972), and other criticism mentioned there. The best biography is Edgar Johnson, *Charles Dickens: His Tragedy and Triumph* (London, 1977), supplemented by Norman and Jeanne Mackenzie, *Charles Dickens: A Life* (Oxford, 1979).

> My faith burns low, my hope burns low,
>   Only my heart's desire cries out in me
> By the deep thunder of its want and woe,
>   Cries out to thee.[20]

As a young man Alfred Tennyson was often profoundly miserable and close to suicide; very uncertain about his own future, even in the field of poetry to which his serious energies were confined from early years; and noted as a heavy smoker and drinker. He spoke about the 'black bloodedness' of his family. One of his brothers spent almost sixty years in a lunatic asylum, and another (who was ordained) was for a time separated from his wife who could not stand his addiction to opium. Other brothers were alcoholic or at least morbid. The shadow was cast by their father, a Lincolnshire parish priest without a vocation. But Alfred Tennyson lived to publish *In Memoriam* in May 1850, to marry next month a devout girl who had previously been alarmed by his irreligion, and to be appointed in November Poet Laureate in succession to Wordsworth. He himself summed up *In Memoriam* as 'my conviction that fear, doubts, and suffering will find answer and relief only through faith in a God of Love.' It was a 'conviction' not entirely convinced; and as eloquent as any confession of faith was the theme that there was no personal immortality in the hands of God, there was nothing left of the dignity of man in an unfeeling universe.

> No, like a child in doubt and fear:
> But that blind clamour made me wise;
> Then I was as a child that cries,
> But, crying, knows his father near . . .
> And out of darkness came the hands
> That reach through nature, moulding men.

He became famous, a peer, a sage – but one of his last poems was *Akbar's Dream*:

> I can but lift the torch
> Of reason in the dusky cave of Life,
> And gaze on this great miracle, the World,
> Adoring That who made, and makes, and is,

---

[20] The best biography is by Georgina Battiscombe (London, 1981).

> And is not, what I gaze on – all else Form,
> Ritual, varying with the tribes of men.

In conversation he once said with emphasis: 'There's a something that watches over us; and our individuality endures: that's my faith, and that's all my faith.'

T. S. Eliot called this faith a 'poor thing' and W. H. Auden once wrote about Tennyson: 'There was little about melancholia that he didn't know; there was little else that he did.' But this was a faith strong enough for Tennyson; and it had a massive appeal to the Victorian public in its religious unsettlement. An American critic has well said that 'from first to last his best poetry raised a psychological protest against the commonplace fact he knew with the intellect or acutely perceived with the senses. In the perspectives of evolutionary theory, he saw perpetual movement as the law of life; but with all his own passion of the past, he intuited a lasting order of values, a peace – both aesthetic and religious – untouched by the bewildering changefulness and relativity of the world.'[21] In his last years Tennyson's highest art went into poetry essentially religious and (what was much harder for him) peaceful. All the evidence of his private life corresponds with his public claim that as he drew towards death he found peace. While a boy he had flung himself sobbing on graves in his father's churchyard, envying the dead. Now he wanted 'no moaning',

> But such a tide as moving seems asleep,
> Too full for sound and foam,
> When that which drew from out the boundless deep
> Turns again home.

Despite his financial independence and the glory of his marriage with a fellow poet, Elizabeth Barrett Browning, Robert Browning spent many frustrated and unhappy years before he acquired his great fame. In his mid-fifties, in 1867, he wrote to a friend: 'The general impression of the past is as if it had been pain. I would not live it over again, not one day of it.' Thus the

---

[21] J. H. Buckley, *Tennyson: The Growth of a Poet* (Cambridge, Mass., 1960), p. 255. The most useful studies are Christopher Ricks, *Tennyson* (London, 1972); Philip Henderson, *Tennyson: Poet and Prophet* (London, 1978); R. B. Martin, *Tennyson: The Unquiet Heart* (London, 1980).

poet was in his own person the despondent Saul, the cynical Karshish, the warped Caliban of some of his most famous poems. The years of his marriage (1841–65) were his most creative period – but part of the reason was that, stirred by the very intensity of his joy in that marriage, he entered so fully into the religious questioning of that time. When he was left a widower he became, at least outwardly, a literary lion who roared in favour of religion and morality, but even in this long, last period some of the most poignant lines in his unending output were moments of self-doubt, of an incurable sadness.

The 'optimism' to be found in so much of his poetry is the faith of an artist who cannot admit that a world so full of beauty can ultimately be pointless. In the early *Paracelsus*, which comes from a materialistic decade, the 1830s, when he was in rebellion against the stifling piety of his Nonconformist home, the beauty of the spring remains; and in that beauty 'God renews his ancient rapture'. Later, Abt Vogter at his organ, building invisible palaces to God, declares: ' 'Tis we musicians know.' And Fra Lippo Lippi finds the truth as a painter, although as a monk he is blatantly immoral:

> The beauty and the wonder, and the power,
> The shapes of things, the colours, lights and shades,
> Changes, surprises – and God made it all!
>   . . . This world's no blot for us,
> Nor blank; it means intensely, and means good;
> To find its meaning, is my meat and drink.

The 'optimism' of Browning is also the faith of a moral man who knows what is wrong with the world but cannot admit that self-purification and self-sacrifice (for example, the Grammarian's total dedication to precise scholarship) will go eternally unrewarded. The 'dread machinery of sin and sorrow' must be designed 'to evolve . . . the moral qualities of man' – in eternal life with God. As Rabbi Ben Ezra exclaims:

> All I could never be,
> All men ignored in me,
> This I was worth to God . . .

In his penetrating satires on religious leaders, something in religion itself is kept inviolate. The fraudulent medium, Mr

Sludge (a type known to him because his wife was a spiritual-
ist), cannot discredit mankind's authentic glimpses of eternity.
The worldly Renaissance bishop who begs his illegitimate sons
to build a sumptuous tomb for him acknowledges something
greater in the Mass to be muttered near that tomb 'through
centuries'. The nineteenth-century bishop, Sylvester Blougram, boasting over the wine that his half-believed faith has
done well for him, glimpses 'the grand Perhaps' although he
holds that 'Creation's . . . meant to hide him all it can'.
Materialism obviously fascinated Browning; his prolonged
delight in the art of the Italian Renaissance was part of the
resurrection which was his marriage. But materialism could
not be enough in the presence of death, that 'fog in the throat'
where human futility had to be encountered finally along with
beauty and love. The answer to the riddle had to be found
beyond the calculations of reason. Bishop Blougram asks the
journalist:

> 'What think ye of Christ', friend? when all's done and said,
> You like this Christianity or not?
> It may be false, but will you wish it true? . . .
> If you desire faith – then you've faith enough. . . .

This bishop's confession voices the mid-Victorian confusion or
scepticism which accompanied the dissatisfaction with materialism. Here is the will to believe amid unbelief, the compulsion
to doubt amid the clinging to belief:

> Just when we are safest, there's a sunset-touch,
> A fancy from a flower-bell, someone's death.
> A chorus-ending from Euripides –
> And that's enough for fifty hopes and fears
> As old and new at once as Nature's self,
> To rap and knock and enter in our soul,
> Take hands and dance there, a fantastic ring,
> Round the ancient idol, on his base again –
> The grand Perhaps! We look on helplessly –
> There the old misgivings, crooked questionings are –
> This good God – what he could do, if he would,
> Would, if he could – then must have done long since:
> If so, when, where, and how? some way must be –
> Once feel about, and soon or late you hit

> Some sense, in which it might be, after all.
> Why not, 'The Way, the Truth, the Life'?

In *Christmas Eve* Browning denounces the 'buffoonery' of papal Rome, and the 'loveless learning' of a German university – but finds himself back in his parents' Nonconformist chapel in South London, asking:

> What is left for us, save, in growth
> Of soul, to rise up . . .
> From the gift looking to the Giver,
> And from the cistern to the River,
> And from the finite to infinity,
> And from man's dust to God's divinity?

The accompanying, rather clumsy, poem *Easter Day*, written while he was in mourning for his mother, begins:

> How very hard it is to be
> A Christian! Hard for you and me . . .

And it ends with the difficulties not so much settled as put aside in a turning to the warmth of life as 'Easter Day breaks'. For it was, in the end, the religion of his parents that seemed to Robert Browning the best source of living warmth for mortals.[22] It was a religion which worshipped not Power but Love.

> The very God! think, Abib; dost thou think?
> So, the All-Great, were the All-Loving too –
> So, through the thunder comes a human voice,
> Saying, 'O heart I made, a heart beats here!
> Face, my hands fashioned, see it in myself . . .'

IMMORTAL DIAMOND

The name of Gerard Manley Hopkins was not known to the Victorian public, but he was one of the first to express frankly

---

[22] The best biographies are *The Book, the Ring and the Poet* by William Irvine and Park Honan and *Robert Browning* by R. B. Martin (London, 1974–82). Critical introductions to the major poetry include those by Philip Drew and Ian Jack (London, 1970–73).

the opinion, prevailing in the twentieth century, that Tennyson and Browning had been over-rated. He privately suggested that Tennyson's *Idylls of the King* should be renamed *Charades from the Middle Ages*. In another letter he wrote of 'Browning's way of talking (and making his people talk) with the air and spirit of a man bouncing up from table with his mouth full of bread and cheese and saying that he meant to stand no blasted nonsense.'

Hopkins has himself been taken seriously by many critics since his friend Robert Bridges edited a volume of his poems in 1918, almost thirty years after his death. He was a musician and an artist, absorbed in the struggle to make words which would be both music and colour, penetrating to the 'inscape' which was the secret of any scene in nature. And he was a Jesuit, made one in 1867 by his fascination with 'elected silence' and compelled by that vocation to keep his poems private when his superiors were alarmed by their strange sensuousness. The longest poem he ever wrote, 'The Wreck of the *Deutschland*', was accordingly suppressed despite its adoration:

> Thou mastering me
> God! giver of breath and bread;
> World's strand, sway of the sea;
> Lord of living and dead;
> Thou hast bound hones and veins in me, fastened me flesh,
> And after it almost unmade, what with dread,
> Thy doing: and dost thou touch me afresh?
> Over again I feel Thy finger and find Thee.

Many of the poems revive ecstasy, as Hopkins contemplates God's glory and Christ's presence in the flight of a falcon, in the gathering of the harvest, in the bugler boy at his first communion in Oxford, in the Liverpool workman anointed for death. But we know that in his isolation he also experienced 'that course of loathing and hopelessness which I have so often felt before, and which made me fear madness.' In his final exile, in Dublin, he wrote six sonnets of desolation and in 1889 – the sad last year of his own life – he mused in his journal about Christ's life: 'Without that, even outwardly the world could be so different that we cannot even guess it. And my life is determined by the Incarnation down to most of the details of the day.' Many of his admirers have persisted in believing that he ought never to have been a Jesuit, but he would never grant that his double vocation had not been of God and at least it can be agreed that for him the imitation of Christ was not a source of sadness. In his most magnificent poem, in 1888, he explained why; and next year he could say that he was 'so happy' to find himself dying. He saw all life within nature destroyed by God's light, now become a fire. Then he saw a resurrection:

Across my foundering deck shone
A beacon, an eternal beam. Flesh fade, and mortal trash
Fall to the residuary worm; world's wildfire, leave but ash:
In a flash; at a trumpet crash,
I am all at once what Christ is, since he was what I am, and
This jack, joke, poor potsherd, patch, matchwood, immortal
    diamond,
Is immortal diamond.

Was that the answer to Charles Darwin or Charles Dickens — the rescue of the spirit of man from the prison house of a brutish materialism?[23]

---

[23] The best short biography summing up the evidence gradually made available is by Paddy Kitchen (London, 1978). Other valuable studies include John Pick, *Gerard Manley Hopkins, Priest and Poet* (Oxford, 1942); Alfred Thomas, *Hopkins the Jesuit* (Oxford, 1969); Donald Walhout, *Send My Roots Rain* (Athens, Ohio, 1981).

CHAPTER NINE

A MISSION TO AN EMPIRE

THE MISSIONARIES

'God is working his purpose out' was a hymn affirming a quite widespread belief that the time was drawing 'nearer and nearer' when 'from utmost east to utmost west' the earth would be filled with a glory – 'the brotherhood of all mankind, the reign of the Prince of Peace.' The hymn was written by an Eton schoolmaster for a festival of the Church Missionary Society in 1894. Churchgoers found it easy to sing because for some twenty years their world mission had seemed a part of their destiny of world empire. All around them they saw peace, if not exactly brotherhood, imposed by the 'land of hope and glory' whose bounds, in an evolution which seemed providential, finally included a quarter of mankind.[1]

No history of English religion could be in any sense complete without some consideration of this movement; for the Victorian missionaries spread Christianity over the almost empty vastnesses of Canada and Australia, began to make Africa south of the Sahara a Christian continent, substituted the Gospel for cannibalism in New Zealand and other islands of the Pacific, powerfully challenged the grip of tradition on India, reached deep into a stagnant China, fought against the slave trade, helped to stop cruel practices such as infanticide and the execution of widows and slaves on the master's death, reduced hundreds of languages to writing, gave women a new sense of human dignity, and planted churches, schools, col-

---

[1] The best introduction to the political history is C. C. Eldridge, *Victorian Imperialism* (London, 1978), and a brilliant attempt to recapture the imperial atmosphere was made in the three volumes by James Morris, *Pax Britannica, Heaven's Command* and *Farewell the Trumpets* (London, 1968–78).

leges and hospitals in many areas where previously the main help expected from religion had been magical. The achievement was possible because a unique opportunity existed. The civilization which Victoria symbolized (Christianity could be introduced as 'the Queen of England's religion') had no equal competitor. Materially and spiritually there seemed to be a vacuum which 'Christian nations' must fill. In a book of 1910 one missionary, Thomas Moscrop, looked back on the growth of *The Kingdom without Frontiers*. He was proud that 'Christian nations' then possessed over eighty per cent of the earth's surface. 'It is very significant that during the nineteenth century the European peoples increased from 170 to 500 millions, and that this increase is likely to go on, whilst the rest of the world, as far as can be seen, is destined to remain stationary.' But it was also significant that his appeal for more missionaries was based mainly on this optimistic forecast of the future progress of the 'Christian nations' and their empires.

No longer was the main motivation a belief that non-Christians would all go to hell. No doubt there were many Christians who still held that belief in 1910, but the tendency in the main missionary societies was more liberal.[2] Non-Christian religions still seemed untrue; but what Thomas Moscrop wished chiefly to stress was that they were uncivilized. 'Indian pantheism does not result in social well-being', he declared. 'Buddhism seems to offer greater promise, but its root-teachings are wrong and so give no hope of social efficiency for the race. China is a large and painful illustration of the social effectiveness of Confucianism. As a social force Mohammedanism is hopeless. The lesser religions of Africa and of the isles of the seas show the same thing in a thousand examples.' For a more concise (if still historically inaccurate) expression of the same missionary imperialism, we may listen to a great empire-builder, Sir Harry Johnston, addressing the Basoga people deep in Africa in 1900: 'We were like you, going about naked . . . with our war paint on, but when we learned Christianity from the Romans we changed and became great.

---

[2] Geoffrey Rowell studied *The Victorians and Hell* (Oxford, 1974).

We want you to learn Christianity and follow our steps and you too will be great.'[3]

Eventually this proud alliance between the Christian mission and the British empire was to end, because the empire collapsed; and the alliance was to be denounced by most Christians. The word 'missionary' was to become almost as offensive as the word 'imperialism'. Mankind was to be amazed that Christians had ever thought it possible to spread a message of humble love from a position of economic, political and cultural strength often amounting to arrogance and exploitation. How, it was to be asked, could the Bible be treated as the Word of God if white men tried to sell that idea along with the trader's gin or opium? How could the Church – or the divided churches exported with all their disputes – grow out of the barrel of the rifle? It is, however, possible to suggest that in the future, when anti-colonial passions themselves belong to history, justice may be done to the Victorian missionaries. They accepted discomfort, loneliness, disease, the danger of violence and a heartbreaking failure to win converts. They sacrificed a normal family life, buried many wives and children in foreign graves, and often died at their posts. Their motives were very mixed but often included exceptional loves for God and neighbour. The results of their work were often unlike the dreams with which they had set out, but these men and women did more than any other group in all previous history or in their own age to make the Christian Church worldwide; and that made other men dream. Addressing the World Missionary Conference in Edinburgh in 1910, the Archbishop of Canterbury declared that 'the place of missions in the life of the Church must be the central place and none other'. And he added that 'if that come true, there may be some standing here tonight who shall not taste of death till they see the kingdom of God come with power.'

The role which the missionaries played in the unprecedented encounter of civilizations and cultures was even more ambiguous than their directly religious role; and it has even

---

[3] Roland Oliver, *Sir Harry Johnston and the Scramble for Africa* (London, 1957), p. 297.

more often been denounced. In the first half of the century they were often drawn from a working-class background, and the committees of the societies which sent them out hoped that their practical skills would not only impress and improve the 'natives' but would also render substantial salaries unnecessary. Some missionaries did indeed prosper on this basis, whether or not they made many converts, but in the process they sometimes became traders or farmers themselves. The alternative was destitution. In the course of the century a different danger to the missionary's spiritual integrity developed. Many middle-class men and women felt drawn to this idealistic and increasingly prestigious work, and although they were prepared for many adventures and sacrifices when they reached settled 'mission stations' they often attempted to reproduce the comfortable homes they had known in England, staffed by many servants; it seemed to be their natural right. They felt obliged to provide employment for converts who had been thrown out of their own families or villages, and thus they became the directors of sizable economic enterprises. In general they were the patrons of the 'native' Christians and this often meant that they were patronizing. 'Natives' could be assistants (the village catechist was in fact the backbone of the worldwide mission) but they could not be colleagues or friends. The missionaries regarded themselves as the allies and social equals of the leading commercial and colonial figures in the area. If they were in physical danger, either they or their supporters expected the colonial authorities to rescue or revenge them – an operation which might involve the extension of the empire. And all these things might compromise them as ambassadors of Christ.

The missionaries often did further damage to their spiritual mission by clumsy failures to understand the inner significance and importance of 'native' customs which seemed to them merely 'savage' or 'barbaric' – customs which for many centuries had regulated sexual relationships and had socialized families, villages and tribes. They were encouraged to admire instead certain customs selected from a British way of life which in other respects was often deplored by these keen Christians: the 'missionary position' in sexual intercourse, teetotalism, the wearing of European clothes, the singing of European hymn tunes, in the towns the building of Gothic stone churches. Converts were also expected to put away all wives except one. This was in accordance with the teaching of the New Testament, but many of the converts felt that the sudden attack on the age old custom of polygamy was not in accordance with local realities or with their own consciences. In a word, the missionaries were intruders.

But those who wish to do justice to them will recognize that it would have been impossible to recruit, or to pay for, an army whose only weapons were the spiritual weapons of the best saints. If there were to be missionaries in any number, then their attitudes had to be more or less the attitudes generally held in the societies from which they came. We should also recall two other facts. It was not rare for missionaries to defend the 'rights' of the 'natives' against traders and government officials, causing intense irritation and contempt. And many of the missionaries recorded observations of 'native' life which laid the foundations of the modern science of anthropology. They were far too clumsy in their attitudes to the traditional way of life which they were helping to destroy; but at least they had bothered to go to these places and to observe strange customs with motives which included love.

Certainly the whole meaning of the Church could be transformed by their activities. The power of the Gospel to convince people in all the continents brought great encouragement, and the need to evangelize rapidly gave the churches a new understanding of their own nature. The Church of England at work overseas could not permanently rely on powers and privileges deriving from the government. Bishops had to be prepared to rough it like other missionaries; the idea of the 'missionary bishops', unfamiliar since Anglo-Saxon days, was revived in America in the 1830s and soon inspired some sturdy evangelists who became heroes in England. By the 1890s there were more than ninety colonial or missionary bishops at work outside the USA. Laymen in the colonies could not depend on the government to pay for clergy, nor could the English system of compulsory tithes be acceptable. In these British colonies, as in the USA, laymen had to take over responsibility for the financial support of the clergy – and demanded in return that the clergy should consult them about the Church's policy. In these ways modern 'Anglicanism', as distinct from support for the Established Church of England, was born in nineteenth-century Canada, Australia and New Zealand. Non-Anglican Churches were also changed. It was not enough to be merely 'Dissent' or 'Nonconformity' when the purpose was to convert the heathen to Christianity and to win or retain the large numbers (more than ten millions) who migrated from the British Isles in the Victorian age. In the free competition for voluntary adherents the non-Anglican Protestants were often more successful than those still burdened with the memory or the image of a privileged Establishment. And Roman Catholics found a new confidence in their claim to universality because they were often the most courageous and most effective of all the Christian missionary forces – although not many of the English were to be found in the ranks of this international army, strictly disciplined under the direct authority of the office called *Propaganda* in Rome.[4]

ANGLICANISM DEFINED IN CANADA AND SOUTH AFRICA

We can begin a Victorian world tour in Jerusalem. This starting point is specially appropriate because the English confusion about the possibility of missionary work based on the Holy City illustrated both the legal problems facing Anglicanism outside the English Establishment and the evangelistic problems facing all the English who wished to address non-Christians. In 1841 a bishopric in Jerusalem was founded by the British and Prussian governments acting jointly. It was to be held by their nominees alternately, and the excuse given was that Protestants in the area needed pastoral supervision. In

---

[4] K. S. Latourette studied the nineteenth century in *Christianity in a Revolutionary Age* (5 vols., London, 1957–61). Max Warren provided a British perspective in *The Missionary Movement from Britain in Modern History* and *Social History and Christian Mission* (London, 1965–67), and Stephen Neill supplied a concise *History of Christian Missions* (Harmondsworth, Middx, 1964). Between them these books list the standard histories of the missionary societies.

fact there were very few Protestants and the aim was political: the bishopric was to be a means of bringing pressure on the Turks, to whose ramshackle empire Palestine belonged. The chief result having been to scandalize those Church of England men (such as Newman) who disliked being reckoned Protestants and those Prussians who opposed their king's liking for bishops, the scheme had to be brought to an end in 1886. But the Act of Parliament which made it possible also made possible the consecration of other bishops for work outside the British empire, and so had some important consequences – for example, in Canada.

The story of Anglicanism in Canada had begun when Sir Francis Drake used the Book of Common Prayer after landing on the west coast in 1578, but the main story is to be dated from the movement up the east coast during and after the Americans' successful rebellion some two hundred years later. Many of the refugees were Anglicans, and many went to Nova Scotia. Among them was Charles Inglis, who had seen Trinity church in New York, where he had been the loudly Tory rector, burned down. It was natural for the government in London to seek to strengthen the existing branch of the Church of England in Nova Scotia, with Inglis as the first bishop in 1787. The number of Anglican clergy in Nova Scotia was never large enough to fulfil the bishop's plans; nor (it was complained) was the annual parliamentary grant large enough. But there was a sustained attempt to build up church life on the traditional pattern. 'We love the place, O God', a hymn which breathes love for altar, font and the rest of the model Anglican church, was written by a lover of St Paul's church in Halifax, the naval base which became the colony's chief town.[5]

Nova Scotia's daughter dioceses were the places where Canadian Anglicanism gained a new self-understanding as a Church not depending on government support. The diocese of Quebec, founded in 1792, was first led by a bishop as conservative as Charles Inglis. This was Jacob Mountain, who remained for thirty-three years; like Inglis he had a son who

---

[5] See William Nelson, *The American Tory* (Oxford, 1961), and Judith Fingard, *The Anglican Design in Loyalist Nova Scotia* (London, 1972).

became bishop of the diocese. The small upper class of English settlers supported Mountain's efforts, and a cathedral was built for him by the Royal Engineers. But it was impossible to establish the Church of England as Mountain wished in 'Lower Canada', since Methodist and other preachers entering from the United States were active and the bulk of the population desired nothing else than that it should remain fervently Roman Catholic, as the old-fashioned 'New France'. The Anglican bishop who was most appropriate to the real, modest, mission in the area was Charles Stewart, who came between the two Mountains. He was an earl's son and a fine scholar who had embraced a life of apostolic poverty, humbly sharing all the hardships of the settlers as a missionary travelling up and down the St Lawrence river.[6]

Another of Nova Scotia's daughter dioceses was Newfoundland, founded in 1839 when it included both Bermuda and Labrador but only eight Anglican clergymen. The second Bishop of Newfoundland was the first bishop in the Church of England overseas to embody the American idea that a bishop could be a hard-living missionary. Sailing up and down the stormy coast, disregarding the cold, reaching his people who were scattered and mostly illiterate, Edward Field, who had once been snug in an Oxford fellowship, was so attractive that one of his many admirers gave him a handsome yacht and enrolled himself as its honorary skipper.

The greatest of the early champions of Canadian Anglicanism was John Strachan, a Scot who was the first Bishop of Toronto (1839–67). When epidemics of typhus broke out (caused by the arrival of destitute Irish immigrants in the 1840s) he never slackened in his pastoral work. When the modern church which served as his cathedral seemed inadequate, he built a stone one; when the stone church burned down, he built another; and when the third cathedral was also destroyed by fire, he built a fourth. When a university was needed, he founded King's College; and when that university was secularized, he led another group which built Trinity

---

[6] T. R. Millman provided biographies of *Jacob Mountain* (Toronto, 1947) and *Charles James Stewart* (London, Ont., 1953).

College. When the government's endowment of the clergy was ended in 1854, he obtained compensation which eased the change to a complete reliance on the generosity of parishioners. His main problem was the leading Methodist preacher, Adolphus Ryerson, whose own character was as indomitable and whose hostility to Anglican pretensions was implacable. Indeed, the Bishop's task was to win voluntary support by being as ready to work among the people as the preacher was. Thus Strachan and the Anglicans who followed him had to refound their Church as a voluntary association alongside others in a democracy – although it remained the 'Church of England in Canada' until 1955.[7]

On this voluntary basis the Anglican and other Churches could flourish as the Canadians multiplied, agreed to their self-governing federation in 1867, and spread to the west. The non-Anglican Churches were far more active in the west – which largely explained the census figures of 1891 when the Anglicans had only 13.5 per cent of the population, the Roman Catholics forty-one per cent, and the Presbyterians and Methodists mostly shared the rest. For the Churches as for the Canadian people, there was plenty of room for expansion. A leading historian of Christianity in Canada and the USA has stressed that 'the religious tone of these two "Christian nations" in the nineteenth century was quite different, for Canada was more cautious, traditional and church-oriented than the United States.' In Canada most denominational schools received some support out of public funds. Part of the explanation is that Canadians fell back on their religious traditions as a barrier against absorption into the USA. But another factor was that the deep division of Canada into British and French traditions meant that it was difficult to invest the nation as such with the religious aura which surrounded 'the Union' in the USA and which had Abraham Lincoln as its prophet.[8]

Canadian Anglicans had found that one of the keys to

---

[7] Philip Carrington wrote a history of *The Anglican Church in Canada* (London, 1963).

[8] Robert T. Hardy, *A History of the Churches in the United States and Canada*, p. 259. The basic book is John S. Moir, *The Church in the British Era: From the British Conquest to Confederation* (Toronto, 1972).

self-supporting strength in church life was the use of synods where bishops could meet their clergy (and their laity, unless one held very High Church views) – and where bishops could meet each other. Such synods had a special meaning in a land where the difficulties of travel were so great; and when in 1865 the Canadian Anglicans' Provincial Synod, covering the eastern half of the country, heard of the problems which had arisen for Anglicans in South Africa, they were sure of the remedy: the bishops of England's colonies around the world must meet.

The South African problems were causing concern because not all missionaries linked with Victorian England were as ready as the Canadians to sink their differences for the sake of their mission. On the contrary, in South Africa there was a clash between the two outstanding English missionaries, a clash about the basic definition of Anglicanism.

One of the rivals was Robert Gray, who sailed out to be Bishop of Cape Town in 1847. Formerly a parish priest in County Durham whose main distinction was that his father had been Bishop of Bristol, he was alarmed to be taking responsibility for a new diocese containing a quarter of a million square miles but very few regular supporters of the Church of England. The descendants of the original Dutch settlers, the Boers, adhered fervently to their Calvinist faith. Although many of them had made the Great Trek to the north in the 1830s and later (rather than accept the abolition of slavery), it was clear that the English would not be able to forget their existence. Among the English colonists such religious activity as took place tended to be Nonconformist. William Shaw, for more than thirty years the pioneer of Methodism in South Africa, managed to be equally active both as a pastor to the settlers whom he joined in 1820 and as a missionary to the tribesmen over the frontier.[9] Bishop Gray, however, turned out to be as hard-working, and as defiant, as any of the Canadians. He never became strong, physically or emotionally. The photographs show a face deeply lined; the

---

[9] *The Journal of William Shaw* was edited by W. D. Hammond-Tooke (Cape Town, 1972).

biographies cannot conceal exhaustions and breakdowns. But he travelled up and down South Africa, rejoicing in the flowers of the unspoiled country although at first rejoicing in little else. Everywhere he tried to plant the Anglican system as he understood it in a moderately High Church way. He called for more bishops.

One of these bishops was the other outstanding missionary of Anglicanism in South Africa, John William Colenso. And with him came trouble. The dean of his cathedral in Pietermaritzburg protested against his doctrine, and Gray felt obliged to adjudicate. Orthodoxy must be vindicated, despite his past friendship with the Bishop and his personal dislike of the Dean. Then this troublesome bishop's book on *St Paul's Epistle to the Romans* (1861) demonstrated that he did not believe that non-Christians such as the Zulus were in danger of everlasting punishment in hell. God did not need to be reconciled to them, for he already loved them abundantly. In order to be saved they did not need to accept personally that Christ had borne the punishment due for their sins. All men were already united with Christ. A later book on *The Pentateuch* demonstrated that Colenso did not believe that it was his duty to assure the Zulus that the Old Testament was entirely the Word of God, including its mathematical impossibilities. Instead, he agreed that the Bible contained some legends not altogether unlike the Zulus' own mythology. For such offences, he was deposed from his bishopric.

Gray took the responsibility for this expulsion of a heretic, and many people in many places applauded. The hymn 'The Church's one foundation' was written during the controversy by one clerical admirer, S. J. Stone. But when appealed to in 1865 the Judicial Committee of the Privy Council refused to uphold his authority, this time pleading that since the Cape Town colony now had its own legislature the Letters Patent from the Crown which had given Gray the right to discipline Colenso had been invalid. In response South African Anglicans drew up a new constitution and in 1870 prohibited any future appeal to the committee on any question of doctrine. But Colenso returned to work as a bishop among his beloved Zulus, defying the bishop whom Gray recognized, and on his tomb was inscribed the one word *Sobantu*, 'Father of the People'. By his stand he had helped to vindicate the right of missionaries to use a liberal generosity in their understanding of their task, and while the official Anglican 'Church of the Province of South Africa' remained doctrinally orthodox and predominantly High Church, its chief distinction came to be a struggle of which *Sobantu* would have approved: the fight to defend the dignity of the black man. This combination of Catholic devotion with broad interests was to be increasingly typical of Anglicanism.[10]

Another result of the Colenso controversy was the birth of the first of the worldwide denominational associations among the heirs of the Reformation.

Anglican Canadians were alarmed by the Judicial Committee's refusal to deal with the legal problems of the Church in South Africa, as well as by its refusal to condemn Colenso's theology. On their initiative seventy-six bishops met in the first Lambeth Conference, in 1867. They decided nothing but their successors met again in 1878 – and in 1888 another Lambeth Conference declared: 'We have realized, more fully than it was possible to realize before, the extent, the power, and the influence of the great Anglican Communion. We have felt its capacities, its opportunities, its privileges.' And Churches without bishops came to think that they, too, would benefit if representatives from the British empire and the United States, with any others who were suitable, met to feel their own capacities, opportunities and privileges. The Alliance of Reformed Churches first met in 1875, the Ecumenical Methodist Council in 1881, the International Congregational Council in 1891 and the Baptist World Alliance in 1905.[11]

---

[10] See Audrey Brooke, *Robert Gray* (Cape Town, 1947). Peter Hinchcliff wrote a history of *The Anglican Church in South Africa* and a biography of *John William Colenso* (London, 1964–65). Norman Etherington presented more detailed research in *Preachers, Peasants and Politics in South East Africa 1835–80* (London, 1978).

[11] Alan M. G. Stephenson studied *The First Lambeth Conference* (London, 1967), and *Anglicanism and the Lambeth Conferences* (London, 1978).

OPENING UP AFRICA

It would of course have been better had nineteenth-century Africa produced of its own Christian heroes abundantly, as twentieth-century Africa was certainly going to do. There were some efforts in this direction. In Sierra Leone Fourah Bay College was set up in 1847 as a training school for African evangelists, and among the tribes on the Gold Coast (now Ghana) Methodism spread almost entirely through African leadership.

In Nigeria a major Anglican experiment took place, thanks to the insistence of Henry Venn, the farsighted Secretary of the Church Missionary Society, on the policy of 'Africa for the Africans'. This policy was carried to the extent of securing the consecration of Samuel Crowther as Bishop on the Niger in Canterbury Cathedral in 1864. Twenty-two years earlier Crowther had been a terrified African boy recaptured from a Portuguese slaver and landed at Sierra Leone. Venn was determined that Bishop Crowther should now manage the mission to the interior, using the great river as a highway. He trusted his man completely and was confident that the experiment would prove the African's capacity for spiritual leadership. After Venn's death, however, the ageing Crowther was accused of financial malpractices and forced to resign.[12]

The hope that the decisive initiatives in the Christian mission to West Africa would be taken by Africans was probably unrealistic in the extraordinary circumstances of the time. The predominant fact was the destruction of traditional tribal patterns by European commerce. Africans were demoralized. The slave trade had already done untold damage (for example, by encouraging the little kingdoms to go to war with other Africans, using muskets supplied by the slavers, in order to secure more slaves). Now to that long-lasting dislocation was

---

[12] See *To Apply the Gospel: Selections from the Writings of Henry Venn*, ed. Max Warren (Grand Rapids, Mich., 1971), and T. E. Yates, *Venn and Victorian Bishops Abroad* (Uppsala, 1978). John Loiello summed up the evidence about Crowther in *Varieties of Christian Experience in Nigeria*, ed. E. Isichei (London, 1982).

added the lure of large profits for the chiefs from other forms of trade with Europe (for example, the export of palm-oil or cocoa beans). The white man appearing from the sea, who might be a missionary, was inevitably fascinating. When malaria had been understood medically (as its name suggests, it had been blamed on 'bad air'), and when steamships had shortened the voyage, there was no shortage of Englishmen eager to convert the kingdoms of West Africa. Thus Crowther was toppled by young Evangelicals fresh out of Cambridge. And when other confident Englishmen tried to 'conquer' the Muslim strongholds in Northern Nigeria and failed dismally, it was psychologically inevitable that they should call for the imposition of as much British rule as could be achieved – and, within this, for as much official encouragement of missionary work as could be extracted out of the nervous colonial administrators.[13]

In East and Central Africa Christianity was planted later than in the west. The chief differences were first that the export of slaves was still flourishing under Arab or Portuguese management, and second that it was possible for Europeans to settle in large numbers in the areas which eventually became Kenya and Zimbabwe. Both these differences increased the challenge to missionary work. The slave trade was, in David Livingstone's phrase, the 'open sore of the world'. The damage which it inflicted on African life intensified under the eyes of the explorers and pioneers, and neither naval patrols nor diplomatic treaties were able to stop it. The Africans seemed helpless, inviting the outsider's intervention by their powerlessness if not by their voices. Every chivalrous instinct in Victorian Englishmen was stirred, particularly since it seemed an opportunity to make amends for England's shameful role in the slave trade from the west coast. And to make

---

[13] African scholars have contributed four illuminating studies: J. B. Webster, *The African Churches among the Yoruba 1888–1922* (Oxford, 1964); F. K. Ekechi, *Missionary Enterprise and Rivalry in Igboland 1857–1914* (London, 1972); J. F. Ade Ajayi, *Christian Missions in Nigeria 1841–91: The Making of a New Elite* (London, 1965); and E. A. Ayandele, *The Missionary Impact on Modern Nigeria 1842–1914* (London, 1966). Shorter studies include those collected in *Christianity in Tropical Africa*, ed. C. G. Baeta (Oxford, 1968), and in vol. v of the *Cambridge History of Africa*, covering c. 1790 to 1870 (Cambridge, 1976).

intervention more attractive, it appeared to be quite easy to establish houses, farms and whole villages under the control of European missionaries, shining as lights in the 'dark continent'. In 1874 a settlement for freed slaves was founded near Mombasa in order to train evangelists for what is now Kenya, but the missionaries maintained such a discipline over the Africans, and treated them so contemptuously, that not even the limited experiment of consecrating another black bishop like Crowther was contemplated.[14] Instead the imaginations of English missionaries and of their supporters at home were seized by a wandering white man. He had a dream that Africa, East and Central, could rapidly be freed from the slavers, and brought into the Christian Church, once it was exposed to European 'commerce'. He was David Livingstone, who at the age of ten had been a lad in a factory in Scotland.

He went to South Africa in 1841 as a doctor-evangelist. He had first chosen China (but there was a war on) and had then been excited by the talk of Robert Moffat. Turned from a gardener into a missionary by Methodist preaching, Moffat claimed to have 'sometimes seen, in the morning sun, the smoke of a thousand villages where no missionary had ever been'. But when Livingstone reached Moffat's mission station at the northernmost outpost of South African Christianity, he found that there were not a thousand inhabitants within ten miles. He found, too, that Moffat (who was best as a translator) did not mind his own tortoise-like progress in making personal contact with Africans. So the impatient Livingstone married Moffat's daughter and found his own life by making great journeys across the Kalahari desert and into the tropical north. At first he told himself that he was looking for more profitable sites for missionary work, but he founded no church, school or hospital. He also discovered that he was happier and more effective when he travelled without any white companion. He sincerely believed that his life would be charmed until his work was done, and in that faith accepted hardships which would

---

[14] A. J. Temu studied *British Protestant Missions* (London, 1972) and Robert W. Strayer *The Making of Mission Communities in East Africa* (London, 1978). T. O. Beidelman, *Colonial Evangelism* (Bloomington, Ind., 1982), drew interesting general conclusions from a study of the work of the CMS in what is now Tanzania.

have broken almost anyone else. His work was simply to get to know and to love Africa and the Africans, recording his observations with meticulous care.

In 1856 he returned to England having crossed Central Africa from coast to coast, having discovered large lakes and dramatic falls hitherto unknown to Europe, and having accomplished the beginning of an understanding of two mighty rivers, the Zambesi and the Congo. Such marvels moved a man grown unfamiliar with English to eloquence as an author and orator. In particular the Zambesi inspired him. To him, it was a river along which legitimate traders could move. That would end the African chiefs' temptations to collaborate with the Arab slavers. With the traders would arrive European settlers who would find the interior highlands delightful. There it would be easy to find coal and to grow cotton and other highly profitable crops. In a very little time churches would be built and crowded by converts. The promise of the Zambesi was what Livingstone meant when he told the undergraduates of Cambridge on an afternoon of December 1857: 'I know that in a few years I shall be cut off in that country which is now open; do not let it be shut again! I go back to Africa to try to make an open path for commerce and Christianity; do you carry out the work which I have begun. I leave it with you.'

Cruel disappointments followed. It was found that the Portuguese who controlled the lower reaches of the Zambesi did not welcome Englishmen, who anyway could not smoothly steam up the river as Livingstone had promised. The mission later called the Universities' Mission to Central Africa was formed and a bishop sent out – who found his apostolic mission bogged down in tribal wars, in conflicts with the Arab slavers, in fevers. Had he not died of dysentery he would probably have been killed in a war, for he used his gun like the others.

Meanwhile Livingstone resumed his journeys – this time, as he maintained, seeking the sources of the Nile. No longer was he an agent of the London Missionary Society; first he was a British consul, then he was merely himself. Spectacularly 'found' by the journalist Henry Stanley in 1871, he deeply impressed that strange man (who had been born John Rowlands, an orphan in North Wales – and who ended up as Sir Henry, a Liberal MP). Instead of returning to civilization penniless and defeated, he wandered off into Africa with Africans – to be found dead on 1 May 1873, kneeling in prayer by his bed in Chitambo's village. Then came the most impressive journey in his story, when his body was taken by his African servants to the far-distant coast and to Westminster Abbey for burial.[15]

Four years after his death, Anglican missionaries arrived in Uganda in response to a letter to the *Daily Telegraph* from Stanley, who had penetrated to the court of a despotic ruler, the Kabaka of Buganda, and been assured that Christianity would be welcome. Two years later White Fathers arrived as Roman Catholic missionaries. The Kabaka, Mutesa I, turned out to be more interested in hoped-for guns and gunpowder than in the rival versions of Christianity, but the missionaries were allowed to teach their faith to the sons of members of the Kabaka's court while they also introduced the wheel, houses with windows and other marvels. The main explanation of this royal welcome – for which there are few parallels in the history of African missions – appears to be that the Kabaka was well aware that his tyranny needed reinforcement against the Arabs coming south from the Sudan; but there is some evidence that the tyrant grew more merciful as the years went by. Unfortunately this king who might have become a Christian died and was succeeded by the eighteen-year-old Mwanga. The new king had learned vices from the Arabs but not much else. He had three of the lads being instructed by the Christian missionaries horribly mutilated and slowly burned alive, and later in 1885 he ordered that Bishop James Hannington, who was arriving to take over the leadership of the mission, should be murdered during his journey. Next year other African men and boys who refused to renounce Christianity were burned; and a

---

[15] The best biographies are Cecil Northcott, *Robert Moffat* (London, 1961); Oliver Ransford, *David Livingstone* (London, 1978); Owen Chadwick, *Mackenzie's Grave* (London, 1959); Richard Hall, *Stanley: An Adventurer Explored* (London, 1974).

period of confusion followed until the British established a 'protectorate' in 1894.[16]

A story involving English Nonconformist missionaries hints at many of the themes running through much of the rest of African history.

The modern missionary presence on the great island of Madagascar began in 1818 with the arrival of agents of the London Missionary Society. They and their immediate successors were men like the pioneers who had broken into India and Tahiti – Evangelical in their religion, uncomprehending towards the local religion, but acceptable to at least some of the 'natives' because they included in their ranks craftsmen whose skills and products were coveted. In the end it was felt necessary to expel them and to persecute their converts because their influence seemed to threaten the ruler's own authority. In 1835 Queen Ranavalona promised highly unpleasant forms of death to all who would not abandon the missionaries' religion, and the persecution continued until her own death in 1861. Within eight years another ruling queen had been baptized as a Protestant. The religion taught by the London Missionary Society gradually became the official religion. Most of the people seem to have admitted that it was the superior religion of a superior people; converts to it were expected to wear European dress, to be attentive during sermons by preachers whom it was difficult to understand, and to accept subordinate positions in church life. Missionaries were often carried by 'natives' bearing litters, instead of walking: it seemed proper. But attacks on customs which had bound the people together were deeply resented, and in the background was the fear that the white man would soon take the land. This fear was justified. The French were allocated this part of Africa by the other European powers; in their turn they acknowledged the British rights on the mainland. In 1895 they occupied Madagascar – and the

---

[16] See John V. Taylor, *The Growth of the Church in Buganda* (London, 1958), and J. F. Faupel, *African Holocaust* (London, 1962). These events were put in the context of colonialism by Roland Oliver, *The Missionary Factor in East Africa* (London, 1952), and were seen through African eyes by Anne Luck, *African Saint* (London, 1963), and by M. Kiwanuka, *A History of Buganda* (London, 1971).

religion of the London Missionary Society became once again a minority creed.[17]

INTO THE PACIFIC

The spread of English-speaking people and of their Churches over the three million square miles of Australia was marked by much of the courageous energy which we have already observed in the history of Canada. In Canada, however, despite all the difficulties missionaries could appeal to many whose sentiments were already favourable to British (or French) Christianity. In Australia, the task facing the Churches was more deeply discouraging. The first clergyman, Richard Johnson, was a humiliated chaplain to transported convicts (in 1788). About 150,000 men and women, almost all from the labouring class and almost all being punished for theft, were transported before this system was ended in 1840 – and even after 1840 the colony of New South Wales and its offshoots remained rough places. In the second half of the nineteenth century Australia had its economic ups and downs, from the gold rush of the 1850s to the depression and drought of the 1890s, without ever experiencing any widespread religious revival like the Great Awakening which had changed American colonial life. By 1870 all state aid for the denominations had been effectively withdrawn throughout Australia, but no popular Protestantism really replaced it. The universities in particular became noted for their atmosphere of secular rationalism, most children having been educated in state schools, where there was no religious instruction as the Churches understood religion.

In such circumstances the Anglican authoritarianism of William Grant Broughton, who became the first Bishop of Australia in 1836, was destined to perish – like the courage of

---

[17] Bonar Gow studied *Madagascar and the Protestant Impact* (London, 1979). Other relevant studies by objective scholars include Robert Rotberg, *Christian Missionaries and the Creation of Northern Rhodesia* (Princeton, N.J., 1965), and T. O. Ranger and John Weller, *Themes in the Christian History of Central Africa* (Berkeley, Cal., 1975).

many of the explorers in the immeasurable desert which formed the interior.[18]

Another dream that perished was the idea that Roman Catholicism in Australia could be shaped by Benedictine monks who would become bishops, use monasteries as cathedrals and establish schools to spread an advanced Christian civilization. It was an idea held tenaciously by Australia's first vicar apostolic, Bishop Ullathorne, and by his successor, John Podling, who was active as Archbishop of Sydney (despite Broughton's fury) until 1877; both were monks. But Benedictine ideals could not survive in control when the bulk of support came from Irish immigrants and when to most Australians a monk was someone to be sent back to the Middle Ages. When the Commonwealth of Australia was formed in 1901 the leading Roman Catholic figure was Archbishop Patrick Moran, a champion of the Irish and of the trade unions.[19]

Nor were these conservative visions the only dreams to end in Australia. In 1836 the colony of South Australia was inaugurated. Instead of convicts, its founders were mainly English Nonconformists. They had ideas not totally unlike those which had driven the Pilgrim Fathers over the Atlantic, and they made some enduring impact; but much of the life of the colony was gradually assimilated into the secular ethos already prevailing in Australia.[20]

It proved very difficult to persuade the 'blackfellows' or aborigines to accept a religion which few of the white Australians seemed to take very seriously, particularly since it meant persuading them to abandon the habit of wandering over vast areas. The main impact of 'civilization' was to destroy them by disease and demoralization – and in Tasmania the aborigines were completely exterminated, many of them being shot down

---

[18] See G. P. Shaw, *Patriarch and Patriot: William Grant Broughton* (Melbourne, 1978), and Ross Border, *Church and State in Australia 1788-1872* (London, 1962). The background was illuminated by L. L. Robson, *The Convict Settlers of Australia* (Melbourne, 1975), and J. M. Ward, *Empire in the Antipodes* (London, 1966).

[19] See T. L. Suttor, *Hierarchy and Democracy in Australia* (Melbourne, 1965), and P. J. O'Farrell, *The Catholic Church in Australia: A Short History* (Melbourne, 1968).

[20] D. H. Pike studied *Paradise of Dissent: South Australia 1829-1857* (Melbourne, 1957). The religious and general development of the nation was presented authoritatively in *A New History of Australia*, ed. F. K. Crowley (Melbourne, 1974).

A Mission to an Empire

in a sporting spirit. But slowly missionary work was done, and from Australia Christianity spread to the evergreen islands of New Zealand.

First came a period when missionaries tried to win the friendship of the Maoris by introducing some of the 'arts of civilized life'; the Maoris, who were cannibals, had never before seen horses, cows, potatoes, corn, wheels or iron instruments. The inspirer of this phase was Samuel Marsden, a small, stout, ruddy and muscular Yorkshireman whose father had been the village blacksmith. Some Evangelicals discovered him in his twenties and sent him to a grammar school and a university, from which he was summoned by William Wilberforce to sail out in 1793 to assist poor Richard Johnson in pastoral work in the Australian penal colony. Unlike Johnson, Marsden stayed on and fought back. He became the first man to build a permanent church in Australia (at Parramatta), and in order to supplement his inadequate salary 'the best practical farmer in New South Wales' (as the hostile governor admitted). He was the first farmer to take Australian wool back to England. But all that did not absorb his energies. When he concluded the first church service ever held in New Zealand, on Christmas Day 1814 at Oiki on the Bay of Islands, his text was: 'Behold, I bring you good tidings of great joy.' But he was sure that it was premature to preach the full Gospel until the Maoris had been persuaded to forget the insults and ill-treatment which their people had received at the hands of visiting English seamen, in those waters mainly in order to hunt whales. That was why, in the seven visits which he paid to New Zealand before his death in 1838, his whole emphasis was the peaceful and utilitarian instruction of the Maoris.[21]

A second period came in which the emphasis was on a more determined evangelism. Methodists crossed over from Australia, as did Roman Catholic priests, and more fervent Anglican missionaries were sent under the leadership of the ex-sailor

---

[21] See A. T. Yarwood, *Samuel Marsden the Great Survivor* (Melbourne, 1977). *Letters and Journals of Samuel Marsden* and *Marsden's Lieutenants* were edited by J. R. Elder (Dunedin, 1932–34), and Eric Ramsden studied *Marsden and the Missions* (Sydney, 1936).

Henry Williams, a strong man who in due course became an archdeacon. Inevitable but tragic steps were taken – the Maoris were persuaded to part with some of their land by 'agreement' with the English settlers, including Williams and other missionaries; and on other occasions they were 'punished' because, being themselves habitually men of war, they had hit back at the white men occupying their country. Pressure grew for larger schemes of English colonization and Edward Gibbon Wakefield, a man who had spent some time in a London prison and who had there composed *A Letter from Sydney*, proved an alluring propagandist. A body of Anglican colonists, the Canterbury Association, went out to found Christchurch; a similar body from Scotland, mainly rebels against the Established Church there, founded Dunedin. Disagreements between the settlers, the missionaries and the Maoris mounted, and in 1840 the Maori chiefs were persuaded to accept the British government's 'protection' in return for a promise that their lands would never be taken away against their will. Archdeacon Williams acted as interpreter during the treaty-making at Waitangi. During the subsequent wars and disasters of the Maoris, that treaty was remembered as the great betrayal. But there followed the full colonization of New Zealand including the building up of church life on the British pattern, the creative Victorian bishop being George Augustus Selwyn.

Selwyn's most attractive activity arose out of his concern for the Melanesian peoples on their many islands to the north. At first his strategy was to gather sons of the island chiefs to be educated in a school which he built next to his cathedral in Auckland. But the school was a failure and another had to be opened on Norfolk Island. Even then Selwyn acknowledged that before enough pupils could be recruited the confidence of their fathers must be won – and the Melanesians had been alienated, like the Maoris, by ruthless sailors. The most notorious culprits were the 'blackbirders' who were virtually slave-traders, but other sailors pursued an alternative policy: in order to clear the islands for settlement by white men they put ashore 'natives' infected with measles, a disease against which there was no resistance. Selwyn saw that the islands must be visited systematically, with courage but also in hope.[22]

To a man of Selwyn's convictions that must mean the recruitment of another bishop. Fortunately non-Anglicans had already shown what could be done. In many of the Polynesian islands to the west, Christian communities had grown in response to missionary work. One missionary, John Williams of the London Missionary Society, had won a special fame by building a boat to get from island to island and by being willing to meet a martyr's death. He had been clubbed to death and eaten on the island of Erromanga in 1839; the islanders had been enraged by the activities of the blackbirders. A Roman Catholic missionary bishop had been killed in similar circumstances in 1845. But in Fiji an astonishing number of conversions had rewarded Methodist missionaries, who had landed in 1835 and who had stayed despite persecutions and despite witnessing the horrors of cannibal feasts. In some Polynesian islands the opposite of martyrdom had awaited missionaries. In the kingdom of Tonga, for example, what was in effect a Methodist State Church was built up while the Christian king who in 1830 took the baptismal name of George reigned until 1893; two missionaries, John Thomas and Shirley Baker, succeeded in each other in almost dictatorial powers. So Bishop Selwyn had a reason to hope that eventually a reward would come. Meanwhile the best plan for the conversion of the Melanesians seemed clear.[23]

He picked a saint who, like him, was an English gentleman, an Etonian and an athlete – but who possessed a gentler character. John Coleridge Patteson was consecrated a bishop for this perilous mission in 1861. He learned the technique from Selwyn: to swim ashore alone and unarmed, pushing in front of him a top hat full of simple presents for the islanders. His great gift for friendship, allied with linguistic ability which had won him a fellowship at Oxford, worked like a charm –

---

[22] John H. Evans wrote a biography of Selwyn as *Churchman Militant* (London, 1964). B. J. Dalton studied the background in *War and Politics in New Zealand 1855–70* (Sydney, 1967), and W. P. Morrell in *Britain in the Pacific Islands* (Oxford, 1960).

[23] A. A. Koskinen studied *Missionary Influence as a Political Factor in the Pacific Islands* (Helsinki, 1953). Niel Gunson's later study of *Messengers of Grace* took the Protestant story to 1860.

until, like Williams before him, he visited an island which had been troubled by the blackbirders; five of its men had been kidnapped. His murder followed. His lifeless body was placed in a canoe and pushed back to his companions. On it was a palm branch, with five knots. In the words inscribed on a cross later built at the place of his death on a converted Nukapu island: 'His life was taken by men for whom he would gladly have given it.'

The mission continued, most of it the work of converts, and the next bishop was Bishop Selwyn's son John, a man as beloved as Patteson. It was too late to save the islands from depopulation, but the Melanesian Church so developed in its faith and its unity that by 1918, when it had a bishop who treated the 'natives' like children, it was able to compel him to resign and go back to England.[24]

TO INDIA

It would obviously be impossible to retrace every step taken by the Victorian missionaries in the east – and it is not necessary, since the patterns repeated themselves. For example, the story of Francis McDougall, who sailed out to Sarawak in 1847 and returned home in 1868 having laid the foundations of a strong Anglican Church amid head-hunting primitive tribesmen, hostile Muslims and Chinese pirates, is in its way as remarkable as the story of his patron James Brooke, the Englishman who was made Rajah of Sarawak; but in its essentials the story of Bishop McDougall is very like the story of Bishops Selwyn and Patteson. We must confine ourselves to an outline of the story of how Englishmen helped to break the dominance of traditional religion over India and China, often with a disastrous clumsiness.

Despite the hopes which surrounded the full admission of

---

[24] Sir John Gutch wrote biographies of Williams and Patteson as *Beyond the Reefs* and *Martyr of the Islands* (London, 1971–74). C. E. Fox wrote a history of the Anglican mission to Melanesia as *Lord of the Southern Islands* (London, 1958).

Christian missionaries into India in 1813, there was no large movement by Indians into Christianity. A modern historian who recorded with praise the decisive influence of Evangelical preachers and administrators on social reform was frank about the missionaries' disappointment as they counted their converts. 'Among the Indians generally, suspicion far outweighed the acquiescence – it can scarcely be described as anything more active – of some of the lower classes and the occasional support of a far smaller number among the higher castes. Sometimes, too, there was open hostility to individual missionaries. From the British government in India the missionaries might look in general for approval extending at times to active support, but an incautious step might produce immediate recriminations'.[25]

For the missionaries almost totally failed to appreciate the Indian point of view. Their pride in their alliance with the men who now ruled India blinded them to the difficulty of securing a hearing for a spiritual message on the basis of that alliance. Indians justly believed that on the whole they were far more religious than their new conquerors, and that their holy men knew far more about the life of the spirit than did the Europeans who tried to use an Indian language to preach from the Bible in a crowded bazaar, or who had to be listened to as the price of receiving a modern education. Indians prepared to see merits in innovations by their conquerors would grant the merit of some social reforms; but they still thought that English talk about morality was hypocritical, for the ending of the East India Company's commercial business in 1833 still left India open to exploitation on a very large scale. Indians observed that the missionaries when they destroyed the centuries-old fabric of custom had no idea about how to replace it from within the Indian tradition. Any convert willing to be baptized had to forfeit his place in his family and his caste, and the almost certain result was that he was economically dependent on the missionaries. In these circumstances the converts were almost certain to be unhappy individuals, people without any

---

[25] Kenneth Ingham, *Reformers in India*, p. 19.

real stake in the Indian society saturated by the religious tradition which Europeans called Hinduism.[26]

In 1857 sepoys in the Bengal Army mutinied. It was the signal for a revolt which included atrocities on both sides. In defending British rule the leading general was an austere Baptist, Henry Havelock, and, specially when he had died of dysentery at the end of this triumph, he became a hero; his last words were to his son – 'Come now, and see how a Christian can die.'[27] But what was needed was more tactful living by Christians, for the causes of the rebellion were clear to all with eyes to see. The British conquest of India had just been completed, and it had been made compulsory for Indian soldiers to serve the British in other imperial wars if so ordered. The threat of the new empire to Indian traditions had been shown by the issue of new cartridges for the troops' rifles; these needed to be bitten off, and so the soldier's mouth would come into contact with grease probably derived from cows (sacred to Hindus) and pigs (unclean to Muslims). The cartridges were withdrawn, but the impression of contempt for Indian religious feelings had been created – or, rather, confirmed.

Despite the smallness of the British army in India (only 45,000 in 1857), the revolt was suppressed because its leadership had no coherent plan and most of the Indians remained either loyal or indifferent.[28] The day of Indian nationalism had not yet come. But Anglo-Indian relations were never the same again. The replacement of company rule by direct government by the Crown did not make much practical difference. The difference was that the degree of innocence, of optimism about the transformation of India, to be seen in British attitudes at

---

[26] The classic modern Indian indictments of the intrusion of the missionaries and their imperial allies were Jawaharlal Nehru, *The Discovery of India* (London, 1946), and K. M. Panikkar, *Asia and Western Dominance* (London, 1953). There was an earlier and more balanced judgement by a leading Indian Christian: K. T. Paul, *The British Connection with India* (London, 1928). For a British scholar's summary, see M. E. Chamberlain, *Britain and India: The Interaction of Two Peoples* (Newton Abbot, Devon, 1974).

[27] See J. C. Pollock, *Way to Glory: The Life of Havelock of Lucknow* (London, 1957).

[28] The best British narrative of *The Great Mutiny* is that by Christopher Hibbert (London, 1978). The best Indian study is S. N. Sen, *Eighteen Fifty-Seven* (Calcutta, 1957).

the height of the Evangelicals' influence vanished. Government officials still talked, often sincerely, about the British having a responsibility for 'the happiness of millions'. But the British now found it harder to think that they could trust, or even understand, the Indians. It was their duty to rule them; but part of their duty was to keep the ruling race uncontaminated.

After the mutiny missionaries were able to take advantage of the policy of the government, introduced in 1854, to bear about two-thirds of the cost of education which it deemed satisfactory. Mission schools gradually made the Christian minority the most highly educated section of Indian society apart from the sections which derived a superior education from an older community's tradition (most notably the Parsees) or from wealth. Some converts from the higher castes were obtained through the chain of colleges established by the missionaries for higher education, but most of the baptisms were of outcasts of the bottom of society or of hill tribesmen. By 1890 there were about 600,000 Indians in churches served by Anglican or other Protestant missionaries, but significantly there were almost a quarter of a million more Roman Catholics, whose priests were seldom English. It is significant, too, that such 'mass movements' into Christianity as did occur did not come in the areas where English influence was felt most strongly. One explanation is to be found in the fact that not until 1912 was an Indian made a diocesan bishop by the Anglicans.[29]

Here was the paradox of the British mission to India. It became well-intentioned but always wounded. It accepted many sacrifices. When independence came in 1947, probably there were two million British graves in India, most of them filled by disease. It contributed much, as independent Indians have often acknowledged. Yet even when it was being self-sacrificial, acting as conscience dictated in justice and kindness, bringing to India Christianity and many other benefits,

---

[29] Relevant studies include Michael Hollis, *Paternalism and the Church* (London, 1962); Mildred Gibbs, *The Anglican Church in India* (New Delhi, 1972); Duncan Forrester, *Caste and Christianity* (London, 1980). An Indian scholar, Sarvepalli Gopal, examined *British Policy in India 1858–1905* (Cambridge, 1967).

the British presence in India was wounding because it was patronizing. The work of Rudyard Kipling shows all this very clearly – although Kipling was bitterly cynical about the work of most of the missionaries, and the vagueness of his own religious beliefs would have shocked his grandfathers, who were both Methodist ministers. He suffered because his parents had left England to earn a living in Bombay. Without any explanation he was deposited with strangers in England at the age of five, and felt an alien when he returned to India in 1881 at the age of sixteen. There were neurotic undertones in much of his work. He contributed much; he wrote about the life of the people of India and about the magic of the land as no one had written before. But in the last resort he could not regard India as his home. Hinduism he despised even more thoroughly than missionary Christianity, and Indians he thought would always need to be commanded while they were being served. Marriage to an American in 1892 meant that he left India except for one brief visit and his dreams.[30]

In 1899 Kipling urged Americans to follow the British example by colonizing the Philippine islands:

> Take up the White Man's Burden –
>   Send forth the best ye breed –
> Go bind your sons to exile
>   To serve your captives' need;
> To wait in heavy harness
>   On fluttered folk and wild –
> Your new-caught sullen peoples,
>   Half-devil and half-child.

TO CHINA

On a Sunday in June 1865 James Hudson Taylor walked by the sea at Brighton. With his agitated mind he saw not the English coast but the Chinese empire. For a missionary to go

---

[30] The best introduction is Angus Wilson, *The Strange Ride of Rudyard Kipling* (London, 1977), and fuller studies include Alan Sandisan, *Wheel of Empire* (London, 1967).

deep into China seemed as difficult as for a non-swimmer to go far into the sea; and eleven years previously Taylor had begun his first, disappointing, experience of the problem when he had joined the missionaries making highly nervous expeditions into the interior from the 'treaty port' of Shanghai. He had returned to England for training as a medical doctor, but his health and his spirits were broken.

To the Chinese, the 'Middle Kingdom' was the only civilization in the world and 'barbarians' must be kept out of it since they only cheated, corrupted and made trouble. Robert Morrison went from Northumberland to China while in his early twenties, in 1807, with the support of the London Missionary Society, but at that time Canton was the only port open to foreigners, who were severely limited to trade on the waterfront. In 1818 he founded the 'Anglo-Chinese College' at Malacca, and the next year he completed a translation of the Bible, but in a quarter of a century he and his few British Protestant colleagues baptized only ten Chinese. Inside China there were remnants of the fairly extensive Roman Catholic missionary work of the previous two centuries, but these remnants were small and persecuted.

In the period 1839–44 wars were fought in order to compel the Chinese to accept the import of opium from India; for the British, too, claimed what Chinese emperors had always claimed – the 'Mandate of Heaven'. The weakness of the imperial government invited a peasant revolt – and for the first time in Chinese history the next revolt, the Taiping rebellion, contained a Christian element, however confused its theology may have been in the eyes of Evangelicals such as Major Charles Gordon, enlisted to stiffen the imperial army.[31] With the defeat of these rebels the missionaries had learned the fatal lesson of dependence on this kind of foreign military intervention in Chinese affairs, but we cannot be surprised that James Hudson Taylor, when he contemplated the Christian mission to China from the Brighton beach in 1865, was depressed.

The son of a Methodist lay preacher who had run a little

---

[31] The best account of this life, which ended dramatically in Khartoum in 1885, is Anthony Nutting, *Gordon: Martyr and Misfit* (London, 1966).

chemist's shop in Yorkshire, his own religious faith was simple. He believed that, without any opportunity to hear and believe the Gospel, the Chinese must die in their sins and be punished everlastingly; he reckoned that a million a month were going to hell. And on that Sunday in 1865 the essentials of a new plan for the evangelization of China suddenly became clear as he pondered and prayed. He would lead a mission which would take full advantage of the promised toleration even if the toleration amounted to little in practice. The missionaries would not live permanently in mission stations, supervising their dependants in the hope that a church would slowly grow. Their message was too urgent for that. Having proclaimed their Gospel, they would move on to other towns and villages. They would not receive regular salaries; God would provide. Meetings held to support them would take no collections, yet no debts would be incurred. They would not be confined to any denomination and they would not be controlled by any committee remaining in England. They would welcome fellow missionaries from any nation and any level of education, and women would be given a wide scope. To symbolize their break with their homes they would wear Chinese dress and speak the local language – but they would preach salvation, not ingratiate themselves by any technical aid.

Fifteen fellow missionaries who accepted Taylor's guidance sailed with him and his wife to China. Thirty years after his Brighton vision the China Inland Mission included 641 missionaries, about half the Protestant missionaries in China. Taylor's letters home breathed the spirit of a mystical union with Christ in prayer and total self-dedication; but he was also a brilliant organizer, able to hold a team together. His courage, shown repeatedly, could not fail to move the Chinese however bewildered they were by his flexible methods or by his uncompromising message. He died in China in 1905.[32]

Three years later the last formidable Manchu ruler of China, the Dowager Empress, died. The imperial dynasty had been fatally discredited by its failure to cope either with the in-

---

[32] The best biography remains that by his son Howard (abridged, London, 1965).

numerable penetrations by offensively over-privileged foreign merchants or with the rebellion of the 'Boxers' in 1897–1900. This rebellion, which murdered some 32,000 Christians, was a great cry of protest against the humiliation of China at the hands of foreigners. But, strangely, it turned out to be a prelude to a time of hope for Christianity. Its violence warned the European powers off the policy into which they had previously been drifting – the policy of colonizing China; and its suppression by a European expedition gave an opportunity to Sun Yat-sen, who had been baptized while a student, to found the Republic of China in 1911. For a time a Republican modernism looking to Japan, America and Europe seemed to promise the regeneration of China. After their long exclusion and their long struggle for recognition, the Christian Churches felt themselves to be on the crest of a wave. Schools, colleges and hospitals proliferated and many students went abroad to study. The Anglicans formed the 'Holy Catholic Church in China' in 1912, uniting their dioceses with much hope for a glorious future; but the chief gains were won by the Roman Catholics and by the interdenominational Protestants of the China Inland Mission. In 1913 the Temple of Heaven in Peking, formerly the 'Forbidden City', was used for a series of Christian evangelistic meetings. The Churches' statistics claimed that the number of their adherents had doubled, to about a million and a half, within ten years of the defeat of the Boxers. It was an achievement to be seen in its context – a population of some four hundred millions. But the progress in China was the largest cause of the optimism reigning in the missionary movement on the eve of the First World War.[33]

How are we to assess this complex story now outlined?

It was often true about the Victorians and post-Victorians abroad, as it was often true about them at home, that 'they pretended to be better than they were. They passed themselves

---

[33] K. S. Latourette, *A History of Christian Missions in China* (London, 1929), remains standard. More recent accounts include the mainly Catholic Columba Cary-Elwes, *China and the Cross* (London, 1957), and the entirely Protestant Pat Barr, *To China with Love* (London, 1972). There is background material, revised in the light of post-1948 studies, in Vincent Shih, *The Taiping Ideology* (Seattle, 1967), and Victor Purcell, *The Boxer Uprising* (Cambridge, 1963).

off as being incredibly pious and moral; they talked noble sentiments and lived – quite otherwise.'[34] But not all the Victorian Christians were hypocrites; and about those who included self-deception in their characters, this was not the whole truth. Their energy and courage flowed from a self-confidence which had its origins partly in Evangelicalism, although also in more secular sources. They were so proud of their technical superiority to other peoples that they came to believe in themselves as the explorers of a world which was somehow 'unknown' before their arrival, as the missionaries of a civilization which was incomparably the best and which included the various denominational interpretations of Christianity. They were slow to see how ready Canada, Africa, the Pacific islands and Asia were to be exploited, governed and to some extent converted – but they did see it and in the end they seized their opportunity, changing the course of history. They gave what they could to the world.

---

[34] Walter E. Houghton, *The Victorian Frame of Mind 1830–1870* (New Haven, Conn., 1957), p. 395. This classic study avoided moral condemnation–unlike the Victorians.

CHAPTER TEN

THE END OF AN ENGLAND

DOMESTIC QUARRELS

There were many warnings to the English Churches. In *The Condition of England* (1909) an Anglican layman, C. F. C. Masterman, paid a tribute: 'The Churches are extraordinarily active, endeavouring in this way and that to influence the lives of the people. Their humanitarian and social efforts are widely appreciated.' But he added: 'Their definite dogmatic teaching seems to count for little at all. They labour steadily on amid a huge indifference.' In 1904 the *Daily Telegraph* printed a long correspondence under the title 'Do We Believe?' It showed much scepticism in the paper's middle-class readership. A book such as *Religion: A Criticism and a Forecast* by Galdsworthy Lowes Dickinson (1905) expressed the superior scepticism of a Cambridge don, the key sentence being the claim that 'religious truth, like all other truth, is attainable, if at all, only by the method of science'. Under such influences, many idealistic and intelligent young graduates who would have been ordained in Victorian times were now turning to the other professions which were being rapidly developed. In the Church of England, ordinations which had reached their peak with 814 new deacons in 1886 were below six hundred a year throughout the period 1901–14. And the autobiography of Eric Gill, a Nonconformist minister's son who was to become famous as a sculptor and as a Roman Catholic, records what he found in a place far removed from the atmosphere of the ancient universities. He was employed with other clerks by the Ecclesiastical Commissioners to serve the Church of England – and he was almost overwhelmed by the contempt for religion which he found among other young men in this office.

An examination of the religious life of Lambeth, the crowded

South London borough which surrounded the Archbishop of Canterbury's palace and Spurgeon's old pulpit, during the early years of the twentieth century has been made by an American scholar. He accepted a survey which suggested that about a tenth of the population could be found in church on a Sunday morning or evening. His broad conclusion agreed with Masterman's verdict: secularization was already strong, although there was still a lot of churchgoing and there was even more charitable activity by churchgoers. The Churches, he wrote, 'intended to persuade the entire nation to attend Sunday services, and there indoctrinate churchgoers with Anglican or Nonconformist values. Instead they persuaded only a portion of the upper and middle classes to attend church, and created a vast parochial and philanthropic network which provided the sacraments and social services to the working classes and the poor.'[1]

Did the remedy lie in more effective religious instruction in the schools? Possibly; but when the Conservatives' Education Act of 1902 subsidized church schools out of the local rates by the payment of teachers and the maintenance of buildings, the Baptist leader, John Clifford, led the 'passive resistance' to this as a holy war against clerical despotism, a war calling for martyrs who would refuse to pay rates. Up and down the country this conflict made relations between Nonconformists and Anglicans worse than they had been for a century and a half. 'Wake up, Oliver Cromwell, wake up the spirit of our Puritan ancestors,' cried Clifford to the Free Church Congress, 'and once more lead us to victories for freedom and for God!' In the end, however, all that happened was that the Anglican church schools survived with a diminishing proportion of the nation's children in them, the Roman Catholic schools survived with greater enthusiasm, and in the new 'council schools' the Bible was taught in a broad way of which most Anglicans and Roman Catholics disapproved. 'A boneless, fibreless, structureless, colourless, tasteless religion, absolutely wanting in every constituent needed to build up the Christian charac-

---

[1] Jeffrey Cox, *The English Churches in a Secular Society* (New York, 1982), p. 6. A. D. Gilbert surveyed *The Making of Post-Christian Britain* (London, 1980).

ter' was how this education was described by a Jesuit, Bernard
Vaughan. But if such criticism of the council schools was partly
justified, the absorption of the denominations in their own
narrow concerns was partly to blame. A few of the wisest Free.
Church leaders, such as the Methodist John Scott Lidgett (a
great man who combined a theology of the love of God with
leadership in London's social work and education), pleaded for
a settlement in the interests of the children. So did the
Archbishop of Canterbury, Randall Davidson, who was defeated in his efforts at a compromise. Agreement about the
syllabus to be used in religious education in the majority of the
nation's schools could not be recorded in an Act of Parliament
until 1944. And by then the mind of England was moving away
from all the Churches. It was partly because they were divided
that the Churches' statistics fell.[2]

Did the remedy lie in the drastic reduction of Anglican
privileges – the only point (it seemed) on which Nonconformists and Roman Catholics agreed? Possibly; but the easiest
point of attack seemed to be the disestablishment of the Church
in Wales, and even this measure was resisted bitterly by most
of the Anglicans, with their Conservative allies. The first
Welsh Disestablishment Bill to be given priority in the government's business was introduced in 1895. The fourth and last
was in its last stages when war broke out. With financial
provisions more generous than the original proposals, it came
into effect in 1920. A direct confrontation with the Church of
England was once again postponed, an important factor being
the diplomatic skill of Randall Davidson. For example, he led
most of the bishops to support the Parliament Act of 1911,
which ended the veto of the House of Lords over Liberal
legislation. As we have seen, many of the broader-minded
clergy and laity were in this period expressing sympathy with
the ideals of Christian Socialism. Thus the identification of the

---

[2] Benjamin Sacks studied *The Religious Issue in the State Schools of England and Wales
1902–14* (Albuquerque, N.M., 1961) and M. Cruickshank *Church and State in English
Education: 1870 to the Present Day* (London, 1963). Sir James Marchant's memoir of
John Clifford (London, 1924) may be supplemented by H. E. Bonsall and E. H.
Robertson, *The Dream of an Ideal City* (London, 1978). J. Scott Lidgett recalled *My
Guided Life* (London, 1936).

Established Church with the Conservative Party, although substantial, was not complete and the Gladstonian tradition of an Anglican presence within the Liberal Party was not obliterated.[3]

Did the remedy lie in more vigorous preaching? In 1904 a large survey of *The Religious Life of London* reached this conclusion although it also argued for a new kind of church around the pulpit – 'large, handsome central halls, well lit and well ventilated, furnished throughout with seats of one pattern' and sponsoring many clubs for 'active, aggressive social work' seeking the 'redemption and development of body, mind and soul'. But the question then arose – what was the preacher to say that was not being said by the politicians or the newspapers? And in each of the denominational traditions into which English religion was now divided, there were sharply conflicting answers.

In the Church of England the challenge was thrown down by the Anglo-Catholic movement, which had increased its attractiveness to churchgoers while the support of duller Evangelical preachers had declined from the 1880s onwards. In 1906 it acquired in the *English Hymnal* the richest collection of hymns yet brought together in the English language. It proclaimed firm doctrines and dramatized them by colourful ceremonies.

When a Royal Commission was appointed to inquire into ecclesiastical discipline in 1904 (by the Conservative Prime Minister, Balfour, in consultation with Archbishop Davidson), 'practices of special gravity and significance' were noted, as demanded by outraged Protestants. Showing how little had been achieved by Victorian discipline, these practices included the interpretation of prayers and ceremonies belonging to the Roman Canon of the Mass, 'the reservation of the sacrament under conditions which lead to its adoration', processions and 'benediction' with the sacrament, the invocation of the Virgin Mary and other saints in hymns and prayers, the observance of the festivals of the Assumption and the Sacred Heart and the

---

[3] See P. M. H. Bell, *Disestablishment in Ireland and Wales*, pp. 225–329, and K. O. Morgan, *Wales in British Politics 1865–1922* (Cardiff, 1963). G. K. A. Bell compiled a masterly biography of *Randall Davidson* (2 vols., Oxford, 1935).

veneration of 'images'. But 'the two main conclusions' of this commission gave the Protestant disciplinarians little hope. 'First, the law of public worship in the Church of England is too narrow for the religious life of the present generation. It needlessly condemns much which a great section of Church people, including many of her most devoted members, value; and modern thought and feeling are characterized by a care for ceremonial, a sense of dignity in worship, and an appreciation of the continuity of the Church, which were not similarly felt at the time when the law took its present shape.' 'Secondly, the machinery for discipline has broken down. The means of enforcing the law in the ecclesiastical courts, even in matters which touch the Church's faith and teaching, are defective and in some respects unsuitable.'

However, if the worship of the Church of England was to be revised in order to accommodate the new richness of Catholic devotion, difficult problems became inescapable. Not only was there the problem of how to persuade Parliament either to produce a Prayer Book acceptable to churchmen or to let the Church produce it for itself. (Between 1880 and 1913 there were 216 bills to regulate ecclesiastical matters introduced into the House of Commons; only thirty-three became law.) There was also the problem of how to secure a new basis of Anglican unity now that the Establishment was cracked wide open, at home and overseas. The Anglo-Catholics reacted touchily, even hysterically, to movements very different but equally Anglican. For example, in 1913 there was a discussion of a possible federation of the Protestant, including Anglican, Churches in Kenya: it aroused the wrath of Frank Weston, Bishop of Zanzibar, and of other Anglo-Catholics. Bishop Weston announced that he was no longer in communion with those who had taken part in the discussion in Africa, and was no less enraged when reports reached Africa of criticisms of their holy book by English Christians. Among some of the clergy as among many of the laity, questions were being asked – however tentatively – about the virgin birth, the miracles and the physical resurrection of Jesus, and about the whole historical basis of Christianity. A few preachers aired their doubts openly and bishops deplored such indiscretions. In 1909 a

theological journal published a much-discussed special number called *Jesus or Christ?*, contrasting Jesus of Nazareth with
the Christ of the Church's orthodoxy. A volume by Oxford
scholars of 1913, *Foundations*, showed that the doctrinal foundations were being shaken in the Church of England, although as
yet only gently.[4]

These winds of theological change blew more fiercely in the
minds of two preachers outside the Church of England – the
Congregationalist, R. J. Campbell, and the Roman Catholic,
George Tyrrell.

Campbell was the great Dr Parker's successor in the marble
pulpit of the crowded City Temple. Whether Parker knew how
much more liberal this young man's views were is a mystery.
The congregation, however, soon saw it; and the crowds
continued to pour in. Campbell's views developed rapidly.
Some words of his criticizing the workers' attitude to Sunday
were reported in newspapers – as many of his words were – and
led to a private meeting with Labour leaders, a novel experience which converted the preacher to a form of Socialism. In
contrast, when he repeated orthodox words about salvation
they seemed to fail to arouse much interest, while all around
him lay the capital of a great empire, full of inequalities but also
full of promises about the progress to come in the twentieth
century. In 1907 two books resulting from his pulpit work were
widely discussed. In *Christianity and the Social Order*, Campbell
maintained with much passion that 'the practical end which
alone could justify the existence of Churches is the realization
of the kingdom of God, which only means the reconstruction of
society on a basis of mutual helpfulness instead of strife and
competition'. This challenge to the Churches was urgent, since
while the contrast between wealth and poverty was shocking
(estimates were quoted that more than one half of the land was
owned by 2,500 people while the average annual income of
11,500 working-class families in York was £85), 'charities
demoralize the poor and gospel missions fail to touch them'.

---

[4] The most important literature is referred to in Roger Lloyd, *The Church of
England 1900–65* (London, 1966), and in Owen Chadwick's study of a controversially liberal preacher, *H. H. Henson* (Oxford, 1983).

The New Theology was even more provocative in its definition
– or lack of definition – of the Gospel. Jesus, Campbell
maintained, 'was God because his life was the expression of
Divine Love'; but he bestowed almost similar praise on progressive humanity. 'Jesus was God, but so are we.' The Spirit of
God dwelt in every man, to such an extent that there seemed no
need for any clear distinction between the Creator and the
creature, or between the Saviour and the saved. 'The *roué* you
saw in Piccadilly last night,' he informed first his congregation
and then his readers, 'who went out to corrupt innocence and
wallow in filthiness of the flesh was engaged in his blundering
quest for God'; and to see the Labour leader, Keir Hardie,
pleading for justice in the House of Commons was to 'see the
Atonement'.

There were many replies to Campbell. The most weighty
came from a fellow Congregationalist, P. T. Forsyth. The son
of a postman and a domestic servant, Forsyth was rather better
informed than Campbell about the conditions of the poor – and
more convinced that the poor needed the 'positive preaching'
of the 'Holy Church' about the 'Holy Father'. He had begun as
a liberal, but had come to see that liberty was not enough; 'now
we want to know what makes and keeps us free, and what we
are free for.' He had found the liberation, the salvation,
required in the gracious God revealed and active through the
divine Christ, and wrote a trenchant book on *The Person and
Place of Jesus Christ* (1909): 'it is through the work of redemption
that I know the person of the Redeemer'.[5]

However, the most immediately effective reply to *The New
Theology* came from Charles Gore, Bishop of Birmingham, an
Anglo-Catholic saint and scholar. The presentation of the
timeless Catholic Faith as the corrective of Campbell's own
hasty and muddled thinking shook him to the core. He became
convinced that 'either Jesus was what the Catholic Church
said he was, or he did not exist; either he was the Man from
heaven, a complete break with the natural order of things, the
representative of a transcendental order, supernatural, super-
rational, super-everything, or he was nothing.' He was con-

---

[5] See W. L. Bradley, *P. T. Forsyth: The Man and His Work* (London, 1952).

firmed and ordained by Gore, and began a thoroughly orthodox, but dull, ministry in the Church of England. His story
sums up the central dilemma of the Free Churches in his day.
Were they to add a touch of down-to-earth Christianity to the
popular causes of the time? Or were they to be more supernatural in their message, and if so was their worship supernatural
enough to defy the current trends? This dilemma was eating
away at their success, although superficially it is true to say
that 'the years 1900 to 1914 seemed to fulfil the extravagant
hopes that the Free Churches had for their future'.[6]

Charles Gore had seemed the obvious man to appoint as the
first Principal of Pusey House, Oxford, when that centre of
Anglo-Catholicism was founded as a memorial to the theological patriarch. But in 1889, only seven years after Pusey's
death, the self-confidence of a new generation of Anglo-
Catholics had been shown by the publication of *Lux Mundi*, a
collection of essays edited by Gore. Throughout that volume
the tone had been optimistic. The mostly young and Oxford-
trained authors seemed to expect the light shining in Beth-
lehem – a light plainly visible to the wise men from Victorian
England – to be welcomed by the world. The beauty of nature
and the strictness of man's own conscience united to testify to
the reality of the Creator and Judge. Mankind's history and the
individual's own experience, although they might include
suffering, united to prepare for the coming of Christ. Christ
emptied himself of divine power in order to be close to men (the
'kenotic' theory of the Incarnation, which brought accusations
of heresy from the ultra-orthodox) – rather like a wealthy
young man from Oxford visiting the London slums. Christ the
incarnate Son taught that all men were sons of God, but called
Christians to an attainable holiness as the salt of the earth,
leaving behind a moral law to guide them, sacraments to feed
them, and the Church to be his continuing Body, 'an organization for the spiritual life'. Into this confidently clear picture of
Lux Mundi it had seemed possible to fit pretty well every fact
significant in the Victorian world, and the book had secured a

---

[6] Paul Sangster, *A History of the Free Churches* (London, 1983), p. 171. R. J.
Campbell retraced *A Spiritual Pilgrimage* (London, 1916).

wide influence as an Anglican intellectual manifesto. It is not surprising that in the 1900s the confused Campbell seemed an upstart to Bishop Gore – and Gore a 'Father-in-God' to him.

Gore was encouraged by Campbell's conversion to affirm still more strongly the power of the everlasting Gospel entrusted to the Church. He rightly declared that no other Gospel had ever been admitted into the foundation documents of the Church of England. The Gospel, in his conviction, produced a Catholicism which was always open to fresh insights (that was why he called himself a 'liberal' Catholic) but which was always fundamentally a coherent whole. He expounded that Gospel by teaching and by a life which to many seemed the best light in all the world. Yet he could not deny that questions about the doctrines in the historic faith, and about the historical facts on which the faith rested, were being asked by men as devoutly Christian as he was himself, as well as by a more sceptical mass of men. If he never felt the full force of those questions in his own mind, that did not prove their unreality or unimportance. An undergraduate once shrewdly compared Gore's mind with an 'awfully jolly' merry-go-round at a fair. The young man's complaint was that the merry-go-round never stopped so that he could make his own way on to it.[7]

Essentially similar cross-currents of thought were to be found in the Roman Catholic community. The unchanging faith was taught with a quiet conviction to growing numbers. It was taught by, for example, Francis Bourne, appointed Archbishop of Westminster in 1903. He was often called the 'quiet' cardinal and that meant 'dull'. Presumably his steady reliability in Roman eyes was the reason why he was appointed, although the youngest of the bishops. He was no saint. His quarrel with Peter Amigo, his successor as Bishop of Southwark, grew so embittered that his old diocese refused to

---

[7] Contrasting assessments were offered in H. D. A. Major, *English Modernism: Its Origins, Methods, Aims* (Cambridge, Mass., 1927), and A. M. Ramsey, *From Gore to Temple* (London, 1960). James Carpenter supplied *Gore: A Study in Liberal Catholic Thought* (London, 1960), and Thomas Langford a survey of English theology, 1900–20, against its social background in *In Search of Foundations* (Nashville, Tenn., 1969). G. L. Prestige wrote *The Life of Charles Gore* (London, 1935). See also Alan M. G. Stephenson, *The Rise and Decline of English Modernism* (London, 1984).

congratulate him when he was made a cardinal and he refused to preach in it. When Liverpool and Birmingham were elevated as archbishoprics in 1911, he was unsuccessfully anxious to have the primacy of Westminster more sharply defined. This touchiness about his status came out again in the following year, when he was invited to Buckingham Palace. But before accepting this gesture of friendship he demanded the proper honours: 'Our position is that the Holy See has, even in the eyes of the Foreign Office, the rank of a Sovereign Power and that the Cardinals are Princes of that Power.' It was not a claim likely to persuade a straightforward ex-sailor such as George V that the Cardinal was as patriotic as he was. But Bourne embodied the religious orthodoxy of his own community, for most of whom the inherited or adopted road to truth was – to use the title of Hilaire Belloc's book of 1901 – *The Path to Rome*.

It was not to be expected that such an ecclesiastic would make any very profound response to the challenge of new thought. In contrast, the movement called 'Modernism' was a theological attempt, marked by a passionate integrity and courage, to come to terms with the questions which destroyed belief for (for example) Edward Elgar. In 1906 that great musician, who had made a master-work out of Newman's *Dream of Gerontius*, and had followed it up with the two oratorios *The Apostles* and *The Kingdom*, ceased to feel loyalty to his inherited Catholicism. And so he ceased to find inspiration in explicitly religious themes. Music continued to pour out of him, often with sincerely patriotic words, but his best music was nostalgic and haunted; and the riddle of a sad world now made his personal philosophy an enigma.[8]

In 1907 Pope Pius X issued an encyclical, *Pascendi Gregis*, in which 'Modernism' was defined and condemned by listing a series of propositions all said to be destructive of Catholicism and of Christianity. The propositions had in common a desire to see the Church adjusting itself to modern thought – for example, by accepting the critical, scholarly study of the Bible.

---

[8] Ernest Oldmeadow wrote a biography of *Francis, Cardinal Bourne* (2 vols., London, 1940–44), and Michael Kennedy a much better *Portrait of Elgar* (revised, Oxford, 1982).

The chief international organizer of Modernism was based on London and it might have been expected that this man, Baron Friedrich von Hügel, would be excluded from the sacraments as Loisy had been. But so far from being excommunicated, the Baron was accorded great honour among Christians of all shades in England, until he was buried in the Benedictine monastery at Downside in 1925. It helps us to understand his immunity if we notice that he was a lay aristocrat. Although a well-known writer of religious books and letters, much sought after as a guide to spiritual progress, he was without a priest's formal responsibility. It also helps to notice that he was a scholarly saint, massive in his sense of the holiness and omni-presence of God, massive in his love of the mystical tradition of the Church, often referred to as Newman's successor; the two men talked over several days in 1876. The motive behind his risky involvement in the Modernist controversy was expressed in a letter on the last day of 1900: 'May this New Year and New Century bring us all much good – much work, and some achievement, visible or invisible, in the direction of a synthesis of Sanctity and Science, in the Church and for the Church.'[9]

An official condemnation was more likely to fall on George Tyrrell, von Hügel's close friend. For Tyrrell was a Jesuit. In that lay both his strength and his trouble. Joining the Jesuit order must have had something to do with his transformation from an idle and feckless Irish schoolboy into an industrious writer with a powerful style, producing many passages of spiritual insight and brave integrity. The Jesuits trained him and then gave him leisure. But they never made him complete-ly happy. Dismissed from the order in 1906, he was dismayed. Forbidden to do more than attend Mass, he ordered that the words 'Catholic priest' should be inscribed over the grave where he was buried in 1909, in unconsecrated ground.

In his posthumously published *Christianity at the Cross-roads* he paid many tributes to what he had called the 'faith of the

---

[9] Recent studies include L. V. Lester-Garland, *The Religious Philosophy of Baron F. von Hügel* (London, 1933); Michael de la Bedoyère, *The Life of Baron von Hügel* (London, 1951); Joseph P. Whelan, *The Spirituality of Friedrich von Hügel* (London, 1971); L. F. Barmann, *Baron Friedrich von Hügel and the Modernist Crisis in England* (Cambridge, 1972).

millions'. 'The Jesus of the first century would be more in sympathy with just those elements of Catholicism that are least congenial to the modern mind – not to say the mind of Modernists – not only with the transcendental, but with the literal, value of the Catholic presentment of the transcendental; with sacraments, priests, temples, priests and altars; with miracles, diabolic possessions and exorcisms; with devils and angels and all the supernaturalism of his own age and tradition. For all these things he had no word, no thought of censure, but only for their abuse and exploitation. . . .' What Tyrrell rebelled against was the Roman insistence that all the historical assertions in the Catholic creeds must be accepted as accurate history. Here his conscience as a modern man overcame his loyalty to a deeply comforting system. To him the virgin birth or the resurrection of Christ was as symbolic as the claim that Christ was seated at the Father's right hand. There was truth here, but it was the same kind of truth as was conveyed by the statue in Prague of the Christ child robed as a king. Artistic, poetic or mystic truth a modern man could accept, if only the Church did not continue to teach 'medievalism'.

Prophetically, Tyrrell rested his hope on a development which he thought might be slow or very rapid. As he moved towards death he wrote: 'It is the spirit of Christ that has again and again saved the Church from the hands of her worldly oppressors within and without; for where that spirit is, there is liberty. Deliverance comes from below, from those who are bound, not from those who bind. It is easy to quench a glimmering light caught by the eyes of a few; but not the light of the noonday sun – of knowledge that has become objective and valid for all. It is through knowledge of this kind that God has inaugurated a new epoch in man's intellectual life and extended his lordship over nature. Shall he do less for man's spiritual life when the times are ripe? and are they not ripening? Are we not hastening to an *impasse* – to one of those extremities which are God's opportunities?'[10]

---

[10] Recent studies include Alec Vidler, *A Variety of Catholic Modernists* (Cambridge, 1970), and David Schaltenover, *George Tyrrell: In Search of Catholicism* (Shepherdstown, W.V., 1981).

THE GREAT WAR

The declaration of war by the British empire against the German empire on 4 August 1914 ended many things, including the post-Reformation phase of English Christianity. Slowly, very reluctantly and often silently, the more perceptive of the church leaders found themselves compelled to acknowledge that here was the end of an England – for here was a horror to which conventional piety and morality seemed largely irrelevant.[11]

The war was a catastrophe which very few expected. In the hot summer of 1914 the church press reflected the nation's absorption in the questions of whether the Unionists would use force in Ireland, whether the strikers would use their industrial muscle successfully, whether the peers would dig their defences against the people, whether the militant suffragettes would make the men surrender, whether the Nonconformists would conquer the church schools. None of these inflexibly determined agitators dreamed that before 1915 was out the war's most popular poem would be published in *Punch* –

> In Flanders fields the poppies blow
> Between the crosses, row on row . . .

On 1 August the Archbishop of Canterbury replied to an invitation to take part in the celebration of the four hundredth year of the Reformation in Germany, in 1917. He was anxious about the international situation, but took the opportunity to say that 'war between two great Christian nations of kindred race and sympathies is, or ought to be, unthinkable in the twentieth century of the Gospel of the Prince of Peace.' On 2 August what was to be called the 'World Alliance for Promoting International Friendship through the Churches' was founded at a conference in Constance. But the unexpected war was supported with an unexpected enthusiasm in the English Churches, including Nonconformity.

---

[11] The best studies are Arthur Marwick, *The Deluge: British Society and the First World War* (revised, London, 1973); Albert Marrin, *The Last Crusade: The Church of England in the First World War* (Durham, NC, 1974); Alan Wilkinson, *The Church of England and the First World War* (London, 1978).

On 7 August the editorial leader of the *British Weekly* was headed 'United We Stand'. Three months later a crowded meeting in the City Temple pledged Nonconformity to the goal of victory. The keynote speech was made by Lloyd George, previously best known as a radical champion of progress, whom the *British Weekly* soon began supporting as a determined war minister. The first Conscription Act of January 1916 created the term 'conscientious objectors' and most of these were Nonconformists or sectarians, but only about 16,500 such men had been registered by the tribunals by November 1918, including about 3,300 who accepted 'non-combatant service'. The total was about a third of one per cent of the men who volunteered or were conscripted during the war. About a third of the men of military age belonging to the pacifist Society of Friends enrolled to fight.[12] The patriotism of the Free Churches was universally acknowledged, and on Sunday 16 November 1918 the King and Queen attended a thanksgiving service in the Albert Hall, the first time that a British monarch had ever attended Nonconformist worship.

The Church of England's patriotism was conspicuously displayed during the recruiting campaigns which were necessary before conscription was thought acceptable; and it was put into practice when thousands of 'padres' (a new word in English) ministered to the fighting men. The Chaplain-General, Bishop Taylor-Smith, a hearty Evangelical stalwart, was so insensitive to the complications of the problems of a much more varied set of chaplains in a much enlarged army that a true saint, Bishop Llewellyn Gwynne of the Sudan, had to be put in charge of the cruelly testing spiritual work in France as Deputy Chaplain-General. Yet Gwynne was no less deeply patriotic than Taylor-Smith. On the eve of the murderous battle of Passchendaele he sat down by the roadside when the last of the troops had gone forward, and prayed with all his might. He thought he heard a voice from the crucifix behind him, saying: 'Only the best can give the best.'[13]

---

[12] See Martin Cleadal, *Pacifism in Britain* (Oxford, 1980).

[13] H. C. Jackson, *Pastor on the Nile* (London, 1960), p. 155. Michael Moynihan assessed the army padres in *God on Our Side* (London, 1983).

The Roman Catholic Church in England similarly identified itself with the sacrifices of the war effort, despite the neutrality of the papacy. It was only slowly that a much more tortured Christian reaction came to the surface in all the Churches and outside them.

In 1916 Henri Barbusse published in French a novel (translated as *Under Fire*) which described a low flight over the front lines one Sunday morning. Sounds from religious services being conducted by army chaplains on the two sides seemed to reach his plane. '*Gott mit uns!* and "God is with us" – and I flew away. . . . What must the good God think about it all?' And now an even harder question was whether there was a God who was both omnipotent and good. It was a question asked by – among many others – Oswin Creighton, a chaplain who was the son of Mandell Creighton, the former Bishop of London. On Easter Day 1918 Creighton wrote to his mother: 'God so hated the world that he gave several millions of English-begotten sons, that whosoever believeth in them should not perish, but have a comfortable life.' He was among the three quarters of a million Englishmen killed in the war.

Up to a point, the questioning can be studied in an impressive series of reports. In October 1916 a National Mission of Repentance and Hope was launched by the Archbishops of Canterbury and York. There was criticism that a 'national mission' was too grandiose, and in fact the mission chiefly influenced the missioners and their already committed supporters, whose thoughts about the ineffectiveness of the Church were stirred. There was also criticism that a nation conducting a crusade did not need to be called to 'repentance', and in fact this call to the nation was often muted at the parish level. But the official outline explained the thinking behind this ambitious venture. 'We have a righteous cause in the great war; but the civil war which seemed imminent in Ireland in the summer of 1914, and the great industrial war for which preparation was then being made, were evidence of something radically wrong among ourselves.' It was acknowledged that the Church had concentrated its message too heavily on the individual. The time had come to proclaim repentance and hope to a whole society in crisis, as the Old Testament prophets had done; and it was this task that made the Church's weakness so painfully obvious. Five 'Committees of Inquiry' were appointed by the archbishops to examine the Church's 'teaching office', worship, evangelism, administration and involvement in industry. When published in 1919, their reports all began with confessions of the Church of England's failure.

The Church's delivery of its message was 'out of touch with the thoughts and ideas of the time'. Its clergy needed to be trained and retrained more systematically, particularly in relation to science and moral and social questions. The clergy had got out of touch with ordinary people – as the chaplains had learned for themselves in the army, where three-quarters of the troops were classified as 'C. of E.' but only a handful would appear at voluntary acts of worship. The Prayer Book urgently needed reform. The laity needed to be involved more in worship and taught how to pray in private.

Evangelism suffered because the Church was regarded as 'the hereditary enemy of the working classes', although among wartime soldiers and peacetime workers there was much 'inarticulate religion' looking for a 'fellowship' often found in the Labour movement. 'The call to service is being found to have more arresting power than the old evangelistic appeal.'

The committee considering industrial problems showed that some notice had been taken of the Russian revolutions of 1917, of the strikes in British factories now expected to become more bitter, and of the unrest in Britain's own armed forces which at the turn of 1918–19 brought the Royal Navy to the edge of open mutiny and forced the government to demobilize the army far more quickly than it wanted. The committee observed that the war 'had a tremendous effect in awakening the social conscience of Christians' and the future would probably look back on 'some features of our industrial system' with the same feelings as they looked back on slavery. Wages, leisure, unemployment benefits, schooling (up to sixteen) and housing must all be improved drastically, and the 'mutual antagonism and suspicion between employer and employed' must be ended. Many more working-class clergy must be recruited.

A much stronger history of identification with the working class led to a warmer welcome to the Roman Catholic chaplains. In his Pastoral Letter for Lent 1918 Cardinal Bourne showed how in this setting even an innately conservative leader could be radical. He announced that 'Capitalism really began with the robbery of Church property' and that 'the army is not only fighting, it is also thinking. . . . They have learned to be suspicious of official utterances and bureaucratic ways. And the general effect of all this on the young men who are citizens of "after the war" is little short of revolutionary.' But it could not be claimed that either the Roman Catholic Church or Nonconformity possessed all the answers to the problems now seen to confront the Church of England. *The Army and Religion* was the title of a report published in 1919 after extensive investigations financed by the YMCA and beginning in 1917. The war had revealed that the results of all religious education were 'strangely small'. Only about twenty per cent seemed to be in touch with any of the Churches. Yet most soldiers were not godless, prayed before battle, showed compassion for each other, and were appropriately buried under a cross.

What did that cross mean? What did Christianity mean in the hearts of Englishmen, whether or not they survived the war?

In reality the problems of the Churches were far more difficult than any report fully acknowledged at the time; for the great war made it harder for millions to believe that the God worshipped in church truly was the sovereign Lord and Judge, punishing the wicked and protecting the faithful or the right-eous. At first it was hoped that the war would be 'over by Christmas' with a resounding defeat of the aggressor; but during four appalling years the reliance on the speedy help of the God of battles in a crusade inevitably grew weaker. It was also believed that one purpose of war within the will of God was to punish both sides for evils which had flourished during peace, and in 1914 the vicar of All Saints, Margaret Street, in London announced that the 'angel of death' had appeared because 'hard, godless women were springing up in multitudes around us, increasing numbers of them refusing to bear chil-dren'. But the suffering of 1914–18 inevitably seemed far beyond anything which a just God could have intended as chastisement for the use of contraceptives by London women, for the use of brothels by soldiers, or for any other sin, even German sin. It seemed to be part of the Christian faith that the believer or the innocent man would be protected, especially if prayed for; but the working creed of the British army came to be fatalism, the belief that 'the bullet will get you if it has your name on it' whatever may be the victim's piety or morality.

Before the war the belief in hell had been losing much of its ancient grip on the Christian imagination, but the belief that an individual's eternal destiny was decided at the moment of his death, so that it was wrong to pray for him after death, had remained ingrained in many Protestants including Anglican Evangelicals. Much evidence suggests, however, that during the war two momentous religious developments occurred in the mind of the average English Christian. First, it became incredible that the good God would sentence many of his children to everlasting punishment when they had already suffered so much through no fault of their own; Flanders was hell enough. Second, all God's children were such a mixture of good and bad that if a Christian prayed for them at all it was right to continue to pray for them when they were dead.

Above every other religious change rose the question: who or what was God? The Christian tradition was that God was the Almighty Father, controlling history and unlimited in his power, dispensing justice unerringly and himself immune from suffering. On that William Paley and Joseph Priestley, George Whitefield and John Wesley, Charles Simeon and John Henry Newman would all agree. But that was now hard to believe. Men were wrestling with mysteries and despairs greater than anything that had afflicted the mind of Browning or Tennyson or Hopkins or George Tyrrell. Nine months before he was killed, Oswin Creighton wrote home: 'I sometimes feel inclined to wonder why God hides himself so inscrutably from our experience. Or is it that the Church has taught us for so long to look for him in the wrong places?' Before the war such a feeling might have produced a faith in a God who was immersed in human progress – R. J. Campbell's City Temple faith, for example. But now the reality of the trenches in France and Flanders overwhelmed any reminders of home and peace and progress, at least for the 800,000 Englishmen who were normally on duty in them; and the wet, slimy, rat-infested, corpse-stinking 'front' was all the more ghastly because it was so near (seventy miles away) that an officer could have breakfast there and dine in his London club that evening. The idea of human progress, presided over by a genial Father, was inevitably one of the casualties in the great war. In 1916 R. J. Campbell collected some recent articles under the title *War and the Soul*. He began with a recognition of 'a widespread feeling of the utter insufficiency of religion, as commonly understood, to interpret for us the terrible situation in which we find ourselves.' Later he asked: 'What ground is there for believing that human affairs must inevitably progress towards betterment?' And he answered: 'None whatever. History almost demonstrates the contrary.'

One answer was to stress the transcendence of God, his holiness in contrast with a world of sin. In 1916 P. T. Forsyth's *The Justification of God* presented this answer in terms of a theology within the limits of a still fairly liberal brand of Nonconformity. The old words sin, evil, forgiveness and grace were restored to the theological currency. Essential to Christian faith was the completed victory of Christ; despite its continuing sins, 'it is a vanquished world'. Here was the English equivalent of the 'neo-orthodox' movement among Protestant theologians on the Continent – a movement which Karl Barth saw to be necessary when in 1914 he read the names of the most honoured theologians of Germany at the foot of an 'appeal' in defence of the Kaiser and the war. And in the Roman Catholic Church, Hilaire Belloc was typical of a militant, defiant neo-orthodoxy responding to the horror unleashed in 1914. He had lost a son whose body was never recovered from the mud at the front. His biographer has explained that 'to proclaim, and where possible to prove, the truth of Catholicism; to show the Church as the salt and savour of such civilization as survived in Europe; to demonstrate the price paid by his own country for the loss of Catholic belief – these now became a single, urgent, public task to which he addressed himself with all the force of his will.'[14]

[14] Robert Speaight, *The Life of Hilaire Belloc* (London, 1957), p. 373.

But even Protestant or Catholic orthodoxy, to which significant numbers clung or returned in this time of troubles, now often included the idea of the suffering God. The idea was proclaimed in the powerful, if rough, 'rhymes' of the best-known of all the army chaplains, Geoffrey Studdert Kennedy. An ugly little man nicknamed 'Woodbine Willie' because he used to distribute Woodbine cigarettes to the troops in France, he was courageous whether in ministering to the wounded in battle or in speaking his mind to generals. He toured the whole army on behalf of the National Mission of Repentance and Hope. After the war he became the chief missioner of the new Industrial Christian Fellowship. His message was now that God had 'the hardest part'; that the crucified Christ was the revelation of the pain in the heart of God. 'How does God deal with sin? . . . He takes it upon himself, and he calls on us to share his burden, to partake of his suffering.'[15]

This God was not often found in the books of Christian theology; but he could be found among suffering men. In a letter written in July 1918, the poet Wilfred Owen described training new troops. 'For fourteen hours yesterday I was at work – teaching Christ to lift his cross by numbers, and how to adjust his crown; and not to imagine his thirst until after the last halt. I attended his Supper to see that there were no complaints; and inspected his feet that they should be worthy of the nails. I see to it that he is dumb, and stands at attention before his accusers. With a piece of silver I buy him every day, and with maps I make him familiar with the topography of Golgotha.'[16] Owen was to be killed a week before the end of the war, joining many of the men he had loved.

Was this idea of the suffering God merely a symptom of a whole civilization's sickness, of the degradation of everything noble, including the idea of the divine holiness? Should it be resisted in the name of the God who was entirely 'other' than sinful man – and in the name of man who needed, more than anything else, to be assured that he could enter the transcendent joy of heaven? So Friedrich von Hügel (for example) now

[15] See William Purcell, *Woodbine Willie* (London, 1983).
[16] *Collected Letters of Wilfred Owen* (London, 1967), p. 562.

maintained. Or was this image of humility at last the truly Christian Gospel of God, destined to replace the bogus orthodoxy of centuries where the thought as well as the life of the Churches had been too much absorbed in power and privilege? Or had the terrible truth to be faced in the twentieth century that God was indeed crucified by tragedies beyond his control? Was God dead, if he had ever existed? If so, would man rise to unprecedented heights of splendour now that he had shaken off the religious illusion? Some hoped so – for example, the Communists who had seized control of Russia. Yet man's demonic cruelty to his own species had been exhibited on a spectacular scale, making him less than the other beasts. If there was no God, was man merely the product of blind chance in an indifferent universe? If so, had he any hope of survival now that he had laid his habitually violent hands on modern technology? If God was dead, could man live?

When the Great War ended with the armistice on 11 November 1918, these were the basic religious questions confronting an England which was no longer Christian in any very substantial sense. The answers were held by the future.

Outline of Events

1738   Conversion experience of John and Charles Wesley
1739   George Whitefield begins open-air preaching
1776   Declaration of Independence of USA
1779   Conversion experience of Charles Simeon
1784   Death of Samuel Johnson; John Wesley's ordinations mean Methodism's split from Church of England
1787   Charles Inglis becomes Bishop of Nova Scotia
1788   First English settlement in Australia
1790   *Reflections on the Revolution in France* by Edmund Burke
1791   Birmingham riots against Joseph Priestley
1793   William Carey sails to India
1794   *A View of the Evidences of Christianity* by William Paley
1797   *A Practical View* by William Wilberforce
1805   Conversion experience of William Wordsworth
1807   Prohibition of slave trade
1811   National Society begins to found church schools; Hugh Bourne begins Primitive Methodist meetings
1813   British India opened to missionaries; prisons opened to Elizabeth Fry
1814   Missionaries begin work in New Zealand
1818   Large government grant for new churches in England
1827   Death of William Blake; *The Christian Year* by John Keble
1828   Repeal of Test and Corporation Acts against Dissenters
1829   Catholic emancipation
1832   First Reform Act despite bishops' opposition
1833   Emancipation of slaves; Oxford Movement begins; Jabez Bunting moves to London as leader of Wesleyan Methodists
1834   Death of S. T. Coleridge

1836   Ecclesiastical Commissioners established; W. G. Broughton becomes Bishop of Australia

1837   Queen Victoria begins reign

1838   *The Kingdom of Christ* by F. D. Maurice

1839   John Williams, missionary to Polynesian islands, murdered

1840   New Zealand taken under British 'protection'

1841   Jerusalem bishopric founded by Anglicans and Lutherans

1844   YMCA founded by George Williams

1845   Irish potato famine causes migration to England; J. H. Newman received into Roman Catholic Church

1847   Ten Hours Act regulates factory work; consecration of Anglican colonial bishops including Robert Gray for Cape Town

1848   Chartist demonstrations in London

1850   Restoration of Roman Catholic hierarchy; Judicial Committee protects Evangelicals in Gorham Case; *In Memoriam* by Alfred Tennyson

1851   Horace Mann's census of churchgoing

1853   Liberation Society begins disestablishment campaign

1854   Florence Nightingale leads nurses to Crimean War

1856   David Livingstone returns to England from Africa

1857   Indian Mutiny

1859   Second Evangelical awakening begins; *The Origin of Species* by Charles Darwin

1860   *Essays and Reviews* arouses controversy over Church of England's doctrine

1861   *Commentary on the Epistle to the Romans* by J. W. Colenso; *Hymns Ancient and Modern*

1863   C. H. Spurgeon opens Metropolitan Tabernacle; *Selections* popularize Robert Browning's poetry

1864   *Apologia pro Vita Sua* by J. H. Newman; Samuel Crowther becomes Bishop on the Niger

1865   Henry Manning succeeds Nicholas Wiseman as Archbishop of Westminster; China Inland Mission founded by James Hudson Taylor

1867   First Lambeth Conference of Anglican bishops

1868   A. C. Tait becomes Archbishop of Canterbury instead

of Samuel Wilberforce; Thomas Barnardo begins East London Juvenile Mission

1869   Irish Disestablishment enacted

1870   Papal infallibility defined by Vatican Council; Education Act establishes state schools; death of Charles Dickens

1871   J. C. Patteson, Bishop of Melanesia, murdered

1873   David Livingstone dies in central Africa

1874   Joseph Parker opens City Temple

1875   G. M. Hopkins writes 'The Wreck of the *Deutschland*'; *The Atonement* by R. W. Dale

1878   Salvation Army named by William Booth

1885   Five hundred societies represented at Lord Shaftesbury's funeral; Bishop James Hannington murdered in Uganda

1886   Josephine Butler secures repeal of Contagious Diseases Acts; Gladstone fails to secure Home Rule for Ireland

1889   London Dock Strike ended by Cardinal Manning; *Lux Mundi* edited by Charles Gore

1890   B. F. Westcott succeeds J. B. Lightfoot as Bishop of Durham

1895   Cardinal Vaughan begins building of Westminster Cathedral

1896   National Council of Evangelical Free Churches formed; Anglican ordinations declared void by Pope Leo XIII

1897   Diamond Jubilee invokes imperialism; Boxers' rebellion in China reacts against missionaries

1901   Death of Queen Victoria

1902   Education Act subsidizes church schools; John Clifford leads passive resistance of Nonconformists

1906   Liberal victory with Nonconformist support; *English Hymnal* enriches Anglican worship

1907   *The New Theology* by R. J. Campbell; Modernism condemned by Pope Pius X

1914   Sudden outbreak of First World War

Index

Also available in Fount Paperbacks

Audacity to Believe
SHEILA CASSIDY

'A story of extraordinarily unpretentious courage in the horror of
Chile after Allende's overthrow. It is easy to read, totally sincere
and sometimes moving. Sheila Cassidy is totally disarming.'

Frank O'Reilly
The Furrow

Prayer for Pilgrims
SHEILA CASSIDY

'... a direct and practical book about prayer ... has the freshness of
someone who writes of what she has personally discovered ... many
people ... will be grateful for this book and helped by it.'

Neville Ward
Church Times

The General Next to God
RICHARD COLLIER
'An absorbing, sympathetic record of the man (General Booth) and
his family and the movement they created.'

Michael Foot
Evening Standard

Also available in Fount Paperbacks

Journey for a Soul
GEORGE APPLETON

'Wherever you turn in this inexpensive but extraordinarily valuable paperback you will benefit from sharing this man's pilgrimage of the soul.'

Methodist Recorder

The Imitation of Christ
THOMAS A KEMPIS

After the Bible, this is perhaps the most widely read book in the world. It describes the way of the follower of Christ – an intensely practical book, which faces the temptations and difficulties of daily life, but also describes the joys and helps which are found on the way.

Autobiography of a Saint:
Thérèse of Lisieux
RONALD KNOX

'Ronald Knox has bequeathed us a wholly lucid, natural and enchanting version . . . the actual process of translating seems to have vanished, and a miracle wrought, as though St Teresa were speaking to us in English . . . his triumphant gift to posterity.'

G. B. Stern, The Sunday Times

The Way of a Disciple
GEORGE APPLETON

'. . . a lovely book and an immensely rewarding one . . . his prayers have proved of help to many.'

Donald Coggan

Also available in Fount Paperbacks

The Mind of St Paul
WILLIAM BARCLAY

'There is a deceptive simplicity about this fine exposition of Pauline thought at once popular and deeply theological. The Hebrew and Greek backgrounds are described and all the main themes are lightly but fully treated.'   *The Yorkshire Post*

The Plain Man Looks at the Beatitudes
WILLIAM BARCLAY

'. . . the author's easy style should render it . . . valuable and acceptable to the ordinary reader.'   *Church Times*

The Plain Man Looks at the Lord's Prayer
WILLIAM BARCLAY

Professor Barclay shows how this prayer that Jesus gave to his disciples is at once a summary of Christian teaching and a pattern for all prayers.

The Plain Man's Guide to Ethics
WILLIAM BARCLAY

The author demonstrates beyond all possible doubt that the Ten Commandments are the most relevant document in the world today and are totally related to mankind's capacity to live and make sense of it all within a Christian context.

Ethics in a Permissive Society
WILLIAM BARCLAY

How do we as Christians deal with such problems as drug taking, the 'pill', alcohol, morality of all kinds, in a society whose members are often ignorant of the Church's teaching? Professor Barclay approaches a difficult and vexed question with his usual humanity and clarity, asking what Christ himself would say or do in our world today.

Fount Paperbacks

Fount is one of the leading paperback publishers of religious books and below are some of its recent titles.

- [ ] THE QUIET HEART George Appleton £2.95
- [ ] PRAYER FOR ALL TIMES Pierre Charles £1.75
- [ ] SEEKING GOD Esther de Waal £1.75
- [ ] THE SCARLET AND THE BLACK
  J. P. Gallagher £1.75
- [ ] TELL MY PEOPLE I LOVE THEM
  Clifford Hill £1.50
- [ ] CONVERSATIONS WITH THE CRUCIFIED
  Reid Isaac £1.50
- [ ] THE LITTLE BOOK OF SYLVANUS
  David Kossoff £1.50
- [ ] DOES GOD EXIST? Hans Küng £5.95
- [ ] GEORGE MACDONALD: AN ANTHOLOGY
  George MacDonald C. S. Lewis (ed.) £1.50
- [ ] WHY I AM STILL A CATHOLIC
  Robert Nowell (ed.) £1.50
- [ ] THE GOSPEL FROM OUTER SPACE
  Robert L. Short £1.50
- [ ] CONTINUALLY AWARE Rita Snowden £1.75
- [ ] TRUE RESURRECTION Harry Williams £1.75
- [ ] WHO WILL DELIVER US? Paul Zahl £1.50

All Fount paperbacks are available at your bookshop or newsagent, or they can also be ordered by post from Fount Paperbacks, Cash Sales Department, G.P.O. Box 29, Douglas, Isle of Man, British Isles. Please send purchase price, plus 15p per book, maximum postage £3. Customers outside the U.K. send purchase price, plus 15p per book. Cheque, postal or money order. No currency.

NAME (Block letters) _____

ADDRESS _____

_____

_____